Mark Slagell

SAMS
Teach Yourself

Ruby
in 21 Days

SAMS

201 West 103rd St., Indianapolis, Indiana, 46290

Sams Teach Yourself Ruby in 21 Days
Copyright ©2002 by Sams Publishing

International Standard Book Number: 0-672-32252-8

Library of Congress Catalog Number: 2001094220

Printed in the United States of America

First Printing: March 2002

04   03   02   01   4   3   2   1

Trademarks

All terms mentioned in this book that are known to be trademarks or service marks have been appropriately capitalized. Sams Publishing cannot attest to the accuracy of this information. Use of a term in this book should not be regarded as affecting the validity of any trademark or service mark.

Warning and Disclaimer

Every effort has been made to make this book as complete and as accurate as possible, but no warranty or fitness is implied. The information provided is on an "as is" basis. The author and the publisher shall have neither liability nor responsibility to any person or entity with respect to any loss or damages arising from the information contained in this book.

ASSOCIATE PUBLISHER
Mark Taber

ACQUISITIONS EDITOR
Katie Purdum

DEVELOPMENT EDITOR
Maryann Steinhart

MANAGING EDITOR
Charlotte Clapp

PROJECT EDITOR
Matt Purcell

COPY EDITOR
Jerome Colburn
(Publication Services, Inc.)

INDEXER
Jason Mortenson
(Publication Services, Inc.)

PRODUCTION EDITOR
Theodore Young, Jr.
(Publication Services, Inc.)

PROOFREADER
Phil Hamer
(Publication Services, Inc.)

TECHNICAL EDITORS
Gene Winston
Dave Thomas
Daniel Solin

TEAM COORDINATOR
Amy Patton

INTERIOR DESIGNER
Gary Adair

COVER DESIGNER
Aren Howell

PAGE LAYOUT
Nina Betterly
Jennifer Faaborg
Jim Torbit
Michael Tarleton
Jessica Vonasch
(Publication Services, Inc.)

Contents at a Glance

Introduction   1

Week 1 The Fundamentals   **9**

Day 1   Getting Started with Ruby   11

2   Hello, Objects!   27

3   Containers   51

4   Iteration and Flow Control   69

5   The Characteristics of Objects   93

6   Ins and Outs   113

7   Catching Up on Details   137

Week 2 Power Scripting   **161**

Day 8   Pattern Matching   163

9   Inheritance and Modules   185

10   Program File Layout, Program Design, and the General Case   203

11   Modules and Classes in Depth   223

12   An Introduction to Recursion   247

13   Mastering the Operating System   265

14   Arguments, Blocks, and Procs   289

Week 3 Making It Work for You   **311**

Day 15   Toward Habitable Interfaces   313

16   Putting It Together (Part I)   337

17   Ruby/Tk   355

18   Ruby/Gtk   389

19   Some Advanced Topics (That Aren't So Hard)   427

20   Working with the Web   449

21   Putting It together (Part II)   475

Appendices 499

A   `irb` Results   501

B   Installation Help   503

C   Debugging, with and without a Debugger   509

D   Essential Vocabulary   517

Index   521

Contents

Introduction   1

Week 1 The Fundamentals   9

Day 1 Getting Started with Ruby   11

  Why Ruby? 11

    Ruby Is Small and Intuitive...12

    Ruby Gives You Immediate Feedback 12

    Ruby Is Free 12

    Ruby Is Portable 12

    Ruby Is Object-Oriented...13

    Ruby Is a Scripting Language 13

    Ruby Supports Regular Expressions 14

  Make Sure You Have Ruby...14

  First Steps 14

    Life in the Command Line 15

    Choosing a Text Editor 15

    Our First Script 16

    Some Experiments..16

    Play-by-Play 17

    Remarks About the Experimental Results...........................18

    The *Shebang* Line 20

  Using Ruby Interactively 21

    An Interactive Tool: `irb` 22

    The `eval.rb` Script 23

  Summary 24

  Is There Homework in This Class? 24

    Exercises 25

    Answers 25

Day 2 Hello, Objects!   27

  What Is an Object? 27

  The First Object: `self` 28

    Teach Yourself Tricks 29

  The Second Object: `other` 30

  Classes..32

    Making Instances of a Class 33

    Appending Methods to a Class 34

    Altering and Removing Methods 35

Everybody's Methods 36

Who Is This "self" Anyway? 37

    Method Arguments 38

    Local Scope for Variables 40

    Communication Within an Object...42

    Communication Between Different Objects 44

    Identifiers and Variables 45

Name Tags, Not Suitcases 45

Summary 47

    Exercises 48

    Answers 48

Day 3 Containers   **51**

A Change in Convention..51

Some Words About Ambiguity 52

Back to Business..54

Strings 54

    Specifying Substrings by Position...54

    Individual Characters..56

    Specifying Substrings by Matching 57

    A Few Useful `String` Instance Methods..58

Arrays 59

    Arrays Containing Arrays 61

    FIFOs and Stacks..62

    Stacks 63

    A Few Useful `Array` Instance Methods..63

Hashes...64

    A Few Useful `Hash` Instance Methods...65

Ranges...66

Summary 67

    Exercises 67

    Answers 67

Day 4 Iteration and Flow Control   **69**

Using Iterators..69

    each 70

    Variations on Iterator Calls 71

    times, downto, upto, step 72

    each_byte 73

    each_index, each_with_index 74

    each_pair, each_key, each_value for Hashes 74

    select, map 75

Flow Control 76

    Conditional Code..76

Loops 78

A Text Filter 78

Interrupting the Flow..80

Odd-Position Elements 81

Testing Multiple Conditions 83

Getting a Value from if or case 84

Grouping Several Expressions into One 86

Why Loop When You Can Iterate? 86

Summary 86

Exercises 87

Answers 89

Day 5 The Characteristics of Objects   93

Instance Variables 94

Mars and the Metric System: A Cautionary Tale 95

Writing a Temperature Class 96

Integers and Floats..98

A Convention for Naming Methods 98

Automatic Accessors 99

Define Your Own Operators 100

Class Constants 103

Access Control (or, A Cure for the Common Code)..............................105

The initialize Method 105

Global Variables 107

What to Name Things...108

Exercises 109

Answers 110

Day 6 Ins and Outs   113

Streams 113

The Standard Streams 114

Files 116

Some Useful IO Methods 117

What About Memory Space? 120

Formatted Output 121

Class Methods..123

Some Useful File Class Methods..125

The Command Line 127

Class Variables 128

Errors and Exceptions..130

Summary 132

Exercises 132

Answers 133

Day 7 Catching Up on Details   **137**

    Numbers in Ruby 138

        Integer Literals..138

        Floating-Point Literals...139

        How Numbers Are Stored 140

        How Numbers Are Presented 142

        Binary Arithmetic 143

    Boolean Logic...146

        Short-Circuit Evaluation 147

    Strings and String Literals 148

    Block Scope for Local Variables 151

    Shortcuts and Tricks 151

        Variable Modification 151

        Chained Assignment 152

        Multiple Assignment 153

    Functional and Imperative Styles 155

        Garbage Collection 155

        Gotchas 156

    Summary...157

        Exercises 157

        Answers 159

Week 2 Power Scripting   **161**

Day 8 Pattern Matching   **163**

    Simple Pattern Matching 164

        Wildcards and Character Classes 165

        Character Ranges...166

        Negation..166

        Abbreviations..167

    Position Anchors...168

    Repetition 169

        Greed 171

    Grouping...172

        Grouping and Repetition 172

        Grouping and Alternation 176

        Grouping and Memory 177

    Switches 178

        Case Insensitivity: /i...178

        Extended Legibility: /x 178

        Multiline Matching: /m 178

    Some Container Methods That Use Regexes 178

Regexes and Matches As Objects 180

Summary 181

　　Exercises 181

　　Answers 182

Day 9 Inheritance and Modules   185

Organizing Organization...185

The Make-Up of Ruby Classes: Some "What" and a Little "How" 186

　　The Basics 186

　　Inheritance 187

Fiddling with Inheritance 189

Play It Again, Ruby: Another Method Call Example..........................193

Modules...195

Resolving Method Ambiguities 197

Summary 198

　　Exercises 198

　　Answers 200

Day 10 Program File Layout, Program Design, and the General Case   203

Program and File Interaction 204

Runtime Extension of Ruby's World: require....................................205

The Argument to require...208

Compiled Extensions 209

　　require and Variables 210

　　require Versus include 211

Examining the Ruby Installation 211

Abstraction and the General Case 213

　　Under- and Over-Abstraction 214

　　Getting Abstraction Right 215

Summary 218

　　Exercises 218

　　Answers 220

Day 11 Modules and Classes in Depth   223

Designing Modules and Classes for Clarity and Reuse 223

　　Some Class/Module Distinctions 224

　　An Exercise in Adjectival Thinking 226

　　Code Reusability 229

Embedded Modules and Namespace Management 229

　　Modules Mixing in Modules..231

　　Classes Defined Inside Modules 232

　　Classes Defined Inside Classes 233

Class-Module Distribution Across Program Files 234

Overriding Methods 235
  Overriding and Aliasing 236
  Overriding an Inherited Method 237
  Handling Arguments in Overridden Methods 239
Summary 239
  Exercises 240
  Answers 244

Day 12 An Introduction to Recursion   247

The Canonical Starting Point: Factorials 247
  A Little Too Much Like Magic? 249
  Recursive Functions 250
Efficiency Concerns 250
  Memoization 252
The Towers of Hanoi 254
Summary 261
  Exercises 261
  Answers 263

Day 13 Mastering the Operating System   265

Motivation 265
Portability Notes 266
Gathering Information 267
Treating Programs As Functions 269
Extended Conversations 272
The Art of Instant Reproduction 275
  Waiting for Children 277
  Pipes...277
How to Control Your Children 278
  Example Spinner #1, Using `fork` 279
  Example Spinner #2, Using `IO.popen` 281
  Example Spinner #3, Using `Kernel.open`........................283
  Summary 283
  Exercises 284
  Answers...285

Day 14 Arguments, Blocks, and Procs   289

Life Without Iterators 290
  Stealthy Approach 291
  A Hands-on Approach..292
  A Hands-off Approach 293
  Final Approach: Very Hands-off 295

Writing Iterator Methods 297

    Hybrid Iterators 298

    New Iterators for Old Classes 299

    Was This Trip Really Necessary? 301

    select_by_index 302

Other Uses for Blocks..303

Summary 304

    Exercises 306

    Answers 306

Week 3 Making It Work for You   311

Day 15 Toward Habitable Interfaces   313

Interface Size and Intuitiveness 314

An IntegerMatrix Class..315

    Initialization...315

    Storing and Retrieving Elements...316

    Accessing Dimensions...318

    Viewing a Matric As a Whole 319

    Providing Iterators 321

    Doing the Math 322

    Multipurpose Methods...324

    A Versatile Constructor Using Default Values 326

    A More Versatile Constructor 327

Summary..331

    Exercises 332

    Answers 333

Day 16 Putting It Together (Part I)   337

The Unjumbler 337

    Getting the Permutations...338

    Finding the Needles in the Haystack..341

    Finished Product 343

    A Portable is_word? Function..344

    Bailing Out Early...345

    Resorting to Wizardry 346

Notes on Language Enhancement 347

An Interactive Process Killer 348

    A Little About the Unix Tools...348

    Designing from the Top Down 350

Summary..331

Day 17 Ruby/Tk   **355**

What Is Tk?..357

Our First Tk Application..357

Geometry Managers 360

Entry Widgets and Buttons 362

Some Other Widgets...366

More Complex Coding 375

Summary...376

    Exercises 377

    Answers 378

Day 18 Ruby/Gtk   **389**

Installation under UNIX 390

Installation under Windows 391

First Ruby/Gtk Scripts 392

Simple Widget Layout 394

    Bin Containers 394

    Box Containers 395

    Table Containers 399

Modular Design for Multiple Windows 400

    Window Subclasses and Test Code 400

    A Table Window 400

    An Application Split into Two Files 402

    Modal Dialogs 403

    The Messagebox Class 403

More Widget Types..406

    Sample 1: Checkbutton and Radiobutton............................406

    Sample 2: AccelGroup, ToggleButton, and HSeparator.............408

    Sample 3: Text 409

    Sample 4: ScrollableWindow 411

A Full Ruby/Gtk Application 411

Summary...419

    Exercises 420

    Answers 421

Day 19 Some Advanced Topics (That Aren't So Hard)   **427**

Sockets 428

    "Hello, World" Using TCP 429

    "Hello, World" Using UDP 430

    A TCP Chat Session 432

    A Simple Web Server 433

    Supporting Concurrent Sessions 438

Threads 440
   Passing Control Around...442
   Establishing a Pecking Order 444
   The Bathroom Pass 445
   When to Thread and When to Fork..446
Summary..446
   Exercises 447
   Answers 447

Day 20 Working with the Web   **449**

Static Content Versus Dynamic Content..450
Server-Side Versus Client-Side 450
Privileges at the Server 451
Configuring Apache: `httpd.conf` 452
   Choose a Root Directory for Web Documents 452
   Enable SHTML 453
   Enable CGI 453
   Set a Uses ID...454
   Activate the New Configuration 454
Test Drives 454
   Using Ruby to Generate an HTML File Directly 455
   A First CGI Script..456
   A First SHTML Script...457
Know Thy Client 458
   Remember the Past 460
   Use DBM to Remember Old Session Information 461
Object-Oriented CGI Support..463
   Session Information Using the CGI Class 465
   Persistent Session Information 466
Embedded Ruby 468
Summary..470
   Exercises 470
   Answers 471

Day 21 Putting It Together (Part II)   **475**

Binary Decision Trees..476
   Script Overview..478
   The BDT Class and Its Relatives...478
   The BDT-sample Class 480
   A Mild Dose of Information Theory 481
   The BDT-set Class 482
   The Full Script..485
   A Test of Intelligence 489

Ideas for Improvements and Enhancements 490
Tk-based Peer Chat...491
What Do We Mean by "Peer"? 492
Top-Level Scripts..493
The TkChat class 494
Testing the Scripts 496
Ideas for Improvements and Enhancements 497
Summary...498

Appendices   **499**

Appendix A   irb Results   **501**

Appendix B   Installation Help   **503**

Unix...503
Step1. Download the Source Code 504
Step 2. Unpack the Archive...504
Step 3. Prepare for Compiling..504
Step 4. make the Interpreter 505
Step 5. Test Before Installing 505
Step 6a. Install (If You're the Administrator) 505
Step 6b. Update PATH (If You're Not the Administrator) 506
Step 7. Test Accessibility..506
Step 8. Set Up the emacs Ruby Mode (Optional)........................506
Microsoft Windows...507
The "One-Click" Installer 507
Unix Wannabe Installation for Windows 507

Appendix C   Debugging, With and Without a Debugger   **509**

Stack Traces 509
Inline Diagnostics 511
The Built-In Debugger 512

Appendix D   Essential Vocabulary   **517**

Index   **521**

About the Lead Author

Mark Slagell. . . .

. . . works as a system administrator and developer, using Ruby as a common language tool to solve problems in a heterogeneous Unix/Windows environment;

. . . has taught C++ programming and developed original course materials at the university level;

. . . holds a Master's degree in computer science and has participated in information security research involving the development of mobile agent tools in Java for distributed intrusion detection;

. . . got his start hand-assembling machine code for the 6502 and Z80 processors back in the dark, misty days of microcomputing (and predictably, has been fascinated ever since with the whole idea of computer *languages*);

. . . enjoys small-town life in Iowa and feels that in a world characterized by high-volume entertainment and fast-moving technology, nothing is more enjoyable than—or should ever take precedence over—a good game of softball.

About the Contributing Authors

David A. Black, Ph.D.. . .

. . . is an Associate Professor of Communication at Seton Hall University;

. . . has written for *Linux Journal*, as well as for numerous critical journals in film and media studies;

. . . is the author of the book *Law in Film*;

. . . was one of the organizers of Ruby Conference 2001;

. . . is active on the `ruby-talk` mailing list and `#ruby-lang` IRC channel.

Hal Fulton. . .

. . . has two degrees in computer science;

. . . has taught at the postsecondary level and has more than a decade of industry experience as a programmer;

. . . is a member of the ACM and the IEEE Computer Society;

. . . is also the author of *The Ruby Way* (Sams Publishing, 2001).

Dedication

To Brian Kernighan and Dennis Ritchie, whose little 1978 book
The C Programming Language *stands today as a model of computer language instruction.*

Acknowledgments

Where can I begin?

Where else but with Yukihiro "Matz" Matsumoto, creator of the breakthrough language you're about to get hooked on.

Warm thanks go to David Alan Black and Hal Fulton for their substantial contributions to this volume, and to Dave Thomas for his careful reading, insights, and just-tactful-enough suggestions. I'd also like to thank Neil Conway for some ideas that helped shape the Ruby/Gtk chapter.

I have Akinori Musha to thank for bringing my English retranslation of Matz's original Ruby tutorial into the mainstream, which seems to be what got me involved in the Ruby community in the first place, and Curt Clifton and Gary Leavens for their early encouragement and interest, which helped me decide to forge ahead with this project.

My friends Susan Yager and David Heddendorf helped me think about the book in a literary sense and suggested one of the better quotations that was used to open a chapter.

To my wife Amy for the patience I have not yet managed to exhaust, to older son Carter for taking on some extra tasks to help free up my time, and to younger son Kenny for asking, as only a five-year-old could, how my "story" was coming: Thank you all.

Tell Us What You Think!

As the reader of this book, you are our most important critic and commentator. We value your opinion and want to know what we're doing right, what we could do better, what areas you'd like to see us publish in, and any other words of wisdom you're willing to pass our way.

As an associate publisher for Sams Publishing, I welcome your comments. You can fax, e-mail, or write me directly to let me know what you did or didn't like about this book—as well as what we can do to make our books stronger.

Note

Please note that I cannot help you with technical problems related to the topic of this book, and that due to the high volume of mail I receive, I might not be able to reply to every message.

When you write, please be sure to include this book's title and author name as well as your name and phone or fax number. I will carefully review your comments and share them with the author and editors who worked on the book.

Fax: 317-581-4770

E-mail: consumer@samspublishing.com

Mail: Mark Taber

           Sams Publishing
           201 West 103rd Street
           Indianapolis, IN 46290 USA

Introduction

The book you hold in your hands is unusual.

You know that it is a book about computer programming, and it is about a language that you may not have heard a lot about; but that much is not, perhaps, unusual. There are many computer languages in existence, you are probably unfamiliar with most of them (isn't everybody?), and you've seen bookstore shelves overflowing with programming titles.

What is unusual is that Ruby is a very advanced programming language, yet this book claims to teach it to you while assuming almost nothing about your expertise or experience. If those two statements sound unrealistic and incompatible, don't immediately put the book down and give up. Instead, consider what it means for a programming language to *be* advanced. You might be inclined to say that an advanced language would be powerful, cryptic, and hard to learn; and would be the province of the highly experienced professional who has been doing it for years, already knows half a dozen languages inside and out, and has found them all wanting in some way.

And you'd be partly right. An advanced language would be powerful. It would also attract highly experienced professionals who found that other languages didn't do what they wanted in quite the way they wanted. But think again about the rest: A truly advanced language might not necessarily be cryptic, because being cryptic cannot be considered a virtue. Nor, by the same token, would it necessarily be hard to learn. And so its usefulness might not be limited to the most experienced programmers.

The world of programming languages has been undergoing sweeping changes in recent years, driven indirectly by advances in hardware. In the good old days, memory was scarce and expensive, and a computer didn't compute all that fast, although it always *felt* fast at the time, as I recall. The lack of cheap speed and cheap storage meant that to get a computer to do anything useful, a programmer had to work at a fairly low level of abstraction. We made our living close to the operating system and, in some cases, the hardware. We had to optimize and tweak on things to get them to run at an acceptable speed (though good compilers and other tools helped with this). Whenever we had collections of information, we thought carefully about how the items were organized in memory. Storage had to be explicitly allocated and freed, and it had to be done just right or things would go to pieces in confusing and seemingly random ways. It was tricky, and it was hard work.

Of course there's nothing wrong with hard work. But there's a good reason to get away from that particular sort of hard work as often as possible. When you write a computer program, you are doing it to solve some particular problem, and that problem usually has nothing to do with the computer, the hardware in front of you, the operating system you're using, the language and compiler you use, and so on. The problem that you want to work on is, in and of itself, interesting. That problem is something you can probably clearly state in words (if you can't, you're in trouble from the start). And therein lies the need for advanced computer languages: When you are thinking about the *problem you wanted to solve in the first place*, you are working mentally at a different and higher level of abstraction than when you've got your hands all over the operating system. It's unnaturally hard to work at more than one level of abstraction at the same time. Not many of us are good at it. So we need high-level languages (what some people are calling "very high-level languages" or *VHLLs*) to help us concentrate on the problem at hand.

What Is Assumed About You

The idea of VHLLs is not new; the need has been present for a long time, and the term has been applied to a number of languages in the recent past. But Ruby is the first language, in my view, to achieve this combination of power, consistency, and readability. Interested people who may not have a programming background can reasonably hope to grasp it. Ruby has made a decisive crossing of the Geek Event Horizon and is the first serious language (as opposed to BASIC and similar toys) to have done so.

Accordingly, this book does not assume that you have any particular experience in programming or computer science. It assumes only that you have intelligence, curiosity, and some time; given those (and perhaps a healthy sense of humor), you can expect to pick up the new skills you are looking for.

On the other hand, neither is it assumed that you are a beginner. If you are a seasoned C, C++, Java, or Perl programmer, Ruby represents a paradigm shift, an opportunity to take a step back and reexamine how you have approached problems. You may find that there are some things you need to unlearn, but your past experience will also certainly prove useful at many points.

What's This About Levels of Abstraction?

Consider a task described as follows: Read a file named raw, extract all the lines containing the word Brighton, sort those lines in increasing numerical order by their third whitespace-separated field, and write the results to a new file named processed. This example will help us understand the motivation for VHLLs in more concrete terms.

Someone trying to perform that task in C would typically think at this level (at least, if trying to solve the problem in haste):

Declare two file handles. Reserve a small number of bytes as a character buffer. Is 80 enough? Yeah, that's probably reasonable. I can always increase it later if I find out differently. And I'll probably want a really big buffer to hold the whole file. But I don't know ahead of time how big the file will be . . . How big is big enough? It's safest to do that after opening the file. Take a deep breath and do it right. I'll ask the operating system for a buffer. So let's see, open the `"raw"` *file in read mode. Do a seek to move the file pointer to the end of the file and a* `tell` *to find out what the absolute position is, meaning that's the total length of the file. Remember that number. Rewind the file pointer back to the beginning. Ask the operating system for enough memory to hold the file. Check the return value in case there's a problem. Now I've got a pointer at the beginning of the big buffer, and I'll make a copy of that pointer. The original will stay put and the copy will move. While not yet at the input end-of-file, read a line into the smaller buffer and use a library function to search for a* `"Brighton"` *in the buffer. If the function returns something nonzero (or was it zero? Doesn't zero mean success? Wait, better look that up, I can never remember), it means the string was found in the buffer, so write the buffer to where the roving pointer points, then move the pointer forward the size of the input line. When at to the end of the input file, close it. Now I've got a buffer containing just the* `"Brighton"` *lines. So far, so good. But how to sort it? It will be hard to sort in place because the lines aren't all the same length. Maybe I should have made an array of pointers at the beginning of each line, then sorted the pointers . . . wait, this will work, I'll keep going through the buffer, picking out the smallest line I find each time, writing that line to the output file and then kind of blanking it out. Ready to proceed, so open the output file with name* `"processed"`. *Make a flag variable, set it to false, I mean 0. Set up a* `do-while` *loop using the flag. Copy the stationary buffer pointer to the roving one again. In the loop, move the roving pointer forward through the line until it sees whitespace twice. I should make an inner loop for that. Now use a library function to convert the text where the pointer is pointing into an integer. Wait, no, a float. Compare that to the lowest number we've seen so far. Hmm, I don't know what the lowest number seen so far is. Better declare a* `lowest` *variable, then initialize it to something impossibly high. Do that before the outer loop starts. If it's lower than the* `lowest`, *copy that value into* `lowest`, *remember where the start of the line was (Wait! I moved the pointer and don't know where the line started anymore. No problem, make a third pointer, copy the second pointer to it every time before you go looking for whitespace), and set the flag to true, I mean 1. At the end of the buffer (how will I know I'm at the end? Better back up and set up a fourth pointer after reading the input file, so we can compare position to that pointer), if the flag is 1, write the line that had lowest value to the output file, then mark the line so it won't be considered again. If the flag is 0, then we must have written all the lines, so we close the output file and we're done.*

Phew. Programming is hard, eh? And that's leaving out quite a few details and resorting to an inefficient and simple-minded sorting method. We also haven't accounted for the debugging phase, which can be counted on to be necessary because something is almost sure to go wrong somewhere. But eventually we'll get it to work—at least until we come across an input file that violates our assumptions, or until someone changes the requirements a little and we find that what we wrote won't easily adapt to the altered task and so we have to go back, Jack, and do it again. We spend our time putzing around with low-level programming details, struggling to come up with some rickety contraption to do the required job, instead of crafting a sensible, adaptable design.

I don't bring this up to disparage the C language. C programs tend to perform with good speed; there are tasks for which it is very well suited; it's possible to write in C and think much more clearly than the above example indicates. There are people who are very good at it. Either they have become so adept at the mental dance involved that they can do it efficiently—even unconsciously—or they have learned to avoid as much low-level thinking as possible and to make prudent use of their own and other people's code libraries, which is a first step toward true high-level programming.

Now let's head for more hospitable latitudes. Suppose you want to perform the same task in Ruby. Here's the likely thought process involved:

Make an array of the lines from the input file `"raw"`. *Get rid of the lines that don't contain* `"Brighton"`. *Sort the array in increasing numerical order by the third whitespace-separated field. Open an output file,* `"processed"`. *Print each line from the array to the file. Close the file.*

Well, that sounds suspiciously like the original problem description, doesn't it? It also suggests a short program. Observe:

```
the_lines = File.readlines("raw")
the_lines.delete_if { |l| l !~ "Brighton" }
the_lines.sort! { |x,y| (x.split)[2].to_f <=> (y.split)[2].to_f }
out_file = File.new("processed","w")
the_lines.each { |l| out_file.print l }
out_file.close
```

What just happened? We concentrated on what the job was about, and the high-level task description translated cleanly into a working program. No pointers, no memory allocation, no loops.[1] Thinking about the problem at hand, we shall see, is the Ruby Way.

Does it all sound too easy? Don't worry. There will be plenty of challenges ahead.

---

[1]*Not that we couldn't write "loopy" code in Ruby too. We can. But it isn't usually necessary.*

But when learning Ruby you'll find life to be pretty pleasant. While it doesn't solve all the big problems for you, it gives you a nice logical framework and a set of tools to handle the most tedious stuff so that you can keep working at a high level of abstraction, completing your jobs quickly, reliably, and maybe even happily.

"The Ruby Way"

We'll keep coming back to discussion about the Ruby Way, which is a phrase often thrown around in the online Ruby developer and user community. As presumptuous as it may be to suggest that there is only one Ruby Way—after all, my view of it, or way of expressing it, may be much different from another's—there is at least some shared intuition about what it is.[2]

The Ruby Way is to avoid sweating the details when it's unnecessary.

The Ruby Way is to solve most problems exactly once.

The Ruby Way is to use your task specifications, whatever they are, to guide the writing of your programs.

The Ruby Way is to test as you go.

Above all:

The Ruby Way is to *use the language as a language* in the conventional, or literary, sense; something that exists to help you express yourself, not an obscure technical maze that keeps getting in your way, begging to be worked around and outsmarted.

Enjoy yourself. It's what we are all here for.

Organization of the Book

This book is organized into 21 lessons, and in keeping with the title, they are numbered by days. While it is undeniably true that everyone learns in different ways and at different speeds, it is suggested that something close to the chapter-per-day pace be observed to ensure that each lesson has a chance to sink in before the next is devoured.

At the end of most lessons there are a few exercises. They are intended to give you opportunities to test and hone your new skills, and also to goad you into contemplating some questions that will motivate you to the lessons yet to come.

---

[2]The Ruby Way *is also the title of a pretty good Ruby book you may want to pick up when you're done with this one.*

Most of the lessons are tied to well-defined topic areas, but there are three special lessons (on Days 7, 16, and 21) whose purposes are not related to single topics. These are explained in the following outline. In deference to Ruby's Unix roots, there are a few areas of Unix-specific material here (including parts of Days 13, 16, and 20), but you will find Ruby's behavior and features to be generally consistent across operating systems.

The lessons in *SAMS Teach Yourself Ruby in 21 Days* include the following:

Day 1, "Getting Started with Ruby," provides a quick overview of the Ruby language, a discussion of what a script is and how to create one, and some very small and simple scripts to examine.

Day 2, "Hello, Objects!," is a gentle introduction to the fundamental concepts of object-oriented (OO) programming (objects, methods, and classes) as they apply to Ruby.

Day 3, "Containers," describes four basic kinds of container objects and shows how to use them to make collections of information manageable.

Day 4, "Iteration and Flow Control," introduces aspects of the Ruby language that facilitate repetition (particularly as it applies to the containers you learn about on Day 3) and decision making.

Day 5, "The Characteristics of Objects," explores ways in which objects of the same class can maintain their own unique characteristics and identities.

Day 6, "Ins and Outs," is about *streams*—the means by which Ruby programs exchange information with the outside world. It also discusses how programs can cope when the outside world does unexpected things.

Day 7, "Catching Up on Details," fills in some important points that had been omitted or glossed over in the first six days. These are language details that are often found in the first couple of chapters of a programming book, but you will probably be in a better position to understand them after a few lessons of a more practical nature.

Day 8, "Pattern Matching," introduces you to the powerful and strange world of *regular expressions*, helping you to concisely express text search patterns that would have otherwise cost many lines of code and hours of frustration.

Day 9, "Inheritance and Modules," shows you how to form hierarchies so that distinct but similar classes need not be rewritten from scratch. It is the first of three lessons dedicated to helping you organize your Ruby code.

Day 10, "Program File Layout, Program Design, and the General Case," shows you how separate class and module files can be managed by scripts. It also discusses in practical terms how to avoid abstracting too much or too little.

Day 11, "Modules and Classes in Depth," describes a kind of programming ecology, suggesting ways to make your code more clear, understandable, and reusable.

Day 12, "An Introduction to Recursion," is an ideological partner to Day 8 even though their topics seem unrelated. Recursion is a technique that allows you to solve what seem like impossibly difficult problems quickly by turning the logic of a program in upon itself.

Day 13, "Mastering the Operating System," shows you how to make Ruby scripts understand and control their computer environment. It also introduces the idea of "forking" one program so that it can become responsible for two (or more) independent entities that run at the same time and can communicate with each other.

Day 14, "Arguments, Blocks, and Procs," explores the information that is passed around among objects. *Blocks* and *procs* make it possible to communicate not only data, but program logic, so you can work at a higher level of versatility and flexibility.

Day 15, "Toward Habitable Interfaces," is a detailed discussion of how new classes can be made easy and intuitive to use.

Day 16, "Putting It Together (Part I)," follows the design and construction of two interesting projects from beginning to end: an "unjumbler" script that takes a scrambled word and makes sense of it, and a "kill-slackers" script that assists with a difficult system administration task in a hybrid Unix/Windows business environment.

Day 17, "Ruby/Tk," introduces the Ruby/Tk windowing library and gets you started writing scripts that exploit the functionality and beauty of a Graphical User Interface (GUI).

Day 18, "Ruby/Gtk," explores GUI programming with the Ruby/Gtk library. Gtk (for GIMP Toolkit) has a highly polished appearance and is easy to work with.

Day 19, "Some Advanced Features (That Aren't So Hard)," leads you through the topics of *sockets* and *threads*. Taken together, these make it possible to design and implement your own original network services.

Day 20, "Working with the Web," is an introduction to a very big topic: how to use Ruby to provide dynamic World Wide Web content. We discuss the difference between server-side and client-side processing, walk through typical configuration of an Apache Web server, and get some experience with CGI, SHTML, and Embedded Ruby.

Day 21, "Putting It Together (Part II)," again follows design and construction of two projects. The first is a simplified artificial intelligence agent that can help you make a decision, based on past experience, such as whether it's a good idea to have a picnic. The second implements a two-way network chat service using a Tk window.

What This Book Is and Is Not

SAMS Teach Yourself Ruby in 21 Days is an instructional book. It does not aim to be comprehensive; neither its intent nor its organization is that of a reference book. There are certain elements of the Ruby language that are not covered and others that are discussed only briefly.

What you will find here is enough know-how to use Ruby in many of the tasks you're likely to see. By the time you get to the end of *SAMS Teach Yourself Ruby in 21 Days*, you can expect to have acquired a good working understanding of Ruby and OO programming, as well as a useful collection of tricks up your sleeves.

WEEK 1

The Fundamentals

1 Getting Started with Ruby

2 Hello, Objects!

3 Containers

4 Iteration and Flow Control

5 The Characteristics of Objects

6 Ins and Outs

7 Catching Up on Details

DAY 1

Getting Started with Ruby

Today we'll talk some in general terms about what the Ruby language is, find out where to get it if it's not already installed, and take our first simple programming steps.

Why Ruby?

The introduction to this book should have convinced you that a very high-level language is worth learning and using. But what's special about Ruby? After all, there are many who consider Java, C++, Python, and Perl to be perfectly good and effective languages, and those are better known.

There are several reasons to look at Ruby, whether you are already proficient in another language, are struggling to be, or are really new at this.

Ruby Is Small and Intuitive

This was the first thing I noticed about Ruby that really intrigued me. It is a language that, for all its expressiveness, does not require a lot of memorization. There is a simple, clean syntax and not too much clutter from special symbols. The vocabulary is mostly made up of sensible single words, not compound words of mixed case. A consistently applied *principle of least surprise* (POLS) means that if you don't know how to do something and you try to say clearly what you mean, there's a good chance that it will work.[1]

Ruby Gives You Immediate Feedback

No compilation phase is needed, so you can quickly see the results of any change you make to a program; just run it and see what happens. You don't have to sit around and wait for an intermediary process to chew on your code and approve it for testing.

Every object in a Ruby program knows something about itself and is willing to share that knowledge when asked. You can treat Ruby almost like a menu-driven language. If your intuition and memory both sputter when you want to know how long a string is, you don't have to go digging for a manual. Ask a string, "What are your methods?" and it will give you a list (length will be in there). Get used to the world being friendly: everybody likes to help you along in conversation.

Ruby Is Free

It's true; Ruby is not owned by a large corporation with its eye on the bottom line. It was created by a nice man called Matz who just wants you to be happy. You can download Ruby from the Internet for free. Whenever a new version comes out, there is no cost to upgrade. If you have ideas for improving the language, its source code is freely available, so you can play with it all you want. Make an improvement to Ruby and you can keep it to yourself, or you can bring it to the Ruby developer community to see if it gets incorporated into the mainstream.[2]

Ruby Is Portable

In the beginning, Ruby was a creature of Unix, but support for DOS/Windows has been catching up quickly, and there are versions available for BeOS and Mac OS X. Portable

---

[1]*Aficionados of some other languages will recognize the POLS concept, but may be pleased at Ruby's more focused application of it. Ruby's POLS helps keep you centered while learning the language ("oh—that works? Okay, I'll remember it") but also tends to complain at the right times, seldom jumping to conclusions and doing the wrong thing when you say something meaningless or ambiguous. This is sometimes referred to as avoiding the "Do What I Mean" syndrome.*

[2]*This, of course, requires that others see it as an improvement!*

graphic libraries like Tk and GTK are supported, so you can write windowed applications on Linux and run them without modification on Windows, and vice-versa. If you really want to, you can write at the Windows-native API level. (Don't expect my help with that.)

Ruby Is Object-Oriented

You don't have to know what this means yet, but it has lots of good consequences. It allows you to do differential programming, which keeps you from reinventing too many wheels. You can also encapsulate information and logic in neat packages to make them easy to deal with. When designing a program, it doesn't feel like you are building a complicated machine so much as orchestrating conversations among intelligent entities.

In contrast to Perl and C++, objects are in Ruby's true nature rather than an afterthought. It's possible to write code in Ruby that doesn't look object-oriented, but under the covers, it's how Ruby *thinks*.[3]

Ruby Is a Scripting Language

There is no strict distinction between a program and a script, but to call something a script is to underscore the fact that it is a simple text file that can be immediately fed to an *interpreter* without compiling in a separate step. The interpreter is a program, usually written in a lower-level language, like C, that reads a script, parses it, and runs it.

Also, a scripting language is often used to instruct the operating system to run other programs, capture their output for processing, and so on. A language that helps you coordinate unrelated programs is sometimes called a *glue* language; perhaps you see why. Thus Ruby is useful for system administration tasks,[4] especially since it is generally much friendlier than standard shell-scripting languages.

---

[3]*Ruby's creator spent considerable effort making the language familiar and comfortable to Perl users, and, as a result, many programmers in the Ruby community are ex-Perlites. Not surprisingly, those people tend to write Ruby code that looks a lot like Perl code! But the actual logic of Ruby is less like Perl's than that of a pure object-oriented language called Smalltalk. Smalltalk has a long and interesting history. It was an ambitious attempt to bring programming to the masses, and the name suggests that its creators hoped even children could use it effectively. But the main thing (in my view) that has kept Smalltalk from gaining wide acceptance is its reliance on a particular graphic environment; you can't easily script with it. Ruby brings us those highly accessible language ideas, and more, in a familiar and conventional form.*

[4]*Here portability necessarily takes a back seat. A Ruby script that orchestrates the execution of Unix-specific system administration programs would be meaningless on a Windows NT machine and would generate "command not found" error messages if you tried to run it there.*

Note

> A rather loose convention in this book is that the word *script* carries a passive and concrete connotation, and *program* carries an active and abstract connotation. That is to say, when we're talking about the program file as something you write or edit, it's a script; but when the interpreter has it and is running it, it's a program.

Ruby Supports Regular Expressions

If you've ever worked with Perl, you know you can't live without regular expressions once you've learned how to use them. They help you do some very impressive things with text processing without writing much code at all.

Okay, let's get on with it!

Make Sure You Have Ruby

To see whether you already have Ruby on your system, open a console window. If you're a Unix user, this will generally be something like an xterm window. If you're a Windows user, look in the Start menu for the MS-DOS prompt.

Now type **ruby -v** and press Return.

```
% ruby -v
ruby 1.7.0 (2001-04-02) [i586-linux]
```

If the response is a Ruby version number and a creation date (not necessarily matching those shown here), we can move forward. If not, visit http://www.ruby-lang.org to download the right Ruby for your system. Installation instructions will come with whatever package you get, but if you need more help, refer to Appendix B of this book.

First Steps

In deference to a tradition started with the classic book that taught so many people how to program in C, *The C Programming Language* by Brian Kernighan and Dennis Ritchie, let's crank out the obligatory "Hello, world!" program. Try typing this directly into a terminal window:

```
% ruby -e 'puts "Hello World!"'
Hello World!
```

Life in the Command Line

Was that really a program? Well, yes. A program that does something simple, such as print a message, needs no elaborate structure. In fact, the program proper lives within the single quotes, and is this:

```
puts "Hello World!"
```

As you might guess, `puts` means to *put* a *string* of characters someplace, in this case the screen.

The code that surrounds the program is our way of starting the Ruby interpreter, `ruby`. The entire line you typed is referred to as the *command line*. The `-e` switch means "evaluate the following expression," which might sound a little odd: What's to evaluate? Is something here supposed to be big or small, good or bad? We'll get to that shortly. For now, if it makes more sense, think of it as *execute* instead of *evaluate*. Also, Ruby makes no real distinction between what in some languages are called statements, instructions, and expressions; *expressions* is the most general term, but since many expressions are primarily designed to "do something" rather than just sit there and be valuable, we will often refer to those expressions as *instructions*.

As you've probably already concluded, we won't accomplish much of interest until we learn how to put some instructions together. We can separate them with a semicolon as follows:

```
% ruby -e 'print "The time is: "; print Time.now,".\n"'
The time is: Fri Feb 15 02:39:28 CDT 2002.
```

But we'll need a text editor before we can be comfortable working with substantive scripts.

Choosing a Text Editor

You can edit Ruby scripts with your favorite word processor, but that generally means taking special steps to save files in plain text format. It will be much more convenient in the long run if you settle on an editor that has plain text as its native format, and many suitable editors exist. Windows provides two: a stripped-down word processor named Notepad, and an anachronism from the DOS days named EDIT. Notepad has the inconsiderate habit of putting a `.TXT` extension on all filenames, which disqualifies it in my estimation. EDIT is okay in a pinch, but there are plenty of better editors to try if you poke around the Internet, and you may already have one you're comfortable with. One of my personal favorites for the Windows platform is PFE (Programmer's File Editor), a freeware editor that is no longer being developed but is still widely available.

On every Unix system you will find the editor vi, which is lightweight and fast. It's also quite confusing if you just fire it up without doing a little reading first, but it's still a fine choice for editing Ruby scripts. Other popular Unix text editors include emacs, pico, joe, jed, nedit, jedit, xcoral, and the editors that come with the Gnome and KDE desktop packages. Mac OS X users can try out BBEdit, or Unix-derived editors like emacs or vi.

Some editors are able to do automatic syntax highlighting and formatting for Ruby scripts, marking your comments, among other things, in distinctive colors.

I generally use emacs when editing Ruby scripts, and recommend it to anybody who needs to do a lot of text editing for any purpose. There is a learning curve involved, and, just like vi, it's confusing if you don't read up on it a bit before trying to use it. But it supports Ruby syntax highlighting, has some nice features including incremental search, is amazingly configurable, and is available for any computer platform.

An improved vi-based editor, vim,[5] provides a more convenient interface than its predecessor. It too supports syntax highlighting in Ruby scripts.

Our First Script

Let's try a script that is a few lines long. Fire up your text editor and type the following, then save using `first.rb` as a filename:

```
print "Say something, please: "
user_input = gets.chomp
print "You said #{user_input}.\n"
print "Backwards, it reads #{user_input.reverse}.\n"
print "The message is #{user_input.length} characters long.\n"
```

Now, back in the terminal window, run the script:

```
% ruby first.rb
Say something, please: Rubber baby buggy bumpers
You said Rubber baby buggy bumpers.
Backwards, it reads srepmub yggub ybab rebbuR.
The message is 25 characters long.
```

If it ran without errors, read on; otherwise check for typographical errors and try again.

Some Experiments

If you're an excruciatingly linear thinker, you can skip ahead and read the "play-by-play" section, then come back here. But if you're like me, you'll enjoy doing a few little experiments first; you might not understand everything that happens, but you'll get nice little teasers burrowing into your consciousness, giving your intuition a head start and helping the explicit answers make more sense when we get to them.

---

[5]*Yes, "vim" stands for "vi improved".*

For each experiment, make the suggested change to the script, then run the program and compare the results to what you got the first time. It is best to undo each change before moving on to the next experiment, so you're examining only one "variable" (in the scientific sense) at a time.

1. Change `print` in the first line to `puts`, or just the single letter p.
2. Remove `.chomp` at the end of the second line.
3. Put an *extra* `.chomp` on the end of the second line.
4. Remove the `#{}` characters surrounding `user_input.reverse` in the last line.
5. Replace the `\n` in the fourth line with a single space.
6. Add semicolons to the end of each line.
7. Insert a pound symbol (#) at the beginning of any line except line two.
8. Change `.length` to `.type` in the fifth line.
9. Leave the script alone, but enter its filename twice on the command line:

```
% ruby first.rb first.rb
```

Play-by-Play

Let's examine how `first.rb` works, and introduce some vocabulary items along the way.

After the `print` instruction in the first line delivers a message to the screen, `gets` ("get string"), in the second line, causes the script to stop and wait for you to type something brilliant at the keyboard.

When you have finished typing the input, you have to press the Enter key to signal that you're done. A special character associated with the Enter key will get tacked onto the end of the input string, but we[6] aren't really interested in that character, so we chomp it off with `chomp`.

Now that we have the input that we wanted, it needs a name. The name is arbitrary; we called it `user_input` because that is accurate and descriptive, but the name could as easily have been inp, i, ui, great_American_novel, wompus, eX9oMjwer, quark, or just about anything else. `user_input` is just a label for a piece of information that we can change whenever we want. We call it a *variable*.

---

[6]*Warning: Be prepared for some anthropomorphizing. As soon as the input has been entered, "we" begin to identify with the program instead of the user. So instead of saying "the program" does this or that, we say "we" do this or that. Don't let it bother you too much; on Day 2 the special name* self *will be introduced—suggesting that the impulse to identify the programmer with the program is part of the language, and so might not be entirely neurotic.*

The equals sign (=) associates a variable with an object, accomplishing what we call *reference* or *assignment*. It is equally correct to say "user_input refers to the user input" or "the user input is assigned the variable name user_input."

In the third line, the input is echoed back to the user. There are two new features here—the #{...} construct enclosing the variable name indicates that what we want displayed is not the variable name itself, but whatever the name refers to; and \n denotes the end-of-line character, without which our output items all get jammed together, end to end, on the same line. \n stands for newline (incidentally, what gets chomped by chomp in line two is also a newline character). Several special characters in Ruby have helpful mnemonics attached to their meanings; two other examples are \t, which moves the cursor to a tab stop, and \a, which sounds an alarm bell.

The fourth line adds something new: the invocation of a *method*. Every object in a Ruby program knows how to do certain things,[7] and method names are the vocabulary with which we can ask objects to perform their various tricks for us. It so happens that strings of characters know how to present themselves in backwards form, and reverse is the method name by which we request that behavior.

Likewise, the last line invokes the length method of a string, which tells us how long it is.

Remarks About the Experimental Results

We'll go through the experiments one by one and see what we learned from them.

1. Changing the first print instruction to puts causes the input line to appear under the prompt message, instead of beside it. A puts ensures that the string ends with a newline character, appending one if necessary.

   Changing print to p has the odd effect of putting double quotes around the output. If the string had contained special characters, p would have displayed them in their symbolic form; for example, print "\a" sounds an alarm bell, whereas p "\a" merely displays "\a" on the screen. As you might guess, p is rarely found in finished scripts, but often has diagnostic uses when you are working on one.

2. If we don't use chomp to remove the newline character, it becomes part of the string assigned to user_input in the second line of the program. The program output now looks strange: The newline is the last character shown in user_input and the first character in user_input.reverse. It also throws off the reported input length by 1.

---

[7]*We will learn shortly that just about everything in a Ruby program is an object in this specialized sense, including the program itself.*

3. Once the newline character has been removed, a second `chomp` has no effect. A `chomp` removes only newlines, so it doesn't steal the last character from your message. On the other hand, a `chop` is less discriminating. (Try it.)

4. If you read the foregoing play-by-play, you already understand what happened here. The `#{...}` is needed to make it clear that we want to see what the variable refers to, not the variable name. It's largely a matter of aesthetics, but some people prefer to avoid this by making a list of different kinds of objects, separated by commas:

```
print "Backwards, it reads", user_input.reverse, ".\n"
```

This is essentially like breaking one `print` instruction into several:

```
print "Backwards, it reads"
print user_input.reverse
print ".\n"
```

5. Removing the `\n` made the forward and reverse output messages appear on the same line. To keep them separate, we could either replace the `\n` or change the `print` in line three to `puts`.

6. Adding a semicolon to the end of a line has no effect. You can put semicolons between instructions on the same line, though this is, in some circumstances, considered bad form. As a general rule, the Ruby interpreter considers the end of a line to signal the end of an instruction, unless it is obvious that the current line is incomplete. The following is legal, since the interpreter can tell the top line needs completion:

```
sum = 2 +
   2
```

But this doesn't work:

```
sum = 2
   + 2
```

Since `sum = 2` makes sense by itself, the interpreter processes it separately before considering the next line. Then it doesn't know what to do with the `+ 2`.

7. The pound sign (#) is a way of placing a comment in a script. Comments mean nothing when the program runs; they're just there for your benefit and for the benefit of any other programmers who see your script. Anything following a #, up to the end of the line on which it appears, generally gets ignored by the interpreter. There are exceptions to this, such as when the symbol appears within quotation marks.

Sometimes you'll find it useful to remove a line temporarily from a script, expecting that you will want it back later. Changing the line into a comment by sticking a # in front of it is a safe and convenient way to accomplish this, and is so common a practice that it has become a universal fixture in programmers' vocabulary (as in, "you should try commenting out those lines and see what happens").

8. The `type` method name is one understood by absolutely every object in Ruby; that is to say, every object is smart enough to at least tell you something about what kind of object it is. You will notice that these type names are always capitalized.

9. Did this one surprise you? The program didn't wait to hear from you; instead the first line of the script itself was used as the input message, as if you had typed it from the keyboard. Keep in mind that we want to be able to get information from files, and not just from the keyboard. We have just demonstrated one of the simplest ways to do it, but it will take a moment to explain.

The idea of objects and their methods is pervasive in Ruby, and `gets` is just another method name, like `length`, `type`, and `reverse`. This means it is a way of talking to an object. Yet, in our example, it appears not to belong to any object. We didn't specify what object the `gets` method was to be applied to, so the Ruby interpreter decided for us. Its logic is simple; if we supply a filename on the command line, it opens the file and relays the `gets` request to it. Otherwise it relays the `gets` request to the keyboard, or more exactly, the *standard input* object, whose name is `STDIN`.

When you typed `first.rb` twice on the command line, the script file was really used twice: once to tell the interpreter which script to run, and again to tell it what data file it should use for input.

Lest you indignantly accuse Ruby of trying to read your mind, this behavior is easy to override: Just specify an object when you make the method call. For example, `STDIN.gets` is a request to the standard input object and causes input to come from the keyboard,[8] regardless of what is on the command line.

The *Shebang* Line

There is a special comment at the top of most Ruby scripts. You'll find something similar at the top of scripts for other languages too. It looks like this:

```
#!/usr/bin/env ruby
```

or sometimes like this:

```
#!/usr/local/bin/ruby
```

This *shebang*[9] line is an exception to the rule that comments are for humans to read. It exists so that on a Unix system you don't have to type **ruby** every time you want to run a Ruby program. Instead you can just type the name of the script file. The idea is that

---

[8]*Well, okay, it's still not that simple:* `STDIN` *can be redirected, but we can wait until Day 6 to talk more about it.*

when given a script to run, the computer needs to know what language is in use; it needs information about which interpreter to pass the script to. We'll discuss this in more detail on Day 12.

The analogous concept in the Windows world is file association, which is taken care of by the "one-click" installer (see Appendix B). Although shebang lines are mostly associated with Unix, they are sometimes seen on Windows too, particularly in the context of Web servers.

Using Ruby Interactively

If you run ruby without providing a command or a program file name, something funny happens. No prompt appears on the screen, but the computer just sits there waiting for you to type things. (You may have already stumbled into this situation.) What's going on? You have invoked the ruby interpreter, and what the interpreter wants to do is to run a Ruby script; that is its only reason for living. Since you didn't provide a script in advance, the interpreter sits patiently, waiting for you to fulfill your obligation and give it something to do.

You can type an instruction or two, or a lengthy script if you want, pressing Enter at the end of each line; when you finish, it will execute the script and return you to your normal command prompt. Now consider: there has to be some way to indicate when you are done typing, since Enter just signals the end of a line, and you can type any number of lines. A special *end-of-file* (EOF) character is provided for this purpose. If you're running Unix, you create this character by holding down the Ctrl key and pressing the D key. Conventionally we denote this key combination as ^D. If you're running Windows, use ^Z, or the function key F6.[10] Here is an example of an interactive session with the Ruby interpreter:

```
% ruby
x = 10**6    # 10 to the power 6
puts x
puts x + 99
puts x.type
s = "EgoMania"
puts s.downcase
puts s.upcase
puts s.type
puts VERSION
^D
```

---

[9]*And why, you ask, is it called something silly like shebang? Well, the pound symbol is also sometimes called a sharp symbol, because of its use in musical notation, and the* she *part is derived from that. "Bang" is an old typesetting term for an exclamation point; in Ruby that symbol is also associated with "destructive" methods, which we'll see on Day 7.*

```
1000000
1000099
Fixnum
egomania
EGOMANIA
String
1.7.0
```

An Interactive Tool: `irb`

Among the more useful sample scripts provided with Ruby is the "interactive Ruby" script. It can be invoked directly from the command line as `irb`. Running irb is a little bit like talking directly to the interpreter, as we did just a moment ago, but it provides incremental feedback. At the end of each line you enter, irb determines whether you have given it something complete enough to execute. If not, it waits for another line. If so, it executes what you gave it, then waits for another expression. But there's a twist— whatever it executes, it displays that thing's *value*.

As I hinted earlier, there's really no difference, as far as the interpreter is concerned, between *execution* and *evaluation*; so when we talk about "something complete enough to execute," what we really mean is "an expression that makes sense." Yes, that's not very intuitive; but all will be explained in a moment.

An expression is something that has a value. Here are some examples:

Expression	Value
9	9
"ABC"	"ABC"
10*4	40
puts "XYZ"	nil

In a sense, evaluating expressions is the only thing the interpreter ever does. It just so happens that some of those expressions have side effects. The side effect of a `print` expression is the delivery of some information, typically to the screen; since that side effect is the only thing we really care about, the value of that expression is something meaningless. But in order to get that desirable side effect, we make the interpreter evaluate the expression.

Now let's play with irb a bit. We'll start by entering the expressions from the preceding table.

```
% irb
irb(main):001:0> 9
9
```

---

[10]*The effect of ^D in Unix is immediate, but in DOS/Windows the ^Z or F6 character is considered part of the input line and is not seen by Ruby until after the next time the Enter key is pressed.*

```
irb(main):002:0> "ABC"
"ABC"
irb(main):003:0> 10*4
40
irb(main):004:0> puts "XYZ"
XYZ
nil
```

The first three expressions were evaluated in the normal sense; irb just gave their values back to us. It is the fourth expression that illustrates the idea of side effects. Notice that two items got displayed instead of one. Since the only thing irb "cares about" is the value of an expression, it printed a nil to the screen. That's Ruby's way of expressing a meaningless, empty value. But in the process of determining that value, the side effect of puts occurred, and XYZ appeared too. If it's not stretching your imagination too much, think of the XYZ as something that we snuck past irb. It didn't mean to print anything but the nil; we tricked it.

What happens if you give irb an incomplete expression? It prompts you again and does not try to evaluate the expression until you finish it. The prompt changes from ">" to "*" to indicate this.

```
irb(main):005:0> (5.99 +
irb(main):006:1* 14.01) /
irb(main):007:0* 2
10.0
```

You might find it handy to run irb in a separate window whenever you are working on a Ruby script. You can quickly try out a new idea, get the value of an expression, learn what the acceptable method names are for an object, and do many other useful things using irb.

Oh, one last thing: I haven't mentioned yet how you tell irb that you're done using it. Just type the word exit. In fact, exit is not a special instruction for irb, but a Ruby expression that, when evaluated, has exactly the side effect you want.

The eval.rb Script

eval.rb is another interactive script provided with Ruby. It's not quite as smart as irb, because it can be fooled about what is a complete expression and what isn't. It also lacks some of irb's text editing capabilities. But it is interesting for two reasons. First, unlike irb, eval.rb is a self-contained script, so a curious beginner can study it. Second, an enhanced version of eval.rb is available that automatically formats code as you type. It also uses color to distinguish expressions, expression values, and side effects. The enhanced eval.rb is available at http://www.ruby-lang.org/~slagell/eval.rb.

Summary

Today we spent most of our time learning what Ruby is about and getting our feet wet with some of the basics of script writing. We wrote our first simple script using a text editor, and were introduced to the interactive tools irb and eval.rb.

We also touched on some of the deeper ideas of the language and bumped up against a few fine distinctions that may seem difficult at the moment. You shouldn't worry about them if they didn't sink in right away. They may not make the language easy to understand in a theoretical sense, but they do make it easy to use. Practice and exposure are what will make them real for you. There are 20 days left. We'll get there together.

Is There Homework in This Class?

We'll end most lessons with a few suggested activities and questions to help you sort through what you've seen. These aren't designed primarily to test your skills but to help you learn, which is an altogether different goal. Do your best before consulting the answers; especially in later chapters, there will be times when an answer you have to struggle for will turn out to be different from, yet just as good as, the one we provide.

For today, you'll just be typing some things into irb and drawing what conclusions you can. Start irb in a terminal window. Type the following expressions on separate lines, notice what values and errors get reported, and see whether you can answer the questions that follow.

```
99 < 100
99 <= 100
100 <= 100
100 == 100
100 = 100
perfect_score = 100
"99" < 100
"99".type
100.type
"99".length
100.length
"99" < "100"
"99" > "100"
99 + 100
"99" + 100
"99" + "100"
"99".to_i + "100".to_i
99.to_s + 100.to_s
99 <=> 100
100 <=> 100
100 <=> 99
99.nonzero?
```

```
"99".nonzero?
"99".respond_to? "nonzero?"
"99".methods
"99".methods.include? "nonzero?"
```

Exercises

We haven't gone very deep into the Ruby language yet, so today's questions will be somewhat different from those you'll see in later chapters. Consider this more like a preview; you won't know all the answers from what you've read so far. Some you might figure out from the results of the foregoing irb session.[11] Others are explained below. As for the unanswered questions, well, just toss them into that stewpot simmering on your mental back-burner; they should be nice and tender by the time we get to the later chapters that will explain all.

1. What are the meanings of < and <= ?

2. What does a pair of equals signs (==) mean, and why can't we use just one?

3. What does the plus sign do?

4. Aren't the results for "99" < "100" and "99" > "100" just wrong?

5. What do the to_s and to_i methods do? And what do the s and i probably stand for?

6. Given that an asterisk means *multiply*, what would you expect the value of the following statement to be?

    ```
    "hubba " * 2
    ```

7. What does that strange <=> thing do, and what use could it possibly be to us? Don't we have several other operators that cover its meaning?

8. Why did "99".nonzero? cause an error, but not 99.nonzero?

9. What does .methods do?

Answers

1. As you might have expected, < means *less than* and <= means *less than or equal to*.

2. The double equals sign tests for equality. We can't use just one, because the single equals sign means something different: We are already using it for variable assignment. You'll have a deeper understanding of this after Day 4.

3. Well, it depends. When used with numbers, a plus sign adds them together. When used with character strings, it concatenates them. (This serves as a quick reminder to Perl veterans; Ruby is not Perl.)

---

[11]*If you're reading this without your computer in front of you, you can see the full results of the irb session in Appendix A.*

4. Consider that what you are comparing are strings, not numbers. The Principle of Least Surprise, as it applies to Ruby, means that the meaning of string comparisons should be consistent regardless of the contents of the strings. To what kind of use, in everyday life, is string comparison most often applied? Alphabetization, of course. Ruby's string comparisons determine *lexicographical* order, which is a generalized kind of alphabetical order. Since a "9" character is lexicographically higher than a "1", we are obliged to recognize that `"99" > "100"` is true in the same way that `"Wilma" > "Fred"` is true.

5. `to_s` converts a number to a string, and `to_i` does exactly the reverse. You probably already figured out that the s stands for *string*. Perhaps less obvious is that i stands for *integer*. We can be specific, because there are different types of numbers. Verify this by comparing the values of the following:

```
"3.14".to_i
"3.14".to_f
```

The f means *float,* which is the usual programming term for numbers that have a fractional part.

6. You'd get `"hubba hubba "`.

7. Instead of true and false values, `<=>` gives us, depending on how its comparison turns out, either -1, 0, or 1; those values correspond to the meanings of the three characters that make up the symbol. In upcoming days we'll see why it is useful to have this specialized comparison operator.

8. It makes sense to ask a number whether it's nonzero. It makes less sense to ask that question of a string of characters. So, `nonzero?` is a method for numbers and not for strings. That might bother you, because the string `"99"` looks like a number and can reasonably be interpreted as one. But if strings were to be allowed to respond to `nonzero?`, some people would just as reasonably expect it to answer based on its length, since all strings have length. Ruby strives to avoid the ambiguities that always plague the pastime of mind reading.

9. `methods` returns a list of all the methods of an object: in other words, the vocabulary you can use when talking to that object. If you think about it, `methods` itself has to be considered a method; sure enough, you can always find it in the list.

DAY **2**

Hello, Objects!

> Just be the ball, be the ball, be the ball.
> —Chevy Chase as Ty Webb in *Caddyshack* (1980)

We will be spending this day learning about *objects* in Ruby, designing them, creating them, examining them, giving them names, and teaching them tricks. We'll cover quite a bit of ground in a short space here, so don't rush through; take your time.

What Is an Object?

Alas, this is a question that shouldn't have to be asked.

Something went wrong years ago when object-oriented programming was a new idea. Maybe C++, the language many of us were first told was object-oriented, didn't quite live up to the billing. Maybe the people teaching it just couldn't break their old procedure-oriented habits. Maybe the language theorists got so happy when burbling about encapsulation, polymorphism, data hiding, and so on, that they forgot to talk plain talk for the benefit of people trying to learn to program. Objects were supposed to make things easier for everybody, but somehow they turned into just one more weird concept to trip over.

But you can let your intuition be correct: an object is what you think it is. Numbers are objects. Files are objects. A program is an object. You can think of yourself as an object if you like. Objects are basically what you refer to when you use *nouns* (and especially, *pronouns*) in speaking and writing.

The things that make objects interesting when you are programming are the same things that make them interesting in the real world. Different objects have different classifications, conditions, capabilities, and limitations. The craft of object-oriented programming more or less boils down to the ability to give objects the right characteristics and to put those characteristics to use later.

The First Object: `self`

The irb program lets us ask the Ruby interpreter some tough questions and see the answers right away. We can start with the most profound question of all, "Who am I?" In other words, evaluate the `self` object:

```
irb(main):001:0> self
main
```

Although that might have been gratifying to the ego, it wasn't very informative. Let's try, "What kind of thing am I?"

```
irb(main):002:0> self.type
Object
```

It's hard to argue with that, isn't it? Still we haven't learned very much yet. How about, "What do I know how to do?"

```
irb(main):003:0> self.methods
["private", "public", "include", "to_s", "kill",
"irb_kill", "fg", "irb_fg", "jobs", "irb_jobs", "conf",
"irb_context", "irb", "source", "irb_source", "cb",
"irb_change_binding", "fork", "quit", "exit", "irb_exit",
"instance_of?", "protected_methods", "inspect", "freeze",
"dup", "__id__", "equal?", "send", "==", "===", "method",
"respond_to?", "kind_of?", "private_methods", "methods",
"frozen?", "taint", "type", "eql?", "instance_eval",
"extend", "=~", "is_a?", "instance_variables",
"public_methods", "to_a", "tainted?", "class", "hash",
"__send__", "display", "singleton_methods", "untaint",
"clone", "id", "nil?"]
```

The actual list of method names you see will depend on the version of Ruby you have installed. Most of these names hold no meaning for us, although one or two might look familiar.

We are going to be adding a new method to self's list shortly. For now, let's put a label on what we just learned so that we can refer to it later. A suitable name for that big list of methods might be "generic methods," but we can't use spaces here, so let's call it generic_methods. Assign the name this way:

```
irb(main):004:0> generic_methods = self.methods
```

 Note

> There are two common ways to deal with word separators. Java programmers usually like to distinguish words by capitalization, as in thisIsAVariableName. I prefer underscores, as in this_is_a_variable_name. You'll see both styles in Ruby programs. A consensus doesn't seem to have emerged yet.

irb lists the methods again when we make the assignment. This could get a little tiresome, couldn't it? When we have added to the method list, we'll want to be able to identify the additions without looking at all that garbage. Having a name assigned to the original method list will help, as you'll see shortly.

Teach Yourself Tricks

It's time to write our first method for self, which we'll call jump. When this method is invoked, self's response will be to put a message on the screen.

A new method has to be *defined*, and the shorthand for *define* is def.

```
irb(main):005:0> def self.jump
```

This code says to the interpreter, "Define jump as a method of self." After this, we supply a definition for the method:

```
irb(main):006:1> puts "How high?"
```

Did you notice the change in the prompt line from :0> to :1>? It means irb is waiting for something, and deferring evaluation while it waits. So unless we want to do or say more in response to a jump command, we had better indicate that we're done defining.

```
irb(main):007:1> end
nil
```

irb digests the new method definition, acknowledges it with a rather noncommittal `nil` evaluation, and changes the 1 back to a 0.

To use the new method, we can explicitly tell `self` to `jump`.

```
irb(main):008:0> self.jump
how high?
nil
```

Note

> Vocabulary note: Since *methods* work like *messages*, when some object has one of its methods called, we call that object the *receiver* of the call.

You will notice again that after invoking the `jump` method we get both the result of the action we asked for, which is the printing of the message to the screen, and the value of the whole `puts "how high?"` expression, which is `nil`. When you're writing scripts rather than experimenting in irb, things will be a little different; you won't see any evaluations unless you ask for them. We'll get back to that thought at the beginning of the next chapter.

To further verify that `jump` has been added to the list of `self`'s methods, you can ask for `self.methods` again and look through the list. Probably you won't have to look far.

Since we are getting back much more information than we really want, is it possible to rephrase the question "What are my methods?" to make the answer more concise and interesting? Sure it is. As we will see over and over again in this book, if there's a simple way to express your wish in natural language, there's probably a simple way to get Ruby to do it. "What are my methods, not including the ones shown before?" can be asked this way:

```
irb(main):009:0> self.methods - generic_methods
["jump"]
```

As you'll find out on Day 3, it's an easy matter to manipulate lists in Ruby and get exactly the information you want out of them. The minus sign in this context means *without*.

The Second Object: other

Programming in Ruby wouldn't be very much fun if only the `self` object were available; it would be no more interesting than living in a world all alone. We would like to be able to populate our universe with more objects.

If we want another object that we can simply call "other," we say

```
other = Object.new
```

This is pretty close to how you would state the request out loud: "Let *other* be a new object." But as it turns out, there is a good reason for the reversal of the last two words in the statement: new is a method name, a message which requests that a new object be created. What receives the message is not an object in the sense that we have so far understood, but a Class object. For now you don't have to worry about what that means; it's mostly important to appreciate that the idea of passing messages between objects is pervasive in Ruby, and the syntax by which it is done is consistent.

We can give other its own methods, too.

```
irb(main):10.0> other = Object.new
#<Object:0x4016f3fc>
irb(main):11.0> def other.philosophize
irb(main):12.1> puts "All men are mortal."
irb(main):13.1> end
nil
```

Ruby uses the funny #<type:address> notation (as in #<Object:0x4016f3fc>) when we haven't given it any better way of describing objects. For now, although it's unsightly, it is at least an effective way of uniquely identifying objects without relying on variable names, which can be handy when debugging. When we get to Day 15, we'll learn how to make the descriptions more readable and informative. It's not important yet.

Our menagerie of objects now includes self and other. Each understands some of the same generic messages, but we have defined things such that their vocabularies are not quite the same.

```
irb(main):014:0> other.type
Object
irb(main):015:0> self.type
Object
irb(main):016:0> self.jump
how high?
nil
irb(main):017:0> other.jump
NameError: undefined method `jump' for #<Object:0x4016f3fc>
(irb):17:in `irb_binding'
irb(main):018:0> other.philosophize
All men are mortal.
nil
irb(main):019:0> self.philosophize
NameError: undefined method `philosophize' for #<Object:0x4017dc68>
(irb):19:in `irb_binding'
```

We can give the two objects different ways of responding to the same message.

Note

In case you're interested, giving two objects different ways to respond to the same message is one of the things language theorists sometimes call *polymorphism*.

```
irb(main):020.0> def self.philosophize
irb(main):021.1>   puts "Eat, drink, and be merry."
irb(main):022.1> end
nil
irb(main):023.0> other.philosophize
All men are mortal.
nil
irb(main):024.0> self.philosophize
Eat, drink, and be merry.
nil
```

Classes

We know how to create methods for individual objects, but that hardly begins to tap into the power of object-oriented programming. Now we can start thinking about how to mass-produce lots of objects from a single set of specifications.

Let's start with the problem of how to make several philosophers who all agree with each other. We could do it the hard way, telling each one what to say:

```
jane = Object.new
def jane.philosophize
  puts "People should behave ethically."
end
howard = Object.new
def howard.philosophize
  puts "People should behave ethically."
end
irma = Object.new
def irma.philosophize
  puts "People should behave ethically."
end
# ...
```

But that looks like a lot of unnecessary work at the keyboard, and of course it is. Since these philosophers obviously all studied under the same teacher, we should be able to define them that way and so avoid all that redundant description. What we are describing, then, is a *class* of philosophers. Continue the irb session as follows. The indentation and comments are to emphasize structure:

```
irb(main):025:0> class Kantian
irb(main):026:1>   def philosophize
irb(main):027:2>     puts "People should behave ethically."
irb(main):028:2>   end   # end of "philosophize" method
irb(main):029:1> end   # end of Kantian class definition
nil
```

There are a couple of things to notice before proceeding. First, the name of every new class, like `Kantian`, always starts with a capital letter. Second, the `end` keyword is used twice here: first to end the method definition and then to end the class definition. When you are writing Ruby scripts, it is a good practice to indent lines so that each `end` is vertically aligned with the first line of whatever is being ended.

Well then, how exactly does a Kantian philosophize? A common mistake among those just learning object-oriented programming is to try to make a class do things directly, something like this:

```
irb(main):030:0> Kantian.philosophize
NameError: undefined method `philosophize' for Kantian:Class
(irb):32:in `irb_binding'
```

Look carefully at that error message. It tells you that `philosophize` is not a method that can be used here, and also helpfully reminds you that `Kantian` is a *class*. Indeed, if you ask for the methods of `Kantian` (using `Kantian.methods`) you will find that `philosophize` is not in the list. But didn't we put it there? Where is it? Try looking at the `instance_methods`:

```
irb(main):031:0> Kantian.instance_methods
["philosophize"]
```

Hmm. It looks like we'd better find out what an *instance* is.

Making Instances of a Class

Look at it this way: What we have created is not a philosopher, but a school that produces philosophers. It is those philosophers, and not the school itself, who know how to philosophize. No good result can come of walking up to a building and shouting, "Tell me the meaning of life!" If we want to hear wisdom, it might make more sense to approach somebody who is walking out of the front door wearing a graduation gown. So what we are after is an individual instance of a Kantian philosopher.

```
irb(main):032:0> jane = Kantian.new
#<Kantian:0x40184e04>
```

Does that look familiar? When we created the `other` object a moment ago, we did it the same way, except that we asked for a new `Object` rather than a new `Kantian`. Consider that `Object` is itself a class. It is, in fact, the most general class in Ruby, so asking for a new `Kantian` (or anything else) is a just a more specific way of asking for a new `Object`. This is part of the concept of *inheritance* that we'll examine later in the book.

Let's find out whether `jane` has had the orthodox Kantian education.

```
irb(main):033:0> jane.philosophize
People should behave ethically.
nil
```

We can churn out some more graduates while we're at it; Kantians in our universe come cheap, and just as we planned, they all think alike.

```
irb(main):034:0> howard = Kantian.new
#<Kantian:0x4017f620>
irb(main):035:0> irma = Kantian.new
#<Kantian:0x40167544>
irb(main):036:0> howard.philosophize
People should behave ethically.
nil
irb(main):037:0> irma.philosophize
People should behave ethically.
nil
```

You will have noticed that the graduates of our school all have names starting with lower case letters. One good reason for this is that it helps us distinguish classes from objects. We'll discuss naming guidelines in some detail before long, but for now it will suffice to remember that class names are capitalized, and variable and method names are not.

Appending Methods to a Class

To make our philosophers seem a little more human, we will next teach them to `rant`. This means creating another method for the `Kantian` class.

One nice thing about Ruby is that it is a dynamic language. That's a vague thing to say, but you'll understand what it means before long, because there are many examples of it throughout the book. To give you an inkling of the idea, it is not necessary to start over and redefine the `Kantian` class if we want to add a method to what is already there, as we can see by continuing the irb session as follows:

```
irb(main):038:0> class Kantian
irb(main):039:1>   def rant
irb(main):040:2>     puts "Nietzsche was a ninny."
irb(main):041:2>   end
irb(main):042:1> end
nil
```

Here, saying "class `Kantian`" does not create a new class, but reopens the old one, letting us get in and tinker with it. The `end` in line 42 closes it back up.

The effect is as if we had defined both methods together when first creating the Kantian class, like this:

```
class Kantian
  def philosophize
    puts "People should behave ethically."
  end
  def rant
    puts "Nietsche was a ninny."
  end
end
```

If we want to, we can verify that our change took effect by looking at the instance method list again.

```
irb(main):043:0> Kantian.instance_methods
["rant", "philosophize"]
```

Now we can ask a new graduate what he really thinks.

```
irb(main):044:0> fred = Kantian.new
#<Kantian:0x40165f64>
irb(main):045:0> fred.rant
Nietzsche was a ninny.
nil
```

Does it matter that jane graduated before the school was making its students so opinionated?

```
irb(main):046:0> jane.rant
Nietzsche was a ninny.
nil
```

It would appear that changes in the curriculum are retroactively applied to alumni! That is to say, when you attach a new method to a class, all objects belonging to that class, regardless of when they were created, become responsive to it.

Altering and Removing Methods

As well as adding new methods to a class, we can improve existing ones. The procedure is to define each changed method as if it were new; it replaces any other method by the same name.

```
irb(main):047:0> class Kantian
irb(main):048:1>   def rant
irb(main):049:2>     puts "Nietzsche was a ninny, and so was Marx."
irb(main):050:2>   end
irb(main):051:1> end
nil
```

And although there is rarely any reason to get rid of methods, it's still good to know that if we regret having defined one, we can undefine it later.

```
irb(main):052:0> class Kantian
irb(main):053:1>   undef rant
```

```
irb(main):054:1> end
nil
irb(main):055:0> Kantian.instance_methods
["philosophize"]
```

Everybody's Methods

So far we have seen how to attach a method to an object by including the object name in the definition line:

```
def spud.a_method_for_object_spud
  # ...
end
```

We can attach a method to an entire class of objects by enclosing the method definition in a class...end block:

```
class Shortstop
  def a_method_for_all_objects_of_type_Shortstop
    # ...
  end
end
```

It is also handy to define methods that belong to *all* objects. This is very commonly done in short scripts that don't require much object-oriented thought.

```
def promiscuous_method
  # ...
end
```

Such methods are sometimes called *top-level* methods. Listing 2.1 is a script that illustrates how a top-level method is accessible.

LISTING 2.1   Accessing a Top-Level Method

```
01:  #!/usr/bin/env ruby
02:  # Define a top-level method named foo.
03:  def foo
04:    puts "The foo method has been called!"
05:  end
06:
07:  # Create an object "ob1", give it a method "call_foo",
08:  #  and let that method call foo.
09:  ob1 = Object.new
10:  def ob1.call_foo
11:    foo
12:  end
13:
14:  # As above, but instead of a single object, define
15:  #  a class and make a couple of instances of it.
```

continues

LISTING 2.1 Continued

```
16:     class FooCaller
17:       def call_foo
18:          foo
19:       end
20:     end
21:
22:     fc1 = FooCaller.new
23:     fc2 = FooCaller.new
24:
25:
26:     # Demonstrate that each object has access to
27:     #  the foo method.
28:
29:     print "self: " ;    foo
30:     print "ob1:  " ;    ob1.call_foo
31:     print "fc1:  " ;    fc1.call_foo
32:     print "fc2:  " ;    fc2.call_foo
```

Running the script produces this output:

```
self: The foo method has been called!
ob1:  The foo method has been called!
fc1:  The foo method has been called!
fc2:  The foo method has been called!
```

Top-level methods are available to the public, but only for *private use*. You can think of this as meaning that no object can be coerced into calling it. If ob1 wants to call foo in one of its methods, as in our example, that's fine, but nobody can directly ask ob1 to call foo.

```
ob1.foo  # This generates an error.
```

The general rule is that a private method cannot have a receiver specified. Whenever no receiver is specified, whatever object made the call is considered the receiver.

Who Is This "self" Anyway?

We've been talking about self as the top-level object; depending on your turn of mind, you might be identifying it with the script, or with yourself as the programmer. But strictly speaking, self is not really one object, but shorthand for the "current object," which is whatever object is in control at any given moment. In a simple script with no defined objects, self is always main, the top-level object, but when other objects exist, they refer to themselves when saying self. After all, this is just how we use the word in ordinary language.

```
#!/usr/bin/env ruby
print "top-level object identifies itself as "
p self
```

```
an_object = Object.new
def an_object.identify_yourself
  p self
end

print "an_object identifies itself as "
an_object.identify_yourself
```

The preceding script produces output like this:

```
top-level object identifies itself as main
an_object identifies itself as #<Object:0x4017052c>
```

Method Arguments

So far, our way of talking to objects has been simple: We invoke a method, and some-thing appears on the screen. That's kind of like pressing a button, watching a light blink, and walking away. But really useful methods can accept, process, and return information. To extend the mechanical metaphor, methods can represent not only pushbuttons, but knobs, dials, switches, and so on.

Information flows into a method through an *argument list*. When defining a method that accepts input of some kind, you put this list within parentheses just after the method name. The list is made of variables separated by commas.

```
irb(main):01:0> def echo_two_args(x, y)
irb(main):02:1>   puts "the first argument was #{x}"
irb(main):03:1>   puts "the second argument was #{y}"
irb(main):04:1> end
nil
```

Similarly, when calling the method, information is passed as a list of comma-separated items within parentheses. (The parentheses can be omitted in some circumstances, but we'll usually leave them in for our examples, at least for a while, just to be consistent and safe.) For each argument, we can either pass the information directly or provide a variable that refers to it. In the next example, a and 0 are the *actual arguments*. The echo_two_args method will assign them to x and y, which are sometimes called *formal arguments*.

```
irb(main):05:0> a = "swordfish"
irb(main):06:0> echo_two_args(a, 0)
The first argument was swordfish.
The second argument was 0.
nil
```

So much for passing information into a method. Getting it out is even simpler; we tell a method what it should return.

```
irb(main):07:0> def eight
irb(main):08:1>    return 8
irb(main):09:1> end
nil
irb(main):10:0> eight
8
irb(main):11:0> eight * eight
64
```

If we had more patience than sense, we could write different methods to return all our favorite numbers.

Here is a method that always gives back a little more than it gets, so to speak:

```
irb(main):12:0> def one_more_than(a_number)
irb(main):13:1>    return a_number + 1
irb(main):14:1> end
nil
irb(main):15:0> one_more_than(5)
6
```

Note

> Experienced C++/Java/Perl programmers will be inclined to try to increment numbers with a ++ operator, only to find that it doesn't exist in Ruby. The author of Ruby has taken some heat for this bit of unorthodoxy, but he has expressed good reasons for standing firm, which we won't go into here. You can't add 1 to x by saying x++, but you can say x+=1, which is more general and only takes one more keystroke. It takes almost no time to get used to.

We can do whatever we like with the value returned from one_more_than, such as assigning a name to it or passing it to another method (or even back to the same one).

```
irb(main):16:0> qaz = one_more_than( - 3.3)
-2.3
irb(main):17:0> qaz
-2.3
irb(main):18.0> one_more_than(one_more_than (qaz))
-0.3
```

It is also permissible to pass multiple values back from a method, as long as you *don't* put parentheses around them. Just separate the returned values with commas.

```
irb(main):19:0> def identify(an_object)
irb(main):20.1>    return an_object.type, an_object.id
irb(main):21.1> end
nil
```

The values will be returned in the form of a list. You can assign them immediately to a list of variables if you like.

```
irb(main):22.0> my_type, my_id = identify(self)
[Object, 537652788]
irb(main):23.0> my_type
Object
irb(main):24.0> my_id
537652788
```

At least for simple methods, you may find it convenient to omit the word `return`. In its absence a method returns the last thing it evaluates. So a method that returns the sum and difference of two numbers can be written either as:

```
def sum_and_diff(n1,n2)
  return n1+n2, n1-n2
end
```

or as

```
def sum_and_diff(n1,n2)
  n1+n2, n1-n2
end
```

Although there is no logical difference between these, in practice the second might execute faster than the first.

Local Scope for Variables

In restaurants, people ordinarily order dishes off the menu and agree that they will pay for them afterward. On the other hand, people ordinarily refrain from wandering back into the kitchen to tell the staff how to do their jobs or look over the cook's shoulder. This is a distinction between *specification* and *implementation*, or between *what* is done and *how* it is done. There is an informal contract between the restaurant and the diner, specified by the menu. The cook provides the meal described in the menu, without the diner interfering. If the meal is satisfactory, the diner pays the required amount (ignore the tip, for our purposes), and everybody is happy.

You're probably wondering what this has to do with Ruby programming. The same distinction between specification and implementation applies to method arguments. When we invoke a method, it is important that we understand what goes in and what comes out; a method has a job to do, a contract to fulfill, corresponding to the specification of a dish on the menu. But it is not important that the user of a method understand its inner workings (corresponding to what the cooks do in the kitchen). In fact, good software engineers understand that it is better in most cases to pretend you don't know how a method works, even if you're the person who wrote it. Only the "contract" should matter.

Let's revisit the `echo_two_args` example from the preceding section. The responsibility of the method is to display the arguments that it is given. The fact that it does so using `puts` instead of `print` is not relevant to the contract, nor is the fact that it internally uses the variable names x and y.

What happens if we're already using the name x for something else, not knowing that the method we are calling will want to use it too?

```
irb(main):25:0> x = "DEADBEEF"
irb(main):26:0> echo_two_args(42.0, x)
The first argument was 42.0.
The second argument was DEADBEEF.
nil
```

2

The string `"DEADBEEF"` has been given the name x, but when the string is passed through the argument list, its name no longer matters to the method; all that matters is *where it appears in the list*. `echo_two_args` sees a list containing two things, and it assigns variables to them in the order specified by its formal argument list. Since `42.0` comes first in the list, `echo_two_args` labels it x. `"DEADBEEF"` comes second and gets labeled y. Both labels are temporary, effective only for the duration of the method's operation.

After the completion of the method call, what happened to the x that used to refer to `"DEADBEEF"`? It escaped quite unharmed.

```
irb(main):27:0> x
"DEADBEEF"
```

If it helps, consider that Ruby's variables usually correspond to *pronouns* in common speech. When you say to someone, "See that pen over there? Please pick it up and hand it to me," the conversation does not have to grind to a halt because you're both worried about what the word *it* refers to (obviously the pen), or about whether you have put your communication at risk by changing the meaning of past or future utterances of *it*. This is what pronouns are good at, after all. They are placeholders, meant to be reused many times with various localized meanings.

Let "that pen over there" be *it*.

Please pick *it* up.

Please hand *it* to me.

Thanks. Now, what were we just talking about?

After that pleasant exchange, the association of the word *it* with the pen object can and should be forgotten. Likewise, formal arguments have meaning confined to the methods using them.

This is also true of Ruby's variables in general, whether or not they are related to method arguments. Unless we say otherwise, they have what we call *localized scope*.

```
#!/usr/bin/env ruby
# Enclosed by def ... end,
#  here is one local scope area for the variable v.
def foo
    v = "ABCDEFG"
    puts "Inside foo, v is #{v}."
end
# Here is another.
v = 1234567
puts "Before calling foo, v is #{v}."
foo
puts "After calling foo, v is #{v}."
```

Here's what the output of this script looks like:

```
Before calling foo, v is 1234567.
Inside foo, v is ABCDEFG.
After calling foo, v is 1234567.
```

We'll learn about scope in more detail in coming days.

Communication Within an Object

People may worry about you if you talk to yourself (unless you keep it quiet), but it's quite common and acceptable for objects in Ruby to talk to themselves. That is to say, an object's methods can call each other and pass information around. Take a look at the script in Listing 2.2.

LISTING 2.2 Talking Methods: ClockWatcher

```
01:   #!/usr/bin/env ruby
02:
03:   class ClockWatcher
04:     def double_report
05:       return look_1 + "\n" + look_2
06:     end
07:
08:     def look_1
09:       e = exact_time
10:       return "First time I looked, the microsecond hand was on #{e}."
11:     end
12:
13:     def look_2
14:       e = exact_time
15:       return "The second time, it was on #{e}."
16:     end
17:
```

continues

LISTING 2.2 Continued

```
18:     def exact_time
19:       t = Time.now
20:       return t.usec
21:     end
22:   end
23:
24:   cw = ClockWatcher.new
25:   puts cw.double_report
```

2

Notice that no methods of `ClockWatcher` perform any output; they merely return information. To create its clock-watching report, the `double_report` method sends out requests to two other methods, each of which asks yet another method what the microsecond component of the current time is. A `double_report` gets assembled like this:

1. `double_report` asks `look_1` to provide its part of the report.

2. `look_1` asks `exact_time` for the microsecond component of the current time.

3. `exact_time` creates a new object of the `Time` class, essentially a snapshot of a clock, and returns its microsecond component (which is itself found by a method call to that object).

4. `look_1` embeds that information into a string and returns it.

5. `double_report` appends a linefeed character to `look_1`'s results, then asks `look_2` for its part of the report.

6. `look_2` learns the time from `exact_time`, embeds it in a string and returns it (as in steps 2-4 above).

7. `double_report` appends `look_2`'s report to what it already had, and returns the whole thing.

Now look at the script as a whole. What causes all of this to happen? An object of the `ClockWatcher` class is created and given the name cw; its `double_report` method is called; the results of the method call are `puts`'ed to the screen. The output of the script looks something like this, depending on when you run it:

```
First time I looked, the microsecond hand was on 737705.
The second time, it was on 737902.
```

On DOS/Windows systems, the resolution of the system clock information is too coarse to be useful for the preceding example. The `exact_time` method can be artificially slowed down to compensate:

```
def exact_time
  t = Time.now
  sleep .5        # pause a half second
  return t.usec
end
```

Communication Between Different Objects

One object may also speak to another by calling one of the other's methods. When this happens, the second object must be named as the receiver of the call.

Suppose Joe can never answer even the simplest of questions without consulting his big brother Frank. To model this situation, we'll go back to writing methods for individual objects instead of defining new classes. Our script is in Listing 2.3.

 Note   Methods that belong to one object, instead of an entire class of objects, are sometimes called *singleton* methods.

LISTING 2.3   Talking Objects: Brothers

```
01:  #!/usr/bin/env ruby
02:  joe = Object.new
03:  frank = Object.new
04:  def frank.weather
05:     return "It's a fine day."
06:  end
07:  def joe.ask_brother(b)
08:     return b.weather
09:  end
10:  puts "Frank says: #{frank.weather}"
11:  puts "Joe says: #{joe.ask_brother(frank)}"
```

Notice the call to b.weather, and contrast it to the previous example, where calls to look_1, look_2, and exact_time had no receiver specified. There, the ClockWatcher object named cw was in each case talking to itself, using its own methods. If we had left the b off here, the receiver of the weather call would have been joe (remember, ask_brother is one of joe's methods, so self refers to joe here) instead of frank. This would have caused an error, because the joe object has no weather method.

The output is

```
Frank says: It's a fine day.
Joe says: It's a fine day.
```

Identifiers and Variables

We have been giving names to objects and methods, and we have so far mentioned only that objects should have names beginning with lowercase letters and that classes should have names beginning with uppercase letters. We can be a little more explicit about this.

You can think of a *variable* as a name that can be given to one thing temporarily, then removed from that thing and attached to something else. The first character of a variable name must, with some exceptions that we'll discuss on Day 5, be either a lowercase character or an underscore (_). The remaining characters may be upper- or lowercase characters, underscores, or digits. So these are legal variable names:

```
last_tango
lastTango

biscuit4
_m
somethingverylongandeasytomisspellwithoutnoticing
```

while these are not:

```
LastTango
ground turkey
4biscuit
pb&j
criss-cross
```

Also, certain words have intrinsic meaning to Ruby, like and, return, and while. A complete list of these *reserved words* is found in Appendix D.

In general, the same rules that apply to variable names also apply to method names.

Name Tags, Not Suitcases

If you're new to programming, or you're used to a reference-oriented language like Java, this part will make all the sense in the world. It might be a problem if you're more used to C or C++.

As mentioned in Day 1, an equals sign (=) accomplishes *reference*, or *assignment*; in other words, it gives an object a name. But the name does not in any way contain the object. By way of illustration, let's use irb to make a String object and give it a simple name:

```
irb(main):01:0> a = "zif"
"zif"
```

2

What does it mean to assign b to a?

```
irb(main):02:0> b = a
"zif"
```

The correct way to think of this is that the string now has two names, a and b. It has not become two strings; no copy has been generated. We can try to alter a and b separately to verify this.

```
irb(main):03:0> a.succ!  # change a to its lexicographic successor
"zig"
irb(main):04:0> a
"zig"
irb(main):05:0> b
"zig"
irb(main):06:0> b << " - zag"   # append something to b
"zig-zag"
irb(main):07:0> a
"zig-zag"
```

You notice that b changes whenever a changes, and vice versa; it would seem that the two names refer to the same thing. If what you want is a copy so that you can change one without affecting the other, you can ask for it via the *duplicate* method, dup:

```
irb(main):08:1> c = b.dup  # "let c be a duplicate of b"
"zig-zag"
irb(main):09:1> c.succ!
"zig-zah"
irb(main):10:1> b
"zig-zag"
```

There are two caveats that need to be mentioned here.

First, copies of objects are very often made implicitly. Most of the time, when you assign a variable name to something, it is not simply an object that has already been named but some meaningful variation on another object.

```
irb(main):11:0> first_name = "Sandra "
"Sandra "
irb(main):12:0> full_name = first_name + "Dee"
"Sandra Dee"
irb(main):13:0> full_name.upcase!
"SANDRA DEE"
irb(main):14:0> first_name # to see if it changed to "SANDRA "
"Sandra "
irb(main):15:0> first_name = "TWEEDLE"
"TWEEDLE"
irb(main):16:0> full_name  # to see if it changed to "TWEEDLEDEE"
"SANDRA DEE"
```

In line 12, `first_name + "Dee"` is a complete, well-formed expression. Ruby calculates that expression's value before applying assignment across the equals sign, and in so doing it creates a new string, which is what gets assigned to `full_name`. So `first_name` and `full_name` are independent, and changes to one cannot affect the other.

Note

> Looking ahead: When x refers to a string, the following two expressions produce the identical result of appending " . . . " to it.
>
>   x << " . . . "
>   x = x + " . . . "
>
> But given the choice, you might want to use the first. Why? We'll answer that on Day 7.

2

The second caveat is really an insignificant technical point. There is an exception to the rule: Simple numbers can each have only one reference, so when you assign another name, you automatically get a copy. The primary reason for this exception is to improve the performance of the interpreter. In practice it can hardly cause confusion, because you can't modify numbers anyway. The value of π (3.141592654. . .) can never really be changed, despite the best efforts of the Indiana state legislature.[1]

Summary

Objects exist so that we can have data and logic in neat little packages. It's not necessary to remember all the time how to manipulate various kinds of data; by giving the objects methods, we teach them how to operate on themselves. That frees us to concentrate on the larger issues of how our programs are to behave.

We also looked at variables today, examining their character and scope. Most Ruby variables behave as pronouns—that is, temporary labels referring to objects and having no meaning outside the structural units (such as methods) within which they are used. More than one variable by the same name can refer to different things, so long as they do not share the same scope.

---

[1]*House Bill #246, 1897. Okay, yes this was a long time ago.*

Exercises

1. In general, you don't have to give a name to anything you don't plan to reuse, as the following code illustrates.

   ```
   # We can instantiate a philosopher named bob,
   # and ask him to rant ...
   bob = Kantian.new
   bob.rant

   # If we don't expect to have a reason to refer to "bob"
   # later, it is equally effective to instantiate an
   # unnamed philosopher and ask it to rant.
   (Kantian.new).rant   # or more commonly, Kantian.new.rant
   ```

   With this in mind, can you rewrite the ClockWatcher example (Listing 2.2) using no variables in the methods? This means getting rid of e from look_1 and look_2, and t from exact_time. Leave cw alone for the moment. Test your modified script and see whether it gives exactly the same results.

2. Here's an exercise in avoiding ambiguity. Take the script you just modified, and get rid of the cw variable, too, so that there are no variables left. If you see an error saying something about an "undefined method 'double_report'," try adding parentheses around the whole thing being displayed by puts.

3. In the example with Frank and Joe in Listing 2.3, why do we have to tell Joe which brother to ask, since he has only one brother? Why can't we do something like this:

   ```
   def joe.ask_brother
     return frank.weather
   end
   puts "Frank says: #{frank.weather}"
   puts "Joe says: #{joe.ask_brother}"
   ```

Answers

1. In general, to get rid of a variable, you can take the thing being assigned to the variable you want to get rid of, and substitute it for the variable wherever you see it.

   ```
   #!/usr/bin/env ruby

   class ClockWatcher
     def double_report
       return look_1 + "\n" + look_2
     end

     def look_1
       return "First time I looked, the microsecond hand was on
             #{exact_time}."
     end
   ```

```
    def look_2
      return "The second time, it was on #{exact_time}."
    end

    def exact_time
      return Time.now.usec
    end
end

    cw = ClockWatcher.new
    puts cw.double_report
```

2. Probably you first tried this to end the script:

```
    puts (ClockWatcher.new).double_report
```

Although it may not seem ambiguous, because you knew what you meant, it may surprise you that it can mean two things. Since

```
    puts (ClockWatcher.new)
```

is a complete expression, it seems reasonable, when reading left to right, to evaluate that expression first and then apply the `double_report` method to the result, as if you had said this:

```
    (puts (ClockWatcher.new)).double_report
```

Of course that wasn't what you meant. It's like the ambiguity you get from sentences like *Last night I shot an elephant in my pajamas.*[2] Ruby isn't able to read your mind, and with no specific instructions from you, it applies standard precedence rules and ends up getting it wrong. To tell Ruby exactly what you mean, surround everything but the `puts` with parentheses.

```
    puts((ClockWatcher.new).double_report)
```

This tells Ruby to evaluate all of `(ClockWatcher.new).double_report` first, then use the result of that as an argument to `puts`. Now the ambiguity is gone, and the script behaves as you intended. *Last night, while I was in my pajamas, I shot an elephant.*

3. In Joe's methods, the name `frank` is out of scope and has no meaning, even though in the rest of the script it refers to a particular object. It will be possible to refer to Frank from within Joe's methods when we have special variables with *global* scope. And we'll get those on Day 5.

---

[2]*Groucho Marx as Captain Spaulding, in Animal Crackers (1930). The punchline: How he got into my pajamas I'll never know.*

DAY 3

Containers

> "It's a Useful Pot," said Pooh. "Here it is. And it's got 'A Very Happy Birthday with love from Pooh' written on it. That's what all that writing is. And it's for putting things in. There!"
>
> —A. A. Milne, *Winnie-the-Pooh*

Today we look at objects whose only purpose in life is to hold other objects. Containers make programming more convenient in the same way that grocery bags make it easier to get your food home from the store: They reduce the number of objects you have to handle and the number of names you have to remember. You don't have to think about which food items are in which bag when you are picking up the bags and carrying them into the house.

Before we pick up that agenda though, there are two digressions to make.

A Change in Convention

Up to this point, most examples you've seen have been either scripts or parts of irb sessions. irb is a nice learning tool, because it lets you see the effects of a line of code immediately. Scripts are the form of the actual work you will do in Ruby, and they let you control exactly what information appears in the output.

From this point forward, to save space and clutter most of our code examples will appear naked, meaning that you can either type them into irb or run them in script form. Let's illustrate with a short piece of code, then walk through an equivalent irb session.

```
ltrs = ("r" .. "u").to_a  #-> ["r", "s", "t", "u"]
ltrs[1].capitalize!       # ltrs == ["r", "S", "t", "u"]
puts ltrs.length          #  4
```

Comments have been added to show some relevant expression values and outputs. When showing the value of the given expression (as in the first line), the comment starts with ->. Some comments will also show value of some other named expression (as in the second line), or the output that appears as a result of evaluating the given expression (as in the third line).

If you ran this example as a script, possibly after inserting the appropriate "shebang" line at the top, you would see only the number 4. No other output was explicitly requested.

An equivalent irb session might look like this.

```
irb(main):001:0> ltrs = ("r" .. "u").to_a
["r", "s", "t", "u"]
irb(main):002:0> ltrs[1].capitalize!
"S"
irb(main):003:0> ltrs
["r", "S", "t", "u"]
irb(main):004:0> puts ltrs.length
4
nil
```

The expression in line 2 failed to show us the whole list of letters, so in line 3 we asked specifically to see the list. Line 4 gave us the output that we were interested in, along with the nil evaluation of the puts statement, which we probably didn't care about. When writing code samples from now on, we'll just document the values and outputs that are interesting to us. You can use irb or write small scripts to verify the results and try your own experiments.

Some Words About Ambiguity

Since we seem to be approaching the craft of programming from a more linguistic than mathematical perspective, we would do well to consider the problem of ambiguity. In general, computer languages cannot tolerate ambiguity, yet in everyday speech we put up with it all the time and make the best guesses we can.

What conclusion do we come to when we hear that "Maria was stung by a bee in a purple bathrobe"? There are two ways to interpret the sentence. We as experienced listeners have a reasonable expectation that people are more likely to wear bathrobes than bees are, which helps us get the interpretation right. But when a listener has no *domain knowledge*, or understanding of the universe that the sentence is talking about, it is necessary to clear up the ambiguity, possibly by rearranging the words.

Maria was stung by a bee that was wearing a purple bathrobe.

Maria, wearing a purple bathrobe, was stung by a bee.

Although it isn't quite proper English, we can use parentheses to remove the ambiguity just as effectively without changing the word sequence.

A: Maria was stung by (a bee in a purple bathrobe).

B: (Maria was stung by a bee) in a purple bathrobe.

When reading either of these, we have to decide what the parenthesized phrase is talking about before we can relate it to the rest of the sentence. Sentence A makes it quite clear that the bee was in the bathrobe when it stung Maria. But in sentence B, even though the bee is the active party, Maria is the subject of the parenthesized phrase. Put another way, the words between the parentheses "evaluate" to a rather sore and angry Maria, and thus it is Maria who wears the bathrobe.

Programmers, at least when relatively inexperienced, shouldn't assume that an ambiguous expression will be interpreted in the intended way. The Ruby interpreter has no domain knowledge to rely on; what it has instead are precedence (or grouping) rules, which may or may not always follow your intuition but are always applied consistently.

We could learn the rules right now if we wanted to, and always try to remember them when writing scripts. Knowing the rules would let us arrange our code in a way that makes it behave as we intend. But that sounds too much like work. For now at least, it will suffice to know that, when in doubt, you can clarify your meaning by grouping expressions with parentheses.

The last exercise of Day 2 is a case in which you need to parenthesize or the interpreter will get your meaning wrong. In the next example it gets it right, so unless you really are wondering what class nil belongs to, you can leave off the parentheses.

```
print [1, 2, 3].type    #-> prints "Array" and returns nil
print ([1, 2, 3].type)  #-> prints "Array" and returns nil
(print [1, 2, 3]).type  #-> prints "123" and returns "nilClass"
```

Back to Business

Now we can get back to talking about object containers. We've already been using some containers without bringing attention to the fact. Strings, by holding characters, qualify as one kind of container. Lists, such as those produced by methods that have to return more than one value, are another kind of container; these are normally called *arrays*. The other types we'll discuss today, *hashes* and *ranges*, we have not yet seen.

Note

> If you already know what a *range* is and have just had your hackles raised by seeing it called a container, I concede the point; it's not a true container. But it acts like a container in the ways that are important to programmers, so it should be introduced with the others. By way of precedent, consider that some languages with "lazy" evaluation (like Haskell) often don't draw a meaningful distinction between them.

Strings

A *string* holds characters and nothing else. It is Ruby's only single-purpose container.

As the name suggests, a string has a beginning and an end; it is an *ordered* container. It might just as accurately have been called a "chain." If the organizing principle were a "bag" instead, then the characters could be scrambled; we would be able to distinguish *list* from *still*, but not *fare* from *fear*.

Two strings are considered equal only if they have the exact same characters in the exact same sequence.

```
"fare" == "fear"      #-> false
"Night" == "night"    #-> false
"nine " == " nine "   #-> false
"rabbit" == "rabbit"  #-> true
```

Specifying Substrings by Position

Each position in a string has a numerical index. In good computer science tradition, Ruby's indices are counted starting with zero instead of one. Segments of a string, or *substrings*, are referred to by their starting positions and lengths. Putting this pair of numbers in square brackets, we can examine or modify individual characters or longer substrings.

```
foo = "wishbone"
foo[0,1]  #-> "w"
foo[2,5]  #-> "shbon"
```

```
foo[0,1] = "f"     #  foo == "fishbone"
foo[5,1] = "a"     #  foo == "fishbane"
foo[0,4] = "wolf"  #  foo == "wolfbane"
```

A replacement string does not need to be the same length as the segment it is replacing.
The affected string expands or contracts as needed.

```
foo[1,5] = "i"   #  foo == "wine"
foo[1,2] = "edg" #  foo == "wedge"
```

It's sometimes more convenient to count from the end of the string than from the beginning. The last character is considered to be in position −1, the next-to-last in position −2,
and so on.

```
bar = foo.upcase + foo.reverse #  bar == "WEDGEegdew"
bar[-1,1]                      #-> "w"
bar[-7,4]                      #-> "GEeg"
bar[-7,4] = ""                 #  bar == "WEDdew"
```

Let's not get lost in notation. If you take a look at bar.methods and scan through the
long list it gives you, you'll see "[]" and "[]=" in there. This means that using square
brackets to feed position information to a string is just another way of applying a method
to an object; the notation may be new, but the concept is no different from what we were
talking about on Day 2. "[]" could have been called "substring" or "slice", and
"[]=" could have been called "replace_substring."

Note

In fact, Ruby offers slice as a synonym for [].

"Radio".slice(2,3) #-> "dio"

If we wanted to be absolutely strictly consistent with method notation, we could do this:

```
qaz = "Mona Lisa"
qaz.[] (0,5)        #-> "Mona "  (refer to substring)
qaz.[]= (3,6,"day") #  qaz == "Monday"  (replace substring)
```

It looks strange, but it works, and it follows the standard dot notation for applying methods: object, dot, method name, and arguments, in that order. Always remember: In Ruby,
all you are doing is applying methods (that is, passing messages) to objects. Sometimes
it isn't obvious, because some specialized notation is provided to let you say things in
another form, but under the hood, it's always the same story.

Providing an alternate way to write something is sometimes known as *sugaring* the syntax; it doesn't make the language any more nutritious, so to speak, but does make it a little more pleasant to work with. This particular syntax sugar is borrowed from Perl, and it
helps Perl programmers feel at home using Ruby's strings.

Individual Characters

The length parameter can be left off when using "[]" or "[]=", in which case the length defaults to one. The results are what you would expect when replacing substrings:

```
s = "012345678"
s[3] = "waffle" #  s == "012waffle45678"
```

But then something surprising happens when you look at an individual character:

```
s = "AaBbCc 012"
s[0]  #-> 65
s[1]  #-> 97
s[6]  #-> 32
s[7]  #-> 48
```

What's that all about? Depending upon your experience, you might or might not recognize the above as ASCII codes, a common way of representing characters as numbers in the range 0 to 255. Ruby doesn't have a separate Character type, so when we talk about characters, we really mean these numbers.

Note

> Don't expect to understand how this works just yet, but if you want to see the ASCII codes of all characters of a string at once, you can try this:
>
> ```
> "Book".split(//).collect{|c| c[0]}
>                  #-> [66, 111, 111, 107]
> ```

Being able to get a visible indication of which ASCII codes are associated with which characters is handy when you're trying to figure out lexicographic (or alphabetical) order. To get characters in this form, you can omit the length parameter to [] as shown above, but to see characters as tiny strings, you can either specify the substring length as 1 or use the chr method to do the necessary conversion. chr is a method of the Integer class.

```
s[0,1]     #-> "A"
s[2].chr   #-> "B"
70.chr     #-> "F"
10.chr     #-> "\n"  (linefeed)
```

You may not often have occasion to use it, but Ruby provides a simple way of expressing characters in ASCII form. A *character literal* is a question mark followed by a single character.

```
87.chr  #-> "W"
?W      #-> 87
?\t     #-> 9    (tab character)
"W"[0]  #-> 87
```

```
"W"[0,1]  #-> "W"
?W < ?X   #-> true (because 87 < 88)
"W" < "X" #-> true (correct lexicographic order)
?W < "X"  # error
```

> **Note**
>
> Here is an example of Ruby refusing to try to read your mind. If comparisons between integers and strings were allowed, you would run into situations like this:
>
> ```
> "4" < ?3
> ```
>
> This is ambiguous because the ASCII code for "3" is 51, which is of course larger than 4. So the comparison might be either true or false depending on which conversion you had in mind.
>
> ```
> "4" < ?3.chr  #-> false  (comparing 1-character strings)
> "4".to_i < ?3 #-> true (interpreting "4" as the number it
>                         represents)
> ```

3

Specifying Substrings by Matching

Often it's useful to deal with substrings based on content rather than position. We've been supplying a position and length to [], but if we supply a string instead, Ruby will search the target string for it and figure out the position and length for itself.

```
footwear = "blue suede shoes"
footwear["suede"]              #-> "suede"
footwear["leather"]            #-> nil
footwear["blue"] = "red"       #  footwear == "red suede shoes"
footwear["socks"] = "sandals"  #  footwear == "red suede shoes"
```

Notice that if the search fails, no replacement happens, but there is also no error; the target string is simply unaffected.

> **Note**
>
> Looking ahead: You can search not only for an exact substring but also for an abstract pattern. Here we replace the first vowel in a word with an asterisk:
>
> ```
> s = "strongbox"
>
> s[/[aeiou]/i] = "*"   #  s == "str*ngbox"
> ```
>
> We'll learn all about string matching patterns on Day 8.

A Few Useful String Instance Methods

<<

Append either another string or a character:

```
x = "one "
x << 49       #-> "one 1"        (49 is ASCII for "1")
x << " two "  #-> "one 1 two "
x << ?2       #-> "one 1 two 2" (same as x << 50)
```

ljust(length), center(length), rjust(length)

Pad with leading and trailing spaces as necessary to grow to the given length.

```
"abc".ljust(7)   #-> "abc    "

"abc".rjust(7)   #-> "    abc"

"abc".center(7)  #-> "  abc  "

"abc".center(6)  #-> " abc  "   (odd spaces go to the right)

"abc".center(2)  #-> "abc"      (no change if length is too small)
```

count(description)

Return the number of characters that match those in the description string. A range of characters can be specified with a dash, as in "a-c".

```
s = "abcde abcde"
s.count("c")    #-> 2
s.count("b-e")  #-> 8
```

delete(description)

Like count, but return a copy with all matching characters removed.

```
s = "abcde abcde"
s.delete("ac-e") #-> "b b"
```

downcase, upcase, swapcase, capitalize

Return a copy with capitalization changed.

```
"aBc".downcase   #-> "abc"

"aBc".upcase     #-> "ABC"

"aBc".swapcase   #-> "AbC"

"aBc".capitalize #-> "Abc"
```

include?(*spec*)

Return `true` or `false` depending on whether the string contains *spec*, which can be a string or a character.

```
"Haystack".include?("needle") #-> false

"Haystack".include?("sta")    #-> true

"Haystack".include?(72)       #-> true (because ?H is 72)
```

index(*spec*, [*offset*])

Find the index where *spec* is found, starting either from the beginning or from *offset*. Again, *spec* can be either a string or a character.

```
"Mississippi".index("ssi")   #-> 2

"Mississippi".index("ssi",3) #-> 5

"Mississippi".index("sp")    #-> nil (not found)
```

rindex(*spec*, [*limit*])

Like `index`, but find the last match instead of the first. The *limit* stops the search.

```
"Mississippi".rindex("i")   #-> 10

"Mississippi".rindex("i",6) #-> 4
```

strip

Remove whitespace (invisible characters such as spaces, tabs, linefeeds, and so forth) from the beginning and end.

```
"  Erie Canal \n".strip   #-> "Erie Canal"
```

tr(*spec*, *repl*)

Short for "translate." Return a copy with characters from *spec* replaced by the corresponding characters from *repl*. The first example here simulates the `downcase` method.

```
"DOS_FILE.EXT".tr("A-Z","a-z") #-> "dos_file.ext"

"Monkey".tr("ym-q","O*:^)?")   #-> "M^:keO"
```

Arrays

An *array*, or list, is very much like a string in some ways: It is a container whose elements can be referred to by their position and whose elements can be examined and changed using the same techniques you have just learned. But there is a big difference between the two. An array can hold objects of any type, not just characters.

Instead of the quotation marks that you use to create a string, surround a new array with square brackets. Elements of an array are separated by commas.

```
veggies = ["corn", "carrots"]
small_primes = [2, 3, 5, 7, 11]
some_objects = ["a string", 44, self]
```

How would you find the second element of the `veggies` array? Knowing what you know about string objects, you should be able to guess. (Remember, we start counting from zero.)

```
veggies[1]                 #-> "carrots"
veggies[1] = "lettuce"    #  veggies == ["corn", "lettuce"]
```

Arrays grow as needed, just as strings do. New storage slots are created on demand, with `nil`s inserted when necessary.

```
veggies[2] = "peas"  #  veggies == ["corn", "lettuce", "peas"]
veggies[8] = "squash"
#  veggies == ["corn", "lettuce", "peas", nil, nil, nil, nil, nil, "squash"]
```

We've seen that for strings, the [*index*,*length*] notation specifies substrings; for arrays, it specifies subarrays.

```
n = [39, 38, 12, 6, 5]
n[2,3]      #-> [12, 6, 5]
n[-2,1]     #-> [6]
```

You can replace subarrays in much the same way you learned with substrings. The lengths of the new and old subarrays don't have to match, so subarrays can be deleted by replacing them with nothing (that is, `nil`), and they can be inserted by "replacing" a subarray whose length is zero.

```
n[2,2] = [100, 101]
   #  n == [39, 38, 100, 101, 5]
n[1,1] = [200, 201, 202]
   #  n == [39, 200, 201, 202, 100, 101, 5]
n[4,2] = nil
   #  n == [39, 200, 201, 202, 5]
n[2,0] = ["two strings", "inserted"]
   #  n == [39, 200, "two strings", "inserted", 201, 202, 5]
```

When defining an array of strings that contain no spaces, you will find that the following syntax sugar saves wear on your fingers and keyboard. The w stands for *words*.

```
%w(black gray green white blue orange)
   #  ["black", "gray", "green", "white", "blue", "orange"]
```

Arrays understand the << and + methods just as strings do. In fact, if you go through the string methods and try each of them on arrays, you'll find that all the ones that make sense for arrays will do what you expect them to, while those with specific meanings that apply only to strings are rejected.

```
a1 = [10, 20, 30]   #->  [10, 20, 30]
a2 = %w(a b)        #->  ["a", "b"]
a2 << "c"           #->  ["a", "b", "c"]
a3 = a2 + a1        #->  ["a", "b", "c", 10, 20, 30]
a3.include? ("b")   #->  true
a1.include? ("b")   #->  false
a3.index (20)       #->  4
a3.capitalize       #  error
```

Arrays Containing Arrays

If an array can hold any kind of object, there's no reason it can't hold another array.

```
pocket = ["wallet", ["house key", "garage key"], "watch"]
```

The second element of `pocket` is a collection of keys, presumably on a key ring. How would you refer to the first key in that collection? If it isn't clear at first, assign a name to the key ring.

```
key_ring = pocket[1]  #-> ["house key", "garage key"]
key_ring[0]           #-> "house key"
```

That's clear, but a little wordy. Unless we expect to refer to the key ring repeatedly in the future, there is no need to give it a special name now. Since they refer to the same thing, you should be able to substitute `pocket[1]` for `key_ring`. It might feel safer to parenthesize when doing this sort of thing, but in this case it's not necessary.

```
(pocket[1])[0] #-> "house key"
pocket[1][0]   #-> "house key"
```

Hardly anyone uses the parentheses for multiple indices, but you can use them, or else just visualize them, if you ever get confused about the order in which to write them. For instance, a square matrix can be expressed as an array of arrays, where each "inner" array corresponds to a row:

```
#  The matrix we want:
#   11  12  13
#   14  15  16
#   17  18  19

m = [ [11,12,13], [14,15,16], [17,18,19] ]
```

Suppose you want the item in the last column and first row. Which do you say: `m[0][2]` or `m[2][0]`? If you remember that the inner arrays are rows, then you know that `m[0]` is the first row, and so `(m[0])[2]` is what you want.

```
m[0][2]    #-> 13
```

It so happens that Ruby is supplied with a powerful `Matrix` class. Later in the book we'll also be defining our own matrix class, which will be somewhat simpler than Ruby's.

You can *flatten* an array if you want to ungroup the arrays within it. This can put all of m's matrix elements in a straight line, and it can take your keys off their ring so that they jangle around loose in your pocket.

```
m.flatten
  #-> [11, 12, 13, 14, 15, 16, 17, 18, 19]
pocket.flatten
  #-> ["wallet", "house key", "garage key", "watch"]
```

We'll list some other useful array methods in a moment.

FIFOs and Stacks

FIFO stands for first in, first out. Conceptually, a FIFO is a one-way pipe: Objects go in one end and come out the other, always in the same order they went in. Ruby offers four methods for implementing variable-length FIFOs, which are `push`, `pop`, `shift`, and `unshift`; but you need only two of them. `push` and `shift` will suffice.

```
pipe = []  # empty array; same as Array.new
 # "push" objects in to the right end ...
pipe.push("one")    #  pipe == ["one"]
pipe.push("two")    #  pipe == ["one","two"]
pipe.push("three")  #  pipe == ["one","two","three"]
 # ... then "shift" them out from the left end.
x = pipe.shift      #-> "one"
y = pipe.shift      #-> "two"
z = pipe.shift      #-> "three"
```

Instead of using `push` and `shift`, we could use `unshift` and `pop`. The array would be organized backward, but in the end the values found in x, y, and z would be the same.

Why such odd names for these method pairs? Because they're not really pairs. `push` and `pop` go together, and were designed for implementing *stacks*. `shift` and `unshift` were designed for dealing with command-line arguments. We will leave the command line aside for now, but we mustn't neglect stacks.

Stacks

Consider a top-loading cafeteria plate dispenser, equipped with a spring so that a single plate is always accessible at the top. The order in which plates are dispensed is exactly the opposite of what you observe in a FIFO. The plate you take off the top had to be the last one put in, often fresh from the dishwasher (ever notice how warm it is?), and conversely, the first plate lowered into the dispenser cannot be taken out until all the ones above it are gone. This is *last in, first out* behavior.

We don't need a fresh example to illustrate a stack. If you modify the FIFO example in the preceding section by replacing each `shift` with a pop, then you'll have a stack. At the end you'll find x=="three", y=="two", and z=="one".

A Few Useful `Array` Instance Methods

min, max

Return the smallest or largest element, respectively.

```
[3,5,2,4].min  #-> 2
%w(Underhill Zamboni James).max  #-> "Zamboni"
```

uniq

Return a copy with only unique elements.

```
[1,2,2,3,3,3,4,4,4,4,5,5,5,5,5].uniq #-> [1, 2, 3, 4, 5]
```

compact

Return a copy with all `nil` elements removed.

```
a = Array.new #-> []
a[6] = "r"    # a == [nil, nil, nil, nil, nil, nil, "r"]
a.compact     #-> ["r"]
```

sort

Return a sorted copy. Later we'll learn how to specify custom sorts.

```
%w(Underhill Zamboni James).sort
 #-> ["James", "Underhill", "Zamboni"]
```

&, |

Perform intersections and unions for sets.

```
s1 = [1,2,3,4,5,7,9]
s2 = [2,4,5,6,7,8,9]
s1 & s2 #-> [2, 4, 5, 7, 9]
s1 | s2 #-> [1, 2, 3, 4, 5, 6, 7, 8, 9]
```

`grep(/`*`description`*`/)`

We'll wait until Day 8 to see the full power of this method (and to explain why the *description* is surrounded by slashes instead of quotes), but for now we can at least make it show us array elements that contain a specific substring.

```
%w(knee ankle foot leg knuckle toe elbow).grep (/le/)
 #-> ["ankle", "leg", "knuckle"]
```

Hashes

Array elements are referred to by numeric indices. A more general approach would be to allow any kind of object, not just a number, to refer to an array element. A *hash*, sometimes also called a *dictionary* or an *associative array*, has this ability.

```
h = Hash.new
h["Alabama"] = "humid"
h["Alaska"]  = "frigid"
h["Colorado"]  = "rocky"
h["Wisconsin"] = "cheesy"

# If you prefer, the above can also be written this way:
# h = {"Alabama"=>"humid",  "Alaska"=>"frigid",
#   "Colorado"=>"rocky", "Wisconsin"=>"cheesy"}

h.size  #-> 4
h["Alaska"]    #-> "frigid"
h["Missouri"]  #-> nil
```

What a hash gives you is essentially a two-column table with *keys* in one column and *values* in the other. Give the hash a key, and it tells you the associated value. If you look up a key that doesn't exist, you get `nil` back.

 Note

To take control of this behavior, specify a default value when creating the hash. If you change the first line of the example to
`h = Hash.new("hospitable")`, `h["Missouri"]` returns `"hospitable"`.
Then again, so does `h["Antarctica"]`.

Hashes are often used for expressing categorizations. Suppose a business is closed on Sundays, and its employees each have Sunday off plus one other day of the week. Then to keep a record of who is off when is to establish six categories of employees, one for each weekday plus Saturday. One possible way of representing that information is with a hash, using employee names as keys.

```
day_off = {
  "Julia" => "Monday",
  "Martha"  => "Saturday",
  "Thomas"  => "Thursday",
  "Alex"  => "Friday",
  "Shamsul" => "Wednesday",
  "Holly" => "Saturday",
  "Jack"  => "Tuesday",
  "Carol" => "Thursday"
}
```

Alternatively, we can organize the same information in six arrays.

```
monday_off  = ["Julia"]
tuesday_off = ["Jack"]
wednesday_off = ["Shamsul"]
thursday_off  = ["Thomas", "Carol"]
friday_off  = ["Alex"]
saturday_off  = ["Martha", "Holly"]
```

It might seem that using arrays would be a more efficient and intuitive way, particularly if there were a very large number of employees. But consider how hard it would be later when you needed to look up Martha's day off. You'd have to pick up each array and scan it, then produce a value that would depend on which array you were looking at when you found her name. That's both inefficient and confusing. Having a hash means you can look up the answer using day_off["Martha"] and be done with it. Hashes can take up more room than arrays, depending on how you use them, but they can also help you do some things more quickly and easily.

A few Useful Hash Instance Methods

keys, values

Return either the keys or values as an array.

```
taste = {"cake"=>"sweet", "lemon"=>"sour",
   "fries"=>"greasy", "pepper"=>"hot"}
taste.keys   #-> ["fries", "cake", "pepper", "lemon"]
taste.values #-> ["greasy", "sweet", "hot", "sour"]
```

key?(x), value?(x)

Test whether x exists as a key or a value.

```
taste.key?("pepper")  #-> true
taste.key?("sour")    #-> false
taste.value?("sour")  #-> true
```

to_a

Get a copy in array form, where each element is a *key, value* array.

```
{ 1=>1, 3=>27, 5=>125 }.to_a
 #-> [[5, 125], [1, 1], [3, 27]]
```

Notice that the hash produces its key, value pairs in a seemingly arbitrary order. Information in arrays is ordered by numbered slots, but hashes cannot be considered ordered containers.

Ranges

How would you describe the array [1,2,3,4,5]? Is it "the numbers 1, 2, 3, 4, and 5," or is it "the whole numbers from one to five"? Of course, either description fits, and neither is much more work than the other to express. But if you want to list "the whole numbers from one to ten thousand," it will take you a while to write them all out in a list. When you want to talk about a sequence of numbers that can be summarized by a starting point and an endpoint, why should we have to talk about all the points in between? We can use a *range* instead.

```
r = (-4 .. 4)
r.type          #-> Range
r.include? (-1) #-> true
r.include? (5)  #-> false
r.length        #-> 9
r.to_a  #-> [-4, -3, -2, -1, 0, 1, 2, 3, 4]
```

Just as with hashes, to_a means "express as an array."

When a range is written as (*start* .. *end*), the endpoint is included. To exclude the endpoint, put an extra dot in the range specification.

```
(0 ... 5).to_a  #-> [0, 1, 2, 3, 4]
```

Ranges can be used not just with numbers but with anything that has a well-defined sequence.

```
parts = ("Part A" .. "Part G")
parts.length                #-> 7
parts.include? ("Part D")   #-> true
```

We'll see the usefulness of ranges when we talk about *iterators* tomorrow. For now it's important to understand that we can use a range instead of an array when we want to describe items in sequence. A range can both save us work and conserve memory (since Ruby keeps track of only the endpoints and doesn't store all the intermediate items).

Summary

Ruby's container classes group items in convenient ways. We looked at four such classes today.

Arrays and hashes are general-purpose containers that accommodate every kind of object. The contents of an array are arranged sequentially and referred to by index, whereas the values in a hash are not maintained in a predictable order and are referred to by objects called keys.

The others are special-purpose containers. Strings can hold only characters. In many ways, strings act like arrays, but they also have some specialized methods, like upcase, that are just for text. Ranges might not be containers in a strict sense, but they describe increasing sequences of numbers and can be treated basically like arrays.

Exercises

1. Suppose you have string1 and string2, and you want to find out whether string2 is a substring of (that is, can be found within) string1. Can you do it without using the include? method?

2. Should this expression evaluate to true or false?

   ```
   ["abc", "def", "ghi"].include?("h")
   ```

3. How could we get an ordered list of all the keys and values of a hash, with no duplicates? For example, how could we get this:

   ```
   [1,2,3,6,8]
   ```

   from this:

   ```
   {1=>8, 3=>6, 8=>2, 6=>2}
   ```

Answers

1. One way to do it would be with the index method. If string2 is a substring of string1, then string1.index(string2) will return a number; otherwise it will return nil. Another way would be to look at the result of string1[string2].

2. It may surprise you that this is false. Consider that the include? method is a message given to an object. What is the object? It's not a string, but an array. The array only looks to see whether it has an element exactly matching "h". It would be beyond its competence to delve into the question of substring matching; that's a job for string objects. Arrays shouldn't concern themselves with it.

On the other hand, (["abc", "def", "ghi"][2]).include?("h") does correctly return true, because it is the string "ghi" that is the receiver of the include? question.

3. First, it should be mentioned that the problem makes sense only when the keys and values are all of a type that can be compared with each other. In this example, they are all numbers, which is fine. If they were all strings, that would work too. A hash like {"six"=>6, "four"=>4} isn't suitable for the problem; we could do everything but the sorting.

That being said, we can take this one step at a time. Let's leave the "ordered" part for last, and start by turning the hash into an array:

```
h = {1=>8, 3=>6, 8=>2, 6=>2}
h.to_a   #-> [[8, 2], [1, 8], [6, 2], [3, 6]]
```

We want keys and values all mixed together, so break up those inner arrays:

```
(h.to_a).flatten #-> [8, 2, 1, 8, 6, 2, 3, 6]
```

Get rid of the duplicates:

```
((h.to_a).flatten).uniq #-> [8, 2, 1, 6, 3]
```

We're almost done:

```
(((h.to_a).flatten).uniq).sort  #-> [1, 2, 3, 6, 8]
```

This kind of method chaining is common in Ruby, and it turns out that the parentheses aren't required; methods are applied in order from left to right.

```
h.to_a.flatten.uniq.sort
```

You can read that as "convert to array, flatten it, select only unique elements, and then sort."

Do you expect it to matter what order you write those four methods in? You can experiment to satisfy yourself.

DAY 4

Iteration and Flow Control

I'd like to thank each and every one of you for stopping by. (Thank you, thank you, thank you, thank you, thank you, thank you, thank you, thank you, thank you, thank you, thank you, thank you, thank you, thank you, thank you, thank you, thank you, thank you, . . .)

—Steve Martin, *Let's Get Small* (1977)

Yesterday we learned about the standard container types and some of the methods that help us manipulate them. Today we will start dealing with containers, and the items they contain, with a great deal more specificity and flexibility. We will also learn many of the logic and control features that we'll need before going much farther.

Using Iterators

Although a container gives us the luxury of not having to name and remember all the things in it, we nevertheless will want to get in occasionally to use its contents. Some of those uses might involve taking the items out of the container (*put away the groceries that are in that bag*), manipulating them but leaving them in the container (*mark all the items in that bag expired*, *then rearrange the bag with the heaviest items on the bottom*), or nonintrusively gathering information about the items (*find the total price of all the items in the bag*; *put together another bag made up of items like those in this bag, except without the vegetables*). To help you accomplish tasks like these, Ruby provides *iterators*.

Generally speaking, iterators are methods that choose pieces from a container and perform on them, individually, whatever repetitive task we care to describe. An iterator call looks something like this:

```
container.iterator { code_block }
```

The *container* is the receiver of the iterator method and holds the objects you want to do something to. The *iterator* specifies how the items are retrieved. The *code block* expresses your instructions on what to do to each item.

each

The simplest and most commonly used iterator is each. It applies to every kind of container.

```
[1,2,3,4,5].each { puts 'We are here!' }
# output:
    We are here!
    We are here!
    We are here!
    We are here!
    We are here!
```

The range (1..5) isn't a proper container, because all it really "contains" are the endpoints 1 and 5, but it behaves like a container in practice. Because the preceding array elements are given in sequence, the example can as easily be written

```
(1..5).each { puts 'We are here!' }
```

For each number in the range 1 through 5, print the message 'We are here!' Notice that we aren't really making use of what the numbers are; we're just ensuring that the code block executes a certain number of times. The output would have been the same if we had iterated over the array [6,2,9,9,14], or over the range (58..62).

Let's incorporate the numbers into the messages: *Print the numbers 1 through 5*, or more precisely, *For each number in the range 1 through 5, print it.* Now the pronoun *it* calls for an iteration variable, a placeholder whose value changes every time the block executes. That variable will go at the beginning of the code block, between vertical bars.

```
container.iterator { |variable| code_block }
```

Here, num is the iteration variable, and it takes on the values 1 through 5.

```
(1..5).each { |num| print "The number is ",num,".\n" }
# output:
    The number is 1.
    The number is 2.
    The number is 3.
    The number is 4.
    The number is 5.
```

Variations on Iterator Calls

Since each is so commonly used to encode instructions of the form *For each item in this container, do that task*, an alternate form is provided to make the code look a little more like natural language.

```
for num in (1..5)
  print "The number is ",num,".\n"
end
```

This may be a little easier to read, but some programmers prefer to avoid it because it applies only to the each iterator, and because it doesn't "look" entirely object-oriented. Since there are other iterators you'll be using, it might be better to use the standard container-dot-method syntax so you can be consistent.

4

Note Also, for does not exactly qualify as a syntax sugar for each, because they handle the scoping of new variables differently: each makes them disappear outside the block, whereas for makes them persist. With experience you're likely to find you want new variables to be confined to the block, making each the better choice.

Another variation is to replace the curly braces with do and end. Typically (but not necessarily) this also means breaking up the code block into separate lines, just as with for.

```
total = 0.0
range = (1..10)
range.each do
  |x|
  total = total + x
end
print "The sum of numbers in the range ",range," is ",total,".\n"
# output:
    The sum of numbers in the range 1..10 is 55.
```

How do you decide which way to write your iterator calls? It is a reasonable rule to use do...end when the code block is relatively lengthy, and go back to the curly-braces variety when the whole iterator call fits neatly on one line. Or you might prefer to find the way that seems more comfortable to you and just stick with it.

times, downto, upto, step

These are a kind of iterator, but they are applied to numbers instead of containers. They are methods applicable to the `Integer` class.

`times` just repeats execution of the block you give it.

```
3.times { print "ni! " }      # output: ni! ni! ni!
```

You can use an iteration variable with `times` if you want, because `3.times` is just another way of saying `(0..2).each`.

```
3.times { |x| print x,' ' }       # output: 0 1 2
```

Since iterating over a range always takes you from the lower to upper limit, a `downto` method is provided to let you go the other way.

```
10.downto(1) {|x| print x,' ' }      # output: 10 9 8 7 6 5 4 3 2 1
```

With `downto` it seems that we have added arguments to the general form of iterator calls. While we're at it, we can make *variable* plural.

```
container.iterator(arguments) { |variables| code_block }
```

An `upto` method is provided as a companion for `downto`. It's not strictly necessary to have it, since `1.upto(10)` means the same thing as `(1..10).each`. But if you ever have occasion to use `downto` in your scripts, it might help your code look sensible and balanced if you use `upto` whenever counting up.

We normally count by ones, but it's also possible to count by twos, or fives, or thousands. For this we have the `step` iterator.

```
# Print the odd numbers from 1 to 19.
# That is to say, "count from 1 to 19 by twos"
1.step(19,2) { |oddnum|  print oddnum,' ' }
# output:
  1 3 5 7 9 11 13 15 17 19
```

If you noticed unexpected output when testing this example in irb, see Exercise 6 at the end of today's lesson.

It's permissible for the iteration variable to pass the end point without landing on it. Changing `1.step(19,2)` to `1.step(20,2)` has no effect; after all, the odd numbers from 1 to 19 are the same as the odd numbers from 1 to 20.

Since upto works just like iteration over a range, you can use it on strings as well as numbers. `"W".upto("Z")` acts exactly like `("W".."Z")`. But you cannot use times, downto, or step with strings.

each_byte

What is a string made of? We have said that it is made of characters, and that is technically correct but simplistic in practice. Long strings, especially those read from text files, will contain many lines, which in turn contain characters. There is some question of interpretation. It's not quite as cut and dried as when we are dealing with arrays; though an array may contain subarrays, those sub-relationships are specified clearly and structurally.

Most of the files we care about will tend to be organized by lines, so when the each iterator is applied to a string, it extracts a line at a time, rather than a character at a time. This choice was made because it seems more reasonable to let you as the programmer break lines up into smaller chunks as needed, than to make you always reassemble lines from the smallest atoms.

But that's only a statement of what we're most *likely* to want. Since there is more than one way to divide up a string, there's no reason why we can't have more than one iterator at our disposal. Notice that in the following example, lines within a string are separated by the linefeed character, \n.

```
text = "one\ntwo\nthree\n"
text.each { |line| print "*", line }
# output:
  *one
  *two
  *three

text.each_byte { |c| print "*", c.chr }
# output:
  *o*n*e*
  *t*w*o*
  *t*h*r*e*e*
```

You can use each_line and each_byte to iterate over strings, if it helps you keep things straight. each_line and each are *aliases*, or two names for the same method.

Note

Looking ahead: each, each_line, and each_byte apply also to files and other "streams," as we'll find on Day 6.

`each_index`, `each_with_index`

It is possible to iterate not only over the objects in a collection but also over their positions within the collection. `each_index` gives only the positions; `each_with_index` gives both the items and the positions.

```
lineup = %w( Northrup McAuliffe Freehan Cash
             Horton Brown Rodriguez Brinkman Lolich )
lineup.each_index { |posn| print (posn+1) }
# output: 123456789

lineup.each_with_index { | man, pos | print (pos+1), man[0,1],' ' }
# output: 1N 2M 3F 4C 5H 6B 7R 8B 9L
```

`times` also provides an alternative way to step through the indices of a container.

```
container.size.times {|idx|...}   # same as container.each_index {|idx|...}
```

This is not very helpful unless the size of the container is known ahead of time, or if the object in question is not a true container and so cannot be iterated over directly. We'll run into this odd situation on Day 15.

`each_pair`, `each_key`, `each_value` for Hashes

When you iterate over a hash with `each_pair`, key/value pairs are assigned to the iteration variables. The iteration works whether you provide one variable or two; if you give two, the first gets a key and the second gets a value, but if you give only one, it gets an array with a key in position 0 and a value in position 1. When you're working with hashes, `each` is an alias for `each_pair`.

```
h = { 'red'=>'primary', 'blue'=>'primary', 'green'=>'secondary' }
h.each_pair { |k,v| print "#{k} is a #{v} color.\n" }
# output:
  green is a secondary color.
  red is a primary color.
  blue is a primary color.

h.each_pair { |pair| p pair }
# output:
  ["green", "secondary"]
  ["red", "primary"]
  ["blue", "primary"]
```

It is also possible to iterate over just the keys or just the values:

```
h.each_key { |k| print k," " }
# output: green red blue
```

```
h.each_value { |v| print v," " }
# output: secondary primary primary
```

If you need to, you can get the same information out of `each_key` that you got out of `each_pair`, by referencing the keys back into the hash.

```
h.each_key { |k| print "#{k} is a #{h[k]} color.\n" }
```

But you can't do that with `each_value`. Hashes are designed to look up values from the keys and not the other way around. What's more, there can hardly be a well-defined answer to the question "What key goes with this value?" when more than one key may share the same value.

Notice that the iterators do not follow the order in which we added keys to the hash. Hashes are not ordered collections as arrays are; they have their own logic of organization, which is tuned for good performance. If you want a hash iteration to conform to some order, you can apply the `sort` method, as we did on arrays in the previous chapter. The sort will be by key, not value, unless we say otherwise. But be careful—the result of the sort is now an array, so you can't use a hash-specific iterator like `each_key` to talk to it afterward. Stick with `each`.

select, map

4

Here are two wonderfully useful iterators. `select` filters unwanted items out of a collection, returning a smaller collection; `map` (also called `collect`) transforms one collection to another in any way you specify.

```
langs = %w( Java Perl Python Smalltalk Ruby LISP Haskell )

# Select the languages with short names.
langs.select { |n| n.length < 5 }
  #-> ["Java", "Perl", "Ruby", "LISP"]

# Select language names that include the letter 'a'...
langs.select { |n| n.include?("a") }
  #-> ["Java", "Smalltalk", "Haskell"]

# ... and those that don't.
langs.select { |n| not n.include?("a") }
  #-> ["Perl", "Python", "Ruby", "LISP"]

# Reverse the names, and take the first 3 letters.
langs.map { |n| n.reverse[0,3] }
  #-> ["ava", "lre", "noh", "kla", "ybu", "PSI", "lle"]

# Take the first 3 letters, then capitalize.
langs.map { |n| n[0,3].upcase }
  #-> ["JAV", "PER", "PYT", "SMA", "RUB", "LIS", "HAS"]
```

```
# Remove all the capital letters and vowels.
langs.map { |n| n.delete("A-Zaeiou") }
   #-> ["v", "rl", "ythn", "mlltlk", "by", "", "skll"]
```

Flow Control

We have seen a few nifty uses for iterators. But there are some limitations on what we can do so far. For example, suppose we had an array and wanted to "select" alternating elements, like this:

```
[60,62,65,70,72,73,75]   #-> [62,70,73]
```

The select iterator won't help here, because it looks at the items themselves and not their positions. It is possible to select the elements that actually are odd numbers (that's one of the exercises at the end of the chapter), but not all the elements in odd positions. In a later chapter we'll learn to write custom iterators; perhaps something like select_by_index or select_with_index would be the right thing here.

```
# How we would use a select_by_index iterator (if one existed)
# to select odd-position array elements:
```

 Note

> There is another test for oddness, i&1 == 1; we haven't learned about that test yet. It executes more efficiently than this one.

```
[60,62,65,70,72,73,75].select_by_index { |i| i%2 == 1 }
   #-> [62, 70, 73]
```

What does that percent sign (%) do? It's like integer division (/), except what it gives you is not the quotient but the remainder. So i%2 is 1 when i is odd, and 0 when i is even.

For now, we'll settle for learning Ruby's basic decision-making tools; in just a little while we'll look at a couple of ways they can help us tackle the alternating-elements problem.

Conditional Code

We have seen expressions that evaluate to true or false; these are sometimes called Boolean expressions. We can make execution of an instruction *conditional* based on a Boolean expression.

```
claim =  70 > 80   #-> false
puts "one"
puts "two" if claim
```

```
puts "three"
# output:
    one
    three
```

This new construction is called an `if` modifier. Since the `claim` evaluated to `false`, the second `puts` didn't happen.

But most expressions are not Boolean; they evaluate to numbers, collections, and all kinds of objects. So we will want to be able to make decisions based on the value of any possible expression. The simple rule is that for non-Boolean expressions, `nil` is considered `false` and absolutely everything else is considered `true`.

> **Note**
>
> This can take some getting used to, depending on your experience. In many languages, the number 0 is considered false, and in Perl, an empty string is considered false. Ruby considers both true.

```
name = "Frederick"
name.index("d")      #-> 3
name.index("u")      #-> nil
puts "#{name} contains the letter d." if name.index("d")
puts "#{name} contains the letter u." if name.index("u")
# output:
    Frederick contains the letter d.
```

It would appear that as far as strings are concerned, `index` can always be used in place of `include?`. Non-Boolean methods conventionally return `nil` to indicate any kind of non-emergency failure (for instance, when something being searched for is not found), making it convenient to use the return values directly in decision making.

You can negate an expression—that is, make it false if it was true or vice versa—by prepending either an exclamation point (`!`) or the word `not`. The difference between these is one of precedence; `not` "binds more loosely" than `!`. We'll explain what that means a little later. If it feels more natural, you can say `unless` in place of `if not`.

An `if` or `unless` modifier is a quick way to attach a condition to the execution of a single statement, but more often than not you will want to make a condition control several lines of code at a time. Writing the condition before the code, and following it all with an end, produces the desired result.

```
if acquaintance.age > 30
  acquaintance.shun
  puts "Never trust anyone over 30!"
end
```

Splitting an `if...end` block with an `else` ensures that one part or the other of the code block will be executed.

```
if Time.now < deadline
  status = "procrastinating"
else
  status = "panicking"
end
```

If you prefer to pack them into one line (this can hurt readability if you're not careful), the condition and code should be separated by the `then` keyword.

```
if q >= 21 then puts "too many" else puts "ok" end
```

Loops

A loop is a section of code that keeps repeating, usually until some condition is satisfied. You construct a loop just like any conditional code block, but use the keyword `while` in place of `if` (or `until` in place of `unless`).

```
count = 5
while count > 0
  puts count
  count = count - 1
  sleep 1                        # pause for 1 second
end
# output (this takes 5 seconds to execute)
  5
  4
  3
  2
  1
```

A Text Filter

We're about ready now to write our first *text filter*, which is a script that takes information from either a file or the standard input, transforms it somehow, and writes the results to standard output. The `gets` method, as we have seen, retrieves one line of text each time it is called. What we haven't known till now is that it returns `nil` when it gets to the end of the file. That fact makes it convenient for use in a `while` loop.

The following filter reverses all the lines in a file. (Some Unixes are supplied with a `rev` program that does exactly this.)

```
#!/usr/bin/env ruby

# Script to reverse all the lines in a file
# Save this as reverse.rb
```

```
while   line = gets
  line.chomp!              # or line = line.chomp
  puts line.reverse
end
```

Note | The main difference between `line.chomp!` and `line = line.chomp` is in performance. We'll talk about the "*bang*" methods, or so-called destructive methods, on Day 7.

`reverse.rb` illustrates the usual form of a text filter script. As long as text is available, read a line, dispose of the newline character, do something to the line, and print it. When you run reverse.rb, you can either type the input from the keyboard or redirect the standard input (and output too, if desired).

```
reverse.rb                      (reads from keyboard, writes to screen)
reverse.rb < infile             (reads from infile, writes to screen)
reverse.rb < infile  > outfile  (reads from infile, writes to outfile)
```

These examples assume that you have marked the `reverse.rb` file as executable. If you have not done this (or cannot, because you are using Windows), invoke `ruby reverse.rb` instead of `reverse.rb` in each case.

Something interesting happens at the top of the script. The result of `gets` is assigned to `line`, but it also becomes the value of the entire expression `line = gets`. As soon as we have reached the end of the file, that value becomes `nil`, making `while` put a stop to everything. Now if the `while` condition starts out false, nothing in the loop executes. That's fine here, because it just means you tried to read an empty file, and so there's nothing to do. But it is not always going to be the behavior you want; sometimes a loop needs to execute at least once, and the first test shouldn't happen till afterward. What works in this situation is to enclose the loop in `begin...end` and then follow it with `while`.

Here is a version of the infamous "cookie monster" script, which keeps prompting the user for input until it finally gets what it wants. Notice the test for an exit condition at the end of the loop:

```
begin
  puts "Gimme cookie!"
  input = gets.chomp
end   while input != "cookie"
puts "Ahh, thank you."
```

4

```
# Sample run:
Gimme cookie!
what?
Gimme cookie!
no
Gimme cookie!
all right already
Gimme cookie!
cookie
Ahh, thank you.
```

We haven't seen it before now, but != is the *inequality* test: it returns the negation of the equality test, ==. It would be equally effective, and perhaps a little more readable, to make the exit condition until input == cookie.

Interrupting the Flow

Now we've seen how to stop a loop at its top or its bottom. Would we ever want to get out from somewhere in the middle? Let's make the cookie monster a little more irritable, so that he complains every time he is given the wrong thing.

```
Gimme cookie!
hockey puck
That not cookie!!!
Gimme cookie!
Frisbee
That not cookie!!!
Gimme cookie!
cookie
Ahh, thank you.
```

This behavior can be achieved only by examining the input after collecting it from the user but before complaining about it, so the exit test really should go somewhere inside the loop. We don't want to stop anywhere else, so as far as the top and bottom are concerned, the loop should seem to be *infinite*. One way to do this is to hardwire the input != "cookie" condition, that is, change it to true.

```
begin
  # ... anything here repeats forever
end   while true
```

But instead, we'll use Ruby's built in quasi-infinite loop construction.

```
loop do
  # ... anything here repeats forever
end
```

When the monster gets our precious cookie, we'll want to `break` out of the loop.

```
loop do
  puts "Gimme cookie!"
  input = gets.chomp
  break if input == "cookie"
  puts "That not cookie!!!"
end
puts "Ahh, thank you."
```

Notice that `!=` changed to `==`, because `break` is interested in knowing when we want to leave the loop, not how long we want to stay in it. (It would also work to say `break unless input != cookie`, but that's an unnecessary double negative.)

Two less common ways to interfere with the operation of a loop are `next` and `redo`. They both cause whatever is left in the loop to be skipped, but the loop is not broken: Execution starts again from the top. The difference between `next` and `redo` pertains to iteration: `redo` starts the iterator block over on the same item as before, and `next` advances to the next item.

```
repeating = true

21.upto(25) do |number|
  next if number==23      # 23 will not appear in output
  puts number
  if number==24 and repeating
    repeating = false
    redo                  # 24 will appear twice
  end
end
  #output:
    21
    22
    24
    24
    25
```

Odd-Position Elements

Let's do a mid-chapter exercise. Recall that we were wondering how to select alternating elements from an array, a task for which the `select` iterator isn't helpful. But we have enough tools to do it now, and in fact we can do it several different ways. We'll leave a relatively nice solution for one of the exercises at the end of today's lesson, and explore a much more awkward solution here. This isn't necessarily a good way to write—it certainly isn't the Ruby Way—but it will help you at least get familiar with Ruby's low-level control constructs, because every once in a great while you really do need to dig them out and use them for something.

There will be three important objects in this code: the original array `orig`, the new array `final` (we shouldn't call it `new`), and a numerical index `idx`. The index will be moving through all the indices of the array, so we'll initialize it to zero.

```
orig = [60,62,65,70,72,73,75]
final = []        # or we could say, final = Array.new
idx = 0
```

Now we need some kind of a loop; a `while` will suffice. The loop should repeat as long as the index is within the boundaries of `orig`.

```
while idx < orig.length   # why '<' instead of '<=' here?
# ...
end
```

What do we want to happen in the body of that loop? We want to grab the element at the position referred to by `idx`, and put it in the `final` array, but only if `idx` is an odd number. This seems to call for testing a condition with `if`, and conditionally appending an array element.

```
if idx%2 == 1            # test for oddness
  final.push(orig[idx])  # or: final << orig[idx]
end
```

One thing is still missing: `idx` never changes. After visiting one array position we should move on to the next one. If we forget this part, the `while` condition will always be satisfied, and as a result, the program will run forever or until some outside force (possibly somebody pressing ^C on the keyboard) stops it; anyway, it won't work right.

```
idx = idx + 1            # or: idx += 1
```

Now we can put everything together. We'll change the conditional block to `if`-modifier form, and add an output line.

```
orig = [60,62,65,70,72,73,75]
final = []
idx = 0
while idx < orig.length
  final.push (orig[idx]) if idx%2 == 1
  idx = idx + 1
end
p final    # output: [62, 70, 73]
```

It's ugly and slow, but it works. How would you start to improve it? If we start at index 1 and add 2 every time instead of 1, we'll never examine any even-numbered locations at all. That means we can eliminate the test for oddness. Can the `upto` iterator help us clean this up further? How about `step`?

Testing Multiple Conditions

We have seen how to express two alternative courses of action, using `if...else...end`. But sometimes we need more flexibility than that. Multiple choices can be expressed with the help of `elsif`.

```ruby
if score >= 90
  grade = "A"
elsif score >= 80
  grade = "B"
elsif grade >= 70
  grade = "C"
elsif score >= 60
  grade = "D"
else
  grade = "F"
end
```

As with `if...end`, an `else` is optional, but must come last if you have it. `else` ensures that exactly one course of action will be taken; without it, one course of action will be taken *at most*.

Look again at the sample above. Doesn't there seem to be some redundancy? Surely there is a simpler way to describe the task. If describing it in words, you wouldn't say "if the score is above. . ." over and over. Ruby provides the more concise `case` construction to approach the description "assign the grade by score, *A* if at least 90, *B* if between 80 and 90, . . .".

```ruby
case score
  when (90..100)
    grade = "A"
  when (80..90)
    grade = "B"
  when (70..80)
    grade = "C"
  when (60..70)
    grade = "D"
  else
    grade = "F"
end
```

We should be careful about details here. Too much extra credit just might earn somebody an F! Since there aren't open-ended ranges like `(90..)`, we might want to change the A range to something like `(90..10000)`.

Note

> Although ranges cannot be open-ended, *infinity* is an assignable value in Ruby, and can be expressed by dividing a positive floating-point number by zero. So we could safely say `(90..(+1.0/0))` here. It just looks a little strange.

Our example can be shortened a bit more by combining lines, since the pieces of conditional code here are quite short. As with `if`, separate the test from the code with `then`.

```
case score
  when (90..100)    then grade = "A"
  when (80..90)     then grade = "B"
  # ...
  else                   grade = "F"
end
```

Getting a Value from `if` or `case`

When looking for ways to eliminate redundancy in a script, we sometimes say we are *refactoring the code*. The term comes from algebra, where simplifying an expression often involves finding common factors and pulling them outside where they can be "distributed" over the rest.

$$5xy + 15x - 40x^2 = 5x(y + 3 - 8x)$$

Changing the `if...end` to a `case...end` accomplished a kind of factoring; in our grading example, it meant we didn't have to mention `score` for every test. But we still ended up assigning something to `grade` every time. We should be able to factor that out too.

Recall that executing code is really no different from evaluating expressions. Whether you are concerned about their values or not, the Ruby code you write is made up of many expressions, often expressions within expressions within expressions, and they can all be counted on to have values. Whenever you see `if...end`, it can be considered as one big expression, and the same is true of `case...end`. The value of an `if` or `case` expression will always be the value of some smaller expression inside: specifically, whichever one is evaluated last. (Recall what happens when you don't explicitly state a return value for a *method*.)

```
angle_type = (if angle == 90 then "right" else "wrong?" end)

# This is the same as:
#    if   angle == 90
#         angle_type = "right"
```

```
#      else
#        angle_type = "wrong?"
#      end
```

The parentheses are added for clarity but are not needed. Notice that `angle_type` is "factored out" by moving it to the front of the expression, much as in algebraic practice. Depending on the size of `angle`, either "right" or "wrong?" will be evaluated, and that will in turn become the value of the whole `if` expression.

Ruby borrows a convenient shorthand from C. `condition ? expr1 : expr2` means the same thing as `if condition then expr1 else expr2 end`. Usually this form is reserved for occasions when the overall expression is relatively small and its value is going to be used for something.

```
# Display a web counter.
print "This page has been viewed ", counter
if counter == 1 then print "time" else print "times" end

# The same thing, a little more compact:
print "This page has been viewed ", counter, " time"
print (counter == 1) ? "" : "s"
```

Before we forget what we were talking about, let's further refactor the grading code by pulling a value out of the `case` expression.

```
grade = case score
        when (90..100)    then "A"
        when (80..90)     then "B"
        when (70..80)     then "C"
        when (60..70)     then "D"
        else                  "F"
      end
```

`case` is quite versatile. We've given it only ranges to test, but it does different kinds of tests for different kinds of objects. Given simple numbers, it tests for equality.

```
angle_type = case angle
             when 90       then "right"
             when (0..90)  then "acute"
             else              "oblique"
           end
```

Whenever `case` comes to a `when` block, it looks at what type of object is associated with it, and calls a special `===` method for that type. For integers, strings, and most other types, it means the same thing as `==`. But for ranges, it means `include?`.

4

Grouping Several Expressions into One

We've seen some ways that Ruby naturally lumps expressions together: if does this, as does case. In a way, every method you write acts like a single expression too. If in some other context you would like to group expressions into one, you can do it with parentheses. For example, an if modifier is designed to apply to single expressions only, and we are accustomed to surrounding multi-expression conditional blocks with if...end. But sometimes it enhances readability to break with convention, if we're dealing with something small enough.

```
(puts "you forgot something!" ; exit) if name == ""

# Same effect as:
#      if name == ""
#         puts "you forgot something!"
#         exit
#      end
```

Why Loop When You Can Iterate?

We have learned a thing or two today about how to write loops, but remember that the best advice is usually to avoid them if at all possible. Loops give you more flexibility than iterators, but at a cost: They make you think at a lower level, often pulling you away from the essence of whatever problem you are trying to solve. They mean typing more code and probably making more mistakes.

Our countdown loop example from the "Loops" section can be more simply expressed on a single line with a downto iterator. As is often the case, making it shorter also makes it more readable.

```
5.downto(1) { |c| puts c; sleep 1 }
```

We'll also see on Day 6 that it is possible to structure text filter scripts around an iterator instead of a while...end loop.

People who are learning Ruby as their first language are likely to find iterators quite easy to use. If you already know one or more other languages, you might catch yourself writing loops when it isn't really necessary, just because it's what you're used to. Try to make your code safe and simple; save your loops for the occasions when there just isn't an iterator that does what you want.

Summary

Iterators are what make containers truly useful. They allow us to apply an operation to everything in a container, or selected elements, without having to think about all of the tedious mechanics of testing and looping.

Although iterators are usually the Ruby Way to deal with objects that live in containers, there are times when there doesn't seem to be an iterator that does exactly what you want. So Ruby also offers a full complement of flow control and logical tools. You can fall back on those tools when necessary, or, as you'll see on Day 14, use them to design an iterator of your own.

Exercises

1. Using the `%` operator and the `select` iterator, how would you find all the odd numbers in an array? Test your code on the array `[10,12,13,15,18]`; try to derive a new array `[13,15]`.

2. Rewrite the odd-position element selection code (see the section "Odd-Position Elements"). Use a `step` iterator, and don't use `if`.

3. We have separate `upto` and `downto` iterators, so why don't we also have separate `step_upto` and `step_downto` iterators instead of just `step`? (Hint: How could you print the odd numbers from 1 to 20 backwards?)

4. What has gone wrong here?

```
marx_bros = %w( Groucho Chico Harpo Zeppo Gummo )
p marx_bros
how_many = marx_bros.size
if how_many = 0
  puts "The Marx brothers never existed."
else
  puts "Relax; all is right with the world."
end

# output:
 ["Groucho", "Chico", "Harpo", "Zeppo", "Gummo"]
 The Marx brothers never existed.
```

5. Look again at our grading example.

```
grade = case score
        when (90..100)    then "A"
        when (80..90)     then "B"
        when (70..80)     then "C"
        when (60..70)     then "D"
        else                   "F"
        end
```

What grade would result from the score 80, since it seems to belong to both the B and C ranges?

6. Explain this behavior of `times` in an irb session.

```
irb(main):001:0> 4.times { |x| puts x }
0
1
2
3
4
```

7. Write three different text filter scripts, one to satisfy each of the following specifications.

7a: Eliminate the blank lines, and double the rest.

7b: Center all visible text within 40 columns.

7c: Swap adjacent pairs of characters (position 0 with 1, 2 with 3, and so on).

Example inputs/outputs:

7a: *input*

```
Abraham Lincoln
Carrie Chapman Catt

Mario Cuomo
Elizabeth Cady Stanton
```

output

```
Abraham Lincoln
Abraham Lincoln
Carrie Chapman Catt
Carrie Chapman Catt
Mario Cuomo
Mario Cuomo
Elizabeth Cady Stanton
Elizabeth Cady Stanton
```

7b: *input* (from Donald Barthelme, "The Glass Mountain," *From Sixty Stories,* Putnam, 1981)

```
          In the streets
    were people
       concealing their calm behind
a facade of vague dread.
```

output

```
           In the streets
            were people
    concealing their calm behind
      a facade of vague dread.
```

7c: *input*

```
He was a little
gray-headed man of sixty.
QRST
QRSTU
```

output

```
eHw saa l tilte
rgyah-aeed dam nfos xiyt.
RQTS
RQTSU
```

Answers

1.
```
[10,12,13,15,18].select { |n| n%2 == 1 }
   #-> [13, 15]
```

2. We start at index 1 and take steps of 2, guaranteeing that we'll pick up just odd elements. Notice that the limit of iteration is not `orig.size` (which here would be 7) but `orig.size-1`, since the legal indices of `orig` range from 0 to 6.

```
orig = [60,62,65,70,72,73,75]
final = []
1.step(orig.size-1,2) { |idx|  final.push(orig[idx]) }
p final    # output: [62, 70, 73]
```

3. The `upto` and `downto` iterators are really just like `step`, except the step value for upto is fixed as 1 and the step value for `downto` is fixed as −1. Since you can supply positive or negative increments, there's no need for separate `step_upto` and `step_downto` iterators. You can count down the odds from 20 to 1 like this:

```
19.step(1,-2) { |n| print n," "}
# output:
   19 17 15 13 11 9 7 5 3 1
```

4. There are too few equals signs in the comparison of how_many to 0. Saying how_many=0 *assigns* 0 to how_many regardless of the value it had before. It's sort of a self-fulfilling prophecy. The comparison-versus-assignment gotcha afflicts most popular languages; it's a tradition going back at least thirty years. There are some languages that use the single = for comparison and reserve something else for assignment; for example in Pascal, `variable := value` is an assignment. This one will probably bite you from time to time if you're a normal person. When Ruby sees code that seems to contain this kind of error, it won't try to fix it, but it will usually give you a helpful warning.

5. The answer is *B*. In `case...when...`, just as with `if...elsif...`, the first successful test is the only one acted upon.

6. It looks like the block is executing one too many times, but it's not. The first four lines are produced by the print instruction, and the last is an artifact of irb. Remember, irb not only executes the code you give it but prints evaluations as it goes along. It so happens that iterator methods typically use their receivers as return values. The number 4 was the receiver of the times iterator.

7a: There are a number of ways to write something that will work.

```
while line = gets
  line.chomp!
  if not line.empty?
    2.times { puts line }
  end
end
```

An alternative choice:

```
while line = gets
  line.chomp!
  (puts line; puts line) if line.size > 0
end
```

Another possibility leaves the newline character undisturbed for printing:

```
while line = gets
  print line+line unless line.chomp.empty?
end
```

7b: Notice that no chomp is necessary if we use strip.

```
while l = gets
  l = l.strip.center(40)
  puts l
end
```

7c: This is the trickiest of the three, but it's still a very short script.

```
while line = gets
  line.chomp!
  0.step(line.size-2,2) { |p| line[p,2] = line[p+1,1] + line[p,1] }
  puts line
end
```

If you examine the iterator block, you'll see that pieces of the string are being replaced in two-character chunks. This explains why the step limit was set to line.size-2, even though line.size-1 is a real index; there needs to be another character to the "right" before a swap can take place. Oddly enough, nothing breaks if we get this one wrong. If there are an odd number of characters, the last attempt to swap will result in `line[p+1,1]` evaluating to an empty string; the last character falls harmlessly back into place.

By the way, what's a better way to express `line[p+1,1] + line[p,1]`? We were bothering with more detail than was necessary. Try `line[p,2].reverse` instead.

4

WEEK 1

DAY 5

The Characteristics of Objects

> "Certainly not," said Socrates, "visible things like these are such as they appear to us, and I am afraid that there would be an absurdity in assuming any idea of them, although I sometimes get disturbed, and begin to think that there is nothing without an idea; but then again, when I have taken up this position, I run away, because I am afraid that I may fall into a bottomless pit of nonsense, and perish. . . "
>
> —*Plato, Parmenides (ca. 370 B.C.E.)*

Now that we've accumulated enough necessary skills, we can get back to objects and classes, clarify the difference between them, and learn how to make individual objects unique and interesting without having to write singleton methods. Along the way we'll learn more about the kinds and scopes of variables and how we can make methods visible only in the places where they're useful.

Instance Variables

The variables that we've used so far have *local scope*. We've likened their use to pronouns in common language: They carry their meaning within some area of communication and then lose that meaning. With only local variables, it would be impossible for an object to remember anything.

```ruby
forgetful = Object.new
def forgetful.store(v)
  contents = v
end
def forgetful.retrieve
  return contents
end
forgetful.store("left wallet on table")
forgetful.retrieve   # error: "contents" is undefined!
```

The variable `contents` has a scope limited to the method in which it appears, so the value stored by the `store` method is inaccessible when we try to get it back in the `retrieve` method; we say that it is *out of scope*. There is in fact no relationship between the `contents` variables in the two methods, other than that they happen to have the same name.

What we need is a variable with more permanence, one whose scope is defined by an object, not the contours of the surrounding code. This is called an *instance variable*.

Note

> The name "instance variable" is not altogether precise for Ruby. An instance variable belongs to an *object,* which is an *instance of a class*. In Ruby, in contrast to most object-oriented languages, you can give an instance variable to an object directly without bothering the rest of the objects of its class. So you might want to think of an instance variable as an *object variable*.

In Ruby, we make an instance variable by starting its name with an "at" symbol (@, also called a *whirl* or a *strudel;* as an Iowa State University alumnus I call it a *cyclone*).

```ruby
babar = Object.new
def babar.store(v)
  @contents = v
end
def babar.retrieve
  return @contents
end
babar.store("peanuts near bush")
babar.retrieve  #-> "peanuts near bush"
```

The instance variable @contents belongs only to babar; anyone else can have an instance variable with that name, and babar won't know and won't care. Even when two objects are instances of the same class, their instance variables can hold different values, and in fact this is generally how objects of the same class are distinguishable from one another.

```
class Philosopher       # let's have dining philosophers...
  def allocate_chopsticks(n)
    @num_chopsticks = n
  end
  def dine
    if @num_chopsticks >= 2
      puts "Mmm, good."
    else
      puts "I don't have enough chopsticks."
    end
  end
end
foo = Philosopher.new; foo.allocate_chopsticks(2)
bar = Philosopher.new; bar.allocate_chopsticks(1)
foo.dine      # output:  "Mmm, good."
bar.dine      # output:  "I don't have enough chopsticks."
```

The number of chopsticks held is a characteristic of a philosopher. We might have made foo and bar alike in every other respect, but one can eat, and the other is hungry.

Mars and the Metric System: A Cautionary Tale

In the fall of 1999, an unmanned NASA spacecraft had been flying for almost a year toward Mars and was beginning to establish orbit when a piece of communication that was expected to be in metric units arrived in English units. The spacecraft went off course just badly enough to brush up against the atmosphere and disintegrate.

Misinterpretation is always a danger when you treat measurements and quantities as simple numbers, with the assumption that everybody agrees on the units.

How much money are you carrying?

25.

Great! You can buy me dinner.

With a quarter? I don't think so.

There are two reasonable ways to deal with this kind of problem. The autocratic approach is to tell everyone that they must all use the same units, but it might not be effective; old habits are hard to break, and you might need to keep reminding everybody for a long time.

5

Another idea is to stop treating measurements as simple numbers; units must always be specified, never assumed. This costs something in efficiency, but promotes safety by removing all misunderstanding.

In an object-oriented language, the second idea can be neatly achieved through a custom data type, one that somehow makes the interpretation part of the measurement. An `Integer` or `Float` (floating-point number) object doesn't have any idea what it means to be a temperature, but we'll make sure that a `Temperature` object does. After storing a temperature, we will be able to retrieve it later without having to remember which units we used when storing it.

```
# Old, unsafe style
room_temp = 64.1      # stored just as a number
# ...  other stuff happens here
air_condition if room_temp > 30     # whoops... was that C or F?
# New, safe style
room_temp = Temperature.new
room_temp.store_F(69.1)
# ...  other stuff happens here
air_condition if room_temp.as_C > 30  # implicit conversion!
```

Writing a `Temperature` Class

Let's create the `Temperature` class as it is described above. We'll want it to be able to store and retrieve a temperature in Celsius, Fahrenheit, and Kelvin units. This calls for six methods; for now we'll name them `store_C`, `store_F`, `store_K`, `as_C`, `as_F`, `as_K`. Also, to distinguish one temperature from another we'll need a single instance variable.

An arbitrary decision faces us: In what units should the instance variable store the temperature? In a way, it doesn't matter, because all we really care about is that the *methods* work as advertised. (A user of the class won't think about how it works, any more than you think about where the wires are routed inside the walls of your house when you flick a light switch on.) To help us remember that Celsius is the native temperature unit, we'll name the instance variable `@celsius`. Two methods will require no conversions, so let's write them first:

```
# Temperature class, first attempt
class Temperature
  def store_C(c)
    @celsius = c
  end
  def as_C
    @celsius   # or, return @celsius
  end
```

We will tackle Fahrenheit next, using the familiar formulas $C = (5/9)(F - 32)$ and $F = (9/5)C + 32$.

```
def store_F(f)
  @celsius = (f - 32)*(5.0/9)
end
def as_F
  (@celsius * 1.8) + 32
end
```

Notice the liberal use of parentheses in these formulas. They aren't necessary in the as_F method, but it doesn't hurt to have them there.

Why type 1.8 instead of 9/5 in as_F? Because we'd rather not make the interpreter calculate 9/5 over and over again. A program that does lots of conversions will run faster this way. Yes, we could do the same thing in store_F, substituting 0.5555555556 for 5.0/9; and yes, we could also divide by 1.8 there; we'll settle all this after a while, but first let's finish the class definition by adding the Kelvin methods.

```
def store_K(k)
  @celsius = k - 273.15
end
def as_K
  @celsius + 273.15
end
end      # this is the end of the class definition
```

Now we can test it out:

```
freezing = Temperature.new
freezing.store_C(0)
freezing.as_F            #-> 32.0
balmy = Temperature.new
balmy.store_F(86.0)
balmy.as_C       #-> 30.0
balmy.as_F       #-> 86.0
balmy.as_K       #-> 303.15
```

5

Note

Looking ahead: Some temperature conversions lead to messy displays. Try storing 57 degrees Fahrenheit, then viewing it in Celsius: it comes out as 13.88888889. In the next chapter we'll learn to take control of how numbers are presented; we can, for instance, specify that a number always be shown rounded to two decimal places (30.0 as 30.00, 13.88888889 as 13.90, etc.).

Integers and Floats

You might be wondering why the 5 is changed to a 5.0 in `store_F`. This is to make sure that dividing doesn't cause everything to the right of the decimal point to get tossed out. 5.0/9 correctly evaluates to 0.555555556 using floating-point division, but 5/9 is evaluated with integer division and the remainder is discarded, leaving us with zero! Sometimes there are good reasons for wanting this behavior (and integer division runs much faster on some hardware), so Ruby supports both kinds of division. Floating-point division is used unless both numbers are integers, so any of 5.0/9, 5.0/9.0, and 5/9.0 will give the results we want.

What if the numbers being divided are stored as variables? You can't just stick ".0" onto the end of a variable name, but you can convert it with the `to_f` method.

```
lives = 9
lives.to_f   #-> 9.0
```

Going the other way requires that we be specific: There are several methods that change a float to an integer, each following a different rounding rule.

```
some_floats = [-5.8, -3.3, 1.4, 6.9]
#  round to nearest integer
some_floats.collect {|f| f.round}  #-> [-6, -3, 1, 7]
#  round down
some_floats.collect {|f| f.floor}  #-> [-6, -4, 1, 6]
#  round up ("ceiling")
some_floats.collect {|f| f.ceil}   #-> [-5, -3, 2, 7]
#  discard fractional part
some_floats.collect {|f| f.to_i}   #-> [-5, -3, 1, 6]
```

A Convention for Naming Methods

The rules for naming methods are not exactly the same as for naming variables. One important difference is that you can end a method name with an equals sign. From this follows a nice convention for storing and retrieving instance variables: Where a variable is named `@foo`, you can write to it with a method named `foo=` and read from it with a method named `foo`. It ends up looking like you're reading and writing the variable directly, but you still have complete control over what those methods do.

```
class Student
  def major=(x)
    @major = x
  end
  def major
    @major
  end
end
```

```
s = Student.new
s.major = "Lunar Hostility Studies"
    # same as: s.major= ("Lunar Hostility Studies")
puts "The student majors in #{s.major}."
    # output:  The student majors in Lunar Hostility Studies.
```

Automatic Accessors

Since these *accessor* methods are so commonly needed, simple shortcuts have been devised for writing them concisely. `attr_reader` supplies a reader method, `attr_writer` supplies a writer method, and `attr_accessor` supplies both.

```
class point
  attr_writer    :x, :y
  attr_accessor :z
end
# same as:   class Point
#                  def x=(value)
#                     @x = value
#                  end
#                  def y=(value)
#                     @y = value
#                  end
#                  def z=(value)
#                     @z = value
#                  end
#                  def z
#                     @z
#                  end
#            end
```

Let's revise the `Temperature` class to follow this naming convention. There should be no apparent outward difference in the treatment of c, f, and k; the user doesn't care that only one corresponds to an instance variable. We just want to be sure the user can manipulate temperatures like this:

```
t = Temperature.new
t.k = 308
t.f        #-> 94.73
t.c        #-> 34.85
```

We can use `attr_accessor` to generate c= and c methods, and write the rest manually. Very little needs to be changed from before, but `attr_accessor` insists that the instance variable name reflect the method names, so it will become @c.

```
# Temperature class, second attempt
class Temperature
  attr_accessor :c
  def f=(f)
    @c = (f - 32)*(5.0/9)
```

5

```
    end
    def f
      (@c * 1.8) + 32
    end
    def k=(k)
      @c = k - 273.15
    end
    def k
      @c + 273.15
    end
  end
```

If f=(f) and k=(k) offend your sensibilities, you can substitute some other argument name.

```
    def k=(value)
      @c = value - 273.15
    end
```

But there is nothing wrong with the way it was written. k=(k) may look like an assignment from something to itself, but k= is a method name and k is an argument name, and the two are distinct. When you assign a value using the k= method, Ruby lets you put a space before the equals sign, even though "k =" is not the name of the method.

```
    t.k= 45.0    # k= is the method name being used, but ...
    t.k = 45.0   # this syntax lets you feel you are manipulating t.k directly
```

Define Your Own Operators

Most languages distinguish between *operators* and *functions*. Operators are the symbols (+-*/%^, and so forth) associated with primitive operations like addition and multiplication and cannot be changed, whereas functions can be defined and redefined as necessary. But in Ruby the distinction is meaningless. The world revolves around *methods,* which encompass the usual roles of both operators and functions. To see that addition is a method in Ruby, consider that 10 + 12 can be rewritten as an invocation of "+" on 10, using 12 as an argument.

```
    10.+ (12)    #-> 22
```

As we saw on Day 1, addition means different things to different kinds of objects.

```
    [10].+ ([12])              #-> [10, 12]
    "Conc".+ ("ate".+ ("nate")) #-> "Concatenate"
```

When we create a new class, we are free to define the behavior we want for the standard operator symbols. We simply have to write the methods. Let's go back to our Temperature class and consider what kinds of operators should be defined for it. Unless we think of a reason to add, subtract, multiply, or divide temperatures, we might as well leave +, -, *, and / undefined. But what about comparisons?

```
arctic = Temperature.new; arctic.f = -50
tropic = Temperature.new; tropic.f = 106
arctic < tropic   #  error: undefined method '<'
```

Surely we'd want arctic < tropic to evaluate to *true*. It's up to us to define a "<" method that does the right thing, and that thing is to "return *true* if your temperature is lower than the one given in the argument, *false* otherwise." Keeping in mind that "your temperature" is kept in the instance variable @c, an excruciatingly literal translation of the task might look like this.

```
class Temperature
  def < (anotherTemperature)
    if @c < anotherTemperature.c
      return true
    else
      return false
    end
  end
end
```

It works, but it's wordier than necessary. Notice that "@c < anotherTemperature.c" is itself a Boolean expression. We want "<" to return *true* if and only if the value of that expression is true; so why not return it directly?

```
class Temperature
  def < (anotherTemperature)
    @c < anotherTemperature.c
  end
end
```

5

That's better. But there's another thing we should probably change. Remember how we wanted there to be no apparent difference between the c, f, and k properties of a temperature? The user needn't know how the information is stored. An important benefit of this approach is that we can safely change the internal workings of the Temperature class any time we please, so long as we continue to support those six accessor methods.

The same principle can be applied inside the class definition. As it stands now, if we ever changed the implementation—perhaps by storing the temperature in Kelvin units—the "<" method would have to be rewritten, because there would no longer be a @c instance variable. But when we know how to make objects talk to themselves, we can avoid such problems. Instead of getting the Celsius value through @c, the object can *ask itself for the value*, invoking the accessor method c just as if it were on the outside looking in.

```
class Temperature
  def < (other)
    self.c < other.c
  end
  # while we're at it, we can define == the same way
  def == (other)
    self.c == other.c
  end
end
```

A disadvantage of this added communication is that it slows performance down very slightly. But it's usually worthwhile, because it results in code that is both more maintainable and more readable.

When defining the other comparison operators, we could follow the same pattern.

```
class Temperature
  def >= (other)
    self.c >= other.c
  end
  # ... likewise for > and <=
end
```

Or, we could ignore the c property and apply some logic to the comparison methods we've already written.

```
class Temperature
  def >= (other)
    not self < other
  end
  def > (other)
    self >= other and not self == other
  end
  def <= (other)
    not self > other
  end
end
```

Now our temperature comparisons work as they should.

```
liquid_nitrogen = Temperature.new; liquid_nitrogen.k = 90
dry_ice = Temperature.new; dry_ice.c = -78
h2o_ice = Temperature.new; h2o_ice.f = 32
h2o_ice == h2o_ice          #-> true
dry_ice < h2o_ice           #-> true
dry_ice <= liquid_nitrogen  #-> false
liquid_nitrogen.c           #-> -183.15
```

> **Note**
>
> Looking ahead: Because the process of defining comparison operators is similar for most classes, it would be nice to have the work "factored out" for us somehow; and indeed, Ruby supplies all the common comparison logic in a *module*. All we really need to define is a "<=>" method and invoke the module, and all the comparison methods anybody will ever need are automagically generated. We'll learn how to take advantage of modules on Days 9 through 11.

Class Constants

The fraction 5/9 is used twice in our `Temperature` class, and our treatment of it was inconsistent. Dividing by it is the same as multiplying by its reciprocal, 9/5, which is 1.8, so we just wrote 1.8 out for the `f` reader method. For the `f=` writer method, we used 5.0/9, partly because its solution is a messy repeating decimal, and partly so we could understand how to make floating-point division happen when we need it. But it's a rather inefficient way of going about things. Every time the `f=` method is invoked, 5.0/9 has to be recalculated. We ought to be able to do the calculation once and keep reusing the result.

A *constant* is like a variable, except that, well, it doesn't vary. It is designed to be given a value and then never changed. We distinguish a constant from a variable by making its first character a capital letter. You might say that we give constants "proper" capitalized names to remind us of their permanence. Ruby does not enforce the constancy of a constant's value in every situation, but it does issue a warning if it sees one being changed.

```
Meaning = 6 * 9  #-> 54
Meaning = 42     # warning: already initialized constant "Meaning"
Meaning          #-> 42
```

To clean up our temperature conversions, we can assign the value of 5.0/9 to a constant, then refer to it whenever needed in the class methods. We'll define the constant inside the class definition but outside any of the methods.

```
# Temperature class, third attempt
class Temperature
  Factor = 5.0/9    # constant assignment happens just once
  attr_accessor :c
  def f=(f)
    @c = (f-32) * Factor
  end
  def f
    (@c/Factor) + 32
  end
  # ... insert same old k= and k methods here ...
end
```

5

Why can't we define `Factor` inside any of the methods? There are two reasons: because
that would suggest that we wanted the constant to have meaning only within that method,
and more importantly, because then the constant would get redefined each time that
method was called. Even if it's the same value as the first time around, in this case Ruby
won't allow the reassignment. The constant should get defined only when the interpreter
reads our class definition the first time. Once that has happened, the constant is firmly
associated with the value it was originally given, as far as the methods of that class are
concerned.

The scope of a constant is limited to the methods of its class. So it would be just fine for
many classes to have a constant named `Factor`. As with local variables, we shouldn't
have to worry what we name them because of possible interference from other parts of a
larger program.

```
class C1
  Konst = "one"
  def what_is_Konst
    Konst
  end
end
class C2
  Konst = "two"
  def what_is_Konst
    Konst
  end
end
C1.new.what_is_Konst  #-> "one"
C2.new.what_is_Konst  #-> "two"
```

It is occasionally useful to look at a class constant from outside. It can be done; scope
limitation doesn't imply any sense of paranoid privacy. We just need to be specific about
which scope we want to look at. Ruby provides a *scope operator* (`::`) for just this purpose. To access `C1`'s `Konst` value when we're not inside a `C1` method, we reference
`C1::Konst`.

It is also possible to define constants that are not inside any class. Those can be accessed
either without a scope operator, or to make it clear that we might be distinguishing one
constant from another of the same name, we can use the scope operator but specify nothing in front of it.

```
Konst = "out there"   # a constant not belonging to any class
Konst                 #-> "out there"
::Konst               #-> "out there"
C1::Konst             #-> "one"
C2::Konst             #-> "two"
```

Access Control (or, A Cure for the Common Code)

While it is not possible to hide class constants from the outside world, it is possible to hide methods. Obviously we wouldn't want to hide the methods that users are going to be invoking directly, but there will sometimes be methods that are used indirectly.

```
class K
  def common_code
    # ...
  end
  private :common_code  # Hide this method!
  def user_method_1
    common_code        # or, self.common_code
    # ... do other stuff
  end
  def user_method_2
    common_code
    # ... do other stuff
  end
end
```

Here we have a class that supports two methods, but those two share some similarity that we were able to factor out into a third method. Since that third method is not part of the user interface, there is no pressing need to give the user access to it; it is only there for the use of the other methods. In fact, there are at least two good reasons to hide it. First, a small interface is less confusing to the user. Second, and perhaps more important, a hidden method is one we can change, eliminate, or rename at will when we are debugging or otherwise improving the class code. As soon as anyone starts using a method from the outside, it might as well be set in stone, and we start having to worry about backwards compatibility with every improvement.

The `initialize` Method

Ruby supports a few special methods that will help us write nice user-friendly classes. We'll deal with most of these niceties on Day 15, but there's one we should learn about right away.

Whenever a new object is instantiated, Ruby looks in its class for an instance method named `initialize` and evaluates it. A simple use of `initialize` can at least help us to prevent this behavior:

```
t = Temperature.new
t.f                    # error: undefined method '*' for nil
```

5

It is a strange looking but perfectly logical error. The f accessor method just attempted to multiply @c by a number, but @c itself isn't a number, at least not yet. Since t hasn't been given a temperature value, its instance variable @c has the value nil. Maybe we *want* an error in this circumstance; but if we don't, the thing to do is make sure every new temperature gets a default value. Let's say we want it to be absolute zero, that is, zero kelvins.

```
class Temperature
  def initialize
    self.k = 0
  end
end
chilly = Temperature.new
chilly.f                    #->  -459.67
chilly.k                    #->  0.0
```

How did all that work? When chilly came into being, its instance method initialize was called, which in turn called the k= method with argument 0. If you look at k=, you see that it gives a value to @c, which means that all the accessors will work; but f returns a value very far away from room temperature. This might be enough to indicate a logic problem, depending on how the temperature is used in a program.

If new is given arguments, it passes them to initialize.

```
class Box
  def initialize (w, h, d)
    @width = w
    @height = h
    @depth = d
  end
  def volume
    @width * @height * @depth
  end
end
b = Box.new (3, 6, 5)
b.volume                #-> 90
```

At the end of the day you'll be asked to apply this idea to the Temperature class so that it no longer takes separate statements to instantiate a temperature object and give it a value.

Note For now, the number of arguments given in a new call must match the number specified by initialize, or there will be an error. On Day 15 we'll learn how to make initialize (and other methods as well) more friendly and flexible.

Global Variables

Up until now we've seen two types of variables: those starting with "@", which have object scope, and those without "@", which have local (or *automatic*) scope defined by where they appear in a script. There are two more kinds we haven't seen yet. We'll discuss *global* variables here, and touch briefly on *class* variables tomorrow.

Starting a variable name with a dollar sign ($) makes it global, which means it is valid absolutely everywhere. Before we look at examples, I'd better lay my prejudices out on the table for you: There is seldom a good reason to create global variables. The more you rely on them, the more trouble you're asking for. I'm afraid you will see them commonly used, but they can usually be replaced with something safer, as we shall see.

That said, let's make a global variable and verify its universal scope.

```
$foo = " accessible from here"

def bar
  puts "top-level method 'bar' says:" + $foo
end
class K
  def bar
    puts "class K's method 'bar' says:" + $foo
  end
end

puts "top-level code says:" + $foo
bar
K.new.bar
# output:
    top-level code says: accessible from here
    top-level method 'bar' says: accessible from here
    class K's method 'bar' says: accessible from here
```

Nothing wrong with that, you say; it must be convenient to have information that can be seen anywhere. But problems arise when your work grows too large to be taken in at a glance, perhaps because you incorporated a finished script into another application. You run the risk of accidentally using the same global variable name twice in different places for completely different purposes; since their scopes overlap, when the second global variable gets defined, it silently overwrites the first. In a language characterized by conversations among objects, letting global variables proliferate results in something like noise pollution: Objects are privy to too much information, and their world becomes confusing.

Do a search-and-replace on the above code using your text editor, changing every $foo to @foo, and test the results. This almost works, because, as it turns out, an instance variable defined in the top level of the script (outside any method or class definition) is visible everywhere except from inside class K. @foo really does belong to an object—that is, the top-level object, which we identify with the entire script or, when in a whimsical mood, with the programmer. Often this is actually the scope that people have in mind when they use globals, so a top-level instance variable can be an effective and less drastic alternative.

Now change every @foo to the constant Foo and test it out again. Visibility is restored everywhere, so we see that a top-level constant has something very much like global scope; but it's still safer, because if another Foo constant is accidentally defined in the top level, the interpreter will notice and issue a warning.

Globals are most useful when we take advantage of the ones provided by Ruby, such as $DEBUG, which reports whether the interpreter was invoked with the -d command line switch.

```
#--- start of script named "hello" (this is line 1) ---
puts "Hello"
puts "We made it to line #{__LINE__}" if $DEBUG
puts "world"
#--- end of script (this is line 5) ---
% ruby hello
Hello
world
% ruby -d hello
Hello
We made it to line 3
world
```

We'll pick up information about some other supplied globals as we go along through the book.

What to Name Things

Naming guidelines have occasioned much argument, pontificating, and browbeating, but here are three simple and intuitive principles that might save you some grief.

1. *Though you see them in examples, never use names like foo or Qaz in a real program.* Those are meaningless words (called "metasyntactic variables") commonly used in language instruction so that the form of a thing can be shown without bringing attention to specific content. When you're doing real work, the content matters, and the variable and method names should reflect it.

Note An authoritative list of metasyntactic variables is found in the *Jargon File*, which any search engine can find all over the Web. It's good reading, full of insight, history, fun, and irreverence.

2. *The smallest names are most appropriate in the smallest scopes.* It would be foolish to name a global variable "$n" in a large program, because it is easy to forget what n means when working on the code; too many important things start with the letter *n*, and you might use it again later without thinking. But a minimal name is often just fine in a small space like an iterator block, at least when context makes it obvious what it refers to.

```ruby
addresses.each {|a|  puts a}             # clear enough
addresses.each {|address|  puts address} # unnecessary
```

3. *Names should be as descriptive as necessary, but no more so.* It can be easy to go overboard with long variable names (some of us remember languages that limited names to a few characters, and get giddy when allowed to make them out of long word phrases). Don't fall into redundancy for the sake of clarity. This is especially applicable to method names: When writing a determinant method for a Matrix class, name it `determinant`, not `matrixDeterminant`, unless you have a Darned Good Reason. Anybody invoking the method probably already knows they have a `Matrix` object on which they're using it.

Exercises

1. "Refactor" the following class by moving redundant code into a private method.

```ruby
class PetLover
  def morning_list
    puts "Feed the cat"
    puts "Feed the birds"
    puts "Scoop the litter"
    puts "Brush teeth"
  end
  def evening_list
    puts "Feed the cat"
    puts "Feed the birds"
    puts "Scoop the litter"
    puts "Do the dishes"
  end
end
```

5

2. Must the `Temperature` class have only one instance variable? Can you think of a way to make it perform better using three? Assume that temperature values are retrieved much more often than they are stored. *Hint: Use Ruby's default reader methods* (`attr_reader :c, :k, :f`).

3. Write a `Counter` class that behaves as follows. You'll probably want one instance variable and four methods.

```
c = Counter.new
c.value     #-> 0
c.advance
c.advance
c.advance
c.value     #-> 3
c.reset
c.value     #-> 0
```

4. A built-in Ruby method, `defined?`, takes a variable name as an argument and returns `nil` whenever that variable is undefined.

```
defined?(frax)  #-> nil
frax = 73
defined?(frax)  #-> "local-variable"
```

Can you use `defined?` to make the `Counter` class work correctly without an `initialize` method? *Hint:* Modify both the `value` and `advance` methods.

5. Modify `Temperature` to support this kind of initialization:

```
t1 = Temperature.new( 100, "C" )
t1.f  #-> 212.0
t2 = Temperature.new( 32, "fahr" )
t2.c  #-> 0.0
t3 = Temperature.new( 400, "K" )
t3.c  #-> 126.85
```

The user should be able to specify "c", "C", "celsius", "Centigrade", and so on. In other words, only look at the first letter, and accept both upper or lower case. (If it's not a valid letter, you can assume Celsius.)

Answers

1. The things our pet lovers do both morning and evening can be viewed as a single care routine.

```
class PetLover

  def care
    puts "Feed the cat"
    puts "Feed the birds"
```

```
      puts "Scoop the litter"
    end

    private :care

    def morning_list
      care
      puts "Brush teeth"
    end
    def evening_list
      care
      puts "Do the dishes"
    end
  end
```

2. Since we're assuming that temperatures will be read much more often than they are stored, we should get all the unit conversions out of the way at storage time so they won't have to be repeated later.

```
class Temperature
  Factor = 5.0/9

  def f=(f)
    @c = (f-32) * Factor
    @k = @c + 273.15
    @f = f
  end
  def c=(c)
    @f = c/Factor + 32
    @k = c + 273.15
    @c = c
  end
  def k=(k)
    @c = k - 273.15
    @f = @c/Factor + 32
    @k = k
  end
  attr_reader   :c, :f, :k
  # omitted: initialize, ==, <, etc.
end
```

3.
```
   class Counter
     def reset
       @count = 0
     end
     def advance
       @count = @count + 1
     end
     def value
       @count
```

5

```
      end
    def initialize
      self.reset   # or just "reset", or "@count = 0"
    end
  end
```

4. When a new `Counter` object is created, the instance variable `@count` will be unde-
    fined, but we can make sure it gets a value as soon as the user tries to do anything
    with the object.

```
class Counter
  def reset
    @count = 0
  end
  def advance
    if defined?(@count)
      @count = @count + 1
    else
      @count = 1
    end
  end
  def value
    defined?(@count)  ?  (@count) : 0
  end
end
```

5. Insert this method into the solution for Exercise 2.

```
def initialize(number, units)
  case units[0,1]        # just look at the first character
    when "F","f"
      self.f = number
    when "K","k"
      self.k = number
    else                 # presumably "C","c"
      self.c = number
  end                    # end of the "case" structure
end                      # end of the initialize method
```

    Or, if you prefer, use upcase to simplify the comparisons.

```
def initialize(number, units)
  case units[0,1].upcase
    when "F"
      self.f = number
    when "K"
      self.k = number
    else
      self.c = number
  end
end
```

DAY 6

Ins and Outs

> The only possible form of exercise is to talk, not to walk.
>
> —Oscar Wilde

Today we delve into how Ruby scripts communicate with the outside world. We've already written some text filters, which are an example of a specialized and very common kind of communication. We've read from the keyboard and written to the screen. But we want more control, more flexibility; our scripts should be able to listen and speak to anything out there, including files, printers, other programs, and the Internet. That sounds like a pretty big topic, and it is. We'll address some of it today, and come back to it throughout the book, especially on Days 13 (where we use Ruby as a *glue* language for coordinating the actions of other programs) and 19 (where we do some fun things with networking).

Streams

There is a level at which everything in the outside world looks alike to a computer program. Unlike the computer memory area allocated for the use of a program, which is a sort of closed system, the outside world is full of moving, changing collections of information, which we can think of as flowing streams. You can dip your hands into a stream of water, take a drink, dip again, and drink again, but the stream is different the second time from the first, and so you are not drinking exactly the same water. Likewise, information gathered from a stream twice in the same way will often differ, whereas assigning a value twice from something that is not a stream almost always yields identical results (with a few exceptions such as rand and Time.now).

```
x = STDIN.gets          # STDIN is the keyboard input stream.
y = STDIN.gets
x == y     #-> false (usually)

x = "a string object"   # A string is not a stream...
y = "a string object"
x == y     #-> true   (of course!)
```

Ruby's most general stream class is named IO, for input/output. An object of the IO class is a stream that can be read from, written to, or both. The class supplies an assortment of instance methods that are quite general and fall into roughly three categories.

1. Control: open, close, pos, rewind, and so forth.

2. One-shot communications: gets, getc, puts, print, read, and so forth.

3. Iterated communications: each, each_byte, each_line, and so forth.

Later in the chapter we'll discuss these methods and a few others.

The Standard Streams

There are three streams that are always open when a Ruby program starts running. One, STDIN, is for input, and the other two, STDOUT and STDERR, are for output. We use STDOUT for normal program output and STDERR when reporting anything strange that happens, at least under Unix (the distinction is less important in the DOS/Windows world).

 Note

> This discussion assumes use of the standard Ruby intepreter. The rubyw version has no standard I/O and is intended for use with graphic user interface (GUI)-only applications; typically these interact through the Tk or Gtk libraries to do windowed communication with the user.

What's the use of standard streams? They make it possible to write simpler, shorter scripts. Sending information to the screen is a very common thing to do, and it would be tedious to have to specify it every time we used puts or print:

```
def greet_user
  STDOUT.puts "Welcome to my program."
  STDOUT.puts "Instructions:"
```

```
   # ... a few more STDOUT.puts statements ...
end
```

Instead we are allowed to say `puts` and omit the receiver, and the information will typically go to the screen.

```
def greet_user
  puts "Welcome to my program."
  puts "Instructions:"
  # ... a few more puts statements ...
end
```

Every now and then we have a reason to take information that would normally go to the screen and send it somewhere else, such as for debugging a script that isn't working properly. Suppose we'd like to send the output of the `greet_user` method to a file so that we can go through it with a text editor later to search for mistakes. One way would be to specify a different receiver for each `puts` statement. (We're about to create our first disk file under program control—are you watching?)

```
def greet_user
  outf = File.open("debug.txt","w") # "w" means open for writing
  outf.puts "Welcome to my program."
  outf.puts "Instructions:"
  # ... a few more outf.puts statements ...
  outf.close
end
```

Of course, that can't be the easiest way. It would be nicer to be able to tell Ruby, "From now on, when I say `puts` without a receiver, assume that I want you to write to the file `debug.txt` instead of to the screen." We can do that, but not by changing the value of `STDOUT`, because, as you may have noticed, it has a name that starts with a capital letter, and therefore it is a constant. Fortunately, Ruby also supplies a trio of global variables that are companions to those constants: `$stdin`, `$stdout`, and `$stderr`. Whenever a Ruby program starts running, these variables refer to the same streams as the constants, but they can be reassigned later if we want.

```
$stdout == STDOUT      #-> true
$stdout = File.new("output.txt","w") # redirect $stdout to disk file
$stdout == STDOUT      #-> false
```

6

A fourth global variable, `$defout`, determines the default output destination whenever Ruby sees an output method invoked with no receiver specified. Usually `$defout` refers to `STDOUT`, but, just like `$stdout`, it can be pointed elsewhere.

```
# Save as "redirect.rb"
def greet_user
  puts "Welcome to my program."
```

```
    puts "Instructions..."
end

puts "This always goes to the screen."
if $DEBUG
  outf = File.new "debug.txt","w"
  $defout = outf
end

greet_user

if $DEBUG
  $defout = STDOUT  # restore standard output
  outf.close
end
puts "Back on screen? Just checking."
```

Since we've made redirection depend on $DEBUG, this script will behave differently depending on whether we run it with the -d flag on the command line.

```
% ruby redirect.rb
This always goes to the screen.
Welcome to my program.
Instructions...
Back on the screen? Just checking.

% ruby -d redirect.rb
This always goes to the screen.
Back on the screen? Just checking.
% cat debug.txt              (or in DOS, "type debug.txt")
Welcome to my program.
Instructions...
```

Similarly, $stdin is where Ruby looks when an input method like gets is invoked without specifying an IO object (except when a filename is given on the command line, in which case a gets by itself tries to read from the file, not from $stdin). Just as $stdout can be redirected, $stdin can also be redirected to read a file that contains some text prepared as the input for your script. That way you can test the script with the same input repeatedly, with utter consistency and without having to wear yourself out typing it in, until the bugs are cleared up.

The other pair of streams, $stderr and STDERR, we'll talk about on Day 13.

Files

Accessing disk files is hardly any different from accessing the screen or keyboard. There are just a few details that set them apart.

Standard input and output are generally available as soon as a script starts, so you can read from and write to them immediately; but files sometimes have to be created before you use them, and in all cases they have to be *opened*. The act of opening a file creates a *file object*. You then interact with that object using I/O methods, some of which you are already familiar with. When you're finished, you *close* the object. This is a new idea to us; we've talked about how to create objects but not, in general, how to get rid of them.

Also, a disk file can be opened in different *modes*. It can be a read-only stream like STDIN, a write-only stream like STDOUT, or both; it can be opened in an "append" mode that allows you to write new information but not overwrite the old.

Finally, "files" are not always files. Operating systems tend to have names for *devices* such as printers, allowing them to be opened, manipulated, and closed just as if they were files. This doesn't make any more work for us; it's just a thoughtful convenience.

Opening a file is a matter of instantiating an object of the File class, using new just as with any other class. We typically supply two arguments when opening a file: the file-name and the mode. Both should be in string form.

```
auto = File.new('C:\AUTOEXEC.BAT', "r")
  # ... read some or all of the contents of the file
auto.close

auto.closed?  #-> true
```

The "r" indicates read mode, so the methods that would write to this file become illegal. As it turns out, the second argument to new is optional, and if it is omitted, "r", being the safest choice, becomes the default mode. Other common modes are "w" for writing, "r+" for read/write, and "a" for append mode.

To provide some parallelism, open is provided as a synonym for new. When you close something, it feels more like real "closure" if it was something you had "opened" rather than "created." (These are not true aliases, because open does something that new can't, under the right circumstances. We will see more on that when we get to *class methods* later in this chapter.)

Some Useful IO Methods

Although these methods are really defined as part of the IO class, you can also think of these as methods of the File class.

6

Note   The issue is one of *inheritance*, which we use all the time, but we won't explore it in depth till Day 9.

All of the examples that follow suppose that `testfile` is constructed as follows:

```
Lord, what fools
these mortals
be.
```

getc, gets

`getc` and `gets` get a single character or a line of text, respectively. A character returned by `getc` is in ASCII form and should be converted using the `.chr` method if you want to see it as a one-character string.

```
f = File.open "testfile"
f.gets        #-> "Lord, what fools\n"
f.getc        #-> 116          (ASCII code for 't')
f.getc.chr    #-> "h"
f.gets        #-> "ese mortals\n"
```

ungetc

`ungetc` "puts back" the last character read, so that it can be read again. This allows you to peek at a stream without really disturbing it.

```
f = File.open "testfile"
f.getc.chr    #-> "L"
f.ungetc
f.gets        #-> "Lord, what fools\n"
```

pos, lineno

`pos` and `lineno` return the current position in a stream, by character (that is, by byte) and by line, respectively. `lineno` only counts how many times you've used `gets`. It does not know your actual position, as `pos` does.

```
f = File.open "testfile"
[f.pos, f.lineno]    #-> [0,0]
f.gets               #-> "Lord, what fools\n"
[f.pos, f.lineno]    #-> [17,1]
14.times { f.getc }
[f.pos, f.lineno]    #-> [31,1]   (lineno is incorrect)
f.close
```

pos=, rewind

The pos= method moves to whatever position in the file you specify. rewind is equivalent to pos=0, except that it also resets the lineno counter to 0.

```
f = File.open "testfile"
f.pos = 6
f.gets          #->   "what fools\n"
f.rewind
f.gets          #->   "Lord, what fools\n"
f.close
```

readlines

readlines reads the contents of the stream and returns it as an array of strings, each element a line.

```
f = File.open "testfile"
contents = f.readlines
f.close
contents.type           #->   array
contents.size           #->   3        (number of lines in file)
contents[-1].chomp      #->   "be."    (reliable way to get last line)
```

read(num_bytes)

Read the specified number of characters and return them as a single string. This method does not care what the characters are, and will cross newlines. If num_bytes is omitted, it reads the entire file; if num_bytes is too large, it reads to the end.

```
f = File.open "testfile"
f.read 20               #->   "Lord, what fools\nthe"
f.read 20               #->   "se mortals\nbe.\n"
f.pos = 12
f.read                  #->   "ools\nthese mortals\nbe.\n"
```

write(string), print(string), <<(string)

These methods write the string at the current position. Although these are not true aliases, they are generally close enough for our purposes. One interesting difference is that the << method returns its receiver; this means you can stack up << invocations on the same string.

```
outf = File.open "fresh.txt", "w"
outf.print "1"
outf.write "2"
outf << "3"
outf << "4" << "5" << "6"
outf.close
File.new("fresh.txt").read      #->   "123456"
```

6

eof?, closed?

eof? and closed? return true or false depending on the state of the stream. These are sometimes useful when writing low-level looping logic on streams.

```
f = File.open "testfile"
f.eof?                       #-> false
while not f.eof?
  print f.pos, "\t"                    #(\t  advances to next tab stop)
  p f.read(10)
end
f.eof?                  #->  true
f.closed?               #->  false
f.close
f.close?                #->  true

# output:
  0        "Lord, what"
  10       " fools\nthe"
  20       "se mortals"
  30       "\nbe\n"
```

What About Memory Space?

The readlines and read methods are convenient, because they make it possible to separate input logic from the rest of what your script does: *read first, process later.* But applying them to very large files can cause problems, because files might end up being larger than the available memory. When you don't know the anything about a file's size ahead of time, you are better off reading it in manageable-sized chunks, such as one line at a time. The read method is safe to use for large files only if you supply a reasonable *num_bytes* parameter.

If you object to the idea of a while loop as the main structural feature of a text filter, but the input files may be too large for the safe use of readlines, check out the ARGF object. ARGF can be iterated over as if it were an array, but it doesn't really read everything at once. Here are three general forms for text filter scripts.

```
# Dangerous for memory, but allows sorting:
all_input = readlines
all_input.each do |line|
  # do something with each line
end

# Safe for memory, but uses an explicit loop:
while (line=gets)
  # do something with each line
end
```

```
# Also safe, and preferable stylistically:
ARGF.each do |line|
  # do something with each line
end
```

Formatted Output

Ruby provides a highly flexible way of formatting information for output, called `printf`. It is borrowed from the C language, and for the convenience of C programmers (including, presumably, the author of Ruby), the formatting specifications are like those used in C's standard I/O library. So if you already program in C and are familiar with how `printf` works, you can skip most of this section; the main differences that you need to know are that `printf` is a method of IO objects (including files) whereas `sprintf` is not (it returns a string).

Let's start with `printf`. You can use it just as you use `print`, except you give it a *format string* as an extra first argument. Certain sequences of characters in the format string will be subsituted with later arguments. That may sound confusing, but some simple examples should make things clearer.

```
x = 25.0/3
puts x                    # output: 1.666666667
printf "%d \n", x         #          1
printf "%f \n", x         #          1.666667
printf "%.2f \n",x        #          1.67
```

In one sense, the job of the format string is to tell Ruby how to print the rest of the arguments. But it's more precise to see it this way: it is *only* the format string that gets printed, after all the percent-sign sequences have been replaced. The most often used sequences are

%d   Show as decimal number

%f   Show as floating-point number

%c   Show as character

%s   Show as string

Some of these are a little misleading. A *decimal* number does not have a decimal point; it's just decimal in the sense of being in base 10, as opposed to base 8 or 16, which are useful in some applications (and can be produced with %o and %x, respectively). A *floating-point* number does have a decimal, but is usually displayed in fixed-point form—which, if you think about it, is usually the reason for using formatting output in the first place.

6

Length specifications can be inserted into these formatting sequences, easily controlling exactly how wide each piece of output is and so making it possible to produce neat vertical columns in reports. To see how this works, here is some code to produce batting averages, given an array of [name, at_bats, hits] triples. First we'll make sure the math seems right, and then clean up the output.

```
batting_data = [
  ["Floyd", 474, 97],
  ["Jenson", 358, 121],
  ["Witt", 399, 82],
  ["Thomas", 203, 58],
  ["Gray", 2, 2]
]

batting_data.each do |name, at_bats, hits|
  print "#{name}  ab: #{at_bats}, ",
        "h: #{hits},  avg: #{hits.to_f/at_bats}\n"
end

# output:
  Floyd  ab: 474, h: 97,  avg: 0.2046413502
  Jenson ab: 358, h: 121,  avg: 0.3379888268
  Witt  ab: 399, h: 82,  avg: 0.2055137845
  Thomas ab: 203, h: 58,  avg: 0.2857142857
  Gray  ab: 2, h: 2,  avg: 1.0
```

The columns are uneven because the names have different lengths, and so do the numbers. Besides that, we're accustomed to seeing batting averages rounded to the thousandths place. Yes, this is a job for printf.

```
batting_data.each do |name, at_bats, hits|
  printf "name: %20s    ab: %4d    h: %4d    avg: %.3f\n",
         name, at_bats, hits, hits.to_f/at_bats
do

# output:
           Floyd    ab:  474    h:   97    avg: 0.205
          Jenson    ab:  358    h:  121    avg: 0.338
            Witt    ab:  399    h:   82    avg: 0.206
          Thomas    ab:  203    h:   58    avg: 0.286
            Gray    ab:    2    h:    2    avg: 1.000
```

That's much nicer, but maybe we don't like that leading 0 in the batting averages, because it keeps a 1.000 average from standing out as it should. There doesn't seem to be a way to suppress the 0 when using printf by itself, but if we could capture some partly formatted output in a string, we could manipulate it in any way before displaying it. sprintf is good at this.

```
batting_data.each do |name, at_bats, hits|

  #  Use sprintf to round the average to 3 decimal places
  #  For Floyd, avg_s becomes the string "0.205"
  avg_s = sprintf "%.3f", hits.to_f/at_bats

  #  Replace first character with a space, but only if
  #  the string starts with "0."
  #  For Floyd, avg_s becomes " .205"
  avg_s[0,1] = " " if avg_s[0,2] == "0."

  #  Use printf as before, but display avg_s as a string.
  printf "name: %20s    ab: %4d    h: %4d    avg: %s\n",
         name, at_bats, hits, avg_s
end

# output:
            Floyd    ab:  474    h:   97    avg:  .205
           Jenson    ab:  358    h:  121    avg:  .338
             Witt    ab:  399    h:   82    avg:  .206
           Thomas    ab:  203    h:   58    avg:  .286
             Gray    ab:    2    h:    2    avg: 1.000
```

Tip

An alias for `sprintf` is `format`, and that's certainly a more descriptive name for what it does. Those of us who prefer calling it `sprintf` are mostly old C programmers.

Another way of getting a formatted string is with the % method. Notice that if there are multiple arguments, % needs them in array form.

```
"Converted character '%c'" % 65   #-> "Converted character 'A'"
"%s: %.3f" % [Time.now, 2.0/7.0] #->
      "Fri Sep 21 15:01:33 CDT 2001: 0.286"
```

Class Methods

6

Up to now we've been rather vaguely referring to the methods of classes, but we should start being more precise now. A class has two kinds of methods: *instance* methods and *class* methods. Most of the methods we've seen have been instance methods, because they are applied to objects, which are instances of a class. But one method we've used quite frequently is a class method. Think about what happens here:

```
x = Philosopher.new
x.allocate_chopsticks(2)
```

When we wrote a dining philosopher class back on Day 5, we defined `allocate_chopsticks` as an instance method, something that was to be applied to individual philosophers. `new` is also a method, but when it is called, its receiver is the `Philosopher` class itself, so `new` must be a *class method*. To bring back an analogy we used earlier, we draw a distinction between the philosophers (objects) and the academy (class) that produces them. When we want wisdom, we will talk to a philosopher, but first we need to get a philosopher, and for that we have to talk to the academy. Thus, for almost any class we can expect the most commonly used class method to be `new`, because the main job of a class is to produce objects.

However, we can define other class methods.

```
def Philosopher.menu
  "rice"
end
```

Notice that we can invoke `menu` using the class as the receiver, but there is no such method for an individual object.

```
Philosopher.menu        #-> "rice"
Philosopher.new.menu    # error: undefined method
```

When writing about methods, we sometimes use this convention to distinguish them: `K#m` is an *instance* method `m` of class `K`, and `K.m` is a *class* method `m` of class `K`.

A more useful example of a class method is found in the `Time` class. When we've created a `Time` object up to now we've used `Time.new` (actually its alias, `Time.now`), capturing the current time. If we wanted to know how many seconds had elapsed since noon of the United States bicentennial in Greenwich Mean Time, we'd want to compare a current time object with one initialized to that earlier point in history. Unfortunately we lack the technology to actually run Ruby in the past, but we do have the `gm` class method.

```
current     = Time.now
bicentennial = Time.gm (1976, "jul", 4, 12, 00)
current - bicentennial    #-> 787312794.8
```

`gm` creates a `Time` object, so it is something like a relative of `new`. In fact, the most common use of class methods is to provide specialized ways of creating objects, often by intercepting arguments and manipulating them before invoking `new` in turn.

```
class X
  attr_reader :foo
  def initialize(f)
    @foo = f
  end

  # Class methods can be defined either inside or outside
  # the class definition (class X ... end); here we do
  # it inside.

  def X.new_discounted(f)
    return X.new (f*4/5)  # the 'return' is optional
  end
```

```
    def X.new_zeroed
       return X.new (0)
    end

  end

  a = X.new(1000)
  a.foo                      #-> 1000

  b = X.new_discounted(1000)
  b.foo                      #-> 800

  c = X.new_zeroed
  c.foo                      #-> 0
```

Class methods are also suitable for certain filesystem operations, because whereas a `File` object is a reference to an open file, not all files should be open when you work with them. There are also `File` class methods that also implicitly open and close files; these are less flexible but more convenient than doing it all yourself.

Some Useful `File` Class Methods

Let's take a look at some of the most useful `File` class methods.

rename(oldname, newname)

The `rename(oldname, newname)` method renames the specified file (or directory), if possible.

read(*filename*)

read(*filename*) reads the contents of *filename* into a single string. (This method is available as of Ruby version 1.7.)

```
  contents = File.read "testfile"
     #  contents == "Lord, what fools\nthese mortals\n"be.\n"

  # Same effect can be achieved by the read instance method:
  #   fobj = File.new "testfile"
  #   contents = fobj.read
  #   fobj.close
```

readlines(*filename*)

readlines(*filename*) is like `File.read`, but returns an array of lines.

```
  File.readlines "testfile"
     #-> ["Lord, what fools\n", "these mortals\n", "be\n"]
```

If you need to divide lines in some unconventional way, you can specify any delimiter by supplying it as an extra argument. (This applies also to the `readlines` *instance* method we saw a little while ago.) To end a line every time "t" is encountered, instead of the usual "\n":

```
File.readlines "testfile","t"
  # -> ["Lord, what", "fools\nt", "hese mort", "als\nbe\n"]
```

open(*filename*)

`open` is a synonym for `new`, unless you treat it as an iterator by supplying a code block. In this case the file is opened, the corresponding file object is passed back to the block, and the file is automatically closed afterward.

```
File.open("testfile") { |f|  print f.gets }

# Same as:
#   f = File.open "testfile"
#   print f.gets
#   f.close
```

dirname(*filename*), basename(*filename*), split(*filename*)

When you use the `dirname(filename)`, `basename(filename)`, and `split(filename)` methods, not only does a file *not* need to be open, it need not even exist. These methods split off the directory information from the basic filename. `dirname` returns the directory information, `basename` returns the basic filename, and `split` presents both in a two-element array. These can be useful, among other times, when working with a file selector in a graphical user interface (GUI).

```
spec = "/home/joeuser/.emacs"
File.dirname spec      #-> "/home/joeuser"
File.basename spec     #-> ".emacs"
File.split spec        #-> ["/home/joeuser", ".emacs"]
```

exists?(*filename*), writable?(*filename*), directory?(*filename*), zero?(*filename*), size(*filename*), mtime(*filename*)

The methods `exists?(filename)`, `writable?(filename)`, `directory?(filename)`, `zero?(filename)`, `size(filename)`, and `mtime(filename)` ask various questions about a file that may appear in a directory listing. These are especially useful when used with the `Dir` class, which provides disk directories.

You can consult Ruby reference material for details on `Dir`, but for now it will suffice to know that `Dir.new(location).entries` returns a directory listing as an array of strings. We can treat it like any other array, for instance by iterating over it.

```
def simple_listing(directory)
  filenames = Dir.new(directory).entries
  filenames.each do |base|
    fullname = directory + '/' + base
    if File.directory?(fullname)
      printf "%30s/\n", base
    else
      printf "%30s %10d\n", base, File.size(fullname)
    end
  end
end
```

The preceding function makes a customized file listing on a Unix system. If the command "`ls -l`" in the current working directory produces this:

```
-rw-r--r--   1 joeuser   root        15071 Sep 19   2000 ChangeLog
-rw-r--r--   1 joeuser   root         4622 Sep 19   2000 Makefile
drwxr-xr-x   2 joeuser   root         4096 Sep 19   2000 src
```

then our `simple_listing` function, called with '`.`' (the current working directory) as an argument, would make the difference between files and directories clearer, show file sizes, and omit all the other details.

```
                        ./
                       ../
            ChangeLog      15071
             Makefile       4622
                 src/
```

We'll do more with directory listings on Day 13.

The Command Line

In case you haven't been exposed to the concept before, most operating systems (including all flavors of Unix, DOS, and Windows) allow strings to be passed into programs when they start running. They are called *command-line arguments* even though in a windowing environment there might be no visible command line where the user is typing information. We have been using command-line arguments in a very narrow way up to now, as a list of input files. The following script reads all the files whose names are on the command line, one at a time, and prints their contents.

```
# Save as cat.rb
while (line = gets)
  puts line
end
```

Do you remember how that works? `gets`, without a specified receiver, tries to open the filenames that are given to the script and read through them in order. A typical command line to call the script might look like this, in DOS:

```
C:\RUBY>ruby cat.rb file1.txt file2.txt file3.txt
```

But we won't always want command-line arguments to be interpreted that way. An argument may refer to an output filename or to something else that is not a filename at all. A constant array provided to every Ruby script holds these arguments in their raw form. The array name is ARGV.

```
#!/usr/bin/env ruby
#
# Script to simply echo the command line arguments
# so we can see them.  Save this as showargs.rb

ARGV.each_with_index { |a,i| printf "arg %2d: %s\n", i,a }
```

Here's a sample run of showargs.rb. Notice that the indices start at 0 instead of 1. This takes a little getting used to if you're used to the way arguments are numbered in C, C++, or some shell languages. On the other hand, it's consistent with the way arrays are handled in the rest of Ruby, so in the long run it will probably make things a little easier for you to remember.

```
C:\RUBY>ruby showargs.rb first second third
 0: first
 1: second
 2: third
```

When a Ruby script reads its command line arguments from ARGV, it is free to do anything with them. That might mean trying to use them as filenames, or just ignoring them.

If you write a script that requires arguments and the user doesn't supply them (or doesn't supply enough of them or the right kinds) you might be prudent to stop its execution right away with an error message instead of letting it crash later.

```
#/usr/bin/env ruby

# Make sure the user supplied the info we need.
(STDERR.puts "usage: myscript.rb arg1 arg2"; exit 1) if ARGV.size<2

# Now do the useful stuff.
# ...
```

Class Variables

If we needed each philosopher to keep track of his or her creation (or graduation) date, it would be a fairly simple task.

```
class Philosopher
  def initialize
```

```
    @graduation_date = Time.now
  end
  attr_reader :graduation_date
end
```

But suppose we also thought that each philosopher should come stamped with a serial number. The `initialize` method would assign a value to an instance variable, say `@serial`, and that number would increment with each new graduate who walked out the door.

It turns out that we'll need a new kind of variable to get the job done, because somehow the academy always has to keep track of what the next serial number should be. Surely this isn't a job for an instance variable; we only want one copy of this information, and it should belong to the school, not one particular student. A global variable would work, but that would introduce the danger of namespace collision (some other class might want to use the same name). What is called for is a *class variable*.

```
class Philosopher
  @@next_serial = 1

  def initialize
    @graduation_date = Time.now
    @serial = @@next_serial
    @@next_serial = @@next_serial + 1
  end

  attr_reader :serial
end

rene = Philosopher.new
emil = Philosopher.new

rene.serial  #-> 1
emil.serial  #-> 2
```

There are three things to mention before moving on.

1. Every `Philosopher` object has access to the class variable `@@next_serial` (remember, `initialize` is an instance method).

2. `@serial` has an attribute reader method but no writer method. We don't want a philosopher's serial number inadvertently changed. We could allow that if we wanted to, via an `attr_writer` or `attr_accessor`.

3. No accessors whatsoever are provided for `@@next_serial`, because we don't want the numbering sequence to be disturbed. But we could allow that too if we chose, by providing the appropriate class method (or even an instance method, because the instances also have access).

6

Errors and Exceptions

By now you've seen what Ruby usually does when an error occurs: It stops and prints a message on the screen. You see a line number, and a description of the problem, and generally you can use that information to go back and fix the script.

But not all unexpected failures are the programmer's fault. There are surprises that don't qualify as emergencies and so should not be allowed to bring a program to a halt. Plenty of strange things can happen when the outside world gets involved. You try to read a file; it doesn't exist. You ask a user for input; you get back something unsuitable. You try to write to disk; the disk is full, or you don't have the right permission, or the file already exists and is marked read-only. So we consider a wider category, *exceptions*, by which we mean events that are out of the ordinary in some way. A well-designed script "expects the unexpected," responding to exceptions in some appropriate way.

There was a time not long ago when it was a programmer's responsibility to check for trouble every step of the way. Open a file, make sure it opened, decide what to do if it didn't; write a line, make sure it got written, decide what to do if it didn't. The practice was confusing and tiresome. Source code that was carefully written tended to be so cluttered with error-handling instructions that it became hard to read. We want to be careful, yet we want to concentrate on what our scripts are supposed to *do*, not how they are supposed to cope with surprises.

Ruby lets you segregate ordinary code from error-handling code in logical chunks. The body of a method definition, or code grouped by begin...end, can be told how to respond to an exception using rescue.

Consider code that keeps track of how many times it has been run by maintaining a times_run file. The normal procedure is to read a number out of the file, add one to it, and write it back. Let's concentrate just on the information-gathering part of the task.

```
counter_filename = 'times_run'
inf = File.open(counter_filename, "r")
count = (inf.gets.to_i) + 1
inf.close
```

But what about the first time this runs? The file doesn't exist yet, so File.open will fail and the program will halt. File.exists? can be used to fix that.

```
counter_filename = 'times_run'
if File.exists? counter_filename
  inf = File.open(counter_filename, "r")
  count = (inf.gets.to_i) + 1
  inf.close
```

```
else
  count = 1
end
```

But we're not being quite comprehensive in our planning. What if, unlikely as it seems, the file gets erased between the time of the existence test and when we try to open it? And is it possible for gets to fail when open has succeeded? Covering all the bases is possible, and costs us nothing extra.

```
counter_filename = 'times_run'
begin
  inf = File.open(counter_filename, "r")
  count = (inf.gets.to_i) + 1
  inf.close
rescue
  count = 1
end
```

This says that if *anything* unexpected happens between begin and rescue, the counter is to be set to 1. The program will not stop. No error message will appear. But the message that would have appeared is still available in the global variable $!, so if you wanted to, you could still print the error without stopping the program.

```
# ...
rescue
  STDERR.puts "An exception occurred: #{$!}"
  count = 1
end
```

Exceptions are objects, by the way, each belonging to a class. You can selectively rescue one kind of error and ignore another, or provide different rescue code for different kinds of errors.

```
begin
  # ...
rescue ScriptError
  # ...
rescue RuntimeError
  #...
rescue IOError
  #...
end
```

If there is some "cleanup" code that you want to make sure gets run whether there is an exception or not, mark it with ensure. ensured code has to come last, after any rescue clauses.

```
begin
  # ... try to do this
```

6

```
rescue
  # ... do this if an exception occurs
ensure
  # ... and then do this no matter what
end
```

Summary

Programs are not closed systems; at least, useful ones aren't. There are many ways they can interact with the world outside, and Ruby's IO objects provide a compact and consistent interface for doing so. When you have an IO object (which might be a file, or a standard input device like the keyboard, or as we will see later, a network "socket"), it responds to a few simple methods like `gets` and `puts`.

Some IO tasks, especially those involving the filesystem, are administrative in nature; files need to be deleted, renamed, and so on. These are usually accomplished by special class methods rather than instance methods.

Finally, since the outside world is annoyingly unreliable, we want to know we can deal with surprises in a comprehensive and graceful way. Ruby's `rescue...ensure` mechanism makes this easy.

Exercises

1. Look at the `sprintf` example in the section "Formatted Output." Suppose we replace this line:

   ```
   avg_s[0,1] = " " if avg_s[0,2] == "0."
   ```

   with this one:

   ```
   avg_s = avg_s[1, avg_s.size-1] if avg_s[0,2] == "0."
   ```

   The effect is that the leading `0` is simply deleted instead of being replaced with a space, and it throws off the columns if somebody has a perfect batting average. Can you think of a simple way to compensate for the change?

2. Look at the example in the "Some Useful IO Methods" section that illustrates the `eof?` method of IO objects. Rewrite it without `eof?`, using `read`, `length` and `step`.

3. Write a script that makes an exact copy of `testfile` and names the copy `test2`. You may assume that there is enough memory to hold the contents of the file. Use your text editor to create a text file named `testfile`, then run your script to verify that `test2` was created and is identical to `testfile`.

4. Using `ARGV`, modify your script from Exercise 3 so that the user must supply the source and destination filenames on the command line. It will end up like a simplified imitation of the Unix `cp` command or DOS `copy` command. Check for error conditions; exit with an informative message if the source file doesn't exist or the user didn't supply two filenames.

5. How can we implement this behavior in our `Temperature` class from Day 5?

```
t1 = Temperature.c(0)
t1.f  #-> 32.0

t2 = Temperature.f(104)
t2.c  #-> 40.0
```

Answers

1. Supply length information for "avg: %s" in the next line:

```
   printf "name: %20s    ab: %4d    h: %4d    avg: %5s\n",
```

2. After using `read` to bring the contents of the file into a string, you can ask the string for its `length` and know ahead of time how far you're going.

```
text = (File.open "testfile").read

count = 0
0.step(text.length-1, 10) do |position|
  print position,"\t"
  p text[position,10]
  count = count + 10
end
```

3. We'll provide two solutions for this problem. The first is fairly symmetric-looking, since it explicitly opens and closes both the input and output files.

```
#!/usr/bin/env ruby

infile = File.open "testfile"
contents = infile.read
infile.close

outfile = File.open "test2", "w"
outfile.write contents
outfile.close
```

The second is more condensed and takes advantage of a class method to do the reading.

```
#!/usr/bin/env ruby

outfile = File.open "test2", "w"
outfile.write (File.read("testfile"))
outfile.close
```

6

Remember, the read method returns a string. We don't have to give it a name if all we're going to do with it is feed it immediately to the write method.

4. The first solution to Exercise 3 is a little more satisfying than the second, so we'll use it as the basis for this modification. Our error checking will not be very sophisticated yet, but we'll get into that in more detail on Day 10.

```ruby
#!/usr/bin/env ruby
#
#  Save as filecopy.rb

if ARGV.size < 2
  STDERR.puts "Usage: ruby filecopy.rb sourcefile destfile"
  exit 1
end

if not File.exists?(ARGV[0])
  STDERR.puts "Error: file #{ARGV[0]} does not exist"
  exit 1
end

infile = File.open ARGV[0]
contents = infile.read
infile.close

outfile = File.open ARGV[1], "w"
outfile.write contents
outfile.close
```

5. Again, here are two solutions. For both, we ask the user to use one of our custom class methods when creating a Temperature object.

The first solution has no initialize method.

```ruby
class Temperature

  # Special "constructor" class methods.
  def Temperature.c (c)
    t = Temperature.new
    t.c = c
    t           # or "return t"
  end
  def Temperature.f (f)
    t = Temperature.new
    t.f = f
    t
  end
  def Temperature.k (k)
    t = Temperature.new
    t.k = k
    t
  end
```

```
# The rest is just our old Temperature class.
Factor = 5.0/9
attr_accessor :c

def f=(f)
  @c = (f-32) * Factor
end
def f
  (@c/Factor) + 32
end
def k=(k)
  @c = k - 273.15
end
def k
  @c + 273.15
end
end
```

You'll notice that each of the class methods is forced to return the object it creates. Invoking new in a more conventional way gets rid of some clumsiness. Here we factor out the conversion functions and present a very different design.

```
class Temperature

  Factor = 5.0/9

  # Make "initialize" expect Celsius units.  This commits
  # "new" to a certain behavior, but we expect users to stick
  # with the specific constructors: f, c, k.
  def initialize(c)            @c = c                     end

  # Define class methods to do all conversions.
  def Temperature.f_to_c(f)    (f-32) * Factor            end
  def Temperature.c_to_f(c)    (c/Factor) + 32            end
  def Temperature.k_to_c(k)    k - 273.15                 end
  def Temperature.c_to_k(c)    c + 273.15                 end

  # Let the constructors all invoke "new".
  def Temperature.c(c)    Temperature.new(c)              end
  def Temperature.f(f)    Temperature.new(f_to_c(f))      end
  def Temperature.k(k)    Temperature.new(k_to_c(k))      end

  # Finally, define all the accessors.
  attr_accessor :c
  def f=(f)                @c = Temperature.f_to_c(f)  end
  def f()                  Temperature.c_to_f(@c)      end
  def k=(k)                @c = Temperature.k_to_c(k)  end
  def k()                  Temperature.c_to_k(@c)      end
end
```

6

Notes on this solution:

a. When all the methods are this short, it sometimes seems to make the class definition more compact and readable to collapse method definitions to one line
each. But if this is done, each method name must be followed with a pair of
parentheses to avoid ambiguity, even if the method takes no arguments.
Otherwise Ruby will try to interpret the body of the method as the name of the
first argument.

b. We end up with two methods each named f, k, and c. But one of each is an
instance method and the other a class method, so there is no conflict between
them. (Where's the other c method, you ask? It's implied by attr_accessor.)

DAY 7

Catching Up on Details

> There are some enterprises in which a careful disorderliness is the true method.
>
> —Herman Melville, *Moby Dick*

When you know a programming language well, you don't use its concepts one at a time; rather, they mesh together in everything you do. Organizing a book of this nature, where prior programming experience is not assumed, is a tricky business. "Chicken and egg" problems abound. It can seem impossible to understand any of the material until you understand all of it. So it just isn't very reasonable to teach programming by presenting everything all at once. Concepts have to be encountered in some order so the understandings can be fitted together as they come, even if this limits the usefulness of the early examples. In the end, the assembled knowledge should have all the pieces in about the same structure as in the mind of an experienced programmer.

The trick, then, is deciding on a useful order. It is traditional to start with numbers and variables, then progress through strings, functions, scope, and eventually (for the dogged reader who makes it that far) classes and objects. But to keep the strengths of Ruby in perspective, we have nearly reversed that pattern up to now. We have been talking about objects, classes, and methods without spending much time on what people are usually shown first when learning to program. Today's lesson is devoted to filling in some of those gaps. You may have already picked up some of what you're about to see from hints and intuitions, but it will be helpful to have it laid out more explicitly.

Numbers in Ruby

Let's start with numbers, which fall into two general categories: those that can have a fractional part (*floats*) and those that cannot (*integers*).

Integer Literals

A *literal* is just a way of expressing something directly in a language, as opposed to using a variable. Writing integer literals is intuitively pretty simple—we've been doing it all along—but Ruby offers some enhancements that help you express yourself readably.

A literal like 863527117 isn't very readable, because you have to look closely and count digits to know its magnitude. Is that in the hundreds of millions, or is it in the billions? When you aren't programming a computer, the convention is to break large numbers up with commas. Saying "863,527,117" makes it plain that we have less than a billion. You can't quite get away with that in Ruby, though, because it would introduce ambiguity:

```
foo = bar(863,527,117)  # looks to me like three arguments.
```

However, it's allowable to break up long integer literals with underscores. The catch is that Ruby doesn't enforce their proper placement, so it's up to you to make sure digits are grouped in the usual threes (also, the underscores mustn't be left hanging off the ends):

```
863_527_117         #-> 863527117
86_35_27117         #-> 863527117
8635__27117         #-> 863527117
86352_7117_         #-> error
_8_63527117         #-> error ("undefined variable"!)
```

To reject an underscore at the end may seem arbitrary, but to reject it at the beginning is necessary so that literals can be distinguished from variables. For instance, this code is perfectly legal (though confusing):

```
_6 = -4    #  _6 is a variable name; -4 is an integer literal
_7 = 6
_6 + _7   #-> 2
```

In some circumstances it is useful to write literals in bases other than ten. Ruby supports bases 2 (*binary*), 8 (*octal*), and 16 (*hexadecimal* or *hex*). Octal and hex are useful mostly because 8 and 16 are powers of 2; this way we get a way to condense binary numbers into fewer digits. Each octal digit represents exactly three binary digits (or *bits*), and each hex digit represents four.

> **Note**
>
> For those of you who slept through math class in junior high school, the *base* of an integer literal refers to how many possible values each of its digits can have. We normally use digits 0–9, so that's base 10. It's probable that humanity got into that habit because we happen to have that many fingers and that many toes (otherwise why would they be called digits?).

Octal isn't used a lot anymore, but for historical reasons Ruby uses it as the default base when interpreting a literal that starts with a zero. Binary and hex literals start with 0b and 0x respectively.

Some integers only make sense when written in a particular base. 3735928559 looks like a meaningless number until you see it in hex as 0xDEADBEEF. That's a value sometimes used to fill unallocated memory so that a hex debugging tool can make it clear at a glance what parts of memory have been disturbed and what parts haven't.

The bit pattern 1110111111111111 might be used for a binary "masking" operation (we'll get to binary operations later in this chapter). To Ruby, though, it's just a number. Expressed in base 10, it becomes 61439, and its meaning is lost. So if you use such a number in a script, you should express it in binary form, or maybe in hex for the benefit of people who know how to do the conversions in their heads (0xE==0b1110, 0xF==0b1111).

```
bit_mask = 0b1110111111111111    # or 0xEFFF
```

Unix file permissions are logically arranged in three-bit groups. That naturally suggests octal form, but it is also fine to write them in binary, perhaps broken up with underscores. The following permission set allows the owner to read, write, and execute a file and everyone else only to read it and execute it.

```
usual_perms = 0755   # or 0b_111_101_101
```

Floating-Point Literals

Although we don't have bases other than 10 to consider when writing float literals, there is still a choice between scientific and standard notation. Scientific notation is useful when dealing with numbers that are very large or very small, and when complete

7

accuracy is not needed. Avogadro's number, which is the number of atoms in one gram of hydrogen, is approximately this:

```
602,000,000,000,000,000,000,000
```

We say "approximately" because in all honesty we can't be sure of all those zeroes. The number might be off by a few quintillion; all that is really important is the magnitude and the first few digits. In scientific notation, Avogadro's number is 6.02×10^{23}. That's a more compact and readable form, and while 23 is a big enough exponent to take Avogadro past our everyday experience, most other scientific notation literals are easily read at a glance, such as 3.5×10^9 for 3.5 billion. A very small number, like the probability of you winning the state lottery on a given day, would live on the other side of the decimal point and so would be expressed with a negative exponent.

Ruby uses an e notation to express scientific notation literals:

```
avogadro     = 6.02e23
lottery_hope = 2e-8     # 0.00000002 in standard notation
```

Floats are not absolutely precise in the way that integers are. If we convert avogadro to an integer, we see that not all those zeroes are for real, and indeed only the first few digits were stored; when we round the result back to the seventh or eighth "significant digit" (or in this case, even the third), we get back the number we literally specified:

```
avogadro.to_i          #-> 601999999999999995805696
```

How Numbers Are Stored

Ruby does a wonderful thing with integers. You won't appreciate just how wonderful it is unless you have had to deal with integer overflows in other languages, so here's a little piece of C code that illustrates the problem:

```
int x = 1000000000;  /* that's 1 billion */
printf (" %d %d %d\n", x, x*2, x*4);

/* output:   1000000000 2000000000 -294967296  */
```

C decides ahead of time to store integers in a certain fixed amount of space. This is usually 32 bits, which allows for $2^{32} = 4,294,967,296$ possible combinations. Allocate half of the combinations to represent negative interpretations, and the result is that integer values have to stay between $-2,147,483,648$ and $2,147,483,647$. Anything outside that range requires too many bits to store, some bits get lost, and what remains seems to make no sense; this is what we mean when we talk about integer overflow. The reason most languages do it this way is for performance. Computer hardware is designed to do efficient calculations on numbers that fit in a fixed space.

Larger numbers can be dealt with pretty much the way you would do it with pencil and paper. Although not all languages include such support, Ruby provides a special large number class called Bignum. Numbers belonging to the Bignum class have an almost limitless range, so there's no overflow. Whenever you give Ruby an integer, it decides what class to put it in based on its size:

```
    10_000_000.type        #-> Fixnum
10_000_000_000.type        #-> Bignum
```

A simple timing test shows that Bignum calculations introduce a speed penalty, which gets more pronounced as the numbers continue to grow:

```
fix = 10_000_000
big = 10_000_000_000
ggl = 10 ** 100
n   = 10000          # number of repetitions

t1 = Time.now
n.times { fix + fix + fix + fix + fix }
t2 = Time.now
n.times { big + big + big + big + big }
t3 = Time.now
n.times { ggl + ggl + ggl + ggl + ggl }
t4 = Time.now

printf "elapsed times: %.3f %.3f %.3f\n", t2-t1, t3-t2, t4-t3

# typical output:
  elapsed times: 0.036 0.138 0.359
```

10^{100} is called a *googol*; it's just a number that was invented to be large. (See Exercise 1 at the end of this chapter.)

In summary, Ruby's integers can be of any size, and they do not overflow. If a Fixnum grows too big through calculation, it is automatically converted to a Bignum and continues to behave correctly. Conversely, Ruby will change a Bignum back to a Fixnum when possible to boost performance.

Note

Of course it cannot be *strictly* true that Ruby's integers can be of any size and that they don't overflow. If you try to store an integer whose Bignum representation cannot fit in your computer's memory, such as a *googolplex*, Ruby converts it to a Float, which then overflows. But it's possible to work with ridiculously large numbers—say, in the 10^{10000} range—if you have a lot of time and memory at your disposal.

7

Although floats can be expressed in standard or scientific form, there is only one method of storing them internally, and only one `Float` class.

It is possible to overflow when working with floats, but the limit—due to the floating-point standard followed by almost all computer hardware, not to a limitation of Ruby itself—is somewhere in the vicinity of 10^{300} (to be a little more precise, 1.79769e+308). When you consider that the number of particles in the universe is estimated to be around 10^{97}, you see that float overflows are unlikely ever to cause you any practical problems. Also, an overflowed float does not become an arbitrary nonsense value, but the special pseudonumber `Infinity`. It no longer represents an actual value, but it still does the best it can in future calculations and comparisons, as the following code shows:

```
huge_pos = 1.0 / 0        #-> Infinity
huge_neg = -huge_pos      #-> -Infinity
huge_pos > huge_neg       #-> true
huge_pos + 1              #-> Infinity
huge_pos / huge_neg       #-> NaN        ("not a number")
```

How Numbers Are Presented

Ruby does not provide specialized conversion methods to show numbers in different forms. `printf` and `sprintf` make them unnecessary, and these are hard to give up once you begin to appreciate their flexibility. The following code illustrates several ways to present the number 27899.

```
n = 27899

# Normal hex, using lowercase digits 'a' through 'f':
nhex1 = sprintf("%x",n)     #-> "6cfb"
# Using uppercase digits and a hex indication prefix:
nhex2 = sprintf("0x%X",n)   #-> "0x6CFB"
# Hex, right-justified in 8 columns:
nhex3 = sprintf("%8X",n)    #->  "    6CFB"
# Left-justified:
nhex3 = sprintf("%-8X",n)   #-> "6CFB    "
# Right justified and padded with zeroes:
nhex4 = sprintf("%08X",n)   #-> "00006CFB"
# Scientific notation, accurate to one digit past the decimal
#   point (this is okay even though n isn't a float):
nsci1 = sprintf("%1.1e",n)  #-> "2.8e+04"
# Using an upper case "E" in the representation, and adding
#   another digit of accuracy:
nsci2 = sprintf("%1.2E",n)  #-> "2.79E+04"
```

We can further massage `nsci2` into an original presentation scheme that looks more like handwritten scientific notation. You won't understand the following example fully before reading the next chapter on *regular expressions*, but this helps show what is possible.

```
sprintf("%s x 10**%d",
        nsci2.gsub(/E.*/,""),
        nsci2.gsub(/[\d\.]*E[+-]*/,"").to_i)
  #-> "2.79 x 10**4"
```

Looking ahead: It turns out to be quite easy to extend Ruby's classes by adding our own methods to them. We could teach integers to do certain canned conversions on themselves, so that just asking for `31722.as_hex` would give us `0x7bea` without making us cook up any of those funny `sprintf` format strings. Relying on such an approach might ultimately mean trading away a little flexibility to gain a simpler, more object-oriented feel in our scripts. We'll have a better understanding of how that is done after Day 14, but for now we will use top-level methods (functions) to do the same thing a little less neatly.

Binary Arithmetic

Here are some odd-looking results. What do they mean?

```
a = 186
b = 9

a | b          #-> 187
a & b          #-> 8
a ^ b          #-> 179
```

Every integer is just a sequence of ones and zeroes when you get down to it. There are lots of situations where it is necessary or at least useful to visualize numbers in that form; at least, nothing of the above example makes any sense unless we do. So here's a function we can use to help us learn about binary arithmetic: given any number, `bin` returns its binary representation, padded out to 8 characters if necessary:

```
def bin(num)  sprintf("%08b",num)  end
```

Let's use `bin` to figure out what the vertical bar operator (|) does:

```
puts bin(a), bin(b), "--------  |", bin(a|b)
# output:   10111010
#           00001001
#           --------  |
#           10111011
```

In case you were wondering, binary `10111011` works out to be 187. Look at each column of output and you see a pattern: The result gets a 1 wherever either of the bits above it is a 1; otherwise it gets a zero. This is called a *bitwise or* operation.

7

The same experiment with the ampersand operator (&) illustrates the *bitwise and* rule: The result gets a 1 only when both the corresponding bits in a and b are 1:

```
puts bin(a), bin(b), "--------  &", bin(a&b)
# output:   10111010
#           00001001
#           --------  &
#           00001001
```

The hat operator (^) applies a somewhat more interesting *exclusive or* rule: The result gets 1 only where the corresponding bits in a and b are not the same:

```
puts bin(a), bin(b), "--------  ^", bin(a^b)
# output:   10111010
#           00001001
#           --------  ^
#           10110011
```

There are two other kinds of bitwise operations: *negations* and *shifts*. Negation is accomplished by the tilde operator (~), as this example shows:

```
puts bin(b),"--------  ~", bin(~b)
# output:   00001001
#           --------  ~
#           ..110110
```

Negation changes each 0 to a 1 and vice versa. The leading dots in the formatted result are Ruby's way of telling you that it would have liked to continue forever printing 1s on the left side.

The operators << and >> specify shifts:

```
puts bin(b), bin(b<<1), bin(b<<2), bin(b<<3)  # shift to the left
# output:   00001001
#           00010010
#           00100100
#           01001000

puts bin(a), bin(a>>1), bin(a>>2), bin(a>>3)  # shift to the right[1]
# output:   10111010
#           01011101
#           00101110
#           00010111
```

Shift any number to the right far enough, and it will become zero. Shifting a number to the left just keeps making it bigger.

---

[1]*Sadly, there is no "stand up, sit down, fight fight fight" operator.*

Here are two situations where you might find binary arithmetic useful.

First, it is possible to represent some group of characteristics as a single binary number rather than to assign each to its own Boolean. A possible benefit of this approach is efficient use of storage space; two possible costs are slower performance and a general straying from the object/method paradigm.

Suppose we want to use a Fixnum to store several Boolean values. A first step is to choose a bit position for each arbitrarily and then create bit masks with descriptive constant names:

```
Four_door          = 0b00000001  # or  1 << 0
Alarm              = 0b00000010  # or  1 << 1
Auto_transmission  = 0b00000100  # or  1 << 2
Spoke_wheels       = 0b00001000  # or  1 << 3
CD_player          = 0b00010000  # or  1 << 4
Air_conditioning   = 0b00100000  # or  1 << 5
```

We can store a set of characteristics into a variable by bitwise-*or*ing their masks together:

```
my_car = Four_door | Alarm | Auto_transmission | Air_conditioning
```

To set a bit to 1 individually is trivially easy (*or* with the mask), but to clear a bit to 0 takes some minor maneuvering in binary arithmetic (first negate the mask, then *and*). Here we use our bit masks to install a CD player and remove the alarm:

```
my_car = my_car | CD_player
my_car = my_car & ~Alarm
```

Testing a condition is always a matter of *and*ing with the corresponding mask:

```
if my_car & Alarm
  # decrease insurance rate or something
end
```

Sometimes it's convenient to test single bits by position:

```
six = 0b110    #-> 6
six[0]         #-> 0
six[1]         #-> 1
six[2]         #-> 1
```

Another common use of binary arithmetic is to try to boost performance on certain kinds of calculations. Every odd integer, when expressed in binary form, ends in a 1; so rather than dividing by two and examining the remainder to determine whether a number is odd, you can as effectively mask against 0b00000001 (that is to say, 1). On some hardware, a binary *and* operation happens to work faster than integer division.

```
puts "#{x} is odd"  if (x&1) == 1    # slower: if (x%1) == 1
```

7

Likewise, shifting an integer three positions to the right can be faster than dividing it by 8, and shifting it two places to the left can be faster than multiplying it by 4, although the results are the same in each case. Still, the performance gains, when they exist at all, may be only marginal, making it seem wiser to resist these attempts at cleverness and just say what you mean.

Boolean Logic

You use Boolean logic to make yes/no decisions. As it happens, there is a considerable similarity between Boolean logic and the binary arithmetic we've just been looking at; both involve *and* and *or* operations as well as *negations*. The main difference is that we no longer care about the individual bits. As far as Boolean logic is concerned, an object can be considered only *true* or *false*, and so it might as well have only one bit.

Recall from Day 4 that Ruby lives by the simple (though perhaps unconventional) rule that the only values that count as *false* are false and nil, and everything else is *true,* as the following code demonstrates:

```
def show_if_true(ob)
  p ob if ob
end

show_if_true false
show_if_true true
show_if_true nil
show_if_true "0"
show_if_true 0
show_if_true [1,2,3]
show_if_true "hello"
show_if_true self

# output:
  true
  "0"
  0
  [1,2,3]
  hello
  main
```

We have before us the basis for making all kinds of yes/no decisions. Testing complex conditions is intuitive; you can use the words and, or, and not, and they will do what you expect:

```
3>2 and not 7>8   #-> true
```

If you are experienced in a language from the C or Java tradition, you will be pleased to find that && is synonymous with and, || with or, and ! with not. These are not exact aliases however; the symbolic forms have a higher precedence, which means they are evaluated earlier (or, as we sometimes say, "bind more tightly"), as shown by the following two lines:

```
! false and false    #-> false
not false && false   #-> true
```

In `! false and false`, the `!` is processed before the and, so the expression is the same as `true and false`. Nothing can be true *and* false, so the end result is `false`. But in `not false && false`, the `&&` is processed first, yielding `false`, which is then negated by `not` to yield `true`.

As always, when in doubt you can use parentheses to impose your own precedence, overriding the defaults:

```
! (false and false)  #-> true
(not false) && false #-> false
```

Short-Circuit Evaluation

For the logical expression `exp1 and exp2` to be true, `exp1` must be true, and so must `exp2`. If you were designing a language interpreter and deciding how it should handle and, a naive approach would be to evaluate both sides and then see whether they both turned out to be true. But if `expr1` is false, is there any need to evaluate `expr2`? Of course not; we know that the whole expression has to be false regardless of `expr2`, so we might as well save time and ignore it. Only if `expr1` were true would it be necessary to proceed to look at `expr2`. (We go from left to right, but we could have looked at `expr2` first.)

Ruby uses this kind of "short-circuit" (or "lazy") evaluation, which means that the interpreter bails out early when it is sure of an answer. Only the left side of an `and` expression is evaluated if it turns out to be false, and, as you might expect, evaluation of an `or` expression halts if the left side is found to be true.

The effect of short-circuiting Boolean logic goes beyond mere efficiency gains. It also gives us more fine-grained control of logic.

For example, it allows us to phrase conditions in "ultimatum" form when it feels more natural to do so. Suppose we have a script that should not be allowed to run except between 9 in the morning and noon. The first line of the script might say "exit if the time is wrong":

```
exit if not (Time.now.hour).between?(9,11)
```

(Note that this is 11 and not 12. If you want to nitpick about whether the exact instant of 12:00:00.000 noon is a permissible time to start the script, you go on ahead. But just changing this 11 to a 12 would let the script start at 12:45 p.m., which we certainly don't want.)

But a more evocative alternate phrasing is "the time has to be right, or I'm leaving!":

```
(Time.now.hour).between?(9,11) or exit
```

7

You might expect and and or always to return `true` or `false`, but in fact they return the value of whichever subexpression they evaluated last, as the following statements illustrate. The effect of this value on a decision the script might need to make later (using `if`, `while`, and so forth) is the same as if it were an actual Boolean value.

```
nil and 6 #-> nil      (alternatively, nil && 6)
nil  or 8 #-> 8        (alternatively, nil || 8)

if nil then "yes" else "no" end    #->  "no"
if  8  then "yes" else "no" end    #->  "yes"
```

Putting this observation to good use, we can concisely provide for default values in situations where a variable might be undefined, as the following example shows.

```
@closing_balance = @opening_balance || 0.0

# Same effect as:
#   if defined?(@opening_balance)
#     @closing_balance = @opening_balance
#   else
#     @closing_balance = 0.0
#   end
```

Strings and String Literals

The two most common ways of specifying a string are in single and double quotes, and we've been doing both ever since Day 1. Often it doesn't matter which kind of quotes you choose:

```
"Parks and Recreation" == 'Parks and Recreation'  #->  true
```

The difference arises when you want to put something unusual in the string, such as a special character or an expression that should be evaluated. We have seen that \n produces a single newline character when enclosed in double quotes. When inside single quotes, though, it produces a backslash character and an n, as if the escape sequence had no particular meaning at all:

```
cooked = "a\nb\nc\n"
raw    = 'a\nb\nc\n'
cooked.length          #->  6
raw.length             #->  9

puts cooked
  # output:
      a
      b
      c

puts raw
  # output:
      a\nb\nc\n
```

Likewise, enclosing an expression in #{...} within a double-quoted literal causes the expression to be evaluated as part of the string, but in single quotes the evaluation doesn't happen:

```
"2 plus 2 is #{2+2}"    #-> "2 plus 2 is 4"
'2 plus 2 is #{2+2}'    #-> "2 plus 2 is #{2+2}"
```

There will be times when you'll want one behavior and times when you'll want the other. Even in the absence of backslash-escaped characters and expressions, single quotes often are used to enclose a string literal that contains double quotes as part of its content, and vice versa:

```
"It's impossible to express this in single quotes."
'"Explain yourself," she said.'
```

What can we do if we want a string literal to contain both single- and double-quote characters? One solution is to enclose it in double quotes; the single quotes inside are no problem, and the doubles can be escaped with backslashes:

```
"\"I can't explain,\" he replied. \"You wouldn't believe me.\""
```

In fact, Ruby allows you to delimit string literals with a variety of characters. You can use pairs of parentheses or square, curly, or angle brackets, as long as you put a percent sign (%) in front and as long as those delimiter characters do not appear, unescaped, inside the string. When this is done, the string is processed for expressions and special characters, as if double quotes had been used; the difference is that double quotes can be part of the string, because the interpreter does not expect them to signal the end. The following example contains both literal double quotes and the "alarm" escape sequence \a (which, depending on your operating system and terminal setup, may produce an audible beep):

```
puts %(Don't be alarmed, but "the bell" tolls\a for thee.)

# Output: Don't be alarmed, but "the bell" tolls for thee.
```

The letter Q, for *quote*, may be placed before the opening bracket. If it is a lowercase q, then the string is not processed for expressions and escape sequences.

Other characters can enclose a string literal too. The vertical bar (|) is often a good choice. The following are all legal string literals:

```
%Q<'Go #{"weST".capitalize}'>  #-> "'Go West'"
%q_a#{3**4}eiou_               #-> "a#{3**4}eiou"
%|][}{{>)|                     #-> "][}{{>)"

%Q_%__                         #-> "%"
```

Finally, Ruby supports *here documents*. They are especially nice for constructing long string literals that contain messages to be displayed for the user. At the beginning of a here document, the operator << introduces a delimiter that can be a string of any length.

7

It's usually pretty easy to come up with a string that you know you won't use inside a literal. Everything encountered up to the next appearance of that string, including line feeds, becomes part of the literal. Expressions and escape sequences *are* processed in here documents. The result of evaluating a here document is a string that can be output immediately, as in the first of the following examples, or assigned to a string, as in the second:

```
puts <<END-OF-LIMERICK
  I don't mean to sound like a spammer,
  But Ruby has such a neat grammar --
  When a task I assail
  Starts to look like a nail
   Then my code starts to look like a hammer!

      -- Hal Fulton
END-OF-LIMERICK

x = <<stopHere
   Oh Wah
   Tay Goo
   Siam

stopHere
            #-> "  Oh Wah\n   Tay Goo\n   Siam\n"
```

Two limitations to the power of the here document are that the delimiter string should not contain spaces and that it should appear in the first column when the literal ends. If you want to be able to place it elsewhere, put a dash after the <<. Then, when you use the delimiter to end the literal, it may be indented, but it still must be the only thing on the line. In the following example, the delimiter is set to STOP with the minus qualifier. The first occurrence of STOP does not qualify as a delimiter, because it is preceded by text. The second STOP is preceded only by spaces, so it delimits the here document:

```
<<-STOP
 one
   two
  This STOP fails
    STOP
         #->"one\n  two\n This STOP fails \n"
```

Here documents can be stacked end-to-end:

```
strings = [<<here1, <<here2, <<here3]
One element ...
here1
Another element ...
here2
Yet another element ...
here3

strings[1]  #-> "Another element ..."
```

Block Scope for Local Variables

Variable assignment inside a block can have a surprising effect if you're not careful. The following code ought to find a nutrient in a list, such that the amount supplied (as indicated by the hash value) is at least 100%, but it doesn't work very well:

```
label = {'Folicin'=>106, 'Vitamin A'=>146, 'Thiamine'=>94}
label.each do |nutrient, percent|
  last_full_rda = nutrient if percent >= 100
end

puts last_full_rda  # error: "undefined local variable"
```

Since `last_full_rda` first appears within the `do...end` block associated with each, its scope is limited to that block. (Not all code enclosures have this property. We'll earn a more intimate understanding of blocks on Day 14.) Making an assignment to `last_full_rda` above the block extends the variable's scope, and fixes the error:

```
label = {'Folicin'=>106, 'Vitamin A'=>146, 'Thiamine'=>94}
last_full_rda = nil
label.each do |nutrient, percent|
  last_full_rda = nutrient if percent >= 100
end

puts last_full_rda  # output: Vitamin A
```

Shortcuts and Tricks

There are three Ruby conveniences—variable modification, chained assignment, and multiple assignment—that you could live without if you really had to, but might make your life easier, and will certainly help you make your scripts smaller by adding descriptive power to little packages. Let's take a quick look at them.

Variable Modification

Almost every script will have at least a few occasions where a variable gets a new value based on its previous value. Something needs to be incremented, decremented, doubled, halved, and so forth. The conventional way to do this is to create a new value and assign it across an equals sign back to the same variable name, as follows:

```
@count = @count + 1
remain = remain - 1
limit = limit * 2
price = price * (1.0+tax)
mask = mask >> 1
flags = flags | 0x80
```

7

Ruby likes to help you get rid of unnecessary repetition in your code wherever possible. The convention that is helpful in this case is borrowed from C: You can rewrite variable variable *operator* expression as variable *operator=* expression. With that in mind, here's how the preceding lines could be written:

```
@count += 1
remain -= 1
limit *= 2
price *= (1.0+tax)    # or, price += (price*tax)
mask >>= 1
flags |= 0x80
```

Note

> If you examine the methods of an integer, you won't find += in the list. These are not really extra methods, but a syntax sugar. You'll appreciate that distinction when you are writing new classes, because when you have decided what the division operator / is going to mean, you don't have to write a new /= method; that would be redundant. Ruby gives its functionality to you for free.

Chained Assignment

When assigning the same value to several variables, it's not necessary to write separate statements for each:

```
a = b = c = d = 99

# same effect as:
#    a = 99
#    b = 99
#    c = 99
#    d = 99
```

This is not a syntax sugar, but a happy consequence of Ruby's order of operations. In contrast to most operations, which are evaluated left-to-right, assignment is evaluated right-to-left. Using parentheses to clarify the point:

```
a = (b = (c = (d = 99)))
```

The subexpression (d = 99) is the first thing evaluated. Its value, sensibly enough, is 99; the fact that d gets *assigned* that value is almost like a side effect. So what value gets assigned to c? 99, of course. And so on.

Multiple Assignment

Several values can be simultaneously assigned across an equals sign:

```
x,y,z = 3,4,5

# same effect as:
#    x = 3
#    y = 4
#    z = 5
```

This makes swapping the values of two variables trivially easy. In most other languages you have to create a temporary holding tank and cycle the values around a kind of triangle, as in the following C example:

```
/* C language example: swapping the values of foo and bar */
int temp;        /* assuming foo and bar are both integers! */
temp = foo;      /* we'll need this later */
foo =  bar;      /* bar's value has been assigned to foo */
bar = temp;      /* this is foo's old value */
```

But in Ruby you can simply say

```
foo,bar = bar,foo    # swap the values of foo and bar
```

How exactly is this happening? If you use irb to experiment with multiple assignment, you'll see that the value of the entire assignment expression is an array:

```
irb(main):001:0> foo=100
100
irb(main):002:0> bar="Ohio"
"Ohio"
irb(main):003:0> foo,bar = bar,foo
["Ohio", 100]
```

So it must be an array that gets carried across the equals sign. After the array makes it across, its values are handed out to the variables on the left, in the order they are given, and the array goes away; it was only a temporary container.

Our first example had the same number of objects on the left and right sides of the assignment. What happens in the event of a mismatch? Here's an example:

```
a,b,c,d = 1,2,3    #-> [1, 2, 3]
   # Results: a==1, b==2, c==3, d==nil
```

Note that the extra variable d doesn't just get left out of the party. If it had had some other value before, it gets overwritten with nil anyway.

It is also possible to have more values than variables:

```
a,b,c = 1,2,3,4,5    #-> [1, 2, 3, 4, 5]
   # Results: a==1, b==2, c==3
```

7

The mechanism of multiple assignment is sometimes used as a kind of shorthand when processing command-line arguments. Suppose we're writing a script that encrypts a file using some kind of key, and, rather than using the traditional filter mechanism (STDIN and STDOUT for input and output), we want the user to supply the input filename, output filename, and key, in that order, on the command line. Then near the top of the script we might say this:

```
in_name, out_name, key = ARGV

# same effect as:
#    in_name  = ARGV[0]
#    out_name = ARGV[1]
#    key      = ARGV[2]
```

This works because ARGV comes to us as an array. If extra arguments are given on the command line, then the size of ARGV is greater than three, and the extras are ignored. If not enough arguments are given, key gets assigned nil; we can test for this and bail out with an appropriate error message if we want to.

We're almost done talking about multiple assignment, but there are a couple of fine points yet to consider. First, we've learned what happens when there are too many values and not enough variables to assign them to: The extras are discarded. Since this may or may not be the desired behavior (as we'll see on Day 15), the last variable in the list can be marked, using an asterisk, as eligible to collect *all remaining values*.

```
a,b,*c = 1,2,3,4,5    #-> [1, 2, 3, 4, 5]
  # result:  a==1, b==2, c==[3, 4, 5]
```

Finally, the following three lines reveal a possible ambiguity to beware of when using multiple assignment:

```
a,b,c = 1,2,3   # result: a==1, b==2, c==3
a,b   = 1,2,3   # result: a==1, b==2
a     = 1,2,3   # result: a==[1, 2, 3]
```

Is the last result surprising? Remember, variables can refer to anything, not just numbers. There is nothing in a = 1,2,3 to tell Ruby that a is to be considered as part of a list of variables, so the obvious conclusion is that we want it to refer to whatever object comes across the equals sign, and here that object happens to be an array. If we want a to receive only one value and not an array, we put a comma after it to indicate that it is to be considered a *list of one variable*. For consistency, a list of any length can be given a trailing comma:

```
a,b,c, = 1,2,3   # result: a==1, b==2, c==3
a,b,   = 1,2,3   # result: a==1, b==2
a,     = 1,2,3   # result: a==1
```

Functional and Imperative Styles

On a few occasions we've used method names that end with an exclamation point. These are *destructive* methods, so called because when one is invoked on an object, the previous state of the object is gone forever. The nondestructive methods we've been using most of the time are sometimes called *functional methods*. To use one or the other sort of method consistently tends to categorize you into a programming style.

Someone who writes in the *imperative* style likes to use destructive methods, operating on objects "in place" as follows:

```
str = "A string\n"
str.gsub!(/[m-z]/,"-")
str.chomp!
str.swapcase!
str               #-> "a --I-G"
```

The *functional* programming style avoids destructive methods. Objects are not transformed directly. Instead, they are implicitly copied, the copy undergoes transformation, and the original is unaffected. A functional revision of the previous example, written out at pedantic length, might look like this:

```
str = "A string\n"
intermediate1 = str.gsub(/[m-z]/,"-")
intermediate2 = intermediate1.chomp
str = intermediate2.swapcase    #-> "a --I-G"
```

Garbage Collection

Nondestructive methods can be chained together. We often do this if we know we won't need to look at the intermediate states later. The entire previous example can be written in this one line:

```
str = "A string\n".gsub(/[m-z]/,'-').chomp.swapcase
```

Neglecting to assign variable names to intermediate objects doesn't actually prevent them from being created. Ruby still goes through the motions; one object is created as a result of the gsub call and another as a result of the chomp call. But their anonymity makes them expendable. They sit there taking up space until the Ruby interpreter gets around to noticing that they don't have names, and so destroys them.

This "garbage collection" process is a central contributor to the convenience of Ruby. It is what keeps you from having to worry about memory allocation. Things exist as long as there might be a use for them, and possibly a bit longer, because Ruby's garbage collection technique tends toward caution.

7

But functional programming, and the extra object creations and disposals that go along with it, can sometimes hurt performance. If you find a program takes up too much memory and runs too slowly, it may be because of an excessive population of objects being invisibly maintained by the interpreter. A good remedy for this is sometimes to rewrite performance-critical portions of your script in an imperative style, using destructive method calls. (A partial, and often less satisfactory, remedy is to tell the interpreter, at strategic moments, to hurry up and take out the trash. The `GC.start` method accomplishes this.)

Gotchas

There are some pitfalls to watch for when using imperative techniques to boost performance.

By convention, a destructive method returns `nil` whenever a call has no effect, making it suitable for plugging into conditional tests (`if`, `while`, and so on). Trying to use the return value in any other way can be a serious mistake, as shown here:

```
s = " xyz "    #-> " xyz "
s = s.strip!   #-> "xyz" (this looks okay ...)
s = s.strip!   #-> nil   (but is dangerous ...)
s              #-> nil   (because you didn't expect this.)
```

The second `strip!` call had no effect on the string, so its return value was `nil`, and the variable s ended up with an unexpected value. The cure is a simple one. Because a destructive method works on an object in place, there's no *reason* to assign a value anywhere. Just do the deed and don't bother with the equals sign. Here's the same example with the offending assignments removed:

```
s = " xyz"     #-> " xyz "
s.strip!
s.strip!
s              #-> "xyz"
```

Once we stop abusing the return values of destructive methods, we see that the redundant `strip!` is no longer harmful.

Never chain destructive methods. They will not work reliably, and worse still, they will seem to do the right thing just often enough to get you good and confused. Consider this example:

```
def silly!(string)
  string.upcase!.chop!.reverse!    # Wrong! Bad! Danger!
end

lang = "ruby"
silly!(lang)    # lang == "BUR"

brand = "GTE"
silly!(brand)   # undefined method 'chop!' for nil
```

Do you see where the error comes from? Because `"GTE"` is already in uppercase, the initial `upcase!` call has no effect and returns `nil`. The `chop!` call, then, has nothing to apply itself to. What we should do instead is call the methods separately, specifying the receiving object each time, like this:

```
def silly_but_safe!(string)
  string.upcase!
  string.chop!
  string.reverse!
end

lang = "Ruby"
silly_but_safe!(lang)        # lang == "BUR"

brand = "GTE"
silly_but_safe!(brand)       # brand == "TG"
```

Also, you should be aware that certain destructive methods are named without an exclamation point. Ruby is not absolutely consistent in this convention, because it was judged important, in possibly an aesthetic more than strictly logical sense, to keep as much extra punctuation out of the language as possible. So for example, `Array#delete_at` is destructive, but its name makes that fairly obvious; it does not currently have a nondestructive equivalent (if there were one, it should probably be named something like `#without_element_at`).

Summary

This was something like a catchup day. Until now we've been exploring wider concepts while overlooking some of the everyday, mundane details that make Ruby tick. After today, though, you're ready to get into some really powerful and fun stuff.

Tomorrow we'll take a step into power programming when we learn about *regular expressions*, a concise language-within-a-language designed just for text processing.

Exercises

1. Since a *googol* is 10^{100}, two ways of expressing it in Ruby are `10**100` and `1e+100`. So why do they not seem to be equal when compared?

    ```
    10**100 == 1e+100   #-> false
    ```

7

2. Somebody has given you a report that contains the information you want, but not all of it is in a form you can read. It is a text file containing lines like these:

    ```
    Jones        Martha      163   01/08/93
    McHugh       Albert      185   09/04/99
    Richards     Kendra      112   11/20/96
    ...
    ```

    Each line corresponds to an employee in your company. The fields are defined by column: Last name in columns 1–12, first name in columns 14–26, "auxiliary" information in columns 28–30, and date of hire in columns 34–41.

    It is the "auxiliary" information that interests you. A long time ago, some demented and forgotten database programmer decided to store several things in there, including the type of health insurance in bits 1 through 3 counting from the right (where bit 0 is the least significant, or rightmost). If bits 1, 2, 3 are all zeroes, the employee opted out of health insurance altogether. But we can't tell by looking which bits are which, because the field is given in base 10 instead of binary.

    As a quick illustration of what's going on, we can use irb to look at the binary form of the numbers from the top two records in the file (Martha Jones and Albert McHugh).

    ```
    irb(main):001:0> sprintf("%8b",163)
    "10100011"
    irb(main):001:0> sprintf("%8b",177)
    "10110001"
    ```

    Count from the right and starting at 0, we see that the bits we care about are "001" for Ms. Jones and "000" for Mr. McHugh:

    ```
    10100011
    11000001
    ```

    So apparently Mr. McHugh is not in the health plan. Ms. Jones has whichever plan "001" refers to; perhaps it's the basic company HMO.

    What you want is a Ruby filter script to read this file and tell us the names of the employees who are not in your health plan. The output should contain no information other than the names. When you test it on the above sample file, you should see Mr. McHugh and Ms. Richards, but not Ms. Jones.

    Test your solution by redirecting its standard input from the text file containing the data, like this:

    ```
    C:\RUBY> ruby my_filter.rb < data_file.txt
    ```

Answers

1. `10` is an integer; raising it an integral power also gives us an integer. But a scientific notation literal always generates a float.

   ```
   (10**100).type  #-> Bignum
   (1e100).type    #-> Float
   ```

   But only in the `Bignum` is accuracy ensured through all 100 digits. Try subtracting either "googol" from the other, and you'll find they're way, way off.

   ```
   (1e+100) - (10**100)   #-> 1.593595576e+83
   ```

2. If you're reading this before having any success at writing the script, it's not too late. Here are some hints you ought to try before looking at a solution.

   First Hint: Look back to the discussion of text filters. Usually it's just a `while` loop that keeps doing `gets` until it runs out of input; inside the loop it looks at each line, makes some decision, and possibly prints something to `STDOUT`. And really, living the Ruby Way means that we would prefer to iterate over standard input rather than to write an explicit loop, so the whole thing might well be built within an `ARGF` iterator:

   ```
   ARGF.each do
     |line|
     # ...
   end
   ```

   Second Hint: You can use the `[start,length]` method to extract substrings by column number. Store each field you care about using a different local variable. Also note that column numbers in reports are usually numbered starting from one, so when you've read a line of a report into a string, something that's supposed to be in "columns 34–41" starts at string position 33 and has width $(41 + 1 - 33) = 9$.

   Third Hint: That auxiliary data field will be in string form. You'll want to bitwise-*and* it with a mask of some kind, but only after it is in integer form; there is no `&` method for strings. Use the `to_i` method of the `String` class to do the conversion.

   Okay, here's one solution. Try not to be too disappointed—the script is a lot shorter than the description of the problem!

   ```
   #!/usr/bin/env ruby
   ARGF.each do |record|
     puts record[0,25] if (record[25,3].to_i & 0b00001110) == 0
   end
   ```

7

The following solution does essentially the same thing, but it is a little more verbose for the sake of a human reader:

```ruby
#/usr/bin/env ruby

health_plan_mask = 0b00001110   # "bits 1-3"
ARGF.each do |record|

  # extract auxiliary info field as an integer.
  aux_info  = record[25, 3].to_i

  # do the rest only if the health plan bits are all zeroes.
  if aux_info & health_plan_mask == 0

    # extract first and last names as substrings.
    first_name = record[0,26]
    last_name = record[13,13]

    # print the employee name
    puts "#{last_name} #{first_name}"

  end  # end "if"
end    # end iterator block
```

If given assurance that the columns between fields will always contain whitespace, you might prefer to ignore column numbers and extract fields using `String#split`. This makes the script much simpler, and possibly also more robust (since it would survive slight changes in the report format):

```ruby
#
#/usr/bin/env ruby
ARGF.each do |record|
  last,first,aux = record.split # discard the last field
  puts "#{last} #{first}" if (aux.to_i & 0b00001110) == 0
end
```

On the other hand, this last solution would fail if the fields themselves happened to contain spaces. For instance, consider what would happen if somebody's first name had been entered as Jo Ann. So it might be best after all to be a little more detail-oriented in this case and trust only the column numbers.

WEEK 2

Power Scripting

8 Pattern Matching

9 Inheritance and Modules

10 Program File Layout, Program Design, and the General Case

11 Modules and Classes in Depth

12 An Introduction to Recursion

13 Mastering the Operating System

14 Arguments, Blocks, and Procs

DAY **8**

Pattern Matching

> Give me a vigorous hypothesis every time. Without one, there's nothing to do but drown in facts.
>
> —Norman Mailer, *Harlot's Ghost*

Some of the most common yet perplexing tasks in computing are in the realm of pattern matching, that is, finding information that satisfies a given description. For many pattern-matching tasks, the tool of choice is the *regular expression*, which we refer to casually as a *regex*.

What exactly is a pattern? On Day 3 we did some pattern matching on strings, using the `String#include?` method:

```
"Hospital".include?("pita")  #-> true
```

We already know how to find the most concrete and simple-minded kind of pattern, which is an exact substring. Maybe we'd like to know whether a string contains a date in the form *mm/dd/yy*, when we don't care what the date is. In that case, looking for a substring isn't good enough. We don't want to limit ourselves to some exact sequence of characters; instead, we are interested in a great many sequences that fit the description.

We know enough to be able to concoct a solution, but it might not be very pretty. Probably the best we can do for now is to step through the string one position at a time, testing for the existence of digits at offsets 0, 1, 3, 4, 6, and 7, and forward slashes at offsets 2 and 5.

```
def contains_date(s) # return true if and only if
                     # s contains a date in form mm/dd/yy
  for posn in (0..s.length-8)
    if s[posn].between?(?0,?9) and
      s[posn+1].between?(?0,?9) and
      s[posn+2] == ?/ and
      s[posn+3].between?(?0,?9) and
      s[posn+4].between?(?0,?9) and
      s[posn+5] == ?/ and
      s[posn+6].between?(?0,?9) and
      s[posn+7].between?(?0,?9)
          return true
  end
end

  # If we got here, then the pattern wasn't matched.
  return false
end
```

Eeeew. . . well, it works, but it's long and repetitive, and muddles in low-level details far too much for my taste. Come to think of it, this would fail to reject nonsensical dates like 33/33/33. Both complicated and incorrect—this can't be the Ruby Way, can it? So much for motivation, then! Let's look at regular expressions in their simplest forms, and come back to the problem of the date pattern in a few moments.

Simple Pattern Matching

There is a class for regular expressions (Regexp) and a "matching" operator (=~). To express a regex literal, we usually surround it with forward slashes. The simplest regular expressions are treated just like substrings.

```
re = /tuv/
re.type        #-> Regexp
re =~ "rstuvwx" #-> 2
re =~ "Tavern"  #-> nil
```

Note   The forward slashes are traditional. Just as with string literals, you can specify some other delimiter; start with %r to make it clear that you want a regular expression. %r[xyz] is the same as /xyz/.

"tuv" is a substring of "rstuvwx" and not "Tavern". Why do we get 2 and nil instead of true and false? Remember, anything other than nil or false is considered true, so we can use these to make yes/no decisions as if they were Boolean values. What =~ really tells us is the position of the match, just as String#index does. If there is more than one match, it tells the position of only the first one found, searching from left to right.

```
/and/ =~ "Lions and tigers and bears" #-> 6
```

Wildcards and Character Classes

The dot character (.) has a special meaning in regexes. It is a *wildcard*, matching any single character.

```
/w.nch/ =~ "w.nch"  #-> 0
/w.nch/ =~ "winch"  #-> 0
/w.nch/ =~ "wench"  #-> 0
```

That raises an interesting question: How would we write a regex that matched "w.nch" but not "winch"? The answer is not far off if you remember the idea of *escaping* in string literals. A character is escaped by putting a backslash in front of it. The backslash some-times imparts special meaning to what follows it, and at other times removes a special meaning; since the dot is special in a regular expression, when we escape it, it becomes just an ordinary dot character.

```
/w\.nch/ =~ "w.nch"  #-> 0
/w\.nch/ =~ "winch"  #-> nil
```

Also special are the forward and backward slash characters, so they too must be escaped if they are to be matched exactly. This unfortunately can make for some confusing-looking code.

```
/\\\// =~ 'vee \/ for victory' #-> 4
# above: \\ matches '\', \/ matches '/'.
# It might be better to change the delimiter so
# the forward slashes are no longer special: %r[\\/]
```

We can make something more selective than a dot wildcard by listing any characters we want matched within square brackets. This is called a *character class*. Be careful: This is not our usual usage of the word *class*—it's simply a specification of which particular characters we want our wildcard to encompass.

8

```
# position 1 must contain a lower-case vowel
/w[aeiou]nch/ =~ "wonch" #-> 0
/w[aeiou]nch/ =~ "wunch" #-> 0

# now we restrict it to just certain vowels
/w[ei]nch/  =~ "winch" #-> 0
/w[ei]nch/  =~ "wanch" #-> nil
```

Notice that this means square brackets are special too. To save time later, let's list all the special regex characters.

```
[ ] ( ) { } * + ? | ^ $ / \
```

To match any one of these as an ordinary character, you have to escape it with a backslash. Got it? Now let's forge on ahead, and by the time we're done with this chapter you'll have meanings attached to each character.

Suppose we want to match all uppercase characters, or almost all characters, excluding only a few. It would then be onerous to have to list all the acceptable characters in the square brackets.

Character Ranges

If several consecutive (by ASCII value) characters are to be included, they can be connected with a hyphen. So [a-z] will match any lowercase letter, [0-9] will match any digit, and [A-Za-z_] will match any letter or an underscore (so it could be used to test the legality of the first character of a local variable name in Ruby). Notice that this makes the hyphen character special, but only inside a character class, and only when surrounded by other characters.

```
/-/       =~ "-"  #-> 0
/[x-z]/   =~ "-"  #-> nil
/[x\-z]/  =~ "-"  #-> 0
/[x-z]/   =~ "abcd-vwx"  #-> 7  (match the x, as it's in the x-z range)
/[x-]/    =~ "abcd-vwx"  #-> 4  (match the hyphen literally)
```

Negation

If a caret ("hat") symbol (^) appears first in a character class list, it negates everything in the list. So [^a-zA-Z] matches any character *other than* a letter. But if the caret does not appear first in the list, it's just a caret, so [x^y] matches any of the three characters 'x', '^', or 'y'. To match an actual caret character, you can either escape it or make sure it isn't placed first in the list.

```
/[aeiou]/   =~ ".^.ruby.^."  #-> 4 (match the u)
/[^aeiou]/  =~ ".^.ruby.^."  #-> 0 (did you expect to match the r?)
/[aei^ou]/  =~ ".^.ruby.^."  #-> 1
```

Abbreviations

Some character classes are in common use and have been given shorter forms. Table 8.1 shows some of these shortcuts.

TABLE 8.1   Character Class Shortcuts

Shortcut	Equivalent	Meaning
\d	[0-9]	Digit
\D	[^0-9]	Nondigit
\s	[\t\n\r\f]	Whitespace (invisible)
\S	[^ \t\n\r\f]	Nonwhitespace (visible)
\w	[A-Za-z0-9_]	Word character
\W	[^A-Za-z0-9_]	Nonword character

From what we've learned so far, we already can say that our date field test could use the regular expression /\d\d\/\d\d\/\d\d/. Look closely: There are three pairs of digits, separated by two (escaped) forward slashes.

Here's a greatly condensed version of the contains_date function we were toying with at the beginning of the day.

```
def contains_date(s) # determines whether s contains a date
                     # in form mm/dd/yy
  /\d\d\/\d\d\/\d\d/ =~ s
end
```

Okay, you got me. This doesn't return true or false. It returns an index within the string, or nil. But that's better than a Boolean: It's more informative, and, as we've pointed out before, it can be used in decisions.

```
input = gets
if not contains_date(input)
  puts "Silly user! You were supposed to specify a date."
end
```

While we're on the topic, the earlier version of the function could have had the same return values; just change its false to nil and its true to posn.

One more thing: We still haven't tackled the problem of nonsense dates. We'll get there soon.

You might find the date regex more readable in one of these alternate forms:

```
%r[\d\d/\d\d/\d\d]
/[0-9][0-9]\/[0-9][0-9]\/[0-9][0-9]/
```

Neither one is all that much easier on the eyes, though. Regular expressions are a highly concise way to express patterns, but they are not as readable as the rest of the Ruby language. There is no magical way to make them clear other than to practice with them. Consider them a language within a language, and devote some time to writing them until you feel comfortable, starting with today's exercises. Look at both versions of our `contains_date` function if you're not sure whether it's worth the effort, because the truth is that one regular expression can replace a lot of conventional code. Even if it takes longer per line to read or write, it will take less time to debug and will save you time and work in the long run.

Note

> Regular expressions have been around in about this same form since long before Ruby was created. Perl and a handful of other languages have tightly integrated regular expressions. They are also often used directly from the Unix command line, via the `egrep` command as well as some of its variants.

Position Anchors

We'll leave character classes aside for a while, and look at the difference between matching characters and positions. There are times when we want to match a pattern only if it is at a certain place, relative to line or word boundaries.

Line boundaries are specified by the caret (^) and dollar sign ($) characters; these represent the start and end of a line, respectively. So `/^Fre/` matches `"Freedom's just another word"` but not `"Cooking with Freya"`. To make sure what you match is on a line by itself, use both, as in `/^INTRODUCTION:$/`.

Line boundary matching respects the divisions within a multiline string.

```
rhyme = "Mary Mary\nQuite contrary"
/ary/   =~ rhyme #-> 1
/ary$/  =~ rhyme #-> 6
/rary$/ =~ rhyme #-> 20
```

Ruby also recognizes the escape sequences `\A` and `\Z` to match a line start and a line end, respectively, but you will more commonly see ^ and $ used, because these have been standardized in other regular expression tools such as Perl, `grep`, and `awk`.

Regex matching does not normally bridge across line boundaries. Even though a newline (`\n`) is a single character, it doesn't get matched by a wildcard dot.

```
/ary.Q/ =~ rhyme #-> nil
```

The *word boundary* anchor \b matches the edge of a word; this usually means a spot wedged between a word character and a nonword character. The start of a line and the end of a line also qualify as word boundaries.

I can't think for a good use for it, but as you might expect by now, \B matches a nonboundary—that is, any spot between characters that doesn't qualify as a word boundary.

Drawing borders between all the characters of a string helps to show how these work.

```
/o\b/    =~ "dodo-grounds"  #-> 3
# what is matched: |d|o|d|o|-|g|r|o|u|n|d|s|
#                      ^^

/-\b/    =~ "dodo-grounds"  #-> 4
# what is matched: |d|o|d|o|-|g|r|o|u|n|d|s|
#                          ^^

/\bdodo\b/ =~ "dodo-grounds"  #-> 0
# what is matched:|d|o|d|o|-|g|r|o|u|n|d|s|
#                  ^^^^^^^^^

/o\Bd/   =~ "dodo-grounds"  #-> 1
# what is matched: |d|o|d|o|-|g|r|o|u|n|d|s|
#                     ^^^

/o\bd/   =~ "dodo-grounds"  #-> nil
# There is an 'o' followed by a 'd', but not
# with a word boundary between them.
```

Repetition

Often we find that some part of a string is unimportant, and what is before and after it is all that we really care about. Placing wildcard dots in that in-between part of a regular expression is fine, as long as we know ahead of time how far apart the relevant pieces are; but we can't always count on that. Suppose we want to locate lines of HTML that contain italic text, enclosed between the start-italics tag <i> and the end-italics tag </i>.

```
But you <i>must</i> pay the rent!
```

The regex /<i>....<\/i>/ would identify the above line as containing some italicized chunk four letters long. That's too specific to be useful; if that were the best we could do, we'd have to test each line against a whole lot of regular expressions before we could be confident: /<i>.<\/i>/, /<i>..<\/i>/, /<i>...<\/i>/, and so on. Fortunately, there are several ways to indicate *variable amounts of repetition* in a regular expression.

The most general way is to follow the repeated character specifier with {min,max}. For example, /<i>.{1,10}<\/i>/ will match a sequence of at least one and at most ten characters. There are two variations on this: {min} matches exactly min characters, and {min,} matches min or more characters. Since it's likely that we don't care about how long the words we find are, a workable regular expression for our example could be /<i>.{1,}<\/i>/. What it says is that we are looking for a pair of HTML italics tags, with *one or more characters* between them.

Can we use {min,max} in our regular expression for date fields? It won't save us any keystrokes, but we might like it better.

    /\d{2}\/\d{2}\/\d{2}/

It not only emphasizes the fact that the digits come in pairs but also makes it plain that we could accommodate another common format with a quick change:

    /\d{2}\/\d{2}\/\d{2,4}/

With a flick of the wrist, we've just recognized dates with two- and four-digit years. Although it looks like three-digit years will slip in too, we can fix that in just a little while when we get to *grouping and alternation*.

That's all fine and good, but as it turns out, the {min,max} syntax is seldom used in practice. Normally programmers are concerned with one of three different repetition tests: Something appears *zero or more times*, *one or more times*, or *zero or one times*. So three special characters are provided as abbreviations for these tests.

Character	Equivalent	Meaning
*	{0,}	Zero or more times
+	{1,}	One or more times
?	{0,1}	Zero or one times

Going back to the HTML example, we can condense /<i>.{1,}<\/i>/ to /<i>.+<\/i>/, and read it at a glance as a pair of italics tags, with something between them.

So what would be meant by /<i>.*<\/i>/? It's almost the same, except it allows for empty tag pairs to be matched as well.

    This <i></i> is legal HTML but might indicate a minor editing screwup.

Think of the question mark quantifier as being used for *optional elements,* because to say something appears "zero or one times" means that it just might be there, and it might not. Finding a (possibly) married woman's title can be done with a regex like /Mr?s\./, because it matches both "Ms." and "Mrs."; the "r" has been marked as optional. Similarly, British and American spelling variants can be encompassed by /valou?r/ and /colou?r/.

Greed

Until now we haven't been noticing precisely *what* gets matched when a regex does its job, just that something does, and that =~ tells us where the match started. It will soon be important to know a little more detail. For this Ruby has a special variable, $&, that records the exact contents of the most recent regex match.

```
# Find a letter 'x' and the 5 characters that follow it ...
/x.{5}/ =~ "The crux of the biscuit"   #-> 7
$&                                     #-> "x of t"
```

Two other useful special variables are $` and $', which hold whatever text came before and after the most recent match.

```
$` #-> "The cru"
$' #-> "he biscuit"
```

With this in mind, we can now look into the concept of *greedy matching.*

```
l = "A <i>line</i> of HTML with <i>two</i> italicized words."

/<i>.+<\/i>/ =~ l #-> 2
$&                #-> "<i>line</i> of HTML with <i>two</i>"
```

That wasn't quite what we were expecting; the match was supposed to be "<i>line</i>" by itself. What happened? To get a clue, let's limit the repetition length and try again.

```
/<i>.{1,10}<\/i>/ =~ l #-> 2$&
                       #-> "<i>line</i>"
```

That's a little better. The match we were looking for was legal, too, but the 10-character limit allowed the regex to distinguish between them. We know that when two matches are possible, the one we get will be the first one found, starting from the left; but sometimes more than one match can start from the same position, and in that case the one we get is *the longest possible* one. This is what is meant by regular expression matching being "greedy."

To find individually italicized words in HTML, we could be a little more specific and replace the wildcard dot with the character class [\w], resulting in the regex /<i>[\w]+<\/i>/. But that still might not really be what we mean. Confronted with a string like `"one <i>italicized phrase</i> and <i>another italicized phrase</i>"`, it would fail to match anything at all.

Happily, we can also request *antigreedy* (shortest possible) matching, by appending a question mark to a repetition specifier. So * becomes *?, {min,max} becomes {min,max}?, and so on. Here are a couple of examples:

```
cheers = "huzzah huzzah huzzah"
/z.*z/ =~ cheers;   $&  #-> "zzah huzzah huzz"
/z.*?z/ =~ cheers;  $&  #-> "zz"

# Antigreedily match HTML italic elements:
sentence = "<i>This is</i> the house <i>that Jack</i> built."
/<i>.+?<\/i>/ =~ sentence #-> 0
$&                        #-> "<i>This is</i>"
```

Note

> What we call *antigreedy* matching is commonly referred to as *nongreedy* matching. I prefer the term *antigreedy* to make it clear that I really want the shortest possible matches, and not something merely shorter than the longest possible matches.

Grouping

To apply repetitive matching to any part of a regular expression, all we need to do is enclose that part in parentheses.

```
/(zub)+/ =~ "zubzub"; $&  #-> "zubzub"
```

It might not be immediately clear that we are doing something new, but consider that until now we've only applied repetition to individual characters or character groups. Grouping in parentheses does not make a character class. Rather, whatever is inside the parentheses is interpreted as a separate regular expression.

```
/(zub)+/ =~ "zzuubb"; $&  #-> nil
/[zub]+/ =~ "zzuubb"; $&  #-> "zzuubb"
```

The regex `/zub/` can't find a match anywhere in `"zzuubb"`, but the character class `[zub]` matches every character in the string. Grouped regular expressions are both far more specific than character classes, and as we're about to see, far more powerful. Repetition is only one of several uses for them.

Grouping and Repetition

We're about to look at a text filter that rejects lines that contain long words. Given input like

```
pig ox hippo
lion emu seal
```

```
monkey rhino
kite hare
```

the filter would produce this output (as you can see, we're defining "long" words as those with five or more letters):

```
lion emu seal
kite hare
```

Here's the entire text filter script, which operates by finding lines made up of zero or more short words, and nothing else.

```
#!/usr/bin/env ruby

no_long_words = /^(\b\w{1,4}\b\W*)*$/
ARGF.each {|line| print line if no_long_words =~ line}
```

Short and sweet! Well, short, anyway. (There's a much simpler way of attacking this problem that involves looking at it from the other side, and we'll get to that better solution in a few moments.)

Note

> What's `ARGF`? We discussed it briefly on Day 6, but a fuller explanation is called for. `ARGF` is an array-like object commonly used in text filter scripts. When a script is given one or more filenames on the command line, ARGF gets the contents of those files, arranged by lines. When the command line is empty, ARGF gets whatever arrives in the standard input stream.
>
> If you run a filter script and it sits there doing nothing, the probable reason is that you neglected to provide input, and it is waiting for you to type something at the keyboard. To help you avoid that situation, here are examples of commands that process an input file through a filter script, saving the results in an output file:
>
> ```
> % ruby filter_script < input_filename > output_filename
> ```
> ```
> % ruby filter_script input_filename > output_filename
> ```
> ```
> % cat input_filename | ruby filter_script > output_filename
> ```
> The `cat` command is Unix-specific; in DOS/Windows, use `type` instead.
>
> In each case, omitting > *output_filename* causes the results to appear on the standard output device, which is usually the screen.

Until you've found a comfort zone working with regular expressions, no_long_words is anything but self-explanatory. Let's analyze the it from the middle outward. First look inside the parentheses:

```
\b\w{1,4}\b\W*
```

Recall that \w matches a "word character" and is equivalent to the character class [A-Za-z0-9_]. So \w{1,4} would match a word (not necessarily a real English word, but something that "looks like" one) containing between one and four characters. The surrounding boundary markers in \b\w{1,4}\b are necessary to make sure a longer word like "monkey" does not get matched; otherwise \w{1,4} would match the first four characters, "monk".

What about the \W* that comes next? Presumably the words that we find will have something between them, such as punctuation and one or more spaces. We don't care how much junk is in between the words, but we do want to be ready if it is there.

It seems we've accounted for the little regex within the parentheses: it matches one "short" word plus whatever comes after it up to the next word. We can slap /.../ or %r[...] delimiters around it and test it on its own, to get a feel for what's going on.

```
test_re1 = /\b\w{1,4}\b\W*/
test_re1 =~ "Purple, red, brown";   $& #-> "red, "
test_re1 =~ "Purple, red, & brown"; $& #-> "red, & "
test_re1 =~ "Purple, green, brown"; $& #-> nil
```

Progressing outward, let's put on the parentheses and the other asterisk. This should match a continuous phrase of short words. Since it is greedy, once it gets started, it will match as long a phrase as it can.

```
test_re2 = /(\b\w{1,4}\b\W*)*/

test_re2 =~ "one, two, three";          $&
test_re2 =~ "testing: one, two, three"; $&  #-> ""
```

That last result is rather surprising. Why did it match an empty string instead of "one, two," again? The answer is that an empty string actually was the first available match. Remember, an asterisk matches zero or more repetitions of something; and sure enough, there were zero short words before "testing". Since the empty match starts earlier than the substantial match, the greed rule doesn't apply.

This little technicality trips everybody up now and then. Sometimes you should use + instead of *; just ask yourself if *once or more* was really what you meant.

Finally, consider what happens when we anchor the ends of the match to the ends of a line.

```
no_long_words = /^(\b\w{1,4}\b\W*)*$/
```

Our finished regex will match *zero or more short words together, which must fill up the whole line!* "one, two, three" won't match because there is not a line end ($) immediately following "one, two, ". The ^ anchor sees to it that "Pocket full of rye" won't generate a match either; without the anchor, a legitimate match would be found starting at "full" and extending to the end of the line. And since the grouped portion of the regex has a star quantifier, we will approve of empty lines, just as if the whole thing were just /^$/. All in all, this seems to produce just the behavior we were looking for, which was to exclude the lines that contain long words. Test the script on a variety of inputs to satisfy yourself. You might try changing either asterisk to a plus sign and see what differences emerge.

What about that better solution, you ask? Instead of accepting lines made entirely of short words, consider rejecting lines containing at least one long word.

```ruby
#!/usr/bin/env ruby

has_a_long_word = /\w{5,}/
ARGF.each {|line| print line unless has_a_long_word =~ line}
```

Hmmm. Now it's almost embarrassing to have done it the hard way, isn't it? But think of it as a little session in the weight room. The hard way gave us some practice with the fairly advanced concept of nested repetition in a regular expression.

Now is as good a time as any to mention two other regular expression operators. !~ is the logical negation of the =~ operator, and it means *does not match*. Thus r !~ s is the same as not r =~ s, and we could have written the last line of the foregoing script as

```ruby
ARGF.each {|line| print line if has_a_long_word !~ line}
```

There's also a case-equality operator for regular expressions, ===. Recall from Day 4 that the === method is aliased to different methods for different classes (we have seen it mean == for integers and strings, but include? for ranges). Sensibly enough, it means =~ when applied to regular expressions.

```ruby
ego = 0
# ... get evaluation_text from somewhere ...
  ego += case evaluation_text
  when /superb|excellent|perfect/ then 2
  when /good|nice/       then 1
  when /disapp|poor/     then -1
  when /terrible|rotten|stinky/  then -2
  else 0
end
```

In the preceding code snippet, each when line compares evaluation_text to a different regex, each time using === (that is to say, =~). When the first match is found, that is the case whose code gets evaluated. In this example, if evaluation_text happens to contain "You did a perfectly stinky job", then /superb|excellent|perfect/ matches first, /terrible/rotten/stinky/ never gets tested, and ego gets an ill-deserved boost.

Grouping and Alternation

No, we're not talking about types of electrical current here. *Alternation* means allowing for alternative matches of sub-expressions within a single larger regular expression. The alternatives are separated by a vertical bar.

```
mm1 = /Mantle|Mouse/ =~ "The Mousetrap" #-> 4
```

Alternation works fine without grouping, but you can't do much beyond the above simple example until you introduce parentheses to distinguish alternative pieces from the rest. /M\w+y(Mantle|Mouse)/ will match "Mickey Mantle" or "Mighty Mouse" but not "Danger Mouse" or "Mantlepiece". Effectively, alternation amounts to bringing some Boolean program logic into a regular expression.

```
 if /M\w+y (Mantle|Mouse)/ =~ line
  # ...
end

# Equivalent code without alternation:
#
#  if /M\w+y Mantle/ =~ line || /M\w+y Mouse/ =~ line
#   #...
#  end
```

Alternation lets us improve the date-field regex example so that some obviously nonsensical dates don't get matched. Months must lie in the range 01–12; that logically breaks down into two small regexes for month matching, 0[1-9] for January through September and 1[0-2] for October through December. So a two-digit month can be matched by (0[1-9]|1[0-2]). Exercise 1 at the end of the day asks you to complete a fairly selective regex for date matching.

```
/(0[1-9]|1[0-2])\/  ... you fill in the rest ... /
```

Grouping and Memory

You already know that Ruby uses the special variable $& to store the part of a string that most recently matched a regular expression. It so happens that there are also numbered variables, $1, $2, $3 and so on, that are used to store partial matches. Which partial matches get remembered? That depends on where you put in parentheses.

```
/(\w+) the (\w+)/ =~ "I punch the clock"  #-> 2
$& #-> "punch the clock"
$1 #-> "punch"
$2 #-> "clock"
```

There needs to be a rule to decide how the partial matches are numbered, because you can nest parentheses.

```
# "any single character, followed by a 3-digit number
#   smaller than 400"

/.(((0-3])\d(\d))/ =~ "867-5309"  #-> 4

$& #-> "5309"
$1 #-> "309"
$2 #-> "3"
$3 #-> "9"
```

Notice that the structure of parentheses is (()()), and that it is the outer parentheses that supply a value to $1. It doesn't matter where the matches end, or even quite where they start: The order in which left parentheses appear in the regex solely determines the numbering of the partial matches.

The most common use of remembering partial matches is a technique called *backreferencing*, in which an early partial match is used to help decide whether some later part of a string should match. A small complication is that match variables such as $1 are not accessible inside a regular expression itself, so a regex like /(M\w+y) $1/ surely won't do what we want; in fact, the dollar sign will try to match against the end of a line. To get at a stored partial match while still inside a regex, we use the escape sequence \1; it holds the partial match that will eventually be assigned to $1. Likewise there is a \2 corresponding to $2, and so on.

```
# Test for a line that starts and ends with the same word.

/^(\b\w+\b).*\1$/ =~ "department of redundancy department"
  #-> 0

$& #-> "department of redundancy department"
$1 #-> "department"
```

Read that regex carefully. The word captured by (\b\w+\b) is recalled later by \1. Also, the dollar sign is unrelated to the variable $1; it does what dollar signs are supposed to do in regular expressions, which is to establish an anchor to the end of the line.

Switches

A regular expression can be followed by one or more *switches*, which are single-letter flags that modify how the regex is interpreted. There are several switches available, but only three that we'll concern ourselves with here. They can be used individually or in combination.

Case Insensitivity: /i

Just as any good text editor supports case-insensitive searching, Ruby supports case-insensitive pattern matching.

```
/APEX/  =~ "apex" #-> nil
/APEX/i =~ "apex" #-> 0

/^(\b\w+\b).*\1$/  =~ "Time after time" #-> nil
/^(\b\w+\b).*\1$/i =~ "Time after time" #-> 0
```

Extended Legibility: /x

It isn't often used, but the /x switch lets you embed comments and spacing in a regular expression. You might find /\b\w{1,4}\b\W*/ more readable in this form:

```
short = /  \b\w{1,4}\b  # a word of 4 or less chars
    \W*    # and then any number of non-word chars
    /x
```

Then again, you might not. Since the /x flag causes comments and spaces to be ignored, you need to escape spaces and pound signs if you want to match them, and that can add some clutter.

Multiline Matching: /m

Regex matching is traditionally line-oriented, but the /m switch treats an entire string as one line, even if it contains newline characters.

```
two_lines = "FIRST\nSECOND"

# Normally, a newline is special and won't be crossed in a match.
/.*/  =~ two_lines; $&  #-> "FIRST"

# A multiline regex treats the newline like any other character.
/.*/m =~ two_lines; $&  #-> "FIRST\nSECOND"
```

Some Container Methods That Use Regexes

We've only looked at the =~ and !~ methods as applied to a regex receiver with a string argument. For convenience, the order can be reversed; the receiver can be a string and the argument a regex, and the results are the same.

```
"Nobody knows the trouble I've seen" =~ /\bt/  #-> 13
```

You can even have strings for both receiver and argument, but in that case Ruby will convert the argument to a regex before testing.

Back on Day 3 you got a glimpse of the `Array#grep` method. The example given there showed only simple substring matching, but now that you know more about regular expressions, you can probably think of more interesting things to do with `grep`. How about finding the methods that can be applied to an `Integer` but whose names are only symbolic, that is, they contain only non-alphanumeric characters?

```
999.methods.grep(/^\W*$/) #->
   [ "[]=", "<<", "<=>", "==", "===", "%", "*", "+",
   "=~", "~", "[]", "<=", "<", ">", ">=" ]
```

sub (substitute) and gsub (globally substitute) are `String` methods that take two arguments: a regex and another string. Whatever matches the regex gets replaced by the string. The difference between the methods is that sub only substitutes for the first match found, but gsub keeps matching and replacing right to the end.

```
"Agriculture".sub(/[aeiou]/i, "--")  #-> "--griculture"
"Agriculture".gsub(/[aeiou]/i, "--")  #-> "--gr--c--lt--r--"
```

Backreferencing is allowed, but again, using \1, \2, . . . —not the $1, $2, . . . —variables.

```
# Reverse each pair of adjacent lowercase letters.
"ab cd ef".gsub(/([a-z])([a-z])/, '\2\1') #-> "ba dc fd"

# Bill Cosby's dentist gag.
"I hope you're satisfied.".gsub(/([aeiou])/, 'ubb\1')
   #-> "I hubbopubbe yubboubbu'rubbe subbatubbisfubbiubbed."
```

You'll notice that the substitution strings are single quoted. If we use double quotes, `"\1"` is interpreted as the one-character string with the given ASCII value (octal 001). Unfortunately, this interpretation happens before the argument is ever seen by the gsub method, and Ruby is simply being consistent: strings are always evaluated the same way, regardless of what might be done with the results. To make sure gsub gets to see those backslashes, we have to either escape them as in `"\\2\\1"` or use single quotes as in `'\2\1'`.

sub and gsub can also be called in iterator form. You provide a regex as an argument, plus a block specifying what you want done with each match. Whatever the block evaluates to is what gets substituted. All kinds of weird transformations can be performed on the matched text.

```
"To be or not to be".gsub (/\w+/) do |word|
   (word*word.length).capitalize.succ
end
#-> "Totp Bebf Oros Notnotnou Totp Bebf"
```

```
# Another way to reverse pairs of adjacent lowercase chars.
"ab cd ef".gsub(/\w\w/) {|pair| pair.reverse}
   #-> "ba dc fe"
```

Since the argument passed back to the block is the original matched text, backreferencing by grouping is often unnecessary. If you do use backreferencing in a block, you need to stick with $1, $2, . . . variables instead of the \1, \2, . . . escape sequences.

```
"07? 0c? 11 3f?".gsub(/([0-9a-fA-F]+)\?/) {$1.hex.to_s}
   #-> "7 12 17 63"
```

Regexes and Matches as Objects

The work we've been doing today has not looked much like object-oriented code. That's a bow to convention and history. Almost all scripts using regular expressions have been written in this highly condensed and cryptic style, and if Ruby is to allow programmers to keep using the regular expression skills they've accumulated over the years, there isn't much that can be done to help with readability. But there is at least one situation when a more modern, OO layout might be advantageous.

There is only one of each of the variables $`, $&, $', $1, $2, and so forth. These hold information about the most recent regex match, so a new match wipes out the old values. Instead, the same information can be encapsulated in a MatchData object; then, if we just maintain separate variables to keep track of separate MatchData objects, old match information doesn't have to get lost.

```
re = /\$(\d*).\d\d/

wow       = re.match("Two large pizzas for $4.99! What a deal!")
fine_print = re.match("(No takeout orders; $12.50 for delivery.)")

# Reading the fine print doesn't make us forget what we saw before:

wow.string    #-> "Two large pizzas for $4.99! What a deal!"
wow[0]        #-> "$4.99"   (the match)
wow[1]        #-> "4"       (backreference $1)
wow.pre_match  #-> "Two large pizzas for "
wow.post_match #-> "! What a deal!"
```

When sending match data to output, the [0] can be left off. Printing a MatchData object produces the matched text.

```
puts "There is a #{fine_print} extra charge."

# output:
#  There is a $12.50 extra charge.
```

8

You are likely to find the explicit use of `MatchData` objects to be unnecessary; in most practical situations a regex match gets processed right away and there is no need to store any of its details for later.

Summary

Today we learned about regular expressions and how to use them to match both simple and highly abstract patterns in text. Their great selling point is their ability to fit extreme expressive power into a tiny space. This is also their biggest drawback. Regexes take time and attention, not only to create and debug, but also simply to read. The /x switch can be used to make a regex more intelligible to a reader, but its use is not commonplace.

Skill with regular expressions will help you not only with Ruby programming, but also with a variety of system administration tasks, particularly if you work on Unix systems. In addition, some text editors, such as emacs, let you conduct searches using regular expressions.

I have heard experienced programmers say, in half jest, "If a regular expression was hard to write, then it should be hard to read." But there's no need to be intentionally obscure. When you have worked hard to write a regular expression that does its intended job, it's a good idea to stop and write comments to explain what the regex does, and also maybe sketch out how it does it. Not only will some future programmer who has to maintain your code appreciate the effort, but you might find that you appreciate it too when you come back to the same script in the foggy future.

Tomorrow we start a three-day unit on the topic of program organization. You'll learn ways to take advantage of other people's work, and also how to keep your thinking clear when building large Ruby projects.

Exercises

1. Finish the refined date-finding regular expression we were working on earlier today:

    `/(0[1-9]|1[0-2]) ... /`

    It should accept something as a date only if the month value is between 1 and 12, the day is between 1 and 31, and the year is a two- or four-digit number. To make the problem simpler, don't worry about months that have 30, 29, or 28 days; April 31 can be allowed as a legal date, and so can February 30.

Test your regex, either by making a function out of it or by wrapping it in a small text filter script. Make sure it accepts these dates,

```
11/30/1944
01/01/95
06/16/1800
```

and rejects these:

```
4/19/85
8/00/7200
41/41/2041
```

2. Further refine your solution to the previous exercise so that the date separator character need not be /. Allow dashes and periods as well. However, the two separators in any date must match. Your solution should accept these:

```
10-04-1961
11.10.2001
```

but reject these:

```
08-14/1988
04.30-1996
```

3. Write a text filter that selects only lines of text that contain equal numbers of the characters *X* and *Y*. Can you come up with a regular expression to do the job? If not, what can you do?

Answers

1. Since we're not worrying about how many days are in each month, we can treat the month, day, and year parts of our regex separately.

```
/(0[1-9]|1[0-2])\/(0[1-9]|[1-2][0-9]|3[01])\/(\d{2}|\d{4})/
```

We're using alternation, `(\d{2}|\d{4})`, to say that either a 2- or 4-digit year is acceptable. We could have used `((\d{2})?\d{2})` there instead: "two optional digits followed by two mandatory digits."

2. Without backreferencing, this would be a very messy problem. We'd have to duplicate the previous solution three times:

```
/( ... complete solution using slashes ... )|
    ( ... with dashes ... )|( ... with periods ... )/
```

Backreferencing means we don't have to duplicate so much. We just have to provide a character class to match the first delimiter, then remember it when matching the second.

```
/(month)([-\/\.])(day)\2(year)/
```

Notice that we want to backreference to the delimiter between month and date, not the month; that's why we use \2 instead of \1.

Plugged into the previous solution, that's:

```
/(0[1-9]|1[0-2])([-\/\.])(0[1-9]|[1-2][0-9]|3[01])\2(\d{2}|\d{4})/
```

3. A regular expression is not necessarily the best tool for solving every problem! It turns out that for all their expressive power, there are both practical limitations on what can be done easily with regular expressions, and theoretical limitations on what can be done with them at all. The "equal numbers of X and Y" script can best be written with conventional Ruby code, using String#count.

```
#!/usr/local/bin/ruby

ARGF.each {|l| print l if l.count("X") == l.count("Y")}
```

You might easily have forgotten that the String class had a count method. If so, writing the lower-level code is not much of a problem in this case. See the example below. But if you're like me, you'll find it worthwhile to have an irb session running in a separate window whenever you're working on a script. Instead of thumbing through a book to find the methods applicable to strings, just click on your irb window, type something like "hello".methods and see what you get. You can use the grep method to narrow the results or to search for something in particular.

```
#!/usr/bin/env ruby

# Filter to find lines with equal numbers of the characters
# X and Y, written without benefit of the String#count method.

ARGF.each do |line|

    num_x = num_y = 0

    line.each_byte do |b|
        num_x += 1 if b==?X
        num_y += 1 if b==?Y
    end
    print line if num_x == num_y

end
```

DAY 9

Inheritance and Modules

"And entitled *A Song in the Time of Order*," came the professor's voice, droning far away. "Time of Order"—Good Lord! Everything crammed in the box and the Victorians sitting on the lid smiling serenely. . .

—F. Scott Fitzgerald, *This Side of Paradise*

The lessons for today and the two following days make up an informal cycle devoted to exploring the matter of program organization. When we do real work in the real world, our scripts can sometimes grow to the point where they are hard to manage and understand. Fortunately, Ruby supports and encourages modular thinking. We're about to learn some of the skills that will make us "scalable" programmers—no job is too big or too small!

Organizing Organization

"Program organization" is a broad, even ambiguous term—and deliberately so.

Program organization has to do with the process of designing your program: figuring out exactly what you want it to do, what classes you need to create, and how they will work together as the program is executed. At the same time, the phrase "program organization" sounds as though it might also pertain to a much more nuts-and-bolts, mundane set of activities—such as deciding what to name your program files, where to store them on your disk, and how to get Ruby to find them.

As it turns out, the cerebral activity of designing a program and the housekeeping activity of managing program files are closely intertwined. Generally, you should begin with the software planning, and let other decisions (such as naming files, or deciding how big to let them get before you split them) develop naturally from the structure of your program.

You can follow that principle only if you know enough about organizing your program files—and enough about how Ruby expects those files to be organized—to develop instincts and habits you can trust. Besides, it's not just a matter of making Ruby happy (though you need to follow certain Ruby-specific conventions, if you expect your program files to be found and executed). There are also benefits to be reaped from intelligent and thoughtful use of the tools and facilities Ruby offers in this area.

When it comes to program organization, in all of its shades of meaning, there's a lot you can do with Ruby. Then there's the art of deciding what you *should* do in any given programming situation. Understanding program organization involves looking at what Ruby considers to be the basic units of code and how those units interact and fit together. In turn, *units* might be classes, modules (*Modules*?! You'll see!), or files.

We'll be looking at all of these aspects of "program organization" over the next few days—separately enough to focus on each in its place, but close enough together to see the connections.

The Make-Up of Ruby Classes: Some "What" and a Little "How"

We're going to start our detailed exploration of program organization by looking closely at classes: what goes into them and what comes out of them.

The Basics

You already know that a class definition includes zero or more methods, variables, and constants. So an example like this

```
class apple
  @@transient = 100 #class variable
  PERMANENT = 200 #class constant
```

```
def say_something
  puts "Hello."
end

end
```

holds no mystery for you. And that's most (though admittedly not all) of what you need to know to write any class in Ruby. (The other part of what you need to know, and eventually will know, has to do with writing class definitions inside class definitions, and a few other things in that vein.)

With a good basic understanding of the individual components that can go into the make-up of a class, it's time for us to turn the corner and look at one of the most important class-related programming techniques of all. It's a technique that doesn't involve putting components into classes; rather, it involves establishing relationships and terms of inter-communication among classes.

Inheritance

So far, we've been piecing our classes together one method, constant, or variable at a time. That's perfectly fine for what we've been doing, but it's not the only way to introduce functionality into the definition of a class. It is also possible for one class to inherit characteristics from another.

Inheritance is more than a Ruby thing: it's an important facet of object-oriented programming in general. The basic idea is that rather than write every class from scratch—and rewrite a lot of the things that two or more classes may have in common—it makes sense to allow a new class to adopt its design and behavior from an existing class. Inheritance works a little differently in each object-oriented language, but the principle remains the same.

Inheritance happens at the time a class is created—not an instance of the class, but the class itself. In your code, you indicate inheritance with the character <. Here, for example, is a barebones illustration of inheritance syntax, building on our earlier definition of class A:

```
class B < A
end
```

Given such a relationship of inheritance, we say that class B is a *subclass* of class A. Correspondingly, class A is called the *superclass* of class B.

Inheritance brings about some quick and powerful results. To start with, class B springs into life already knowing about the class variables and constants defined in class A. You can test this by adding a telltale method to class B:

```
class B < A
  def show_perm
    puts "Constant PERMANENT is set to #{PERMANENT}."
  end
end

baker = B.new
baker.show_perm     #output: Constant PERMANENT is set to 100.
```

In addition—and very importantly—instances of class B will respond to the same methods as instances of class A:

```
apple = A.new
apple.say_something    #output: Hello

baker = B.new
baker.say_something    #output: Hello
```

Very magical, considering that we never actually typed a #say_something method into our definition of class B.

In fact, it's even more magical than it appears.

At first glance, it might look as though inheritance is just a trick for saving a few keystrokes: baker does what apple does, and all we had to type was < A. But inheritance is not a typing shortcut. The method #say_something in class B is not just a method with the same name and behavior as class A's #say_something method—it *is* class A's #say_something method.

Let's unpack that statement a bit.

When baker, an instance of class B, receives the message say_something, its first response is, "I don't know what to do with that message. I don't have a method called #say_something." But then it thinks a little more and says, "Wait a minute—let me ask my class's superclass!"

The class of baker is B, and B's superclass is A. Sure enough, it turns out that our little object baker can respond to #say_something, because its class's superclass offers a way to do so.

Let's extend the previous example to produce graphic proof that class B's #say_something is literally the same method as class A's #say_something. When we change class A's version, the changes pop up in, or through, class B:

```
class A
  def say_something
    puts "We're redefining this method!"
  end
end

# No surprise here.
apple.say_something     # output: "We're redefining this method!"

# But new objects of class B also inherit the redefined behavior ...
boyscout = B.new
boyscout.say_something  # output: "We're redefining this method!"

# ... as do old class B objects.
baker.say_something     # output: "We're redefining this method!"
```

The same thing applies to class variables: class B's variable @@transient, for example, is class A's variable @@transient. Changes to that variable in one class will affect the value in the other class, because you're really just assigning to, or retrieving the value of, exactly the same variable.

(Constants are a little different. A subclass can define a constant with the same name as a constant in its superclass, but with a different value, without altering the value of the superclass's constant.)

We'll make several passes through this material. For now, just keep in mind that inheritance is a way to streamline your program design, but it is *not* just a typing shortcut. Inheritance creates deep, powerful structures and relationships among classes.

Fiddling with Inheritance

Now let's crank it up a notch by looking at a somewhat more extended, though still small example. We'll start by doing it wrong.

Not really *wrong*—our example will run—but wrong in the sense that it could be done more easily and reliably with some redesign. That redesign, as you might guess, will take the form of establishing one or more relationships of inheritance among classes.

Let's say we wanted to write a set of Ruby classes to model the members of the violin family. We might reasonably start with the violin itself:

```
class Violin
  attr_accessor :strings

  def tuning
    %w{ g d a e }
  end

  def tune
    @strings = self.tuning
  end

  def untune
    @strings = false
  end

  def in_tune?
    @strings
  end
end
```

To represent the tuning of a violin's strings, we've used an array of, well, strings—called @strings, as it happens. The #tune method sets the instance variable @strings to the value of tuning. The #untune method sets @strings to false, to flag incorrect tuning. The method in_tune? tests the instrument for correct tuning, as reflected in the value of @strings.

Now, on to the next instrument:

```
class Viola
  attr_accessor :strings

  def tuning
    %w{ c g d a }
  end

  def tune
    @strings = self.tuning
  end

  def untune
    @strings = false
  end

  def in_tune?
    @strings
  end
end
```

If you scrutinize class `Viola`, you'll see that it differs from class `Violin` in only one respect (other than its name), namely the tuning. With that single exception, all we've done is retype class `Violin` with a new name. That's a sure sign of loose program design. It also means that we're in danger of doing too much work in the future—not only when creating new classes (`Cello` and `DoubleBass`), which will also involve retyping, but also in the event that we want to make a change that affects several instruments.

The process of tuning, for example, might be a candidate for change. We haven't taken a very sensible approach to it. The way things stand, the instance variable `@strings` can be changed to anything by anyone, and there's nothing to guarantee that it won't be changed to something meaningless (like, "Hi. I'm this instrument's strings."). Perhaps we do want to be able to change the tuning of the instrument—after all, Bach's *Fifth Suite for Cello* calls for the A string to be tuned down to a G. But perhaps we've made `@strings` a little *too* changeable.

Furthermore, there's an imbalance in the design. To tune the instrument to its standard tuning, we use #tune. But if we want to tune it to anything else, we have to set the value of `@strings` explicitly. Having two ways to tune the instrument, depending on what we're tuning it to, isn't very elegant.

We can fix these problems by taking away the capacity to modify `@strings` directly, and giving #tune an optional argument. If we call #tune without an argument, our instrument gets tuned to its standard tuning. If we supply an argument, the instrument gets tuned to the tuning we specify. We'll throw in a little bit of argument-checking, just to make sure that the argument to #tune is a valid tuning. (Well, almost sure. This is a rather skimpy argument check, but it will filter out the worst offenses.)

Here's our new `Violin`:

```
class Violin

  def initialize
    tune
  end

  def standard_tuning
    %w{ g d a e }
  end

  def tune(t = self.standard_tuning)
    if t.is_a?(Array) && t.size == 4
      @strings = t
    else
      puts "Sorry, '#{t}' is an invalid tuning"
      puts "Tuning has not been changed!"
    end
```

```
    end

    def tuned_to
      @strings
    end

    def in_tune?
      @strings
    end

    def untune
      @strings = false
    end
  end
```

Note
> The form `t = self.standard_tuning` in the parameter list of #tune means that t is an optional argument, and that if it isn't supplied in the call to #tune, it will take on a default value (namely, the value of `self.standard_tuning`). You'll see this technique closer up in a few days.

As things stand now, we have to go back and type this code into each of the classes we've written. This isn't convenient. Moreover, it isn't safe. The more you have to type (or even cut and paste), the more room there is for errors and inconsistencies to creep in.

Enter inheritance. (Did you guess?)

Let's start again and clear the remaining cobwebs from our program design. This time, we'll take the sensible approach by extracting as much common information and behavior as possible from all the instruments, and put it in a parent class:

```
  class ViolinFamilyMember

    def initialize
      tune
    end

    def standard_tuning
      false
    end

    def tune(t = self.standard_tuning)
      if t.is_a?(Array) && t.size == 4
        @strings = t
      else
        puts "Sorry, '#{t}' is an invalid tuning"
```

```
      puts "Tuning has not been changed!"
    end
  end

  def tuned_to
    @strings
  end

  def in_tune?
    @strings
  end

  def untune
    @strings = false
  end
end
```

9

Now writing the classes for the instruments is easy. For each instrument, we rewrite or *override* the method #standard_tuning (which, as you can see, is just a placeholder ViolinFamilyMember). Everything else can be inherited unchanged from the parent class.

Here's the new Violin:

```
class Violin < ViolinFamilyMember
  def standard_tuning
    %w{ g d a e }
  end
end
```

And we continue in the same way for the rest of the family.

Play It Again, Ruby:
Another Method Call Example

Just for good measure, let's walk through another method call in our violin family. What we're doing is getting a feel for how Ruby finds methods, or *resolves* method calls. It's worthwhile to gain some facility with this, since the strength of your program design will often depend on how you deploy inheritance.

Let's say we have created a Cello class:

```
class Cello < ViolinFamilyMember
  def standard_tuning
    %w{ c g d a }
  end
end
```

And now we create a `Cello` object

```
c = Cello.new
```

and we want to play the Bach *Fifth Suite* on it:

```
c.tune( %w{ c g d g } )
```

What this does, as you can verify by looking back at the example, is set the instance variable `@strings` to the appropriate letter values.

Let's go over that method call once more, this time thinking along with Ruby.

Ruby sees `c.tune`, which means, "Send the message `tune` to the object to which the variable `c` is a reference." That object, of course, is an instance of class `Cello`. Ruby now must find out whether instances of class `Cello` are in the habit of responding to the message `tune`.

Looking at the definition of class `Cello`, we see that there is no visible evidence of a method called `tune`. In other words, if all we had to go on were that class definition, we (and Ruby) would conclude that instances of class `Cello` do not respond to the message `tune`.

However, we (and Ruby, but let's stop saying that) have a thread that we can follow. The `Cello` class inherits from the `ViolinFamilyMember` class. So `ViolinFamilyMember` is the next stop along the way.

Sure enough, `ViolinFamilyMember` does define a way to handle the message `tune`—namely, an instance method called `tune`. By inheritance, `Cello` objects have access to that method.

"is a"

The inheritance relation in object-oriented programming is sometimes described as an *"is a"* relation: a violin "is a" stringed instrument, a square "is a" rectangle, and so forth. This provides a good test for whether one of your classes should inherit from another one. Can you say "X is a Y" (or, if it sounds better, "all Xs are Ys")? If so, then as you design your program you might want Y to inherit from X. If not—for instance, if you would not say "a cello is a violin"—then the parent-child relationship implied by inheritance probably doesn't apply.

Modules

Now that you've internalized the idea that the fundamental unit of a Ruby program is the class, you might be interested to learn that classes are merely one variety of something called a *module*.

That's the attention-grabbing way to put it. In fact, classes really are the fundamental unit of object-oriented design, and therefore of programming Ruby. But it is also true that classes are a type of module. Class `Class` is a subclass of class `Module`. That alone puts modules front and center in the Ruby language world.

Not all modules are classes, though. Modules have traits of their own that figure very prominently and powerfully in Ruby program design.

A module looks a lot like a class:

```
module MyFirstModule
  def say_something
    puts "Hello from inside a module."
  end
end
```

If we replaced `module` with `class` (and maybe changed the name to something with `Class` in it, just to be consistent), we would indeed have created a class. So how is a module different?

In fact, there are several differences between classes and modules—but if you want to see the most significant one, try to create an instance of a module:

```
m = MyFirstModule.new # Wrong!
```

Modules do not have instances. There is no such thing as a `MyFirstModule` object. That's the main difference between modules and classes.

Like a class, but incapable of spawning instances. . . . Sounds really useful, like a car without a steering wheel. Why bother writing a module if you can't have instances of it?

Modules, as the name suggests, are "pluggable" units of code—specifically, "pluggable" into classes. Or, to put it in more Rubily accurate terms, a Ruby class can, if it chooses, *mix in* one or more modules. This is accomplished using the keyword `include` with the name of the module as an argument.

Broadly speaking, when a class mixes in a module, the elements of that module—its methods, variables, and so on—become elements of the class that has mixed it in.

You can easily see this in action. Put the definition of `MyFirstModule` into a file, followed by these lines:

```
class SomeClass
   include MyFirstModule
end
```

When you do this, it means that instances of `SomeClass` will have access to the methods in `MyFirstModule`. In other words, instances of `SomeClass` will respond to messages corresponding to methods in `MyFirstModule`:

```
s = SomeClass.new
s.say_something   #output: Hello from inside a module.
```

As was the case with inheritance, the method to which the instance has access actually is the original method—meaning, in this case, `MyFirstModule`'s method #say_something. Any changes you make to the methods inside a module will therefore affect what happens when those methods are called by an instance of a class that mixes in that module. (The same holds for class variables defined in a module.)

Note

> Some object-oriented programming languages allow what is called "multiple inheritance", where a class can have two or more "parent" classes. Ruby does not allow multiple inheritance; each class in Ruby has either zero parents or one parent. But by using the module mechanism to organize your code, you can give your classes as much derived and shared functionality as you need to.

I'm My Own Grandpa

If you get curious and try to diagram what's a class and what's a module in Ruby, you'll find a bit of a paradox toward the top of the family tree. Let's say you start with the object `String`, which is an object of type `Class`. Now you want to know more about `Class`. You evaluate `Class.type`, and you find out that `Class` is also an object of type `Class`. Hmmmm. . . . What about superclasses? Well, the superclass of `String` is `Object`, and `Object` has no superclass. That makes sense. On the other hand, the superclass of `Class` is `Module`, while `Module`'s type is. . . `Class`. How can `Module` be the parent of `Class` if `Module` is an object of type `Class` in the first place? The answer lies in the Ruby core. When Ruby starts up, it knows enough internally about what constitutes a class that it can get itself started before class `Class` exists. Think of it this way: Even though class `Class` is what enables you, the programmer, to create new classes, it's really just a gateway to something that Ruby can already do internally.

Resolving Method Ambiguities

Following the method-finding trail through the path of inheritance and/or module inclusion seems like a more obscure way of understanding things than simply saying, "Cello has the method #tune because it got it from ViolinFamilyMember." But there are cases where the question of whether an object responds to a given message is trickier than this.

Let's say you write a class that mixes in two different modules (a perfectly legitimate thing to do). What happens if those two modules, by coincidence, define methods with the same name?

Consider this case:

```ruby
module Nice
  def salute
    puts "Nice to meet you."
  end
end

module Military
  def salute
    print "To show my respect, I'm hitting my forehead "
    puts "with the side of my index finger."
  end
end

class Person
  include Nice
  include Military
end

p = Person.new
```

What will happen if we call p.salute?

The answer is that we'll get the military salute. The reason is simply that Military was included after Nice, so Military's version of #salute overrides Nice's version.

There's nothing particularly obscure about this; it's quite logical that the most recent definition you've provided for a method is the one that Ruby turns to when you call that method. (The other definitions actually still exist, but you don't know about that yet because it's still Today, not a day or two from now. Understand?) The method call isn't even very ambiguous, from Ruby's point of view.

But if you don't realize what's going on—and if you don't know how to follow Ruby's footsteps to see which version of the method is being executed and why—you could end up having a lot of trouble debugging your program.

To put it less fatalistically: Since you do know that Ruby follows a trail, make sure that the names you use in your modules are distinctive to the point where the likelihood of their being duplicated in other modules (at least, others that have any chance of being mixed in along with yours) is minimal.

Summary

We've just been introduced to a couple of concepts that are central to object-oriented programming with Ruby. *Inheritance* is a standard OO technique that allows us to program incrementally. It lets us establish categorical relationships among classes, specifying only the differences, and so keeping our code from becoming too repetitious. But *mix-in* of modules is more specific to Ruby. It lets us easily bring various kinds of functionality into a class without complicating the inheritance structure.

Inheritance is the broader concept of the two, because it implies both what an object "is" and what it can do; mix-in is mostly just concerned with capability, not identity.

Tomorrow we'll start to work on the organizational and logical skills that tell us when to use subclasses and modules. At the mundane technical level, we'll also see how Ruby lets us separate those pieces into manageable files.

Exercises

See whether you can predict the result of running each of the following small programs (Exercises 1–5) before you run it. Try to come up with an answer for each one before you look at the next one. (And keep in mind that there's just a tad of deviousness behind at least some of these.)

1. Program 1:

```
module Friendly
  def interact
    print "What's your name? "
    name = gets.chomp
    puts "Hello, #{name}."
  end
end

interact
```

2. Program 2:

```
include Friendly
interact

module Friendly
  def interact
```

```
          print "What's your name? "
          name = gets.chomp
          puts "Hello, #{name}."
        end
      end
```

3. Program 3:

```
   module Friendly
     def interact
       print "What's your name? "
       name = gets.chomp
       puts "Hello, #{name}."
     end
   end

   include Friendly
   interact
```

4. Program 4:

```
   class Person
     def initialize
       @species = human
     end
   end

   class Friend < Person
     include Friendly
   end

   f = Friend.new
   f.interact

   module Friendly
     def interact
       print "What's your name? "
       name = gets.chomp
       puts "Hello, #{name}."
     end
   end
```

5. Program 5:

```
   module Friendly
     def interact
       print "What's your name? "
       name = gets.chomp
       puts "Hello, #{name}."
     end
   end

   class Person
```

```
        def initialize
          @species = "human"
        end
      end

      class Friend < Person
        include Friendly
      end

      f = Friend.new
      f.interact
```

6. Let's say you want to branch out beyond the violin family and play the guitar. What changes would you make to our violin example, in order to make writing a `Guitar` class as easy as possible?

   Hint: The guitar is not part of the violin family, but it is a stringed instrument. And so are violins, and cellos, and. . . .

Answers

1. Program 1 dies with an unrecoverable error. Here, we've called `#interact` after defining it inside a module—but we haven't *mixed in* (included) the module. So our "top-level" program doesn't actually know anything about a method called `#interact`.

2. Program 2 produces another unrecoverable error—and, admittedly, throws you a bit of a curve ball. This time, we've used `include` to mix in the module. The problem is, we've used it too soon: at the time of the mix-in, module `Friendly` doesn't exist. Ruby has to have already executed a module's definition before you can mix in that module. (We'll develop this theme tomorrow when we look at how Ruby retrieves code from separate program files stored on disk.)

3. Program 3: All is well.

4. Program 4 is another broken program, for the same basic reason as Program 2: we've jumped the gun by mixing in a module that hasn't yet been defined. (If you're rolling your eyes at the repetition and obviousness, at least you've learned something!)

5. Program 5: All systems are go.

6. In order to accommodate a guitar, we're going to have to think beyond just the violin family. We'll need something along the lines of a `StringedInstrument` class. And `ViolinFamilyMember` will inherit from that.

Actually, `StringedInstrument` can be almost identical to `ViolinFamilyMember`. The main thing that needs to be changed is the number of strings. We've been testing the tuning array to make sure it has only four strings. Guitars have six. A harp has. . . Well, let's not drive ourselves crazy.

We're going to have to modify the "four string" test, leaving the details up to child classes.

```ruby
class StringedInstrument

  def initialize
    tune
  end

  def standard_tuning
    false
  end

  def tune(t = self.standard_tuning)
    if t.is_a?(Array) && t.size == self.string_count
      @strings = t
    else
      puts "Sorry, '#{t}' is an invalid tuning"
      puts "Tuning has not been changed!"
    end
  end

  def tuned_to
    @strings
  end

  def in_tune?
    @strings
  end

  def untune
    @strings = false
  end
end
```

Next, we deal with the basics of the violin family. . .

```ruby
class ViolinFamilyMember < StringedInstrument
  def string_count
    4
  end
end
```

9

. . . and the specific instruments (illustrated by `Violin`):

```ruby
class Violin < ViolinFamilyMember
  def standard_tuning
    %w{ g d a e }
  end
end
```

And now, what we all came to see—the guitar:

```ruby
class Guitar < StringedInstrument
  def string_count
    6
  end

  def standard_tuning
    %w{ e g b d a e }
  end
end
```

WEEK 2

DAY 10

Program File Layout, Program Design, and the General Case

> And I reckon that by the time there ain't any boats left at all, the
> Commission will have the old thing all reorganized, and dredged out, and
> fenced in, and tidied up, to a degree that will make navigation just simply
> perfect, and absolutely safe and profitable; and all the days will be
> Sundays...
>
> —Mark Twain, *Life on the Mississippi* (1883)

Today we continue to explore the processes of program organization in Ruby.
We're going to split our time between some of the nuts and bolts of program
file management—in particular, the process of splitting your program up into
multiple files—and some more theoretical questions—specifically, the roles of
abstraction and generalization in the process of program design.

That means we'll be playing both sides of the theory/practice border today. In this case, the two are closely related. Once you get a feel for some of the design principles we'll be talking about today, you'll be in good shape for tomorrow's lesson.

Besides, you don't want to spend a *whole* day learning about storing programs in files, now do you?

Let's start there, though.

Program and File Interaction

As you saw yesterday, Ruby finds methods by following certain rules, expecting the program to be arranged in a certain way. Ruby also has some expectations when it tries to locate the source of its programming instructions.

What that slick segue means is that we're going to take up the topic of program file layout, storage, and retrieval. This constitutes part of "program organization" in the broad (some might say sprawling) sense that we've defined that term.

In most cases, Ruby receives programming instructions by reading in one or more disk files. (As you know from using irb, that isn't the only possibility, but that's our focus here.) You already know about the "one" in "one or more disk files" because each of our examples has been contained in one file. In this section we'll take a look at the "more" in "one or more"—that is, how to split your program into multiple files, and what Ruby needs to know from you in order to find those files at runtime.

All the techniques we've learned up to now, including mix-in of modules and creation of classes and subclasses, can be practiced easily if you put everything in one file. Indeed, for small projects, that is a reasonable way to work.

If you write programs of any significant length, however, you are likely to find that you want to split your program among two or more files. This tends to make things much easier when it comes to maintenance, distribution, and reuse of code.

Moreover, Ruby programs tend to depend heavily on separately packaged *extensions*, each adding a specific functionality to the language (CGI programming, the `Matrix` class, reading and conversion of date formats, and so on). The Ruby distribution itself includes many such extensions, and more are available on the Ruby Application Archive and elsewhere. If you want to take advantage of anything like the full power of the Ruby language, you need to know how to get these extensions to be recognized by your program so that you can use what they offer. So that's exactly what we are about to learn.

Note

The Ruby Application Archive (RAA) is a place established for Ruby authors to share contributions of many kinds, including applications, extensions, and documentation. At the time of this printing it can be found online at `http://www.ruby-lang.org/en/raa.html`.

Runtime Extension of Ruby's World: `require`

By far the most important tool for getting a program in one file to see what's in other program files is the `require` method.

At its simplest, `require` causes a running program to pull in, and evaluate, the code from a file on disk. You can try this out easily. You need to create two files. Call the first **req.rb**, and put these lines in it:

```
def speak
  puts "Hello."
end
```

The second file should be called **reqtest.rb**, and its contents should be this:

```
require 'req'    # leave off the .rb extension
speak
```

Now test `reqtest.rb`. It's the top-level script, but when the interpreter runs it, both files are consulted.

```
% ruby reqtest.rb
Hello
```

As you can see, the `require` line in `reqtest.rb` caused the code in `req.rb` to be read in and executed. (Ruby added the `.rb` file extension to the name for you.) The output, in this example, is the same as it would have been if you took out the `require` line and pasted in the definition of #speak.

When you `require` a Ruby code file, it's almost as if you'd typed the contents of that file into your program file right at the point where you typed `require`. (We'll elaborate on that "almost" at a couple of points later today and tomorrow.)

`require` belongs to a standard Ruby module called `Kernel`. All `Kernel` methods are available as top-level methods (that is to say, ordinary functions), without our asking for them explicitly. That's a very Good Thing in this case, because otherwise we'd have to `require` the `Kernel` module before we could use the `require` method, and we'd end up stuck in our tracks.

Most of the time, `require` statements occur near the beginning of program files, but they don't have to. You can `require` at any point in a program.

Let's look at a more complex and somewhat more realistic example. We conquered the realm of music yesterday, so for our next example we'll turn to one of life's other great pleasures: food. Along with illustrating the mechanics of `require`, this example sneaks in a bit of reflection on when and *why* you might want to split your code among multiple files.

Let's start with a simple class hierarchy. Our classes are modeled on dishes (using the term "dish" in the food sense, not the crockery sense). Dishes can inherit from other. So our class structure will look, at least along one branch, like this:

```
class Dish
end

class ChickenDish < Dish
end

class ChickenCacciatore < ChickenDish
end

class KungPoChicken < ChickenDish
end
```

Obviously we're using "stub" classes here; a fuller implementation would include various methods and variables.

We do not live by chicken alone, so let's create a similar class hierarchy for beef. We add the following classes to the ones we already had, and save the whole thing as food.rb:

```
class BeefDish < Dish
end

class BeefWellington < BeefDish
end

class SteakTartar < BeefDish
end
```

We now have two separate class hierarchies, based on the main ingredient. They have a common ancestor—class `Dish`—but below `Dish`, on the class family tree, the two hierarchies branch apart.

Now, let's switch gears. Let's say we wanted a way to differentiate *cooked* dishes from *raw* dishes, regardless of the main ingredient.

We could scrap the whole thing and start again with `RawDish` and `CookedDish` classes. However, we've already decided to base our object structure around the main ingredient, and that's probably a better way to do it, since it corresponds to how most people would categorize the dishes most of the time. But we still want a way to indicate whether each dish is cooked or raw.

This is a case for modules. Our modules will look something like this:

```
module Cooked
  attr_accessor :temperature
end

module Raw
  attr_accessor :bacteria_count
end
```

Add those modules to the *beginning* of food.rb.

Now we want to do the cooking (or not, in the case of raw dishes). This is a matter of *mixing* in the appropriate modules. (That's not a food metaphor; as we saw in yesterday's lesson, you really do "mix in" modules in Ruby. The modules that are mixed in are often referred to as *mixins*.) We achieve this by adding include directives to three of the classes we've defined:

```
class ChickenDish < Dish
  include Cooked
end

class BeefWellington < BeefDish
  include Cooked
end

class SteakTartar < BeefDish
  include Raw
end
```

Our program file now includes two modules and several classes in two branches of the Dish class family tree. Note that the way we've used our modules introduces a kind of asymmetry. In the chicken hierarchy, we stipulate *cooked* at the top: any class that represents a specific chicken dish (that is, any child class of class ChickenDish) has the characteristic of being cooked. In the case of beef, however, the cooked/raw distinction doesn't kick in until we get to the level of the individual dishes.

This asymmetry is perfectly acceptable. Our Cooked and Raw modules neatly "plug in" where needed, and only where needed. Mixins in Ruby do not have to follow the patterns of the class hierarchies into whose classes they are mixed.

So all is well in the kitchen.

The only snag is that everything is in one file. There's not all that much code, so it probably doesn't strike you as a big problem. But what if we create lots of classes, with lots of dishes? What if we decide, purely for reasons of file-naming neatness, to put all the chicken classes into a chicken.rb file and all the beef classes into a beef.rb file? Or maybe split them up into poultry.rb and redmeat.rb?

Easy, you say. Put all the *whatever*-related classes into `whatever.rb`. End of problem.

Not quite. What about the modules? If you put this class

```
class SteakTartar < BeefDish
  include Raw
end
```

into a file with a bunch of other classes, but without the `Raw` module, then what sense will that `include` statement make?

In order for Ruby to `include` a module, it has to be able to *see* that module. If the module is actually in the program file where the `include` happens, then Ruby can see it. Otherwise, if the module is in a different file, you have to `require` the file before you can `include` the module.

To achieve this arrangement in our example, follow these steps:

1. Put the code for the `Cooked` and `Raw` modules into a separate file, called `doneness.rb`.

2. Delete the code for the modules from the original file, `food.rb`.

3. Make sure that `food.rb` and `doneness.rb` are in the same directory.

4. Tell Ruby that, during program execution, you want the new module file to be read in. To do this, put the following line:

   ```
   require "doneness"
   ```

   at the top of `food.rb` (or on the line after the shebang line, if there is one).

Now, when `food.rb` is run, `doneness.rb` is read in when Ruby encounters the `require` statement. At that point, the modules defined in doneness.rb are visible to Ruby—so that when certain classes include those modules later, Ruby knows what to do.

The Argument to require

The argument to `require` is a filename—sort of. Actually it's the name of an *extension*, and Ruby extensions are kept in files. So it's a filename. Sort of…

When you say `require "mymodule"`, Ruby doesn't take `mymodule` as a straight filename. If it did, it wouldn't find it, since you have no file called `mymodule`—only one called `mymodule.rb`. But Ruby does find your file, because Ruby adds the extension `.rb` to the argument to `require`, if that extension isn't there already.

Ruby also respects path information that you include in the argument to `require`. If you provide an absolute path (such as `/home/mydir/rubystuff/mymodule`), Ruby treats it as an absolute path (still performing the trick of adding `.rb` on the filename at the end).

If you provide something other than an absolute path—namely, either a plain filename or a path to a file, such as `tests/mymodule`—Ruby treats it as a relative path. But relative to what? Not just your current directory. In fact, Ruby maintains a list of directories to search for required extensions. This list by default includes the main Ruby installation on your system. It also includes the program's current working directory, whatever that happens to be.

Ruby's extension directory list is stored in the global variable `$:` (as you can see if you evaluate `$:` in irb). When you require a file, Ruby goes through the list in `$:` and looks for it in each of the directories in that list.

If you look at `$:`, you see that `"."`, the program's current working directory, is last on the list. Because Ruby looks in all those other directories first, if you're requiring a file in the current directory, it's important that the file have a different name and path from any files earlier in Ruby's search path.

For example, suppose you create a file called `matrix.rb` and then put `require "matrix"` in your program in the same directory. Ruby looks for `matrix.rb` in all the other directories on the list first. There happens to be a `matrix.rb` distributed with Ruby itself, so Ruby loads that one instead of yours.

You can make this issue moot by putting the current directory first in the search path, as follows:

```
$:.unshift(".")
```

But it's still a good idea to try not to give your extension files the same names as ones that come with the Ruby distribution.

Note   Ruby raises a `LoadError` exception if you try to `require` a file it can't find.

Compiled Extensions

The purpose of `require` is to load Ruby extensions during program execution. But you may be surprised to learn that the extensions themselves may not all have been written in Ruby. Many are written in C, and `require` loads those extensions also.

C extensions are compiled to binary files of a type that, confusingly, are called *shared object files* (for reasons having nothing to do with Ruby or object-oriented programming). The names of these shared object files usually have the extension `.so` (for shared object) or `.dll` (for dynamic link library), depending on which platform you're using.

During the process of searching for the Ruby extension you have asked for with require, Ruby looks for binary files of these types, as well as Ruby source files. If you say require 'something', Ruby searches the various directories stored in its search path (the $: variable), trying on different filename extensions like a shopper trying on different hats.

This means that require is more than a shortcut for sticking Ruby code into a file at a given point. It's a tool for loading Ruby extensions at runtime, whether those extensions take the form of Ruby code files or (non-Ruby) shared object files.

---

require's Cousin load

The less frequently used *load* method is similar to require, but with some important differences. It loads only Ruby source files (not binary files); it doesn't automatically add the .rb extension to the filename; and when you load a file, the file will be loaded whether it was loaded previously or not. (This differs from require, which keeps track of the extensions it has loaded and loads each extension only once per program run.)

---

require and Variables

In a couple of respects, require is also less than a shortcut for sticking code into a file. Which is to say: require doesn't behave quite like a cut-and-paste mechanism. It almost does.

(Yes, you've heard that already. Here, as promised, we'll look more closely at part of that *almost*.)

When you require an extension, local variables defined in that extension are not visible. You can see this in the (lack of) action in the following test. First, create a file file1.rb:

```
require 'file2'
puts "Value of var is #{var}"
```

Second, create a file file2.rb:

```
var = "Hello.  I'm var."
```

If you run file1.rb, your program blows up. (That's the term favored by professional programmers, who are very rigorous in their use of technical language.) This is because file2.rb's local variable var does not become visible or available in the scope doing the requiring.

Class variables, however, do make the journey from the `required` file to the requiring scope. You can see this if you change `var` to `@@var` in the preceding example. (Also change the wording in the strings, just to keep things logical.) The same is true of constants; change `var` to `CON` and you'll see.

`require` Versus `include`

`require` and `include` often figure together in a kind of one-two punch: An extension gets `required`, and then one or more modules defined in that extension get mixed in or `included`.

The exact terms of this partnership can sometimes be a source of confusion. If you do not find yourself confused, you might want to skip over this, just so that no ideas get planted in your head. Otherwise, keep reading. (C programmers who are used to an `#include`—which actually is more like Ruby's `require` than Ruby's `include`—this includes you. It even requires you.)

Here's how `require` and `include` relate to each other:

- `require` means "Go look for an extension, somewhere among the disk files on the system, and evaluate it according to the known rules."

- `include`, on the other hand, has nothing to do with files. When you `include` a module—more precisely, when you mix in a module by using the `include` directive—you import (under certain constraints) that module's methods, variables, and constants into the namespace that's doing the including.

In order to `include` a module, the module has to be visible to Ruby. That means either it has to be in the current file (remember our all-in-one-file exercise?), or it has to be part of an extension that has been found and successfully added, using `require`.

You can `require` an extension and then not `include` any modules from it. You can `include` a module that's already visible to Ruby, without requiring an extension. The two directives often go together, and for good reason (wanting to `include` a module that resides in a file that you need to `require` is a common scenario). But they are not the same and are not always linked.

If it helps, you can think of it as, "I `require` that you find this file because I might want to `include` one or more of its modules."

Examining the Ruby Installation

Somewhere on your computer system, there's a Ruby installation. It contains the many files that Ruby needs to run. You can learn much from studying what's in this installation. For one thing, you can study Ruby's idea of program file organization close up.

In order to do this, you need to find the Ruby installation directory. (On a Unix or Linux system, this is typically `/usr/local/lib/ruby`.) You may have to hunt around a little. The actual files may be in a further subdirectory named for a Ruby version, such as `/usr/local/lib/ruby/1.6`. When you find a directory with upward of sixty files whose names end in `.rb`, along with subdirectories called `irb` and `net`, you're there.

Note   If you can't find your Ruby installation directory easily, look again at the contents of the `$:` global variable. It may give you more paths than you need, but it should include the starting-point directory you're looking for.

The base Ruby installation directory contains a core library of extension classes and modules, many of which, over time, you will quite likely use in your code. On this trip to the installation, however, we're not reviewing what these programs and extensions actually do (although you should feel free to explore that if you like). Rather, we're looking at them as examples of program file organization in Ruby.

irb is an old friend, so let's have a look at it. In your Ruby distribution's main directory, you'll see a file called `irb.rb`. This file itself gets required by the `irb` program. If you open `irb.rb` in your text editor, you will see the following (or something like it) near the top:

```
require "irb/init"
require "irb/context"
require "irb/extend-command"
require "irb/workspace"

require "irb/ruby-lex"
require "irb/input-method"
require "irb/locale"
```

When irb starts up, it loads all of these extensions. The code for the irb program is broken up, for convenience and clarity, across several separate files. As you can see from the syntax of the arguments to `require`, most of those files are located in an `irb` subdirectory, which can be found next to irb.rb in the Ruby installation.

Next, have a look at the file `cgi.rb`, which is the core of Ruby's CGI programming interface.

A few screens into the file (feel free to do a search, if that's too vague a description), you will find the line `require 'English'`. Let's follow the trail. `require 'English'` means that the program is expecting to find an extension called `English` somewhere in the Ruby runtime load path (the directories stored in the `$:` variable).

Since `cgi.rb` comes with the Ruby distribution, the only place it can be certain to find `English.rb` is in the distribution itself. So let's make a wild guess and look for a file called `English.rb` right alongside `cgi.rb` in the main Ruby installation directory.

Sure enough, there it is. `English.rb`, by the way, provides English-language aliases for some of Ruby's more cryptic variables. So if you `require` it, you'll be able to say `$CHILD_STATUS` instead of `$?`, `$LOAD_PATH` instead of `$:`, and things like that. Examine the `English.rb` file to see the full list of available aliases.

To see more of Ruby's extension search behavior up close, have a look at some of the subdirectories, especially `net`. If you want to use one of the extensions in `net`, you have to include the (relative) path—for example, `require 'net/telnet'`.

This brings us to the end of today's pass through program-file and extension management techniques. We'll turn now to more theoretical matters. As for `require`: Hold that thought.

10

 **Caution**   When you open Ruby installation files in your text editor, be careful not to change them. Such changes may have unexpected effects on the behavior of your scripts, or the extensions that your scripts depend on, and as a result you may find that you have to reinstall Ruby to get things back the way they were. So if your editor lets you open files "read-only," do it that way.

Abstraction and the General Case

In common speech, the adjectives "abstract" and "general" have connotations of vagueness, lack of substance, or unsuitability for real-life problems of one kind or another. ("His argument was rather abstract." "That's too general a solution to apply to my situation.")

In the realm of computer programming, however, abstraction and generalization have to do with some very nonvague habits of thought and program design.

"To abstract" comes from a Latin root meaning "to pull or draw [something] away." When you abstract from something, you pull or draw from it what you consider its essential, defining features. Abstract imagery works on this principle. A simple circle might represent a head, the sun, a coin, or the endless cycle of existence, because circularity is a property you can abstract, or "pull away," from each one of those things. It's an essential quality they share.

When you create classes in an object-oriented program, you engage in a process of abstracting: You abstract properties that are shared among several objects. You saw this several days ago with the `Kantian` class. Instead of writing the same methods over and over again for each object, we created the Kantian class to embody in an abstract manner the properties shared by all Kantians. That class could then serve as a type of factory for any number of Kantian individuals (or instances).

Yesterday's violin-family example illustrated this, too, bringing the technique of inheritance to bear on the process of abstraction of object properties. The parent class ViolinFamilyMember comprised everything we could abstract out of *all* the children. Only when we hit the wall of specific, irreducible differences between one child and the next (in the area of tuning) did we split the "family" tree.

Under- and Over-Abstraction

The ViolinFamilyMember class served to represent the most general case possible, in the context of the real-world objects we were trying to model.

That bit about the "context" is important. We stopped generalizing when we had what our situation seemed to call for. In yesterday's "guitar" exercise, we resumed the generalization process, abstracting back from members of the violin family to stringed instruments—again, because that was what the task required. And then we stopped.

In theory, we could have kept the process going even further: StringedInstrument could have had a parent class called MusicalInstrument, which could have had a parent class called Tool. . . And, indeed, part of the art of abstracting is to know when to go a little bit past your immediate needs for the sake of designing classes that might be general enough to fit into another program.

But the leap from stringed instruments to all musical instruments is a big leap conceptually, and one we didn't need. Since we weren't branching out into any nonstring types (like brass or percussion), generalizing to "musical instrument" wouldn't have added anything very rewarding to our structure. In fact, a MusicalInstrument class is likely to be quite simple. The hard part is modeling the different types of instruments, as well as the individual instruments.

The principle of covering the general case applies to method-writing as well as class design. So does the principle of stopping when it makes sense to stop. For example—a slightly sledge-hammerish example, but an example nonetheless—suppose you're writing a quick, simple method to convert miles to kilometers. On the one hand, you want it to be general, within the framework of its purpose. You're not going to write it so that it's handcuffed to a specific set of cases, such as:

```
# Bad!
def m2k(m)
  if c == 0
    then return 0
  elsif c == 1
    then return 1.6093
```

```
    elsif c == 2
      then return 3.2186
    ...
  end
```

Rather, you will craft the method to handle the general case:

```
def m2k(m)
  return m * 1.6093
end
```

That's probably the right level of abstraction for the problem. But now, for the sake of argument, let's say you really, really wanted your #m2k method to anticipate every imaginable case, if not more. So you decide to make it even more general. "Hmmmm," you hum. "Just look at that hard-coded, inflexible, nonabstract number! Shouldn't I allow more flexibility than that?"

In the flush of enthusiasm for generalization—and it's a very catchy process—you might come up with a version where the caller could pass in the final value in the formula, such as:

```
def m2k(m,n=1.6093)
  return m * n
end
```

Yes, this is a more general solution, but it's general to the point of absurdity. No one who needs to convert from miles to kilometers is going to want to override the conversion rate. Anyone who did would just be multiplying two numbers anyway, and there is no need to go to the trouble of writing an #m2k method to do that.

Getting Abstraction Right

The moral of the story is: Design your code to model objects and behaviors as generally as it can, consistent with a realistic evaluation of what the purpose of writing the program is in the first place.

"Talk about 'abstract'!," you interject bitterly. "Why not just say 'Do the right thing' and get it over with?"

So how abstract *should* you get? How general is the general case?

There's no way around the fact that decisions about object modeling must be made relative to each program you're designing and each problem you're solving. But that's not a bad thing. One of the nice qualities of object-oriented programming is that it offers "hooks" into familiar, real-world object structures and relationships—which means, in turn, that you can bring at least some of your real-world judgment to bear on questions like how general to make your classes.

Not every case will be as transparent as "violin family" versus "stringed instrument". But you will find that you can use, and frequently trust, the instincts about abstraction and generalization that you have from dealing with object categorization in real life.

For example: Let's say you're writing a chess program. You have to write code to handle the board, and you have some options. Do you hard-code the 8×8 dimensions of the board? Or do you write methods which adapt themselves to any size board, in case someone wants to use your code to create a 9×9 or larger chess game—or to create a board, possibly not even a square one, for use in some other game?

Let's look at some of the factors you would have to reckon with in deciding whether to write code that worked only with an 8×8 board, as opposed to code that would work with a two-dimensional board of any size. Consider the impact of the decision on one particular, hypothetical method. We'll call it #adjacent_to. The idea for this method is that, given an *X-Y* coordinate on the board, it returns an array of all the squares that are adjacent to that square.

If you were going all-out in hard-coding a traditional 8×8 chessboard, you could economize on calculations (and therefore running time) by storing all possible values in advance. You could do this in an array. Assume that the board's 64 squares are numbered from 0–63. Your array will contain 64 elements, with each index corresponding to a particular square. Each element of the array will itself be an array, containing the numbers of the squares adjacent to the square corresponding to the index. We'll store this array (in shortened form) in the constant NEIGHBORS:

```
class ChessBoard
  NEIGHBORS = [ [1,8,9],        # adjacent to square 0
                [0,2,8,9,10],   # adjacent to square 1
                ...
                [55,56,62]      # adjacent to square 63
              ]
```

Now if we want a method that can tell us any square's neighbors, we just have to add this version of #adjacent_to to class ChessBoard:

```
def adjacent_to(sq)
  NEIGHBORS[sq]
end
```

That will certainly work for an 8×8 board. It won't, however, help someone who wants to write a Boggle™ program, which traditionally uses a 4×4 grid and sometimes 5×5. Nor would it help someone writing a tic-tac-toe program.

This is a case where you have to decide among several choices:

1. Stick to your guns and hard-code the 8×8 dimensions, as above. This will run fast, because it stores values instead of calculating them. But it's inflexible.

2. Write a generalized version of #adjacent_to, so that it works for a two-dimensional board of any size. Put it in a class called Board, and have ChessBoard inherit from Board. This approach is slower, but it's nicer to people who might want to write BoggleBoard or other such classes. (We're not nice enough actually to write it, though. We'll keep it hypothetical.)

3. Create the flexible version of class Board, as in the preceding choice. Then, every time a new Board object is created, calculate all the neighbor relations among the squares. Do this calculation just once, storing it somewhere for future retrieval.

4. Create the flexible version of class Board, as in the second choice. Then, write class ChessBoard as a subclass of Board—and rewrite or override the inherited #adjacent_to method, using a hash.

The point of spelling all this out is to give you a sense of what's involved in thinking through design and implementation decisions, specifically in the realm of abstraction and planning for the general case. There's no one formula for success. You have to decide what makes sense.

In this particular case, there probably isn't going to be too much at stake. If some other programmer has to write a board implementation from scratch, not all that much time or effort will be lost (especially since Ruby comes packaged with a Matrix class, which could do some of it for us—but that's another story). Further up the scale, however, when projects get big and writing components of projects takes serious time, the kind of hard-coding that prohibits code reuse can be a real impediment to development. Still, a bit of brainstorming reveals strategies for striking a balance between a general solution and a chess-specific solution. If there's any payoff at all, in terms of saving time later or writing code that has more than one possible use, it will have been worth finding and considering those strategies.

Note   You've seen method overriding briefly already, and we'll see it again later today. The point of mentioning it here is simply to include it among the coding strategies at your disposal in addressing the Board problem.

Summary

We've learned today about Ruby's support for maintaining different areas of program logic in separate files. A script can take advantage of the functionality of the code in other files by the use of the `require` and `include` methods. Those other files may have been written by you, or they may have come from other authors who solved certain problems so that you wouldn't have to.

Also, we have started to wrestle with the ideas of abstraction and generalization. It is possible, we have found, to make our solutions too general or not general enough. Finding the most useful abstractions for each situation is a skill that comes with experience. It's a worthwhile skill to develop, because the Ruby Way is to solve most problems exactly once. Every now and then you are faced with a task that looks somehow similar to a task you have worked on before. If you did a good job of abstracting when solving it the first time, you can simply invoke the old solution.

Tomorrow we'll gain more experience in program organization, concentrating on how to write reusable code, before moving on to new topics.

Exercises

1. Here's a little script. Pay attention; you will be rewriting this.

```ruby
def help_student
  puts "Hello student"
end

def help_teacher
  puts "Hello teacher"
end

print "Student (1) or teacher (2)? "
choice = gets.strip

if /^1/.match choice    # or: choice =~ /^1/
  help_student
elsif /^2/.match choice
  help_teacher
else
  puts "Unknown choice #{choice}"
end
```

We're going to play a little game of "move the code around."

First, move the definition of #help_student to a separate file, called student.rb, and rename the method to #help.

Second, move the definition of #help_teacher to a separate file, called teacher.rb, and rename the method to #help.

Now, from the original code, you should have just the main body of a program left, without any method definitions.

Here's the challenge: Rewrite the main body of the program so that it works the way it did when the two "help" methods were defined right there with it. You may use only one require statement.

2. For this exercise, you'll need to create two files.

   The first is called complex.rb and contains this code:

   ```
   def shrink
     puts "I think you have a complex."
   end
   ```

   The second is called runcom.rb and contains this code:

   ```
   #!/usr/bin/env_ruby
   require 'complex'
   shrink
   ```

   What do you predict the output of running runcom.rb will be?

   Now run it.

   Did it do what you expected? If not, can you figure out why not?

3. We'll start this exercise today and work on it some more tomorrow. It's intended as much to get you thinking and brainstorming about program organization questions as to get you to write a full, working program. (Not to discourage the latter activity, but right now we're focusing on the design and abstraction muscles in your brain.)

   And the exercise is: Design a program that creates, shuffles, and deals hands (of whatever size you specify) from a standard deck of playing cards.

   Don't worry about the shuffling part; you'll be provided with a method for that. (Writing a shuffling method is hard, and it's not relevant to what we're doing right now.) For the moment, just think about how you might go about organizing the code for this program.

   Let's assume there's going to be a class called Deck. Is it a subclass of a higher, more abstract or general class? Does it have subclasses? Does it gain its behavior from one or more modules—and, if so, what are they?

   And what about the cards themselves? Do you need a separate Card class, or can you just create cards as part of class Deck?

   We'll provide some code and discussion in our solution, but not a complete program. To get the most out of the exercise, be sure to give yourself some time to work out your own solution before looking at ours.

10

Answers

1. There are a couple of ways to do this, depending on how you interpret the word "use" in the instructions.

   If "use" means "type"—that is, if you're only allowed to type one `require` statement—you could rewrite the program like this:

```
print "Student (1) or teacher (2)? "
choice = gets.strip

if /^1/.match choice
  req = "student"
elsif /^2/.match choice
  req = "teacher"
else
  puts "Unknown choice #{choice}"
end

require req
help
```

Note that the name of the extension we require is not a literal string but a variable containing a string. That's perfectly legitimate. And it lets us postpone the `require` until we know what we need to require. Then, once we do it, the `#help` method we get will be the right one.

If you interpret the word "use" to mean "execute," then you can type two `require` statements, as long as only one of them gets executed! That would look like this:

```
print "Student (1) or teacher (2)? "
choice = gets.strip

if /^1/.match choice
  require "student"
elsif /^2/.match choice
  require "teacher"
else
  puts "Unknown choice #{choice}"
end

help
```

In practice, it's relatively rare to `require` an extension based on a condition (such as the value of some user input). Most calls to `require` are straightforward and usually happen at or near the beginning of a program. But seeing it done in a somewhat more elaborate way illustrates the fact that `require` is a normal method that takes a `String` argument and can be executed anywhere in a program.

2. If you didn't expect `runcom.rb` to fail with an error, it's because you didn't realize that there's already a file called `complex.rb` in Ruby's runtime search path. So when you did the `require` call, the extension you got was Ruby's complex extension, not your own. As a result, your program could do all sorts of tricks with complex numbers, but it didn't know anything about a method called `shrink`.

   To fix this, you might put the program's runtime directory at the front of the `$:` variable (in the manner we saw earlier today), or provide an absolute path as the argument to `require`. Or you might just rename `complex.rb` to something else.

3. A deck of cards is very similar to an array. It's a two-dimensional data structure, and it has a fixed order. (You can change the order by shuffling it, or dealing from it, but at any given moment it's in a particular order.)

   So you might want to use inheritance to piggyback on Ruby's very own `Array` class:

   ```
   class Deck < Array
   end
   ```

   You might consider whether there's anything more general than a deck and less general than an array—that is, whether `Deck` should inherit from some other class, which would in turn inherit from `Array`. The answer is probably no. A deck of cards is so array-like that it makes sense to have it inherit directly from `Array`. (But you should still think about things like this before you commit to a design.)

   When a new deck is created, it needs to be filled up with 52 cards. (We're not going to bother with jokers.) You can already sketch this out placeholder-style in Ruby:

   ```
   class Deck < Array
     def initialize
       # fill self with 52 cards
     end
   end
   ```

   We could `fill self with 52 cards` like this:

   ```
   self[0] = "two of hearts"
   self[1] = "three of hearts"
   ...
   ```

   ...but that's about as elegant as our hard-coded kilometer converter.

   Maybe this is a sign that we should think seriously about having a `Card` class. Then each of the deck's fifty-two "elements" (to use array terminology) can be a `Card` object.

   And to create (initialize) a card, you probably need to pass it a suit and rank....

10

Tomorrow we'll return to this exercise. And we'll start with a short but working version of the program, based on today's preliminary analysis, moving on from there to add some enhancements and do some refactoring.

So feel free to spend some time between now and then coming up with your own version of it. Even if it's not identical to the one in tomorrow's exercise, you may be able to hone your skills on both versions.

Do get a little sleep, though.

DAY 11

Modules and Classes in Depth

> Genius detects through the fly, through the caterpillar, through the grub, through the egg, the constant individual; through countless individuals, the fixed species; through many species, the genus; through all genera, the steadfast type; through all the kingdoms of organized life, the eternal unity.
>
> —Ralph Waldo Emerson, *History*, from *Essays: First Series* (1841)

Today, part III of our program organization trilogy, we'll look at designing modules and classes for reuse, embedding modules, and class-module distribution. We'll also explore overriding methods. As you can tell, we've got a lot to cover today, so let's get started.

Designing Modules and Classes for Clarity and Reuse

When writing a program in Ruby, you organize your code into classes and modules. As we've seen, your efforts have to mesh with certain constraints in the way Ruby organizes and finds code at the class or module level and also at the disk file level.

But even in cases where it's going to be self-evident what to call the files and where to put them, you still have to make decisions about class and module hierarchies. A lot of that decision making has to do with deciding what should be a class and what should be a module.

Classes and modules are very closely related. In almost any case you could, if you felt like it, cut methods from a class, paste them into a module, and then mix the module into the class, without changing the behavior of the program. Given that the class/module border is so easy to cross, when do you write a module and when do you write a class? And why?

Design decisions at this level have a lot to do with abstraction. They also have to do directly with the creation, storage, retrieval, and reuse of program files. This is why abstraction, in the sense in which we've been using the term, is not "abstract" in the common negative sense of "vague."

Some Class/Module Distinctions

As you think about and start to design the data structures in your program, one of the major areas of decision-making is often that of the class/module distinction: What types of functionality should be put in modules as opposed to classes? If classes share characteristics, is that a case for inheritance (passing those characteristics down in a straight line) or for a module (dishing the characteristics out to any class that needs them)?

Sometimes the choice is obvious. Sometimes it isn't, and sometimes a case can be made for at least two very different ways of designing a program. You can't predict the right thing to do in every case. No one can. But you can help yourself a lot by understanding what's at stake in the decisions you make and by thinking about the underlying reasoning behind class/module distinctions.

Here are a few things to think about:

- The basic unit of organization and behavior in your program is the class. Modules represent a kind of code preorganization stage.
- Classes get instantiated, so if you want there to be an object in your program that is "a Thing," then you need a class called Thing.
- Modules do not get instantiated. Modules contain behaviors and characteristics that do not belong to any one class—in fact, they do not belong to any one family of classes.
- The names of many modules are *adjectives*, whereas class names tend to be *nouns*. A *class* is a template for a thing. A *module* is a cluster of characteristics.

Let's look more closely at that last point.

The decisions you make regarding your class and module design have a lot to do with the process of abstraction. When you abstract from a set of classes (or real-world things that are candidates for being classes) and still end up with a thing (like Vehicle as an abstraction of Car, Bus, and Train), you probably have a good candidate for inheritance. When you abstract to the point that what you've abstracted are, themselves, abstract characteristics—words that end with -ability, -ness, or the like—you have probably reached the stage where a module is the best choice.

(Yes, words that end with the suffixes -ability and -ness are nouns. But they're nouns yearning to be adjectives. When you've abstracted to the max and find yourself about to create a class called Communicability or Shapelessness, what you probably really want to do is create a module called Communicable or Shapeless.)

You can see some very important cases of adjectival naming in the Ruby core language itself as well as in the core library. There are, among others, modules called Enumerable, Observable, and Comparable. You can mix these into your own classes—and even if you don't, you're using at least some of them anyway, because Ruby's built-in types use them. (Class Array mixes in Enumerable, for instance.)

Concepts like "enumerable" and "comparable" are indeed very abstract, but they're extremely useful and directly pertinent to the behavior of Ruby objects. For example, the Comparable module (as its name suggests) adds certain facilities for object comparison to any class that mixes it in. Lots of different types of things lend themselves to being compared. Thus you might see this:

```
class PrizeHog
  include Comparable
...
```

and, elsewhere, this:

```
class LibraryOfCongressCatalogNumber
  include Comparable
...
```

Being "comparable" is not exclusively a trait of objects of a particular class, nor even those of a particular hierarchy of classes. It's more like a seasoning that can be added to classes across the board and across the organizational chart of class family trees. (You still have to do some work to get your classes to know what the criteria of comparison are in each case; but given a little bit of such intelligence, Comparable automatically provides several comparison methods.)

An Exercise in Adjectival Thinking

Not all Ruby modules correspond to adjectives, either in name or in spirit. But a lot of them do—and, in any case, thinking adjectivally is a good way to train yourself in the difference between classes and modules.

Let's expand both our adjectival and our musical horizons by designing a program (albeit a rather sketchy one) to log sound recordings by medium, title, and duration.

Recording media lend themselves to class inheritance; that is, the various media—CDs, LPs, 78s, and so forth—have enough in common with each other that it makes sense to design them as subclasses of a general, abstract RecordingMedium class.

We're going to take generalization and abstraction even further. What is it about a recording medium that's so characteristic? Well, it represents a finite resource, and that resource gets used up bit by bit. At any given point, a certain amount of the resource has been used, and a certain amount remains.

All of this sounds so abstract that it's hard to tell we're describing a recording medium. We could be describing enrollment in a limited-seating college course, or planning a car trip on one tank of gasoline, or writing checks against a dangerously low bank balance. In other words, we're not talking only about LPs and CDs and cassette tapes: we're talking about *things that can be used up*, or *consumed*. We're going to embody this in our program by creating and using a module called Consumable. This module will encapsulate the behavior of any number of consumable things (bank balances, cassette tapes, gasoline), without actually naming any of them. The module will be mixed in by the class RecordingMedium.

Enough talk of what we're going to do: let's do it. Listing 11.1 is a complete program containing a usable Consumable module, record.rb.

LISTING 11.1 record.rb

```
01:  module Consumable
02:    attr_accessor :capacity, :used
03:
04:    def remaining
05:      @capacity - @used
06:    end
07:
08:    def finished
09:      @used >= @capacity
10:    end
11:
12:    def room_for?(x)
13:      @used + x <= @capacity
```

LISTING **11.1**   Continued

```
14:     end
15:
16:     def consume(x)
17:       @used += x
18:     end
19:   end
20:
21:   class RecordingMedium
22:
23:     include Consumable
24:
25:     def initialize
26:       self.used = 0
27:       @tracks = []
28:     end
29:
30:     def record(title,duration)
31:       if room_for?(duration)
32:         @tracks.push(title)
33:         consume(duration)
34:         return true
35:       else
36:         return false
37:       end
38:     end
39:   end
40:
41:   class CD < RecordingMedium
42:
43:     def initialize
44:       self.capacity = 70
45:       super
46:     end
47:   end
48:
49:   # Some test cases:
50:
51:   cd = CD.new
52:   if cd.record("Minute Waltz", 1)
53:     puts "Recorded the Minute Waltz"
54:   else
55:     puts "Couldn't record the Minute Waltz"
56:   end
57:
58:   if cd.record("Messiah", 120)
59:     puts "Recorded Messiah"
60:   else
61:     puts "Couldn't record Messiah"
62:   end
```

11

Note

> That super you see in class RecordingMedium's #initialize method means that after you've done this initialization, run the #initialize method of the parent class. We'll see super in more detail later.

Like a fine stereo system, all the components of this program—the module, the general class, the subclass of the general class, and the main program code—work together seamlessly. Let's go back to that module, Consumable. As we've already seen, it models the behavior of many things in the world. It's a pity to limit its usage to just one little program. What if we want to write that checkbook utility? Or that trip planner? Or…?

Modules often serve this convenient, auxiliary purpose. But don't get in the habit of thinking of modules as second-class (so to speak) citizens of the world of Ruby program design. For one thing, class Class is actually a child class of class Module. Moreover, certain modules, such as Enumerable from the Ruby core, stand second to none as important components of Ruby software.

In some respects, coming up with a good module requires more imagination than creating a class tree. Vehicle as a parent class for Car, Bus, and Train is a fairly obvious thing. Realizing that you've got a useful, adjective-level functionality on your hands is often less obvious. But looking for such things can help you streamline and strengthen your program design, as well as potentially give you something you can reuse in the future.

Did someone say "reuse"?

Modules and Multiple Inheritance

As you know from Day 9, Ruby does not support multiple inheritance (MI); that is, every class has exactly zero or one parents. Some object-oriented languages do support MI. In such languages, you could make Salted a class, and then have ChickenCacciatore inherit from both ChickenDish and Salted. Ruby keeps things simple (MI can actually lead to some weird class hierarchies) yet full-featured through the use of modules. In spite of the lack of MI in Ruby, you have complete, fine-grained control over what your classes can and cannot do, thanks to modules.

Code Reusability

There's a certain intellectual and even aesthetic appeal to a well-organized, neatly abstracted object-oriented program design. It's a nice feeling when the little light bulb above your head goes on and you realize that cars and buses are vehicles, or that cassette tapes and bank balances share certain abstract characteristics that can be encapsulated in a module. The effort you put into object-oriented design and abstraction is not necessarily its only reward. You will, at least sometimes, also have earned the reward of code reusability. Planning for code reuse is not only a way to save typing; it's a way to give life, and longevity, to your code. If you write a module that can be mixed into multiple classes, or a class that's designed to be inherited by other classes, then there's always a possibility that in the future someone will use your code, even for purposes you didn't envision. (It's not likely that there will be new, unforeseen members of the violin family coming along, but you never know.)

Reusability is not solely the domain of object-oriented programming. Other programming styles have the same goal, although they tend to go about it differently. But when you're designing and writing object-oriented programs, you cannot, and should not, escape the concern of reusability, from the beginning of the process to the end.

This does not mean that all the code you write will be reusable. It does, however, mean that you should consider whether and how you might make your code reusable. You'll write plenty of one-shot code over time, and that's perfectly fine. The main thing is to be sure that you're not missing opportunities to write for reuse because you have not considered it.

11

Embedded Modules and Namespace Management

Most of our module examples have involved what might be called the classic or "bread-and-butter" usage of modules in Ruby: A class mixes in a module with an `include` statement, probably at the very beginning of the class definition, and that module's methods and class variables become accessible to instances of the class that's doing the mixing in.

That, along with inheritance and a few other techniques, is enough to get you streamlining your program design nicely. However, there's somewhat more variety to how classes and modules can interact.

Remember how definitions of modules and classes can `include` methods, constants, and variables (of various kinds)? Well, if you liked that, you'll love this: Definitions of modules and classes (which really means modules, because classes are a type of module) can also include definitions of other modules, other classes, or both.

Listing 11.2 is simple example:

LISTING 11.2   nested.rb

```
01:  class Outer
02:    @@transient = 100
03:    PERMANENT = 200
04:
05:    def say_something
06:      puts "Hello."
07:    end
08:
09:    class Inner
10:      def greet
11:        puts "Hello from inside class Outer::Inner!"
12:      end
13:    end
14:  end
```

We've got a class-inside-a-class. Now, what do we do with it? Specifically, how do we create an instance of that inner class?

How you get at a class-inside-a-class depends on where you are. If you're still inside the definition of the outer class (or inside it again because you've reopened it), then you can create an instance of the inner class in the familiar way:

```
# Reopen class Outer
class Outer
  i = Inner.new
  i.greet                #output: Hello from inside class Outer::Inner!
end
```

If you're anywhere else and you want to create an instance of that class, you can't just call Inner.new. When you're outside of class Outer, you need to find a pathway through class Outer to get to the classes defined inside class Outer.

As spiritual as finding a pathway sounds, finding this pathway is very down-to-earth. You just have to tell Ruby what you're looking for.

Ruby tags the inner class with a kind of double-barreled name consisting of both its own immediate name (Inner, in our example) and the name of the class it's enclosed by (Outer). This double-barreled name is written using :: as a connector, and it's what you use to specify the inner class from outside both classes:

```
oi = Outer::Inner.new
oi.greet                #output: Hello from inside class Outer::Inner
```

Putting a class inside a class this way means, among other things, that even if you have another class called `Inner` somewhere in your program, its name won't conflict with the name of this `Inner`, because the name of this `Inner` has to be expressed as `Outer::Inner`. This is what we mean when we say that this kind of nesting or *embedding* of classes and modules offers a way to organize, protect, and essentially manage namespaces.

You can embed classes and modules as deeply as you wish, using as many `::` connectors as is needed to fish them out. If things get too deep, you might want to reconsider your program design. But there are good reasons to do things this way, at least in certain circumstances.

We're going to survey some common permutations of embedded class and module coding, along with commentary on how they work and when you might want to use them. As you'll see, there are usually ways to get around the multibarreled naming syntax, but it's not always a good idea to do so.

You don't have to memorize all of these permutations today. The main thing is to look at them and understand them, so that you get a sense of the possibilities at your disposal in designing your class and data structures. (Even if these techniques don't leap to the top of your Ruby toolkit, at least you'll be able to recognize them when you see them used elsewhere.) Be open to the possibility of permutations and usages you don't see here; this is just a survey of some of them, not a catalog.

11

Modules Mixing in Modules

One module can mix in or `include` another, just as a class can mix in a module. This can be an effective technique for organizing hierarchies of modular functionality:

```
module Polygonal
  def perimeter
    pe = 0
    sides.each {|s| pe += s}
    pe
  end
  ...
end

module Pentagonal
  include Polygonal
  ...
end

class USMilitaryHeadquarters
  include Pentagonal
  ...
end
```

Given this arrangement, class `USMilitaryHeadquarters`'s instances have access to Polygonal's #perimeter method. (Come to think of it, there probably won't be too many instances of that class, but you get the idea.)

Classes Defined Inside Modules

Classes can be defined inside a module. This provides a way to organize, and protect, your namespaces.

Consider this code, where we define *two* classes called `Spine`:

```
module BookParts
  class Cover
  end

  class Spine
  end
end

module BodyParts
  class BigToe
  end

  class Spine
  end
end
```

The saving grace here, aside from the unlikelihood of writing these particular modules, is that you can differentiate—in fact, you must differentiate, assuming you're outside their definitions—between the two `Spine` classes, by *fully qualifying* their namespaces:

```
s1 = BookParts::Spine.new
s2 = BodyParts::Spine.new
```

(We're assuming that both of these module definitions are in our scope—that is, either our main program code is in the same file as both modules, or we've required one or more files so that Ruby can see the modules.)

Now, while we have tackled the problem of how to get at both `Spine`s in a clear and unambiguous manner, we have not done the thing we usually do with modules—namely, mix them in with include. What happens if we do?

Well, as you mix in modules, their internally defined classes and modules enter your namespace, in the order mixed in. So if we `include BookParts`, we can then create a `BookParts::Spine` object without much typing effort:

```
include BookParts
s = Spine.new
```

The danger of this approach is that if we also include BodyParts, then whichever Spine class was defined most recently will be "our" Spine class. The necessity of specifying the longer name-path protects you from accidentally clobbering a name with a newly mixed-in namesake.

> **Note**
> This is very similar to our "salute" example in Day 9. In that example, we clobbered a method name by mixing in two modules. Here, we're clobbering a class name. The underlying issue is the same.

Classes Defined Inside Classes

This is where we started earlier, with Outer and Inner, so we don't have to linger here too long.

Defining classes inside classes provides a namespace management facility similar to that provided by defining classes inside a module. There are times when you might want to do this. Perhaps the class you're defining has its own little universe of internal classes, each of which contributes something to the overall structure of the enclosing class but would be meaningless outside of that class.

This ChristmasTree class defines an inner Light class. For something to be an object of that inner class means that it's not a traffic light, or a flashlight, but a ChristmasTree::Light.

```
class ChristmasTree

  class Light
    attr_reader :color
    def initialize
      @color = [ :red, :green, :blue, :yellow, :white ].rand(5)
    end
  end

  def initialize
    @lights = []
    50.times { @lights.push Light.new }
  end
end
```

Here, it's reasonable to have a class whose name to the outside world is ChristmasTree::Light—since that class's main purpose, in any case, is to serve as a kind of helper or building block for class ChristmasTree.

Sometimes, however, embedded classes start showing up where it would make more sense to have a relation of inheritance. Consider this example:

```
class Book

    class Paperback
    end

    class Hardcover
    end

end
```

The use of embedded classes, in this case, cries out to be reworked into an inheritance-based structure:

```
class Book
end

class Paperback < Book
end

class Hardcover < Book
end
```

When deciding whether to create inner classes, keep an eye out for cases where they're not doing much more than echoing an inheritance hierarchy. If so, they shouldn't be made inner classes, but placed outside and made into subclasses as shown in this example. The same reasoning also applies when deciding whether to define classes inside a module.

Class-Module Distribution Across Program Files

When it comes to deciding which classes and modules to put in what files, Ruby allows all sorts of permutations. You have to consider what you, and perhaps other people, might want to do with your code later.

One option that you have is to put each class in a different file. You can also group more than one class in one file, if you want.

There's a convention in other object-oriented languages of creating one file for every class defined. When you write something in Java, for example, you end up with many files, each containing the code for a single class.

This practice is less strictly followed in Ruby; you'll often see a program source file with more than one class definition in it. When it comes to modules, especially those that are designed for very widespread usage, the one-per-file practice is fairly common.

You can also put one class in more than one file. What could that mean? Recall that Ruby lets you "reopen" classes and change methods. If you do this in a file other than the one in which the class was originally defined, then you can say that the class definition is in more than one file.

Moreover, thanks to the dynamic nature of Ruby, you can make certain decisions about all of this on-the-fly. You could, for example, write a program that `requires` one of two other files, depending on user input. Each of those two files might change the behavior of a class in a particular way.

Another variation on the theme would be cases where you want to write a module that is designed to be mixed in by just one class. This isn't exactly a shining example of writing generalized, reusable code—but if it helps with what you're writing, there's nothing necessarily wrong with doing it.

An example of this can be found in matrix.rb, a standard Ruby library extension. As you'll see if you look at that file, the code starts with the definition of module `ExceptionForMatrix`; a little further down, class `Matrix` mixes in that module.

This is a case where creating a one-use module makes sense, because it helps internally organize the code. It doesn't mean that the author of the `matrix` extension doesn't grasp the principle of reusability. Far from it: `matrix` is extremely abstract and reusable.

11

Overriding Methods

Ruby is very open-minded about letting you add components to your classes and modules, and even individual objects, after they've already been initially defined:

```
class Thing
  def talk
    puts "hi"
  end
end

t = Thing.new
t.talk      #output: hi

# Re-open Thing and add a new method.
class Thing
  def shout
    puts "HI!!!"
  end
end

t.shout     #output: HI!!!
```

```
# Add a singleton method to object t.
def t.whisper
  puts "(hi)"
end

t.whisper    #output: (hi)
```

This is just the tip of the iceberg when it comes to the kinds of runtime power Ruby offers you in the area of class and object modification. (And not just your own classes, either. Ruby doesn't put much of the core language behind locked doors.) Here, we're going to put the spotlight on a particular flavor of class alteration: namely, the practice of rewriting or *overriding* existing methods. This is something that arises constantly in the process of mapping out and implementing the various kinds of class/module relations and intertwinings we've been looking at.

Overriding and Aliasing

Overriding a method is easy. You don't have to ask; you just do it:

```
class Thing
  def talk
    puts "hi"
  end

  def talk
    puts "hello"
  end
end
```

Actually, even though that's the simplest scenario, it's not necessarily the best. If you run that last example using the -w flag, you'll get a warning: discarding old talk. What that means is that when you redefine the method #talk, the old method #talk is no longer available.

"But," you interject, "isn't that the idea? Why create a new #talk if we're going to mourn the loss of the old one?"

Here's why. Sometimes a new version of a method is really there to act as a kind of doorway to the old version. That sounds very mystical; let's look at an example. To understand this example, you need to know that alias is a way of saving the old method—actually, a copy of the old method (freeing up the original old method to be discarded)—under a new name.

```
class Thing
  def talk
    puts "hi"
  end
end
```

```
# Re-open class Thing:
class Thing
  alias :oldtalk :talk

  def talk
    puts "I used to say"
    oldtalk
    puts "but now I say 'Hello'."
    puts "Hello"
  end
end
```

In the middle of the new #talk, we call our "backup copy" of the old version—namely, #oldtalk.

This ability to copy methods before overriding them puts an enormous amount of power in your hands when it comes to code design and customization, even in the core Ruby language.

Let's say, for example, that you wake up one morning wishing that Ruby's Array class would warn you if you asked it to sort arrays with more than 10,000 elements. Here's what you could do:

```
class Array
  alias :oldsort :sort
  def sort(&block)
    if size > 10000
      $stderr.puts "Warning: sorting large array"
    end
    oldsort(&block)
  end
end

(0...15000).to_a.sort   #output: Warning: sorting large array
```

Overriding an Inherited Method

We've seen that you can manually reopen a class and change its methods. Your classes can also override methods that they inherit.

Remember how inheritance works: If class Child inherits from class Parent, then instances of Child can respond to messages corresponding to Parent's methods. This works because the child class can, in effect, forward messages to its parent.

But a child class can also reimplement or override the methods of its parent. Here is a simple example:

```
class Parent
  def talk
    puts "I am the parent."
  end
end
```

```
class Child < Parent
  def talk
    puts "I am a child."
  end
end
```

Now, if a `Child` object is asked to #talk, it finds that it can respond to the message talk (without resorting to the "Wait a minute—let me ask my class's superclass!" strategy we saw on Day 9).

Furthermore, the new version of the method in the child class can, if it wants, still call the parent's version. This is accomplished with the `super` keyword. Earlier we glimpsed super walking down the street in sunglasses. Now we really meet it:

```
class Child < Parent
  def talk
    puts "My parent class sounds like this:"
    super
    puts "but I sound like this:"
    puts "I am a child."
  end
end
```

The keyword `super` means "Call the parent class's version of the method we're currently in." This, by the way, might mean calling the parent class's own parent class's version. Whatever it takes—however far up the inheritance tree we have to go to find the method—that's what we want when we use `super`.

Like `alias`, `super` is a doorway back to methods you've overridden. This means that you never have to lose any power or functionality when you override methods. Not that you will always call the old versions, but you can.

When "Is a" Isn't

The inheritance relation between two object-oriented classes can, as mentioned earlier, be thought of as an "is a" relation: a `Car` "is a" `Vehicle`, `ChickenCacciatore` "is a" `ChickenDish`, and so on. In Ruby (wouldn't you know it?), the "is a" way of looking at inheritance doesn't always work. That's because of how flexible Ruby is about letting you alter and extend the methods and attributes—or *interface*—of classes and even individual objects. If you can add a #change_tire method to a `Cello` object, does it still make sense to say that a `Cello` "is a" `ViolinFamilyMember`? And you can apply the same skepticism to the object itself: is a cello that changes tires still even a `Cello`? You can use the "is a" approach productively up to a point in Ruby; but keep in mind that, in the long run, every object can "be a" thing unto itself.

Handling Arguments in Overridden Methods

When you override a method and then call the old version of the method, you'll often have to (or want to) do something about the arguments to the method. Most commonly, you'll end up wanting to pass them along to the old method, perhaps having changed or examined them along the way.

This means that your new method should be written to handle the same arguments the old method did. Here's an example where the new version of the method intercepts the arguments and changes one of them to all uppercase:

```
class Thing
  def speak(who,what)
    puts "#{who} says: #{what}"
  end
end

t = Thing.new
t.speak("Hamlet", "To be or not to be...")

class Thing
  alias :oldspeak :speak

  def speak(who,what)
    oldspeak(who,what.upcase)
  end
end

t.speak("Hamlet", "To be or not to be...")
```

If you simply want to pass the arguments along unchanged, without worrying much about what they are, you can define your new method with the argument list (*args,&block), and then call the old method with the same list. *args will sponge up any regular arguments, and &block will pass along the block, if there is one. This isn't the sleekest way to do it; generally, you should write something to match the actual arguments. We'll understand this better in coming days. But the sponging-up approach does protect you against changes in how the method you're calling handles its arguments.

Summary

Over the last three days, we've been discussing the skills and tools that make it possible to confidently develop and maintain projects of any size with Ruby.

We knew about classes and methods almost from the start, but now we know how to use inheritance to concisely express relationships in and among families of similar classes, and how to group related methods into modules so they can be mixed in anywhere they are needed. We've also learned how—and to some extent, when—to separate modules and classes into reusable files.

Taking advantage of these techniques will ensure that even in large programming projects, each piece can be seen, understood, and maintained independently of the whole. That's easy to say, but it's not always easy to accomplish if you lack the luxury or discipline of advance planning; indeed, nearly every programmer has been involved in projects whose scope was not foreseen at the beginning, and which somehow just kept growing. To keep things manageable when that happens, you need to be vigilant. Keep rethinking, refactoring, asking yourself questions, testing the pieces. Have patience! Such skills are developed only with time and experience, but their practice, once you learn to trust yourself, keeps each job under control and your mind at ease.

Tomorrow we step away from these practical concerns and into the Zen-like world of recursive thinking, where problems which at first glance seem nearly impossible turn out to have absurdly simple solutions. Does that sound like fun?

Exercises

1. Look again at Listing 11.2, where we defined class `Outer` and class `Inner`. Save that listing to a file, if you haven't already.

   At the end of the file insert the code shown below, which adds a new class and some :

   ```
   class Other < Outer
   end

   oi = Other::Inner.new
   oi.greet
   ```

   If you run this program now, it will output `"Hello from inside class Outer::Inner!"` even though `oi` is an instance of class `Other::Inner`. How can you get it to say hello from inside class `Other::Inner` instead?

2. Follow these instructions, and then predict what you think the output will be before you run the program:

   First, create a file called `inner.rb`, containing just these lines:

   ```
   class Inner
   end
   ```

   Now, create a file called `outer.rb`, with these lines:

   ```
   class Outer
     require "inner"
     end
   ```

```
end

oi = Outer::Inner.new
puts "oi is an instance of #{oi.class}"
```

What would you expect the output from running outer.rb to be? (*Note:* This is another sneaky, nasty, trick question, slipped in here to cover a potentially useful point that we haven't discussed yet. All will be revealed.)

3. Back to our deck of cards (from Exercise 3 in Day 10):

Here's a reasonably full implementation of the deck of cards program, based on yesterday's analysis of the task. Some test code is included at the end, so you can save this as a file and run it directly.

Look at this along with yesterday's discussion, to get a sense of how this implementation addresses the various questions we raised. Then keep reading, because we're doing more with this today.

```
module CardData
  @@suits = %w{ h d c s }
  @@ranks = %w{ 2 3 4 5 6 7 8 9 10 j q k a }
end

class Card
  attr_accessor :suit, :rank

  def initialize(s,r)
    self.suit = s
    self.rank = r
  end
end

class Deck < Array
  include CardData

  attr_reader :shuffled

  def initialize
    @@suits.each do |s|
      @@ranks.each do |r|
        push Card.new(s,r)
      end
    end
    @shuffled = false
  end

  def shuffle!
    size.downto(1) do |n|
      push delete_at rand(n)
    end
```

11

```
      @shuffled = true
    end

    def deal(n)
      if size - n < 0
        puts "Not enough cards to deal #{n}"
      else
        if not shuffled
          puts "Warning: dealing from unshuffled deck."
        end
        slice!(0,n)
      end
    end
  end

  d = Deck.new
  hand = d.deal(5)    # should generate shuffle warning
  p hand              # should spew lots of card object guts
  d.shuffle!          #
  hand = d.deal(5)    # no warning this time
  p hand              # more card object guts
  hand = d.deal(100) # should fail because too big a hand
```

> **Note**
>
> Notice that we've named our shuffling method with an exclamation point.
> This is because the method directly changes the deck of cards. There's no
> way to unshuffle them back to their previous state. That makes #shuffle! a
> destructive method; review Day 7 if this concept seems unclear. We would
> normally name the method #shuffle if it did not modify the deck of cards
> directly, but returned a shuffled copy of the deck. (Strictly speaking, #deal is
> also destructive, but we'll let that pass. The *bang* naming convention is not
> strictly observed in Ruby, and perhaps #deal is intuitively less destructive
> than #shuffle!.)

There are lots of ways to shuffle arrays. Different ways of doing it vary widely in terms of speed. This one is fairly fast for small arrays. It also doesn't take up much space, so we're using it. But keep in mind that entire books could be—and have been—written on how best to implement data operations like shuffling.

Today's deck-work consists of a few modifications and enhancements.

1. Let's say we decide that the #shuffle! method is so useful that we want it to be part of class Array. Then class Deck will have access to it, through inheritance.

   It's not hard to reopen Array and define the method. But notice that our #shuffle! involves setting the variable @shuffled, which serves as a flag to indicate the shuffled state of the deck.

If we put #shuffle! directly into class Array, we don't want to include any reference to @shuffled. That's too deck-specific.

So, how do we do this? How do we "promote" the method #shuffle! to class Array, and still track shuffled in class Deck?

2. To deal cards, we're using the method Array#slice!, which removes elements from an array. (The version with no exclamation point just captures elements, without altering the array itself. That's not what we want, since dealing from a deck does alter the deck.)

The way we've done it, we check to see whether there are enough cards left to deal a hand of the requested size, and then if there are, we deal it.

We might be tempted to do it another way. Why not just go ahead and do the slice! —then, if there aren't enough cards, the slice! will presumably return nil (because it couldn't comply with our request to slice *n* elements), and we'll know that it didn't work?

The reason is that slice! will *not* return nil in those circumstances. If an array has, say, three elements, and you slice! four, the array will be empty and the three elements will be returned by slice!:

```
a = [1,2,3]
s = a.slice!(0,4)
p a          #output: []
p s          #output: [1, 2, 3]
```

So, since slice! won't oblige us by returning nil if we ask for too many cards—er, elements—let's take the bull by the horns and rewrite slice!!

To summarize: Reopen class Array (hey, you're doing that anyway for #shuffle!) and modify #slice! so that if the requested number of elements is greater than the size of the array, it will return nil; otherwise, it will behave as usual.

3. Put your modifications to class Array in a separate file, called cards.rb. While you're at it, put the CardData module in that file, too. Put the main code (the Deck and Card classes, and the little tests) in a second file, called deck.rb. (If you want to be really slick, you can put the tests in a separate file.)

11

Answers

1. The object `oi` is an instance of class `Other::Inner`. It's finding the `#greet` method by following its chain of inheritance backward.

   In order to get `oi` to greet you from its own class, you can override `#greet`. Replace your definition of class `Other` with this:

   ```
   class Other < Outer
     class Inner
       def greet
         puts "Hello from inside class Other::Inner!"
       end
     end
   end

   oi = Other::Inner.new
   oi.greet
   ```

   But there's an even better way to do it—a way that saves you the trouble of overriding the method if you create more classes that use it.

   Instead of including the name of the enclosing class (`Outer` or `Other` or whatever) in the string, get the name of the class and then print the string. Here's just the revised output command:

   ```
   puts "Hello from inside class #{self.class}!"
   ```

   If you do it this way, the output will automatically "know" what class name to fill in.

2. This answer brings you the next installment in the ongoing saga of how requiring an extension is almost, but not quite, like typing the code into your file.

   You might expect the output to be `"oi is an instance of Outer::Inner"`. Indeed, if you take out the `require` statement and stick in the definition of class `Inner` from inner.rb, that's what you'll get.

   What you get from the way we've done it, is `"oi is an instance of Inner"`. What this tells us is that even though you did the `require` inside a class definition, the definition of class `Inner` ended up as a top-level definition (`Inner`), not a nested one (`Outer::Inner`).

   This kind of "promotion" of definitions to a higher scope is something to be aware of when using require.

3. After making the requested changes, you should end up with two files. The first, `cards.rb`, looks like this:

   ```
   class Array
     def shuffle!
         size.downto(1) do |n|
         push delete_at rand(n)
   ```

```
      end
    end
    alias :oldslice! :slice
    def slice!(*args)
      n = args[1]
      if n
        if size - n < 0
          return nil
        end
      end
      oldslice!(*args)
    end
  end
  class Card
    attr_accessor :suit, :rank
    def initialize(s,r)
      self.suit = s
      self.rank = r
    end
  end
  module CardData
    @@suits = %w{ H D C S }
    @@ranks = %w{ 2 3 4 5 6 7 8 9 10 J Q K A }
  end
```

11

The second, deck.rb, looks like this:

```
class Deck <Array
  require 'cards'
  include CardData

  attr_reader :shuffled

  def initialize
    @@suits.each do |s|
    @@ranks.each do |r|
        push Card.new(s,r)
      end
    end
    @shuffled = false
  end

  def shuffle!
    super
    @shuffled = true
  end

  def deal(n)
    if not shuffled
      puts "Warning: dealing from unshuffled deck."
    end
```

```
      hand = slice!(0,n)
      if hand == nil
        puts "Not enough cards to deal #{n}"
      end
      return hand
    end

  end

  d = Deck.new
  hand = d.deal(5)    # should generate shuffle warning
  p hand              # should spew lots of card object guts
  d.shuffle!          #
  hand = d.deal(5)    # no warning this time
  p hand              # more card object guts
  hand = d.deal(100) # should fail because too big a hand
```

Note that we've used both of the techniques we've studied for gaining access to classes we've overridden: the super keyword, in cases where the old method belongs to the superclass; and alias, in cases where we want to create a "backup copy" of the old method so that the new method can pass the buck to it.

There's plenty of additional tweaking you could do here (not to mention developing actual games using this as a base). Feel free to explore and test. It's the best way to learn.

DAY 12

An Introduction to Recursion

> The journey of a thousand miles begins with a single step.
> —Lao Tzu

Today we'll be exploring a simple and powerful programming technique. When you apply *recursion*, you boil down a problem into some fundamental observation, then use that observation to solve the problem at an abstract level. The programming language takes care of the details. We saw on Day 4 that iterators sometimes make it unnecessary to bother with writing loops, but today we'll see that recursion can make it unnecessary even to use iterators.

The Canonical Starting Point: Factorials

Almost every textbook and lecture that teaches recursion starts with *factorials*. That really is a fine way to introduce the technique, so we won't buck tradition today.

The factorial of a positive integer is calculated by multiplying it by all positive integers smaller than itself. (Factorials are undefined for negative numbers, and the factorial of 0 is defined to be 1.) Standard mathematical notation for the factorial of a number *n* is *n*!, so we say, `5! = 1 × 2 × 3 × 4 × 5 = 120`.

Factorials are often used for problems of probability and counting. For instance, how many ways can a standard deck of cards be shuffled? For each of the 52 cards that can end up on the bottom, there are 51 possibilities for the card above it, meaning there are 52×51 possible combinations for the bottom two cards. For each of those pairs, any of the remaining 50 cards could be next, and so on. Follow the process to its conclusion, and you see there are 52! possible ways to stack the deck.

We can teach the `Fixnum` class to calculate factorials by writing a new instance method. Without recursion, we would write a loop or, more likely, employ an iterator like `upto`.

```
class Fixnum
  def factorial
    result = 1
    2.upto(self) {|factor| result *= factor}
    return result
  end
end
```

This is called an *iterative solution*. It lays out in advance what work needs to be done, then proceeds in a linear way from beginning to end. It starts with 1, multiplies it by 2, multiplies the result of that by 3, and keeps going until the number it multiplies by is `self`, which is the `Fixnum` object receiving the method call. Let's test the method on some small numbers and, while we're at it, see how many possible ways there are to shuffle a deck of cards.

```
0.factorial                     #-> 1
(1..6).map{|n| n.factorial}  #-> [1, 2, 6, 20, 120, 720]

52.factorial  #->
    80658175170943878571660636856403766975289505440883277824000000000000
```

Notice that when the `factorial` method is called to calculate 0! or 1!, the `upto` iterator does nothing, because `self` is less than 2, but the answers come out right. Also, we could just as correctly have started iterating at 1 instead of 2.

A *recursive solution* looks much different, and relies on our making a useful observation about the nature of the problem. What relationship does any factorial have with the one below it? Look at 3! = 6 and then 2! = 2. Clearly, 3! is three times as big as 2!. In turn, 4! is indeed four times as big as 3!, and in general, it is in the nature of factorials that $n! = n \times (n - 1)!$. We can say this only "in general," because it isn't true when *n* is zero.

Actually, we have just made two observations about factorials, not one. That's the way recursion typically works: There is one rule that applies almost all the time (here, that rule is $n! = (n \times -1)!$) and at least one other rule that applies only in some special circumstance (here, it's $0! = 1$). These are referred to as the "recursive case" and the "base case," respectively. To solve the problem we'll need them both.

Mathematicians like to define things recursively because it lets them use more precise language. To define $n!$ formally, we don't have to say "up to" or "everything between" or anything like that; instead, we can say

$$n! = \begin{cases} n \times (n-1)! & \text{when } n > 0 \\ 1 & \text{when } n = 0 \\ \text{undefined} & \text{otherwise} \end{cases}$$

Brushing aside the undefined part (we'll let $n!$ be 1 when n is negative), it's simple to rewrite this definition as Ruby code.

```
class Fixnum
  def factorial
    return (self * (self-1).factorial) if self > 0
    return 1
  end
end
```

A Little Too Much Like Magic?

There is something startling about recursive code. Where's the rest of it? It looks like it shouldn't work! Surely if whenever somebody asked you what day of the month it was, you said, "Oh, it's the day after whatever it was yesterday," your friends would get rightly irritated with you. So how can we get away with that kind of answer here, since we know that you can't calculate 10! without multiplying a few numbers together?

The answer is that the question turns into a series of questions. When we ask the number 10 to tell us what its factorial is, it doesn't know the answer, except that it must be 10 times as big as 9!, so it turns around and asks 9, "Okay, what's *your* factorial?" The question makes its way down to 0, the only number equipped with a ready response. The answer then makes its way back up, with a single multiplication performed at each step. For instance, when 4 learns that 3! is 6, it calculates 4×6 and tells 5 that 4! is 24. A lot of talking is going on, but whoever asked the original question is only listening only for the answer it will get from the number 10, and doesn't hear any of the other conversations.

This leads us to the one real weakness of this technique. Recursion may not be a perfect cure for all our problems, because it turns out to be less efficient than doing things iteratively. Sometimes the difference is hardly noticeable, but other times it's prohibitively expensive in terms of processing time, or memory, or both.

12

Although calculating factorials isn't one of those tasks that causes trouble when you use recursion, if you were writing a factorial method that you really wanted to use, you'd probably end up doing it iteratively, because it's simple enough to think about that way. As it turns out, though, there are problems that almost nobody can solve or even understand without resorting to recursion. We'll see some of those a little later, and learn a cute way of getting around that performance problem.

Recursive Functions

As you might remember, there is no strict difference in Ruby between functions and methods, but we informally refer to a method as a function if it takes arguments and returns a value, especially if it is a top-level method not attached to any particular class. Traditional recursion is done with functions, and does not involve the creation of lots of new objects, although it still consumes memory. In a sense, you can think of recursive functions as *calling themselves*; or perhaps a little more precisely, calling new copies of themselves. Here's the factorial solution written and tested as a recursive function:

```ruby
def factorial(n)
  if n>0
    n * factorial(n-1)
  else
    1
  end
end

factorial(0)  #->  1
factorial(5)  #->  120
```

As this suggests, recursion is not limited to Ruby or to OO languages in general. You can write recursive code in all languages that support functions—which is to say, just about all languages.

Efficiency Concerns

This pattern appears frequently in nature and in mathematical puzzles:

```
1, 1, 2, 3, 5, 8, 13, 21, 34, 55, 89, ...
```

If you've seen the Fibonacci sequence before, you already know how to calculate its next element, which is 144. The rule is simple: To get any number in the sequence, add the previous two.

The script in Listing 12.1 contains two functions to find the *n*th element (counting from zero, as usual) in the Fibonacci sequence: one iterative and the other recursive. When run, it shows that both functions get correct results; but there is a dramatic difference in the performance numbers.

LISTING 12.1 fib_test_1.rb

```ruby
01: #!/usr/bin/env ruby
02:
03: # A performance test of iterative and recursive functions
04: # that calculate elements of the Fibonacci sequence.
05:
06: # The iterative version is not very elegant.
07: def fib_iterative(n)
08:   if n<2
09:     1
10:   else
11:     prev_1 = prev_2 = 1
12:     new_elt = 0            # (scope is important, value isn't)
13:     2.upto(n) do
14:       new_elt = prev_1 + prev_2      # get the newest element
15:       prev_1,prev_2 = prev_2,new_elt  # update the stored elements
16:     end
17:     new_elt
18:   end
19: end
20:
21: # The recursive version is much simpler, but runs slower.
22: def fib_recursive(n)
23:   if n<2
24:     1
25:   else
26:     fib_recursive(n-2) + fib_recursive(n-1)
27:   end
28: end
29:
30: 5.step(35,5) do |n|
31:   t_start = Time.now
32:   answer = fib_iterative(n)
33:   t_end = Time.now
34:
35:   printf "fib_iterative(%2d) = %10d;  took %7.2f seconds\n",
36:     n,answer,(t_end - t_start)
37:
38:   t_start = Time.now
39:   answer = fib_recursive(n)
40:   t_end = Time.now
41:
42:   printf "fib_recursive(%2d) = %10d;  took %7.2f seconds\n",
43:     n,answer,(t_end - t_start)
44:
45: end
```

12

Typical results:

```
fib_iterative( 5) =           8;  took     0.00 seconds
fib_recursive( 5) =           8;  took     0.00 seconds
fib_iterative(10) =          89;  took     0.00 seconds
fib_recursive(10) =          89;  took     0.00 seconds
fib_iterative(15) =         987;  took     0.00 seconds
fib_recursive(15) =         987;  took     0.01 seconds
fib_iterative(20) =       10946;  took     0.00 seconds
fib_recursive(20) =       10946;  took     0.09 seconds
fib_iterative(25) =      121393;  took     0.00 seconds
fib_recursive(25) =      121393;  took     1.01 seconds
fib_iterative(30) =     1346269;  took     0.00 seconds
fib_recursive(30) =     1346269;  took    11.75 seconds
fib_iterative(35) =    14930352;  took     0.00 seconds
fib_recursive(35) =    14930352;  took   129.30 seconds
```

The speeds reported on your machine might vary, but even if you have very fast hardware, I don't recommend adjusting this script so that it goes up to 50. You'd have to wait a very long time for it to finish.

What's happening? The recursive function is doing some redundant work. To determine `fib_recursive(10)`, it has to calculate `fib_recursive(8)` twice. Do you see why? The plot thickens: Finding `fib_recursive(35)` involves recalculating `fib_recursive(5)` more than 100,000 times.

 Note

> It's not hard to verify something like this. Use an instance or global variable as a counter. Set it to zero before starting a recursive calculation. Inside the recursive function, add 1 to the variable whenever some condition is met (in this case, whenever n == 5). Examine the variable after the calculation finishes.

Since the iterative version does the same job almost instantaneously, it might seem that attacking a problem recursively is just too impractical to bother with. But since recursive thinking is often so much simpler, it sure would be nice if we could find a way to make it efficient as well. (Drum roll. . .)

Memoization

No, that's not a typo. *Memoization* is a technique for eliminating the performance penalty from recursive code. Here's the idea: Even though recursively calculating elements of the Fibonacci sequence is slow because certain elements get recalculated over and over, the results of those calculations don't change; `fib(5)` is always 8 no matter how many times you crank it out. So why not store each new result somewhere and reuse it later?

Typically when you memoize, you start with an ordinary recursive algorithm but then add on a simple data structure like an array or a hash. In the example in Listing 12.2 an array is suitable. Initially we make it empty. Every time the recursive function is called, it first looks in the array to see whether it has already calculated the answer that is being asked for. If so, it just returns it. If not, it fills that array slot and then returns the answer. Each calculation is done exactly once.

LISTING 12.2   fib_test_2.rb

```
01:  #!/usr/bin/env/ruby
02:
03:  # A performance test of recursively calculating elements
04:  # of the Fibonacci sequence, with and without memoizing.
05:
06:  # Iterative version
07:  def fib_iterative(n)
08:    if n<2
09:      1
10:    else
11:      prev_1 = prev_2 = 1
12:      new_elt = 0            # (scope is important, value isn't)
13:      2.upto(n) do
14:        new_elt = prev_1 + prev_2       # get the newest element
15:        prev_1,prev_2 = prev_2,new_elt  # update the stored elements
16:      end
17:      new_elt
18:    end
19:  end
20:
21:  # Recursive version with memoization
22:  @memo = []    # initially empty results array
23:  def fib_memoized(n)
24:    # If we don't already know the answer, we have to find it.
25:    if not @memo[n]
26:      if n<2
27:        @memo[n] = 1
28:      else
29:        @memo[n] = fib_memoized(n-2) + fib_memoized(n-1)
30:      end
31:    end
32:
33:    # At this point, we always have a stored answer to return.
34:    @memo[n]
35:  end
36:
37:  5.step(35,5) do |n|
38:    t_start = Time.now
39:    answer = fib_iterative(n)
```

continues

LISTING 12.2 Continued

```
40:     t_end = Time.now
41:
42:     printf "fib_iterative(%2d) = %10d;  took %7.2f seconds\n",
43:       n,answer,t_end-t_start
44:
45:     t_start = Time.now
46:     answer = fib_memoized(n)
47:     t_end = Time.now
48:
49:     printf "fib_memoized(%2d)  = %10d;  took %7.2f seconds\n",
50:       n,answer,t_end-t_start
51:
52:   end
```

Running the script, we find that memoization gives us, at least in this case, the best of both worlds. We still solve the problem recursively, but the performance is more like that of the more difficult iterative approach:

```
fib_iterative( 5) =          8;  took   0.00 seconds
fib_memoized( 5) =           8;  took   0.00 seconds
fib_iterative(10) =         89;  took   0.00 seconds
fib_memoized(10) =          89;  took   0.00 seconds
fib_iterative(15) =        987;  took   0.00 seconds
fib_memoized(15) =         987;  took   0.00 seconds
fib_iterative(20) =      10946;  took   0.00 seconds
fib_memoized(20) =       10946;  took   0.00 seconds
fib_iterative(25) =     121393;  took   0.00 seconds
fib_memoized(25) =      121393;  took   0.00 seconds
fib_iterative(30) =    1346269;  took   0.00 seconds
fib_memoized(30) =     1346269;  took   0.00 seconds
fib_iterative(35) =   14930352;  took   0.00 seconds
fib_memoized(35) =    14930352;  took   0.00 seconds
```

The Towers of Hanoi

You may have heard of this logic puzzle involving three vertical pegs and a some disks of various sizes. All disks start on the same peg, arranged in order of size, biggest on the bottom. The object is to move all the disks to another peg, but you can move only one disk at a time, and you must never place a larger disk on top of a smaller one.

It's extremely difficult to solve the Towers problem if you don't think recursively. One of the legends about the puzzle is that a despot, faced with solving it, called in a close advisor who was supposed to be pretty smart, and asked for his help. The advisor said, "Oh, that's easy; to move seven disks from the first peg to the last, first move the top six disks to the middle peg, then move the bottom disk to the last peg, and then move those six disks again to the last peg." The despot decided he was being mocked—how can those six disks be moved all at once? So the story goes, he had the advisor beheaded.

The advisor actually had the right idea. The thinking behind recursion, always, is to deal with the simplest case when it's in front of you, and when it's not, to find a way to reduce the problem just a little bit. To move a stack of n disks, if $n = 1$, you just move that one disk; it's your simplest case. Otherwise, what you have to do is "recursively" move the top $n - 1$ disks to an intermediate peg, move the bottom disk by itself, then "recursively" move the $n - 1$ disks again. That's all there is to it; you don't have to worry about how the recursive part works.

Many solutions to the Towers problem have been written as computer programs. Some of them are extremely short, occupying less than a dozen lines of code. The central logic of our solution will be about that simple, but we'll build some animation into it, too, just for fun.

You'll need an ANSI terminal to run this. ANSI is the standard terminal type for Unix machines, and it's also provided with Windows. In some Windows installations, ANSI works "out of the box;" for instance, this is usually true for Windows 98. To test whether your Windows terminal is ANSI-enabled, run this one-liner from the command prompt:

```
ruby -e 'print "\e[7m REVERSE VIDEO \e[m"'
```

The message "REVERSE VIDEO" should appear with foreground and background colors reversed, typically black on white, and the "\e[7m" and "\e[m" should *not* appear. Otherwise, you'll need to configure your system to use ANSI. Here's one way to do it.

Locate the file named ANSI.SYS, perhaps by selecting Find after right-clicking My Computer on the desktop. Now use Notepad or another text editor to load C:\CONFIG.SYS (in Windows 95, 98, or ME) or %systemroot%\system32\CONFIG.NT (in all other Windows versions). Edit the file so it includes a line like the following, adjusted according to where you found ANSI.SYS:

```
DEVICE=C:\WINDOWS\COMMAND\ANSI.SYS
```

You may have to reboot to make the change effective. The next time you open a command window, it should be ANSI-enabled. (Some Windows 2000 users report that they must use command.com as the command shell instead of cmd.exe to make ANSI work.)

12

The organization of our solution will be centered around `Peg` objects. To keep things simple, a `Peg` will have just three methods that matter to the outside world:

1. `initialize(position, size)`

   When a new `Peg` is created, `position` will determine which peg of the puzzle it is (either 0, 1, or 2), and `size` will determine how many disks it can hold. If `position` is 0, the peg is given a full pile of disks; otherwise it's empty.

2. `drop(size)`

   Drop disk of the given size onto the peg.

3. `lift`

   Lift the top disk off the peg and return its size.

The `Peg` class will take care of all the display details, so for now we'll concentrate on the high-level logic of the job, in a script you can save with filename `towers.rb` (see Listing 12.3). It will use the `Peg` interface described previously. We'll worry about the workings of the `Peg` class a little later.

LISTING 12.3　`towers.rb`

```
01:    #!/usr/local/bin/ruby
02:
03:    # A Ruby script to solve and animate the Towers of Hanoi puzzle.
04:
05:    require 'peg'
06:
07:    def main
08:      # Get user input for initial height, defaulting to 7.
09:      @height = (ARGV[0] or 7).to_i
10:
11:      # Make an array of three Peg objects.
12:      @pegs = [0,1,2].map {|x| Peg.new(x,@height)}
13:
14:      sleep 2                 # Take a little pause for drama ...
15:      move_tower(0,2,@height)  # ... then move the stack!
16:    end
17:
18:    # Recursive function to move the top 'n' disks
19:    #    from peg 'src' to peg 'dst'.
20:    #
21:    # In the recursive case:
22:    #    move all but the bottom disk to the intermediate peg,
23:    #    move the bottom disk to the destination peg,
24:    #    and then move the others on top of it.
25:    #
26:    # In the base case, just move that 1-disk stack.
```

LISTING 12.3 Continued

```
27:    #
28:    def move_tower(src, dst, n)
29:      if n>1    # RECURSIVE CASE
30:        intermediate = 3 - (src + dst)      # think about it...
31:        move_tower(src, intermediate, n-1)
32:        @pegs[dst].drop(@pegs[src].lift)
33:        move_tower(intermediate, dst, n-1)
34:      else      # BASE CASE
35:        @pegs[dst].drop(@pegs[src].lift)
36:      end
37:    end
38:
39:    main  # Script actually executes here.
```

towers.rb employs a simple top-down code structure. A function named main expresses the basic agenda. Support functions are below that, and the whole thing gets underway when main gets invoked at the bottom. This kind of script is one you can look at and see what really happens without having to scroll down. Here, we have just one support function: move_tower, which does all the recursive work.

Now we'll put the Peg class into a file named peg.rb (see Listing 12.4). We'll assume the existence of an ANSI module that will know how to place the cursor, clear the screen, and so on. Every ANSI method or constant yields a string that we can print to STDOUT. The constants Reset, Clear, Normal, Bold, and so on do what their names suggest. The methods fore_color and back_color will take a single numeric argument and set the text foreground or background color accordingly. For cursor placement, we'll have a locate function.

12

LISTING 12.4   peg.rb

```
01:  require 'ansi'
02:
03:  class Peg
04:    include ANSI
05:
06:    # Create a peg in position 'c' that can hold 'n' disks.
07:    def initialize(c,n)
08:      print Clear if c==0
09:      @contents = []
10:      @column = c
11:      @disks = n
12:      1.upto(n+1) {|p| show_blank(p)}  # show the peg, empty
13:      if c==0
14:        @delay = 0
```

continues

LISTING 12.4 Continued

```
15:         n.downto(1) {|disk| drop(disk)}
16:     end
17:     @delay = 2 ** (2-n)  # adjust delays to size of puzzle
18:   end
19:
20:   # Place a disk of width 'w' on the peg.
21:   def drop(w)
22:     @contents.push(w)
23:     show_disk(size,w,@delay)
24:   end
25:
26:   # Take a disk off the top of the peg, and return its width.
27:   def lift
28:     show_blank(size)
29:     @contents.pop
30:   end
31:
32:   ### PRIVATE METHODS FOLLOW.
33:   private
34:
35:   # Place the cursor at the given height on the peg.
36:   def set_cursor(position)
37:     print locate((@disks*2+2)*@column+4, @disks+4-position)
38:   end
39:
40:   # Show a disk at position 'p' with width 'w'; delay 'd' seconds.
41:   def show_disk(p,w,d)
42:     set_cursor p
43:     print " "*(@disks-w)
44:     print back_color(1+(w % 6))  # map disk widths to colors
45:     print " "*(w*2+1)
46:     print Normal
47:     update
48:     sleep d
49:   end
50:
51:   # Erase the disk at position 'p'.
52:   def show_blank(p)
53:     set_cursor p
54:     print Normal
55:     print " "*@disks + "|" + " "*@disks
56:     update
57:   end
58:
59:   # Return the occupancy of the peg.
60:   def size
61:     @contents.size
62:   end
```

LISTING 12.4 Continued

```
63:
64:    # Update the display.
65:    def update
66:      print locate(1,1)
67:      STDOUT.flush
68:    end
69:
70:  end
```

There was no pressing need to have the Peg class in a separate file; it's obviously tailored for use in the Towers of Hanoi puzzle, so we could have as easily defined Peg in the main towers.rb file. It is prudent, though, to have the ANSI module in its own file, because basic ANSI functionality might be reusable in all kinds of contexts. It's a cheap way to get some simple, portable graphics when ordinary text doesn't quite do what you want.

This module in Listing 12.5, to be saved as ansi.rb, has a little more functionality than is needed by the Towers of Hanoi puzzle:

LISTING 12.5 ansi.rb

```
01:  # A very simple ANSI module.
02:  # This could be enhanced considerably.
03:
04:  module ANSI
05:    Reset         = 27.chr + "c"
06:    PRE           = 27.chr + "["   # the ubiquitous ANSI escape prefix
07:    Clear         = PRE + "2J"
08:    Normal        = PRE + "0m"
09:    Bold          = PRE + "1m"
10:    LowIntensity  = PRE + "2m"
11:    Underline     = PRE + "4m"
12:    Blinking      = PRE + "5m"
13:    Reversed      = PRE + "7m"
14:    Up            = PRE + "A"
15:    Down          = PRE + "B"
16:    Right         = PRE + "C"
17:    Left          = PRE + "D"
18:    Home          = PRE + "H"
19:    WrapOn        = PRE + "?7h"
20:    WrapOff       = PRE + "?7l"
21:
22:    def fore_color( c )
23:      sprintf "%s3%dm",PRE,c
24:    end
```

12

continues

LISTING 12.5 Continued

```
25:   def back_color( c )
26:     sprintf "%s4%dm",PRE,c
27:   end
28:   def locate( x, y )
29:     sprintf "%s%d;%df",PRE,y,x
30:   end
31: end
```

This is a substantial project and lives in three files. You might want to test it first on a simple version of the problem:

    C:\RUBY>**ruby towers.rb 4**

If you don't specify a size, the default is 7 disks. The fixed dimensions of a terminal in DOS/Windows means you can get only up to 12 disks on a peg before the display runs out of horizontal room. Figure 12.1 shows `towers.rb` hard at work after being started with 12 disks.

If you are using some kind of an X terminal in Unix, you might try resizing it and animating a larger version of the puzzle (but remember that each time you add a disk, you double the number of moves it takes).

FIGURE 12.1

`towers.rb` *in action.*

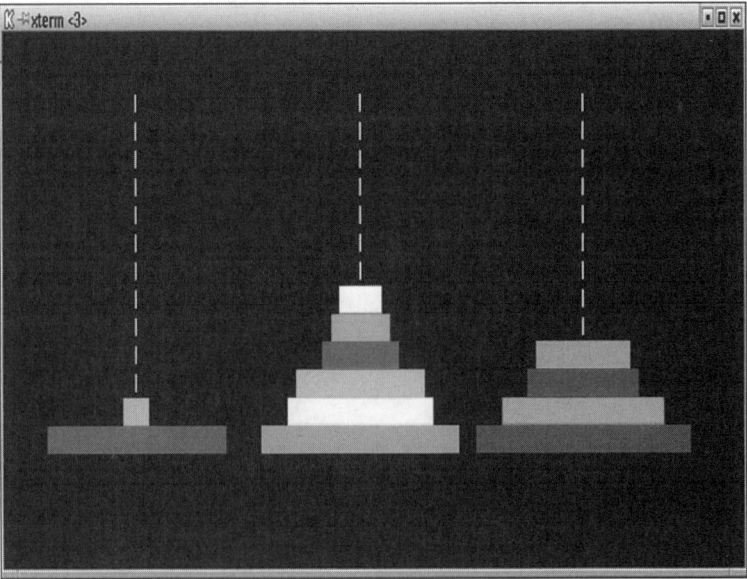

Summary

Today we learned about recursion and discussed its advantages and disadvantages. We explored memoization as a way to make recursive code remember past results, thus speeding it up dramatically in some situations.

Remember, recursion is your friend. Faced with a journey of a great distance, the iterative thinker says "This is going to take a lot of steps," but the recursive thinker says "I will take one step, then start a brand-new journey that is slightly shorter than this one." Guess who suffers less stress.

When you have a knotty logic problem in front of you, be on the lookout for ways to divide it into a recurrence relation (what "one step" in the solution should look like) and a base case (how you can recognize when the task is almost done). If you can do that, you can solve your problem recursively.

Tomorrow we'll get into a challenging and rewarding topic, which is the use of Ruby to get a grip on a computer's operating system. We'll be creating and managing multiple processes, and learning to take advantage of system tools and information.

Exercises

1. Factorials are defined for all positive integers. So why didn't we make `factorial` a method of the `Integer` class? Wouldn't it work just as well? After all, `Fixnum` is a subclass of `Integer`.

2. Is there any particular reason we used `upto` instead of `downto` in the iterative version of the factorial method? *Hint:* Think about error conditions.

3. In the memoized version of the Fibonacci sequence test, why is `@memo` an instance variable, and why is it initialized outside the function? Is it possible to do the same thing with a local variable?

4. This exercise is rather silly and useless; it's just here as a warmup for the next exercise, which will be slightly meatier.

   Write a recursive function that returns the length of a string. The only `String` instance methods you're allowed to use are `empty?` and `chop` (using `length` or `size` is definitely cheating). The function should behave as follows. (*Hint:* The length of a string is 0 if it's empty; otherwise it's the length of a slightly shorter string, plus 1.)

   ```
   length_recursive("")       #-> 0
   length_recursive("rhythm") #-> 6
   ```

12

Alternatively, you can make it a new instance method of the `String` class so that it is invoked like this:

```
"Snark".length_recursive     #-> 5
```

5. Below is a `Node` class and code to create some `Node` instances. The nodes form a kind of tree with one "root" and many "leaves." Each node has a value, which is just a number, and optionally some children.[1]

```
class Node
  attr_reader :value
  attr_accessor :children

  def initialize(v)
    @value = v
    @children = []
  end
end

a = Node.new 12     # Make some nodes with some values.
b = Node.new 9
c = Node.new 34
d = Node.new 31
e = Node.new 5
f = Node.new 12

a.children = [b,c]   # Make a the parent of b and c.
c.children = [d,e,f] # Make c the parent of d, e and f.
```

The last two lines establish family hierarchy. Conventionally, a tree is drawn upside down, with the "root" at the top and the "leaves" at the bottom. The tree generated by this code is visualized in Figure 12.2.

FIGURE 12.2

A tree with six nodes.

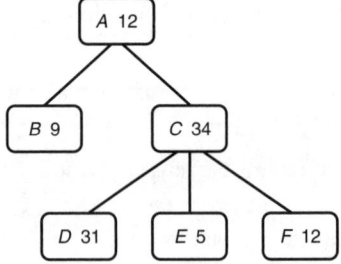

---

[1]*Yes, that's a mixed metaphor. The root is the parent of whatever nodes are directly attached to it. To be a leaf means to have no children.*

The Node class already has an instance method value (created by attr_reader) that returns the value of any individual node.

```
a.value  #-> 12
c.value  #-> 34
e.value  #-> 5
```

Your job is to write another instance method that finds the value of a node added to the values of all its descendants. Call it subtree_value. Look at the following sample results, and make sure you know what's going on before trying to solve the problem. Notice that a is the ancestor of the whole tree, so a.subtree_value should be the values of all the nodes added together. c has a few children; e is childless.

```
a.subtree_value  #-> 103
c.subtree_value  #-> 82
e.subtree_value  #-> 5
```

As with most recursive solutions, this one is quite simple once you see it (which makes it that much more frustrating if you don't see it, of course). If you come up with a solution that seems to work, test it on some more trees of your own.

Answers

1. *n*! is a function that grows extremely fast as n grows. For example, 1000!, which looks manageable at first glance, turns out to be more than 2,000 digits long when multiplied out. The factorial of any Bignum would be so big that it would not be representable as any kind of number Ruby knows about.

2. If we used downto and tried to find the factorial of a negative number, the function would get stuck in a pattern of infinite recursion, multiplying by numbers that were more and more negative. Eventually, Ruby would run out of "stack space" and stop, which, while a little less unpleasant than the consequences of a true infinite loop, is still less than ideal behavior. To be completely correct, we might put the following line at the top of the function, and then it won't matter which iterator we use:

```
return nil if n<0
```

3. This boils down to an issue of scope. If we made memo a local variable for the fib_memoized function, it would be created and destroyed each time the function ran. If we think of the function as running lots of copies of itself at the same time, then each copy of the function has its own array, which is guaranteed to be empty when tested for previous answers. We need the scope of @memo to extend a little farther; this way it gets created only once and can accumulate information over many function calls.

12

4. Look at the hint again. It can be translated almost directly to code.

```
def length_recursive(s)
  if s.empty?
    0
  else
    length_recursive(s.chop) + 1
  end
end
```

Here's the same solution as a `String` instance method.

```
class String
  def length_recursive
    if self.empty?
      0
    else
      (self.chop).length_recursive + 1
    end
  end
end
```

5. Remember that recursion works by invoking slightly smaller versions of the original problem. So you don't really want to try to add the values of all descendants of the node you started with directly; that's iterative thinking, and in this case it would make your job very difficult. Rather, add up the subtree values of the immediate children of the node you started with. Don't work harder; work smarter! That's recursive thinking.

```
class Node
  def subtree_value
    total = @value
      children.each {|c| total += c.subtree_value}
    total
  end
end
```

DAY **13**

Mastering the Operating System

I'm king of a house! And, what's more, beyond that,
I'm king of a blueberry bush and a cat!

—Dr. Seuss, *Yertle the Turtle*

We've referred to Ruby as a "glue language" a couple of times, and now let's flesh out what that means. Today's material is a little more difficult than most of what we have dealt with so far, and none of it is really essential to learning the Ruby language, so don't despair if you have some trouble following along. But being able to interact fluently with the operating system and the facilities it provides can give you one heady feeling.

Motivation

Many complicated tasks are best handled by delegating parts here and there. An automobile manufacturing plant doesn't build a vehicle from scratch; it buys assemblies from other plants, builds others, and assembles them all into a car.

Similarly, a program file written in C is not directly changed into an executable program file in one step; a preprocessor, compiler, linker, assembler, and optimizer each handle a part of the process. Whenever responsibilities are split, somebody or something has to coordinate the work.

Most of us are system administrators to some extent: We keep our computers running, clean up after unexpected problems, install and uninstall applications, and so on. In the Windows world, some of these tasks are taken care of by supplied system programs and the rest is usually left to rebooting, so detailed administration is rendered in one sense impossible and in another sense unnecessary. The Unix operating system, on the other hand, as all of its administrators and many of its users know, is much more accessible and controllable, but on the debit side there's an old axiom in technology: "Anything you *can* control you *must* control." We have a strong motivation to find ways to automate administration duties flexibly.

Finally, there is the matter of performance. A *parallelized* script is one arranged in such a way that there are different subtasks running at what appears to be the same time. When a computer has a single microprocessor, there's no way for two things really to be happening at once (the operating system interleaves tasks by rapidly switching between them), so it might seem a waste of effort to arrange things so that two subtasks run together but each at half speed. In practice, however, each subtask needs more resources than just the processor. If a subtask has to wait for some event to happen over the network or for a disk drive to complete a seek, another subtask may be able to make use of that otherwise wasted time.

We call Ruby, Perl, and some others "*glue languages*" because they make it possible to coordinate the actions of several programs. If we are to be precise, we should say *process* where we've usually been saying *program,* because we will soon see programs that can reproduce themselves, so as far as the operating system is concerned, one program may account for many processes.

Ruby also provides powerful tools for gathering system information: It's a simple matter to look at a disk directory or a group of directories, even with all their subdirectories, learn the search path for executables, find out about the existence, the size, and other characteristics of a file, and so on.

Portability Notes

As mentioned earlier in the book, Ruby's primary development began and remains in the Unix world, and the language has since been adapted to other platforms. Most of what we see today is tailored for Unix, and parts are not entirely portable. A few of the Unix-specific features will work under Windows when run from within the Cygwin `bash` shell. Since some of today's examples will be given in more than one variant form, you might find that one form or another is better suited to a Windows environment.

To turn the tables around, Windows itself is not without its modular aspects. Ruby comes with Object Linking and Embedding (OLE) support that allows it to be used as a Windows glue language, too.

 **Note**   In the Windows world, the work of glue languages is usually called *automation*. The Win32OLE package was developed by Masaki Suketa.

Gathering Information

Some primary sources of system information for your scripts are the `ENV` object, the `Dir` and `File` classes, and the `Find` module.

Every Ruby script has access to a special body of data known as the *environment*. It contains information that may vary from machine to machine or user to user, arranged as pairs of strings. For instance, "`COLUMNS`" might be associated with "`80`" to indicate that a standard-width terminal is in use. All this information is accessed through a special object named `ENV`. It behaves like a hash: We can access any value by enclosing the associated key in square brackets:

```
ENV['LINES'] #-> 24    (this is 25 in DOS/Windows, typically)
ENV['HOME']  #-> /home/slagell
```

Of special interest is `ENV['PATH']`. It is a colon-separated list of directories that are to be searched when a new application is run. You may know that the DOS PATH is traditionally semicolon-separated because directory names may contain colons, but for the sake of portability, Ruby does a small transformation on DOS directory names, so in every case we can use Unix naming conventions. (Actually, it is the Cygwin compatibility layer under the most popular Windows Ruby distribution that is responsible for this. Not all Windows Ruby distributions will necessarily do it exactly the same way.) Backslashes are turned forward, and drive letters are substituted with a standard prefix. For example, `C:\LOCAL\BIN` becomes `/cygdrive/c/local/bin`.

There was a time when reading a disk directory was a tedious task involving multiple system calls and complicated data structures, but not any longer. The `Dir.entries` class method will read any directory you specify and return the results all at once in an array.

13

```
# Suppose the current directory contains:
# file1, file2, dirA/file3, dirA/file4, dirB/file5, dirB/file6

# '.' always refers to the current directory.
# '..' refers to the 'parent' directory, one level up.
Dir.entries('.') #-> [".", "..", "file1", "file2", "dirA", "dirB"]
Dir.entries('dirA') #-> [".", "..", "file3", "file4"]
```

Find.find also searches directories, but does so recursively, including the contents of subdirectories in the search. It does not return an array; instead, Find.find is an iterator, so you supply a block that is to be applied to each filename. The following example below prints only the filenames, but if you want an array of all the names, you have to collect that information using the iterator code (see Exercise 1 at the end of the Day). The Find module is not automatically included in your scripts, so you have to ask for it.

```
require 'find'

Find.find('.') {|filename| puts filename}
 # output:
  .
  ./dirB
  ./dirB/file6
  ./dirB/file5
  ./dirA
  ./dirA/file4
  ./dirA/file3
  ./file2
  ./file1
```

Specific directories may be excluded from the search by pruning inside the iterator block:

```
Find.find('.') do |fn|
 if fn == './dirA'
  File.prune
 else
  puts fn
 end
end
 # output:
  .
  ./dirB
  ./dirB/file6
  ./dirB/file5
  ./file2
  ./file1
```

The `File` class mixes in the `FileTest` module, which gives you quick information about files. Most of its methods answer yes-or-no questions, for example:

`File.exists?(name)`	Does the file exist?
`File.directory?(name)`	Is it a directory?
`File.executable?(name)`	Is it either an executable program or a directory?
`File.writable?(name)`	Am I allowed to write to it?

Treating Programs as Functions

If you've ever written even a very simple DOS batch file or Unix shell script, you're familiar with the idea of calling an external program as if it were a function. That's primarily what shell scripts are for:

```
#!/bin/sh

# A typical Unix shell script
echo "I'm going to call two other programs now."
prog1        # execute a program named prog1
prog2        # then another program named prog2
echo "All done."
```

We need to make note of two things before moving on. The first point is that it doesn't matter what language those external programs were written in. They might be compiled programs, Ruby scripts, or scripts in some other language. Secondly, the operation of `prog1` and `prog2` is sequential. In other words, `prog1` has to finish running (or more precisely, return control) before `prog2` can start, and the "all done" message doesn't appear until after `prog2` finishes.

One way to write shell scripts in Ruby is with the Kernel module's `system` method:

```
#!/usr/bin/env ruby

puts "I'm going to call two other programs now."
system("prog1")
system("prog2")
puts "All done."
```

13

Standard command shells like `tcsh` and `sh` lack some of the control structures that we have come to rely on after learning a general-purpose language. In most command shells it tends to be cumbersome to express something like "execute the following command a hundred times." But Ruby's iterators can be mixed freely with external calls. For instance, we can take readings of the number of users logged on to a Unix system over the space of one minute like this:

```
6.times { system('who | wc -l'); sleep 10 }
```

Note

> External programs might exist in one operating system and not in another, which naturally raises portability issues. Also, some commands (such as mkdir) span operating systems, but in Unix they are implemented as separate programs, whereas they are hidden inside the command processor in DOS/Windows. In such a case you can try launching a separate command processor in DOS, perhaps using ENV['COMSPEC'] /C command.

Kernel.system's return value is true or false depending on whether the command succeeded—that is to say, whether it finished "normally" or with some kind of error code. (A false return value can also mean the program that was invoked couldn't be found.) When we invoke another program, it is usually because we are interested in what it has to say, so, instead of letting that program write to the screen, it would be nice to be able to capture its standard output in a string. We'll see how that's done in a moment, but before going any further, let's write a couple of simple Ruby scripts that we can refer to in examples. Save the following script as greet.rb:

```
#!/usr/bin/env ruby
puts "Greetings from sunny Spain."
```

Now save this one as repeat.rb:

```
#!/usr/bin/env ruby
input = gets.chomp
doubled = input.gsub(/(.)/, '\1\1')
puts doubled
```

If you invoke these scripts using system, they will run as if you had typed their names at the command line. Because repeat.rb requires input, it will stop and wait for you to type something. Both scripts send their output to the screen:

```
system("greet.rb")
  # output:
    Greetings from sunny Spain.
system("repeat.rb")
  # you must type something here ...
    As You Like It
  # output:
    AAss YYoouu LLiikkee IItt
```

The above assumes you've made `greet.rb` and `repeat.rb` executable in a Unix environment, typically by using the `chmod` command and making sure the current directory (`'.'`)
is in the `PATH`. Otherwise you must invoke the Ruby interpreter with the name of the
script as a command line argument, for example, `system("ruby repeat.rb")`.

Without getting too deep into the workings of shells here, it's possible to redirect a pro-
gram's input from the outside by using the vertical bar (pipe) character (`|`); we say we
"pipe" input to the program:

```
system("greet.rb")
system("echo Pipe-job | repeat.rb")
 # output:
   Greetings from sunny Spain.
   PPiippee--jjoobb
```

The `system` method is rarely used in practice, because quoting with "backticks" is more
useful and requires fewer keystrokes. The *backtick* is the backward-sloping single quote
character (`` ` ``) typically found above the Tab key on a U.S. keyboard. To surround a
command with backticks is to capture its output; that is to say, it makes a Ruby
expression whose value is the output of the command. Output no longer goes straight
to the screen:

```
gr = `greet.rb`
 # output: none, but gb now refers to
 # the string "Greetings from sunny Spain."
```

If you don't like the look of backticks (or if for some reason you'd like to use backticks
themselves as part of a quoted command), an alternate syntax for `` `command` `` is
`%x{command}`. Think of the x as meaning *execute*. In either syntax, the command is
processed like a double-quoted string before execution, so special characters can be
escaped, variables evaluated, and so on. We can capture the output of one script, modify it
if needed, and feed it to the other:

```
intermediate = `greet.rb`
final = `echo #{intermediate.chomp.upcase} | repeat.rb`
 #-> GGRREEEETTIINNGGSS FFRROOOMM SSUUNNNNYY SSPPAAIINN..
```

External programs can duplicate many of Ruby's built-in features, but it's better to stay
inside the language when possible. `` `ls` `` will generally do a fine job telling you the contents of the current working directory on a Unix system, but `Dir.entries('.')` is
portable. It also happens to be more secure: If somebody has stealthily broken into your
computer, then there will be system commands that can't be trusted (typically `ps`, `ls`,
and a few others), but it's very unlikely that a hacker will have thought to install Trojan
substitutes for your Ruby interpreter or libraries.

13

Extended Conversations

There's a definite limitation to the kind of communication just shown. It's fine if one program has to ask another a single question and it is satisfied with that, but what if some slightly more involved protocol needs to be negotiated? Consider a meeting between spy1 and spy2, who have never before seen each other face to face. spy1 needs a secret from spy2. spy2 is willing to tell the secret but needs to be assured of the identity of spy1, and spy1 isn't entirely sure of the identity of spy2 either. Consequently, when planning to meet for the first time, they agree on specific pleasantries that will be exchanged before getting down to business. If either spy says the wrong thing during the first three messages, somebody must be an impostor, and the deal stops right there.

spy1: What are Bostonians wearing this winter?

spy2: The mice got into the bread pudding again.

spy1: Your children must be very happy.

spy2: Okay, here's what you need to know. . .

We're going to model this conversation with a pair of scripts. If the spy1 script uses backticks to exchange information with spy2, they can get only as far as the bread pudding, because spy2 has to be done running before spy1 can move on to the next message.

To have a true conversation in which each script is able to wait for the other one, we need a way to overlap their execution in time. Ruby's IO module has a popen method that does that. It starts another program running and returns an IO object, which is a stream that can be written to, read from, and closed just like a file.

Conventionally we refer to the processes now as parent and child; the parent is the one that used popen. When the parent wants to say something to the child, it writes to the IO stream, and the child reads it as standard input. When the child wants to say something to the parent, it writes to its standard output, and the parent reads it from the IO stream. The *p* in popen refers to the *pipes* through which the two communicate. There is one pipe going each direction.

Let's start with spy2.rb in Listing 13.1. Since it communicates only through STDIN and STDOUT, it's the simpler of the two to write, and we'll be able to test it without creating pipes.

FIGURE 13.1

Pipes and IO objects.

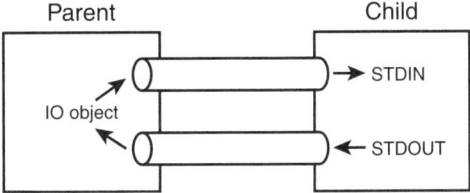

LISTING 13.1 spy2.rb

```
01:  #!/usr/bin/env ruby
02:
03:  m1 = gets.chomp
04:  if m1 =~ /Bostonians/
05:    puts "The mice got into the bread pudding again."; STDOUT.flush
06:    m3 = gets.chomp
07:    if m3 =~ /children.+happy/
08:      puts "The secret ingredient is boric acid."
09:    else
10:      puts "No secrets for you!"
11:    end
12:  else
13:    puts "Pardon me, I thought I knew you."
14:  end
```

There's just one odd thing here. STDOUT is usually buffered to help performance, and in certain situations we need to force the information to be nudged out of the buffer to prevent conversation from dragging to a halt. When STDOUT is really the screen, this isn't usually a problem, because in that case there's an automatic flush every time a newline character comes through. In this example an explicit flush is necessary only after the first reply (line 5), because after the next one, spy2.rb ends its execution, resulting in a flush. As we'll see in a moment however, it's possible to tell Ruby not to buffer STDOUT, so that all output appears immediately.

Before writing spy1.rb, let's test spy2.rb by itself, entering input as if we were *spy1*:

```
%ruby spy2.rb
What's up?
Pardon me, I thought I knew you.

%ruby spy2.rb
What are the Bostonians wearing this year?
The mice got into the bread pudding again.
Darn those mice.
No secrets for you!
```

13

```
%ruby spy2.rb
What are the Bostonians wearing this year?
The mice got into the bread pudding again.
Your children must be very happy.
The secret ingredient is boric acid.
```

Now that we're confident spy2.rb understands the protocol, here's spy1.rb (Listing 13.2). It is the coordinating or "glue" script in this example, not because it initiates conversation, but because it starts spy2.rb running in the first place. (Imagine *spy1* waking *spy2*, who has been asleep on a park bench.)

LISTING 13.2   spy1.rb

```
01:  #!/usr/bin/env ruby
02:
03:  companion = IO.popen("ruby spy2.rb","w+")
04:
05:  companion.puts "What are Bostonians wearing this winter?"
06:  m2 = companion.gets.chomp
07:  if m2 =~ /bread pudding/
08:    companion.puts "Your children must be very happy."
09:    secret = companion.gets.chomp
10:  else
11:    companion.puts "Pardon me, I thought I knew you."
12:  end
13:
14:  puts "Mission accomplished: #{secret}"
15:  companion.close
```

The close at the end is not strictly necessary, but it's good discipline to close whatever you open.

When we test the scripts together (by running only spy1.rb), we don't see the conversation between them, just the final result from *spy1*'s perspective:

```
%ruby spy1.rb
Mission accomplished: The secret ingredient is boric acid.
```

Here's a case when we can take advantage of STDERR (which was introduced in Day 6). When trying to debug a child invoked by popen, we can't simply use puts to display messages, because STDOUT no longer points to the screen. STDERR, however, has not been redirected; anything sent to STDERR is going to appear on the screen to facilitate debugging. To verify that the first message arrived at the child through a pipe, we can do this:

```
m1 = gets.chomp; STDERR.puts m1
```

Or we could make the printing of debugging info conditional on the $DEBUG flag, which depends on the Ruby interpreter being launched with the -d switch (but be careful—two interpreters are running, so make sure that the right one gets the switch turned on, or that both do).

```
m1 = gets.chomp; STDERR.puts m1 if $DEBUG
```

 Note See Appendix C for a more extended discussion of debugging techniques.

The Art of Instant Reproduction

Something special happens when we supply the special filename "-" to IO.popen. Instead of starting an external program, the Ruby interpreter makes an exact copy of itself as a new process, running the same script as before:

```
IO.popen("-", "w+")

# Now there are two of me!
["fee", "fie", "foe"].each {|x| STDERR.puts x}

 # output: feefee
          fie
          foe

          fie
          foe
```

The duplicate script does not start at the beginning but from the point immediately after the IO.popen call. Parent and child are running overlapped in time—or if you prefer, at the same time—so there is no guarantee of the order in which their output to STDERR will appear. That's why we see their output interleaved. Here, one has rudely interrupted the other before it can spit out the newline character at the end of its first output line.

The child is born with pretty much the same history as the parent, including the same variables with the same values, so it would seem hard to tell them apart. But there is a difference in the way the two handle their input and output. Remember, the child's STDIN and STDOUT are its way of getting to the communication pipes that connect it with the parent (which is why the child had to use STDERR to send something to the screen). The parent gets to those pipes by referring to the IO object that was returned by IO.popen. When the child starts running, it thinks it is the one that just completed an

13

IO.popen call, but it can have no real use for the return value, so the value it gets is nil. That's handy. As we see in the following example, it gives the parent and child a way to determine who is who.

```
who = IO.popen("-","w+")
if who.nil?
  sleep .5  # (Pause to show respect for my elders!)
  STDERR.puts "I am the child."
else
  puts "I am the parent."
  who.close
end

# output:
 I am the parent.
 I am the child.
```

We've introduced a short pause into the child's code to keep it from interrupting the parent. But also notice that we haven't been using the pipes at all. If parent and child have no particular need to communicate, then IO.popen might be more than we need.

A more primitive way to do the same thing is with Kernel.fork. Just like IO.popen, fork splits a running program into two nearly identical processes that can be identified by the return value of the fork call. In contrast to IO.popen, the child's input and output are not redirected, and the return value to the parent is not an IO object, but something called a process identifier. A fork call is typically made like this:

```
pid = fork

if pid.nil?
  # child's code goes here
  ...
else
  # parent's code goes here
  ...
  Process.wait  # This will be explained shortly.
end
```

There's an alternative syntax for fork that you might prefer. Instead of testing the return value against nil, supply fork with a block of code. Only the child will run that block, and whatever follows it belongs to the parent:

```
fork do
  # child's code
  ...
end

# parent's code
...
Process.wait
```

Waiting for Children

We're nudging up against the mysteries of system programming here, but it's important for a parent to `wait` for its children to finish running before it stops. In the world of computer operating systems (in contrast to the way it's done in nature), parents are supposed to outlive their children. This is because parents are considered responsible for children, and irresponsible parents put the system at risk of accumulating a population of rogue processes, which have wonderful descriptive names like runaways, orphans, and even (shudder) zombies. Preventing this, as we'll see shortly, sometimes involves a presumptuous use of the process ID returned by `fork`.

The `Process.waitpid` method is more specific than `Process.wait`. It looks at a single child specified by ID, given as the first argument (whereas `Process.wait` waits for any child). If the second argument `Process::WNOHANG` is given, the method returns immediately and never really waits. Thus the parent can keep busy if a child dawdles. The return value of `Process.waitpid` indicates the state of the child: if `nil`, the child is still running:

```
STDOUT.sync = true  # Turn off buffering, make flushes unnecessary
kid = fork do
  print "Child about to sleep"
  sleep 1
  puts "child done sleeping."
end

sleep .1 # to allow for child's initial message
until Process.waitpid(kid, Process::WNOHANG)
  print "."
  sleep .1
end

# output:
 Child about to sleep.........child done sleeping.
```

Pipes

A highly flexible communication scheme is to use `fork` with pipes that you have created explicitly beforehand. `IO.pipe` returns a pair of `IO` objects, of which the first is read-only and the second is write-only. These objects represent the two ends of the pipe that was just created. If we create two pipes, we end up with four `IO` objects, which both the parent and the child can use to converse with each other after the `fork`. The effect is similar to `IO.popen`, but the child's standard IO streams are undisturbed, and piped messages are no longer subject to buffering concerns. Here's an example of communication with pipes after a `fork`.

13

```ruby
parent_to_child_in, parent_to_child_out = IO.pipe
child_to_parent_in, child_to_parent_out = IO.pipe

fork do
  # child code
  child_to_parent_out.puts "Hi, Mom!"
  reply = parent_to_child_in.gets.chomp
  puts "My Mom said: '#{reply}'"
end

# parent code
message = child_to_parent_in.gets.chomp
puts "My child said, '#{message}'"
parent_to_child_out.puts "Go to bed"
Process.wait

 # output:
 My child said, 'Hi, Mom!'
 My Mom said: 'Go to bed'
```

You may be wondering why pipes are considered unidirectional. After all, if they were bidirectional, we could get away with just one pipe, right? But then trouble would arise when a process sent a message and then immediately listened for a reply. If the sender listened on the same pipe it spoke into, then unless the receiver was very quick in pulling the message out, the sender might hear itself in the pipe and be unable to tell who was talking. Thus we need two pipes. To underscore the fact, it's considered good practice to make the parent and child close the ends of the pipes they know they won't use, immediately after the return from fork, like this:

```ruby
...
fork do
  child_to_parent_in.close  # child won't need these ...
  parent_to_child_out.close
  ...
end

child_to_parent_out.close  # and parent won't need these
parent_to_child_in.close
...
```

How to Control Your Children

One rather entertaining use for a child process is to convince the human user that something productive is happening during a long calculation. When generating large Fibonacci numbers using our old inefficient recursive function, it might be comforting to see a little spinning bar at the text cursor position until the answer comes back.

Mind you, our "progress spinner" isn't a real indication of progress. It's just eye candy, a little psychological trick. If the calculation somehow got stuck in an infinite loop, the spinner would keep spinning, giving false assurance that all was right with the world. (Think of it like the animation Windows shows when copying files on the desktop, or like that infamous "your call is very important to us" message loop you hear when you try to talk to someone at the phone company.) It is in fact the spinner that will be running in an infinite loop, and our challenge will be to stop it cleanly when the calculation is done.

We'll split this example into a top-level script and a few alternative Spinner class files, because we'll be trying different spinner implementations. Listing 13.3 is the main script, which creates a Spinner object for the duration of the calculation, then stops it.

LISTING 13.3 spintest.rb

```
01: #!/usr/bin/env ruby
02:
03: require 'spinner1' # Edit this line to try different spinners.
04:
05: # Our slow recursive Fibonacci function.
06: def fib(n) (n<=2) ? 1 : (fib(n-2)+fib(n-1)) end
07:
08: print "Please wait while I calculate a large Fibonacci number."
09:
10: animation = Spinner.new
11: result = fib(28)
12: animation.stop
13:
14: puts
15: puts result
```

Now it's time to figure out how to make spinners behave as they should.

Example Spinner #1, Using fork

Repeatedly displaying the sequence of characters \, |, / and - in the same position on the screen creates an animation of a bar rotating clockwise. When a Spinner object is created, it "forks off" a new child process whose job is to print a \ character at the cursor position, backspace, print |, backspace, and so on until the parent tells it to stop. But stopping is a little tricky. If we use fork without first creating pipes, there's no communication set up between parent and child. Still, we can rely on simple violence: since the parent knows its child's process ID, it can kill the child whenever it pleases, using Process.kill. (Being civilized folk, we should admit that we've strained the biological metaphor to the breaking point.) Save Listing 13.4 as spinner1.rb, and test it by running Listing 13.3, spintest.rb.

13

LISTING 13.4 spinner1.rb

```
01:  class Spinner
02:    Baton = '\|/-'
03:    def initialize
04:      STDOUT.flush
05:      @child = fork do
06:        trap('SIGHUP') do
07:          print " \b"
08:          STDOUT.flush
09:          exit!
10:        end
11:        rotation = 0
12:        loop do
13:          printf "%c\b", Baton[(rotation+=1) & 3]
14:          STDOUT.flush
15:          sleep .2
16:        end
17:      end
18:    end
19:
20:    def stop
21:      Process.kill 'SIGHUP', @child
22:    end
23:  end
```

There are some new techniques and subtleties here that could stand explaining.

First, trap('SIGHUP') in line 6 is a Unix idiom. trap sets aside a block of code to be executed only if a particular signal is received. There are various signals that processes may send to each other, and sighup is considered among the least impolite. The block attached to this trap says: "When given a 'hangup' signal, I should erase the last character of the animation, backspace to restore the cursor to its original place, flush the output stream, and quit." (See, despite the use of the word *kill*, the whole interaction is not really so violent after all.) Using exit! instead of exit is conventional for child processes. In this particular case it doesn't matter, but sometimes Ruby scripts are set up with one or more *exit handlers*, or pieces of code that always run at exit time. Usually these are relevant only to a parent process, so exit! prevents them from being run in the child.

Line 13 is a bit dense. Let's take it from the inner parentheses and work outward. rotation+=1 has a dual purpose. It increases the value of rotation by one, and it also returns that new value. When we do a bitwise *and* with 3, the result is to cycle through the values 0, 1, 2, 3 over and over again. It's just a faster way of getting the remainder of rotation/4. Since the contents of the square brackets always evaluates to a number between 0 and 3, `Baton[(rotation+=1) & 3]` returns a single character from the `Baton` string. The `%c` in the `printf` format string makes sure the character gets printed as a character instead of as a numeric ASCII value, and `\b` is the backspace that keeps the animation from wandering across the screen. The line could have been broken up like this:

```
rotation = rotation + 1
remainder = rotation % 4
char_to_print = Baton[remainder]
printf "%c\b", char_to_print
```

Have you tried running `spintest.rb` (Listing 13.3) yet? Good. It even works under Windows, surprisingly—well, it almost works. The spinner leaves a little mess behind in some cases.

If you're running Unix and feeling brave, try it again but with the `Process.kill` line removed or commented out. What happens? Uh-oh. A runaway process! The child is still spinning a baton, and you've just animated your text cursor. To stop it, you can either close the window, or find and kill the child process. You might run the `ps` command to find the process ID of the still-running Ruby interpreter, and `kill` that, or you might get away with just saying `killall ruby`.

The moral here is that `fork`ing is not a thing to be done carelessly. Parents need to be good citizens and diligently keep track of their children. The stakes are particularly high when a `fork` is done inside some kind of loop structure, as with the one-line script `loop {fork}`. That's known as an *Evil Wabbit*. It goes on reproducing forever and wreaking all kinds of havoc, at least on operating systems that lack good safeguards against wabbits.

Example Spinner #2, Using `IO.popen`

If we use `IO.popen` instead of `fork` to start the child process, then there is a communication channel through which the parent can tell the child to stop spinning. But even that isn't quite as simple as we'd like. If the child tries to get input using conventional means, and it doesn't know ahead of time when that input is coming, it can't do its animation while waiting. For this we need another traditional Unix function, `select`. A popen-based spinner class is given in Listing 13.5.

13

LISTING 13.5 spinner2.rb

```
01: class Spinner
02:   Baton = '\|/-'
03:   def initialize
04:     STDOUT.flush
05:     @child = IO.popen('-', 'w+')
06:
```

continues

LISTING 13.5 Continued

```
07:     if @child.nil?
08:        rotation = 0
09:        until select([$stdin], nil, nil, .2)
10:           STDERR.printf "%c\b", Baton[(rotation+=1) & 3]
11:        end
12:        gets          # read the 'stop' message
13:        STDERR.printf " \b"  # erase the last baton character
14:        exit!
15:     end
16:  end
17:
18:  def stop
19:     @child.puts("stop yer spinnin") # message content is unimportant
20:     @child.close
21:  end
22: end
```

Change the third line in spintest.rb as follows,

```
03:  require 'spinner2' # Edit this line to try different spinners.
```

and try out the new spinner by running spintest.rb again. On some Windows systems, the popen technique seems to work a little more reliably than fork.

The call to select glances at $stdin and sees whether there is any input there waiting to be picked up. Actually, *gazes* is a better word, because we've set it up so that it watches for up to 0.2 seconds and then exits with a nil return value if it didn't see anything. Since we've built a delay into select, there's no need for a separate sleep statement. When no input is present, the child can do something else (rotate the spinner) and come back later to look for input again.

Again, we can probably get along without the @child.close invocation, but it's here as a matter of good hygiene.

Also, we no longer have an infinite loop, and therefore we don't have to set up a signal trap for when we get out of it. Instead, when a message from the parent comes, select returns something that isn't nil, and the while loop exits normally. So the cleanup code can happen below the loop instead of above it.

Example Spinner #3, Using `Kernel.open`

There's no need to put the full code here for `spinner3.rb`. Just make a copy of `spinner2.rb` (Listing 13.5), with one small edit. Change

```
@child = IO.popen('-', 'w+')
```

to

```
@child = open('|-', 'w+')
```

We've seen the `open` method of the `File` class, but this `open` method is slightly different. It belongs to the `Kernel` module. Put as simply as possible, when the first argument starts with a vertical bar character, `Kernel.open` acts like `IO.popen`; otherwise it acts like `File.open`. This is mostly a way of saving a few keystrokes.

Summary

We've had a taste today of the powerful things that can be done when your scripts control the environment around them. Here's a brief recap.

The hash-like `ENV` object and the methods of `File`, `Dir`, and `Find` all provide a script with information about the situation within which it operates. Ruby scripts can run external programs either sequentially, optionally capturing their output for later use, or in parallel; they can also split themselves into separate processes. Processes running at the same time can communicate through `IO` objects called pipes, which are either created implicitly by `IO.popen` or explicitly by `IO.pipe`. Parent processes can and should keep track of what their children are doing. They can communicate with children not only through pipes but also by sending signals with `Process.kill` and eavesdropping with `Process.waitpid`.

That's a lot of ground to cover in one day. You can get much deeper than this by learning more about the operating system and other applications that you use.

13

Tip

> Looking ahead: While `fork` and `IO.popen` are ways of splitting a Ruby program into simultaneous processes, another popular way of doing essentially the same thing is by threading, a concept we'll explore on Day 19.

Exercises

1. Extend the `Dir` class with a new class method `entries_recursive`. You may use `Find.find` as a tool. `entries_recursive` should return an array just as `entries` does (except the "`..`" element will be missing, since `Find.find` omits it), but it should recursively search all subdirectories. It should behave as shown here:

   ```
   # Suppose, as before, that the current directory contains:
   # file1, file2, dirA/file3, dirA/file4, dirB/file5, dirB/file6
   Dir.entries_recursive #->
     [".", "./dirB", "./dirB/file6", "./dirB/file5",
      "./dirA", "./dirA/file4", "./dirA/file3",
      "./file2", "./file1"]
   ```

   If you like, tweak the results so that every leading "`./`" is suppressed, and the single "`.`" entry is not returned. Remember that the `Find` module has to be explicitly required when you test your method.

2. Write a script that uses `fork` to create a child. The parent and child should then count from one to ten, with the parent printing the odd numbers and the child printing the even numbers. Though it's not entirely reliable, manipulate parent/child timing using `sleep` to get the output to come out in the right order. The output should look something like this:

   ```
   Parent says 1
   Child says 2
   Parent says 3
   Child says 4
   Parent says 5
   Child says 6
   Parent says 7
   Child says 8
   Parent says 9
   Child says 10
   ```

3. Improve the previous solution by setting up a pair of pipes before forking off the child process. Let the parent and child coordinate their actions by talking through the pipes. Neither should sleep; both should react immediately to messages.

4. Try the same thing using `IO.popen` instead of `fork`. Remember that `IO.popen` essentially gives you a pair of pipes, so you don't have to create any.

5. Is it possible to have a true progress spinner for the Fibonacci function, one whose animation indicates the function is doing something? How would it have to be different from our examples?

6. Write a function named `executables` that returns an array of all the executable files in your search path. *Hint:* First get an array of all the directories in your search path.

Answers

1. The information we're looking for is the same as that provided by `Find.find`, so the simplest solution is to gather up what it finds into an array.

```ruby
require 'find'

def Dir.entries_recursive(initial_dir)
  results = []
  Find.find(initial_dir) {|f| results.push f}
  results
end
```

For cleaner results, examine each entry before putting it in the results array.

```ruby
def Dir.entries_recursive(initial_dir)
  results = []
  Find.find(initial_dir) do |f|
    if f != '.'
      results.push(f.gsub(%r{^\./}, ''))
      # the regular expression above could be written /^\.\//
    end
  end
  results
end
```

2.
```ruby
01:     #!/usr/bin/env ruby
02:
03:     fork do
04:       # child code
05:       sleep .5
06:       2.step(10,2) do |num|
07:         puts " Child says #{num}"
08:         sleep 1
09:       end
10:     end
11:
12:     # parent code
13:     1.step(9,2) do |num|
14:       puts "Parent says #{num}"
15:       sleep 1
16:     end
17:     Process.wait
```

3.
```ruby
01:     #!/usr/bin/env ruby
02:
03:     a_in, a_out = IO.pipe
04:     b_in, b_out = IO.pipe
05:
06:     fork do
07:       # child code
```

13

```
08:        a_out.close; b_in.close
09:        2.step(10,2) do |num|
10:          a_in.gets
11:          puts " Child says #{num}"
12:          b_out.puts "your turn, Dad"
13:        end
14:      end
15:
16:      # parent code
17:      a_in.close; b_out.close
18:      1.step(9,2) do |num|
19:        puts "Parent says #{num}"
20:        a_out.puts "your turn, kid"
21:        b_in.gets
22:      end
23:      Process.wait
```

4.
```
01:      #!/usr/bin/env ruby
02:
03:      STDOUT.sync = true
04:      child = IO.popen('-', 'w+')
05:      if child == nil
06:        # child code
07:        2.step(10,2) do |num|
08:          gets
09:          STDERR.puts " Child says #{num}"
10:          puts "your turn, dad"
11:        end
12:      end
13:
14:      # parent code
15:      1.step(9,2) do |num|
16:        puts "Parent says #{num}"
17:        child.puts "your turn, kid"
18:        child.gets
19:      end
20:      child.close
```

5. It would be hard to do it in a neat and modular way. But this works:

```
01:      #!/usr/bin/env ruby
02:
03:      Fib_baton = '\|/-'
04:      @fib_counter = 0
05:      @fib_rotation = 0
06:
07:      def fib(n)
08:        # deal with the spinner once in a "great while"
09:        if (@fib_counter += 1) == 20000
10:          @fib_counter = 0
11:          printf "%c\b", Fib_baton[(@fib_rotation+=1)&3]; STDOUT.flush
```

```
12:        end
13:        # now do the actual calculation
14:        (n<=2) ? 1 : (fib(n-2)+fib(n-1))
15:     end
16:
17:     print "Please wait while I calculate a large Fibonacci number."
18:     result = fib(28)
19:
20:     puts " "  # erase the animation character
21:     puts result
```

There is no child process. The `fib` function is doing its own animation. The speed of the spinner is tied not to the wall clock, but to the actual speed of calculation.

Since a recursive function doesn't really know which invocation of itself is being called from outside (all but one are generated by some other copy), the erasure of the animation character has to happen in the calling code.

6. This will take a little explaining.

```
def executables
  results = []
  directories = ENV['PATH'].split(':')
  directories.each do |dir|
    results +=
      Dir.entries(dir).
      map  {|f| File.join(dir,f)}.
      reject {|f| File.directory?(f)}.
      select {|f| File.executable?(f)}
  end
  results
end
```

To test the function in a script, use the line `puts executables`. More usefully, you can iterate over the results; in some environments, such an idea might reasonably be used in a virus-scanning script.

```
executables.each do |filename|
  examine the file for virus signatures
end
```

The PATH comes to us as a single colon-delimited string, but `split(':')` turns it into an array so that it can be iterated upon. Each directory in `directories` is now examined using `Dir.entries`. `files` is an array of filenames, some of which are executable programs.

13

Now we do a series of useful transformations on that array, chained together into a statement that spans several lines. The map prepends directory information to each entry (so for instance, indent might become /usr/bin/indent). The reject gets rid of directory names, including the meaningless '.' and '..' entries. Finally, after the select, nothing remains but names of executable files.

Each directory in the PATH yields another of these nicely processed arrays, and they get combined using += into the results array that accumulates the final product.

The same logic, but in a somewhat tidier style, is shown in the following code. Since we started with one array and ended with another, the whole transformation can be summed up in another map iterator call.

```
def executables
  paths = ENV['PATH'].split(":")

    Dir.entries(d).map {|f| File.join(d,f)}.
      flatten.
      reject {|f| File.directory?(f)}.
      select {|f| File.executable?(f)}
  end
end
```

WEEK 2

DAY 14

Arguments, Blocks, and Procs

> "I came here for a good argument!"
>
> "No you didn't; you came here for an *argument*."
>
> —Monty Python's Flying Circus, "The Argument Sketch"

This news just in from the Keen Grasp On The Obvious Department: The enterprise of object-oriented programming is all about objects. They are the basic building blocks, the unit of currency, of our scripts.

As we've seen all along, objects bundle information and logic into neat packages by incorporating instance methods and instance data. An object's methods are designed to work with its own data so that other objects don't need to know how to. Communication with an object is accomplished by passing information via arguments to methods, and what do those arguments refer to? Yup, other objects.

A friend of mine describes OO programming as analogous to speaking in a language dominated by nouns, as opposed to traditional (or procedural) programming, which is more like speaking in a verb-centric way. It's a powerful, consistent, and fairly simple way to approach most programming problems, but, as with any paradigm, there are situations that it doesn't fit easily. Today we'll see how Ruby lets you pass *logic* to methods. Don't be alarmed; we've been doing it all along but without quite understanding how it works. Today we'll learn some things about the mechanism and will use that understanding to start writing our own iterators.

Life Without Iterators

Let's play dumb for a while: Suppose we've never seen iterators, and we would like to give an object foo a completely new task to do. We mean this in a very general sense; although the object has its own methods, which are the tricks it already knows how to perform, we'd like to be able to tell it to do something arbitrary and unfamiliar. In other words, we'd like to pass it some code. How can we teach an old dog a new trick?

Here's a little game to make the problem a little more concrete. Secretive is a class whose objects each own a number @r chosen randomly somewhere between 0 and 1.

> **Note**
>
> That's strictly less than 1, although possibly equal to 0. (It will probably take you a lot of tries before you see it come out to exactly 0.)

```
class Secretive
  def initialize
    @r = rand
  end
end
```

When we make a new Secretive object by saying foo=Secretive.new, we don't know what its instance variable @r contains. We also neglected to write any accessors, so there's no good way to find out. Our challenge is to find out what @r is without writing an accessor.

> **Note**
>
> Actually, if we're writing this code in irb, it will immediately tell us the contents of foo's instance variables, like this:
>
> ```
> irb(main):002:0> foo=Secretive.new
> #<Secretive:0x40265564  @r=0.2343148718>
> ```

Stealthy Approach

There are several ways to win at this game. The first is almost cheating—it's a strange technique that lies on the edge of the scope of this book (and so won't be exhaustively explained right now), but it's presented in Listing 14.1 just so that you can see that in a dynamic language like Ruby, almost anything is possible.

LISTING 14.1   stealth-1.rb

```
01:    #!/usr/bin/env ruby
02:
03:    class Secretive
04:      def initialize
05:        @r = rand
06:      end
07:    end
08:
09:    class Inquisitive
10:      def getSecret(other, context)
11:        # Temporarily attach a "sing" method to the Secretive class.
12:        code_1 = "class Secretive\n "+
13:                 " def sing\n "+
14:                 "   puts \"My secret number is \#{@r}\"\n"+
15:                 " end\n" +
16:                 "end\n"
17:        eval(code_1,context)
18:
19:        # Invoke the method.
20:        other.sing
21:
22:        # Now get rid of the method.
23:        code_2 = "class Secretive\n"+
24:                 " remove_method :sing\n"+
25:                 "end\n"
26:        eval(code_2,context)
27:      end
28:    end
29:
30:
31:    sec = Secretive.new
32:    inq = Inquisitive.new
33:    inq.getSecret(sec, binding)

    # sample output:
    My secret number is 0.7309132419
```

14

How is this almost cheating? The Inquisitive object *dynamically modifies* the Secretive class. It actually builds the sing method as a string, invokes the Ruby interpreter via the `Kernel.eval` method to attach it to `Secretive`, then calls the method to make sec divulge its secret. Afterward it removes the new method. Awfully sneaky, wouldn't you say? Of course, the main rule of our game was that we couldn't write an accessor method; but we can claim we didn't really cheat, because it was the `Inquisitive` object that wrote `Secretive#sing`. We just gave it the tools to do the job; we didn't do anything bad, at least not directly. (Similar argument: *I didn't break the wine glass; I only dropped it, and the floor broke it.*) `Kernel.eval` takes a string of arbitrary Ruby code to be evaluated, plus optionally a "context" argument, which in this case was filled in from the outside using the `Kernel.binding` method.

Temporarily modifying another class at a time like this is a lot like swatting a fly with a sledgehammer. It's a powerful and dangerous idea that generally shouldn't be used except in extraordinary circumstances; and even then, you can usually get away with using `instance_eval`, as in Listing 14.2, to confine your meddling to an object instead of the class to which it belongs.

LISTING 14.2   `stealth-2.rb`

```
01:    #!/usr/bin/env ruby
02:
03:    class Secretive
04:      def initialize
05:        @r = rand
06:      end
07:    end
08:
09:    class Inquisitive
10:      def getSecret(other)
11:        other.instance_eval('puts "My secret number is #{@r}"')
12:      end
13:    end
14:
15:    sec = Secretive.new
16:    inq = Inquisitive.new
17:    inq.getSecret(sec)
```

A Hands-on Approach

We can avoid wantonly interfering with the structure of the `Secretive` class if we arrange ahead of time that its objects will agree to be examined. In human terms, imagine a child who is allowed to read anything in his room as long as he leaves the door open. By prior arrangement, a parent can walk in at any time and say, "Give me that book." In Listing 14.3, an exchange of method calls takes place: `inq` calls `sec.obey`, and in response, sec calls `inq.what_to_do`. In this way sec actively gives away information, rather like the child giving the parent the book.

LISTING 14.3 `hands-on.rb`

```
01:    #!/usr/bin/env ruby
02:
03:    class Secretive
04:      def initialize
05:        @r = rand
06:      end
07:
08:      def obey(master)
09:        master.what_to_do(@r)
10:      end
11:    end
12:
13:    class Inquisitive
14:      def getSecret(other)
15:        other.obey(self)
16:      end
17:
18:      def what_to_do(data)
19:        puts "My secret number is #{data}"
20:      end
21:    end
22:
23:    sec=Secretive.new
24:    inq=Inquisitive.new
25:    inq.getSecret(sec)
```

This is different in a subtle but important way from the first solution. Here, sec does not own the code it is calling; rather it calls a method in inq, a fact that clearly implies some trust. Still, the trust is not necessarily total and involuntary. In line 9, sec has explicitly given inq access to its secret data. If instead it had said `master.what_to_do(.3)`, then inq would not have known it was being lied to.

A Hands-off Approach

Imagine the parent unobtrusively slipping a note under the door instead of walking in and taking charge in person. The next solution is like that. It involves passing a small object to sec: not the object inq in its entirety, but a *procedure* (or *proc*) *object*.

Ruby has a `Proc` class for procedure objects. You construct one like this:

```
p = Proc.new {some code}
```

14

More commonly, you use an abbreviated syntax:

```
p = proc {some code}
```

At this point the variable p refers to a proc object with a few of its own methods. The important one is Proc#call, which actually executes (evaluates) the code.

```
a_sum = proc {1+2+3}
a_sum.call       #-> 6
```

A proc object is like a piece of frozen logic; it doesn't get executed when first created. So, even if its code is rife with errors, they might not get noticed right away.

```
p = proc {a load of nonsense}  # no problem yet
p.call          # error: "undefined local variable or method"
```

Procs, like methods, can take parameters. Any arguments passed to Proc#call are later assigned to the variable names given between the vertical bars, and the usual multiple-assignment tricks apply:

```
product_of_two = proc {|factor1, factor2| factor1 * factor2}
product_of_two.call(9,6)        #-> 54

product_of_many = proc {|*factors|
                        result = 1
                        factors.each {|n| result *= n}
                        result}
product_of_many.call(13,14,15,16)   #-> 43680
product_of_many.call(11,12)         #-> 132
product_of_many.call(10)            #-> 10
product_of_many.call()              #-> 1
```

Listing 14.4 shows how we might use a proc object in the Secretive/Inquisitive problem.

LISTING 14.4   hands-off.rb

```
01:   #!/usr/bin/env ruby
02:
03:   class Secretive
04:     def initialize
05:       @r = rand
06:     end
07:
08:     def follow(procedure)
09:       procedure.call @r
10:     end
11:   end
12:
13:   class Inquisitive
14:     def getSecret(other)
15:       do_this = proc {|num| puts "My secret number is #{num}"}
```

LISTING 14.4 Continued

```
16:        other.follow(do_this)
17:      end
18:    end
19:
20:    sec=Secretive.new
21:    inq=Inquisitive.new
22:    inq.getSecret(sec)
```

As before, sec explicitly makes @r available. The subtle difference between this script and the previous one is that sec never sees inq and never invokes any of inq's methods. All it sees is the procedure object it is given, like that piece of paper the parent slides under the child's door.

At this point we should mention two other Proc instance methods. Proc#arity returns the number of arguments the proc expects, or a negative number if the last argument is there by itself or is given with an asterisk.

```
whatkind    = proc {|x| x.type}
sum_of_3    = proc {|a,b,c| a+b+c}
pf_wrapper = proc {|fmt,*args| printf(fmt, args)}

whatkind.arity     #->  -1
sum_of_3.arity     #->   3
pf_wrapper.arity   #->  -2
```

Also, Proc#[] does the same thing as Proc#call. You may prefer myproc[arg1,arg2] as a more compact alternative for myproc.call(arg1,arg2).

Final Approach: *Very* Hands-off

Finally we're about to see where all this is heading, which is into the heart of the concept of iterators. Our concluding solution is something like having the parent speak some instructions through a closed door. The "piece of paper" no longer exists; there are just some disembodied words, which the child is supposed to obey.

Let's go straight to the code (Listing 14.5) and then talk about how it works.

LISTING 14.5 Final Solution: iterator.rb

```
01:    #!/usr/bin/env ruby
02:
03:    class Secretive
04:      def initialize
05:        @r = rand
06:      end
```

14

continues

LISTING 14.5 Continued

```
07:
08:     def follow
09:       yield @r
10:     end
11:   end
12:
13:   class Inquisitive
14:     def getSecret(other)
15:       other.follow  {|num| puts "My secret number is #{num}"}
16:     end
17:   end
18:
19:   sec=Secretive.new
20:   inq=Inquisitive.new
21:   inq.getSecret(sec)
```

That's not very different from the previous example at first glance, but look at the definition of the Secretive#follow. Do you see what's missing? There is no argument list! The instructions that are to be followed are evidently not coming in the form of a proc object or, for that matter, any kind of object at all. There is no variable name assigned to them. Yet, yield @r somehow causes the instructions to be obeyed. How is this possible?

To answer that question, we need to re-examine what we mean by a *block*. We've used the word fairly loosely up until now when referring to a collection of related code in some kind of enclosure: a class definition, a method definition, begin...end, case...end, and so on. But for today's purposes we'll be very specific: A block is a collection of code enclosed by either do...end or curly braces, as in {...}.

The fundamental characteristic of this kind of block is that *it cannot stand alone*, as a little experiment in irb illustrates:

```
irb(main):001:0> 9999
9999
irb(main):002:0> begin 9999 end
9999
irb(main):003:0> do 9999 end
SyntaxError: compile error
(irb):2: parse error
do 9999 end
    ^
        from (irb):3
```

A block cannot be evaluated or executed by itself, so it is useless until combined with other code that tells how and when to evaluate it. Put Proc.new or proc in front of a block, and it gets made into an object to be evaluated later via Proc#call. Put an iterator call in front of a block, and the iterator will evaluate the block. If the iterator method invokes `yield` more than once (possibly in a loop), then the block gets evaluated more than once, too.

```
(proc {p self}).call   # output (usually): main
3.times {print "z"}    # output: zzz
```

Put `loop` in front of a block, and the block executes forever, or until something explicitly stops it. `loop` is not in fact a syntax feature of Ruby, but just another iterator method; it belongs to the `Kernel` module.

In a way, an iterator doesn't exactly execute the code block that it is given. Since no object changes hands, you might say the iterator never gets possession of a block. Rather, it *yields to the caller*, and what it yields is both data and control. It is the caller that executes its own code block, using the data yielded by the iterator. (Perhaps determining who's doing the work is not very meaningful, because in larger architectural terms it is the interpreter that does everything. Objects don't burn calories, so to speak.) The `yield` statement distinguishes an iterator from an ordinary method. `yield` is the iterator's way of telling its caller, "You have my blessing to execute arbitrary code using this data." But the iterator method gets something back in exchange for that trust: Whatever the block evaluates to also becomes the value of the `yield` in the iterator.

```
def baz
  value = yield("father")
  puts "The value of the yield expression was '#{value}'"
end

baz {|s| s.sub(/fa/, 'mo')}

    # Output: The value of the yield expression was 'mother'
```

Writing Iterator Methods

Standard Ruby iterators cover so many situations that you don't often have to write your own. Inheritance sees to it that any class descending from a common container class like `String`, `Array`, `Hash`, or `Range` will have a working `each` method. But many classes contain other containers without being descended from them; often it is useful to provide iterators that link those inner containers to the outside world:

```
class Foo
  def initialize
    @my_data = %w{ Washington Adams Jefferson }
  end
  def each
    @my_data.each {|element| yield element}
  end
end
```

14

```
Foo.new.each {|x| puts x}
   # output:  Washington
             Adams
             Jefferson
```

Foo is not a descendant of the Array class, but Foo#each allows Foo objects to be iterated upon just as if they were arrays.

Hybrid Iterators

It's possible for a method to be an iterator some times and not at other times. Kernel.block_given? allows methods to determine how they were called. Let's expand the previous example:

```
class Foo
  # ...
  def data
    if block_given?
      @my_data.each {|element| yield element}
    else
      @my_data
    end
  end
end
```

Now we have a single method that can mean, depending on how it is called, "Give me your data" or "Do this with your data."

```
f = Foo.new
f.data        #-> ["Washington", "Adams", "Jefferson"]
f.data {|pres| puts pres[0,3]}
   # output:  Was
             Ada
             Jef
```

Some of the methods that we've already seen have this capability, for instance File.open. Normally we are responsible for closing what we open, but if we give File.open a block, it will pass the new file object to the block and close the file itself when the block finishes. The code

```
File.open("nash_wapiti.txt","r") {|file| puts(file.gets)}
   ...
```

prints the first line of a file, just as the following does:

```
poem = File.open("nash_wapiti.txt","r")
puts poem.gets
poem.close
```

We saw another method that swings both ways yesterday. Notice the two ways of invoking Kernel.fork—one treats it as an iterator, and the other does not.

`yield` simplifies the passing of logic into methods. It's a little limiting, insofar as only one block can be passed (there's no mechanism for saying *which* block should be yielded to, were there more), but it is hard to imagine a situation where multiple blocks would ever need to be given to a method. On the other hand, if such a situation ever arose, extra blocks could be made first into objects using `Proc.new` and then passed as ordinary method arguments; the iterator would invoke them using `call` instead of `yield`.

Before moving on, we'll note in passing that there are ways to convert between blocks and procs in iterator calls. First, you can pass an iterator a proc object instead of a block, provided you preface it with an ampersand (&):

```
square = proc {|num| num*num}
[1,2,3].map &square  #->  [1,4,9]

   # same effect as:  [1.2.3].map {|num| num*num}
```

Going the other way, an iterator can convert the block that it was given into a proc object by using `Proc.new` by itself:

```
def my_iterator
   instructions = Proc.new   # wrap the block up as an object
   instructions.call(17)
end

my_iterator {|x| x+1}   #->  18
```

Alternatively, the given block can be assigned to a proc object through the last element of the method's argument list. An ampersand is used to distinguish the block from the other arguments:

```
def num_op(number, &operation)
   return operation.call(number)
end

num_op(7) {|a| a*(a-1)}  #->  42
```

If num_op is called without a block, `operation` will be `nil`.

```
num_op(88)  # error: undefined method 'call' for nil
```

New Iterators for Old Classes

Let's try adding iterators to a couple of standard classes. These will be fairly trivial, as they just take some logic we might normally apply from the outside and move it inward. First, let's write `Array#backwards_each`. It should behave like this:

14

```
a = [1,3,5]
a.backwards_each {|num| puts ("@"*num)}
  # output:  @@@@@
            @@@
            @
```

To attack this problem, consider how you could do it with the tools Ruby already offers. Say out loud, if necessary, what you want: *Get a reversed copy of the array, then apply the block to that copy.* It could be done like this:

```
the_copy = [1,3,5].reverse    #-> [5,3,1]
the_copy.each {|num| puts ("@"*num)}
```

If we're going to work this logic into an `Array` instance method, it will mean dealing with an array named `self`, because, as with most instance methods, we're teaching objects of a class some new way to operate on themselves. Here's the whole solution:

```
class Array
  def backwards_each
    the_copy = self.reverse
    the_copy.each{|elt| yield elt}
  end
end
```

Take a moment to test it out. Then accept my humble confession that this is a reinvention of a wheel, because Ruby already has an `Array#reverse_each` method.

Our second iterator is `IO.choose`, which should examine a text file whose name is given, and return an array of the lines that satisfy some particular condition. Ideally we would like to name this `IO.select`, because it acts so much like `IO#select` and `Array#select`. Unfortunately, the name already belongs to a different method (which we used yesterday, as you might recall). So given this text file,

```
snrfw
poj i
4fubb
p mk
```

we would want to be able to, for example, ask for the lines containing at least one vowel.

```
IO.choose("sample.txt") {|l| l =~ /[AEIOU]/i}
    #-> ["poj i\n", "4fubb\n"]
```

Again, how would we do the job without extending a class? *Get an array of all the lines; then, from those, choose the ones that contain a vowel.* `IO.readlines` will be useful here.

```
whole_enchilada = IO.readlines("sample.txt")
whole_enchilada.choose {|l| l.include? "aeiouAEIOU"}
```

Remember the form of class methods. We don't want to start with `class IO ...` `def choose`, because that would leave us with an instance method; instead we should start with `def IO.choose`. As it turns out, there's not much more to write. `IO.choose`, like `Array#backwards_each`, is an insignificant bit of fluff.

```
def IO.choose(filename)
  all = IO.readlines(filename)
  all.select {|l| yield l}
end
```

Chain those method calls, and the body shrinks down to one line. (We could do the same thing with `Array#backwards_each`, too.)

```
def IO.choose(filename)
  IO.readlines(filename).select {|l| yield l}
end
```

Since `IO.readlines` returns an array, our solution is relying on `Array#select` to do its job. We can use `IO#select` instead, if we first generate an `IO` object with `File.open`.

```
def IO.choose(filename)
  File.open(filename).select {|l| yield l}
end
```

Was This Trip Really Necessary?

The preceding examples may be of marginal usefulness. We could easily live without them. One of Ruby's charms is that, being a young language, it hasn't accumulated a huge repository of standard classes and methods. It's possible to really *know* the language, to keep the bulk of it in your head and work without a reference book in front of you. The Ruby development community generates a continuous buzz of discussion about proposed extensions, most of which are borrowed from other languages and generally sound like great ideas; yet in most cases a few individuals quietly point out some straightforward and concise way of getting the job done without extending Ruby, there is a collective sigh of appreciation, and the proposal falls by the wayside. Ruby seems to consistently cover the fundamental ideas, and its toolbox has so far remained, somehow, comprehensively sparse.

The best advice I can offer about iterators is this: When defining a new class, teach it to support the most common iterator methods (especially `each`), at least when those methods seem to have some natural meaning and inheritance doesn't make it happen without your intervention. We'll come back to the idea of language extension later on in the book, but let's dabble a little more first, because there's an idea we left hanging out there on Day 4. . . .

14

select_by_index

Do you remember this problem?

```
[60,62,65,70,72,73,75].select_by_index { |i| i%2 == 1 }
    #-> [62, 70, 73]
```

We were looking for a way to extract array elements from odd-numbered positions, and we thought an Array#select_by_index iterator would be handy. It doesn't exist, but that's no problem now, because we know enough to be able to write our own.

Here's one way of going about it. Start with an empty result array. Iterate over the *element, index* pairs of self, yielding the indices back to the caller for its judgment on which ones fit the bill and pushing the corresponding elements into result. Then return result when we're done.

```
class Array
  def select_by_index
    result = []
    self.each_with_index do |element,idx|
        result.push element  if yield idx
    end
    result
  end
end
```

That works, but was there any need to grab all the elements? Wouldn't it be more efficient to iterate over just the indices, and grab the corresponding elements only after the indices have checked out?

```
class Array
  def select_by_index
    result = []
    self.each_index do |idx|
        result.push self[idx]  if yield idx
    end
    result
  end
end
```

Yes, this performs a little better; but the advantage is small enough that if you find the first form of select_by_index easier to think about, it should probably be left alone.

At the end of today's lesson, you'll be asked to write a select_with_index iterator so that array elements can be selected by criteria that relate to both position and content.

Other Uses for Blocks

`BEGIN` and `END` are special constructs that are not commonly used, but they can help you make your scripts robust and well-behaved. Regardless of where it appears, a block attached to the keyword `BEGIN` executes before the rest of your script, and a block attached to `END` executes last:

```
#!/usr/bin/env ruby

BEGIN { puts "Starting..." }
END   { puts "Done." }
puts "Working..."

   # Output:  Starting...
   #          Working...
   #          Done.
```

`END` is particularly useful, because it can help a script clean up after itself. If you use use the ANSI module we wrote back on Day 11 and get careless, your programs might exit leaving the terminal window in a strange state, maybe even with flashing blue text on a pink background. Spare yourself that embarrassment. An `END` block prevents such aesthetic offenses, regardless of how the script exits:

```
END { print ANSI::Normal }
```

Another use for blocks is *signal trapping*. Processes receive signals from each other and from the operating system. We saw an example yesterday: A parent process sent a "hang up" signal to a child process using `Process.kill`, and the child had previously been set up with a *trap* which defined its response to that signal. The response code was given in the form of a block, but it can make more sense to wrap it up as a proc object if the code itself is large and will need to be applied to more than one kind of signal.

Note
> There are signals that indicate various error conditions related to the operation of the processor unit (such as segmentation violation), interprocess communication, timed alarms, and so on. If you're on a Unix system, you can say `man 7 signal` to see a complete list of available signals.

```
trap_handler = proc do
  # complicated trap handling code goes here ...
end

trap "SIGINT", trap_handler
trap "SIGKILL", trap_handler
trap "SIGPIPE", trap_handler
  # etc.
```

14

Summary

The object-oriented paradigm tends to make us see things in terms of what they are instead of what they do. To communicate in the form of instructions rather than objects, Ruby provides the mechanism of passing *blocks* to *iterators*. We have used iterators before; today we learned to write them ourselves.

We also were introduced to procedure objects, which wrap blocks up so that they can be assigned to variable names and passed around just like other objects.

Before we can produce truly reusable code (or, as some folks say, *reuseful* code), we'll need to know how to design nice intuitive interfaces. So tomorrow we'll be using what we learned today to follow up on the discussion from Day 11. The goal will be kind of informal protocol, or etiquette, of interface design.

Exercises

1. Listing 14.6 is yet another variation on the `Secretive/Inquisitive` problem we were playing with. Why doesn't it work?

LISTING 14.6 buggy.rb

```
01:    #!/usr/bin/env ruby
02:
03:    class Secretive
04:      def initialize
05:        @r = rand
06:      end
07:
08:      def follow(procedure)
09:        procedure.call
10:      end
11:    end
12:
13:    class Inquisitive
14:      def getSecret(other)
15:        do_this = proc {puts "My secret number is #{@r}"}
16:        other.follow(do_this)
17:      end
18:    end
19:
20:    sec=Secretive.new
21:    inq=Inquisitive.new
22:    inq.getSecret(sec)

    # output:
      My secret number is
```

2. Write an `Array#select_with_index` iterator. Test it on an array of numbers by asking for the elements that satisfy two conditions: They must be even, and they must reside in even-numbered positions. Your solution should support this test code:

```
msnums = [1,3,4,6,7,9,10,12,13]
nums.select_with_index {|n,i|  n&1==0 && i&1==0}
    #-> [4,10]
```

3. Write an `Array#shuffled_each` iterator. It should iterate over all elements, but in an unpredictable order. What's challenging about this is that there is no `Array#shuffle` method built into Ruby (although we did work on a "destructive" `Array#shuffle!` method on Day 11, which you might want to go back to study or reuse in some way). So you have two choices: Either do the shuffling inside your iterator, or write `Array#shuffle` separately and then refer to it in a much simpler iterator. The second idea seems more harmonious with the Ruby Way; after all, you may want that shuffling logic for some other use. If you like, by using `block_given?` you can write a single `Array#shuffle` method that iterates when appropriate; that would let you make `Array#shuffled_each` an alias for `Array#shuffle`.

Note

This is just an exercise, of course. Keep in mind that the existence of a working `Array#shuffle` method would by itself make shuffled iteration trivial, since `anArray.shuffle.each {...}` is clearly just as easy to say as `anArray.shuffled_each {...}`.

Since any first attempt at a solution can be expected to destroy or damage the array being operated on, you need to know that `Object#dup` can make a copy of just about anything. Make a disposable copy of the array, do your work on that, and the original will be undisturbed.

Three solutions will be provided.

The following example illustrates the usage. Be sure your solution preserves the original order of the array after `#shuffled_each` has been called, as shown here.

```
nums = (1..7).to_a                  #-> [1,2,3,4,5,6,7]
nums.shuffled_each {|n| print n}  # output: 3164527
nums.shuffled_each {|n| print n}  #          4753162
nums.shuffled_each {|n| print n}  #          1724536
nums                                #-> [1,2,3,4,5,6,7]
```

4. On Day 1 we looked at the `<=>` method and found that it compares two objects (often numbers, but they may be something else) and returns either -1, 0, or 1 depending on their ordering; x<=>y should be -1 when x<y, 0 when x==y and 1 when x>y. Ruby's

built-in sort facility uses <=> unless it is given a block to use instead, in which the case the block takes two objects, compares them by any criterion, and returns -1, 0, or 1. Thus, an array of integers is sorted from most negative to most positive,

```
[30,-12,9].sort   #-> [-12, 9, 30]
```

unless we tell it, perhaps, to sort by absolute value:

```
[30,-12,9].sort {|x,y| x.abs <=> y.abs} #-> [9, -12, 30]
```

Try writing an Array#my_sort method that behaves like a standard Ruby sort, using <=> if it is called with no block. Don't worry about efficiency, as long as you get it to work. The solution we'll present will be a simple-minded implementation of the rather slow "bubble sort" algorithm:

Walk through the array from one end to the other, swapping each element with the one after it if they are out of order. Repeat the process until you've made a pass without swapping anything, which indicates that the array is sorted.

Again, return a sorted copy of the array; don't disturb the original.

Answers

1. This is a scope problem. It is the Inquisitive object, inq, that generates the code for the procedure object do_this, so when sec runs the proc in line 9, it is trying to print *inq's* @r, which of course doesn't exist. To verify this, see what happens when you insert "@r = 1000" at the top of the getSecret method, between lines 14 and 15.

2. A tiny modification to select_by_index does the job.

```
class Array
  def select_with_index
    result = []
    self.each_with_index do |element,idx|
      result.push element  if yield(element,idx)
    end
    result
  end
end
```

3. As promised, here are three solutions, corresponding to the ideas given in the problem. First is a single Array#shuffled_each method, presented with the disclaimer that it is not a very good example of the Ruby Way. In a loop, it grabs one element randomly, yields it to the caller, then deletes it from the array until the array is empty. Since that would destroy our original array if we weren't careful (causing total self-destruction, you might say), the operation is carried out on a copy:

```
class Array
  def shuffled_each
    c = self.dup
    while not c.empty?
      index = rand(c.size)
      yield c[index]
      c.delete_at index
    end
  end
end
```

The second solution is split into two methods: `Array#shuffle` and
`Array#shuffled_each`. Keeping them separate means that `#shuffle` can be
used for other purposes later. This `#shuffle` follows the hint by making one pass
through the copied array, swapping each element with some random other element:

```
class Array
  def shuffle
    c = self.dup
    s = c.size
    c.each_index do |i|    # or: c.times do |i|
      r = rand s
      c[r], c[i] = c[i], c[r]
    end
    c
  end

  def shuffled_each
    self.shuffle.each {|elt| yield elt}
  end
end
```

The last, and most elegant, approach is to reuse a known solution and provide a
single hybrid iterator, which can be called with either name:

```
class Array
  def shuffle!  # "destructive" method from Day 11
    size.downto(1) {|n| push delete_at rand(n)}
  end

  def shuffle
    c = self.dup
    c.shuffle!
    c.each {|elt| yield elt} if block_given?
    c
  end
  alias shuffled_each shuffle
end
```

14

4. Granted, this was a minor exercise in masochism. It's fortunate that you don't have to write Ruby code at this level most of the time, because the dirty work has been done for you; and in the present case, Ruby's various `sort` methods (found in the `Enumerable` module and the `Array` and `Hash` classes) do a much more efficient job than ours anyway. Listing 14.7 shows the solution.

LISTING 14.7 Solution: `bubble-1.rb`

```
01:    class Array
02:      def mysort
03:        copy = self.dup
04:        all_done = false  # the bubblesort completion flag
05:        until all_done
06:          all_done = true
07:          (copy.size-1).times do |idx|
08:            if block_given?
09:              if (yield copy[idx], copy[idx+1]) == 1
10:                all_done = false
11:                copy[idx], copy[idx+1] = copy[idx+1], copy[idx]
12:              end
13:            else
14:              if (copy[idx] <=> copy[idx+1]) == 1
15:                all_done = false
16:                copy[idx], copy[idx+1] = copy[idx+1], copy[idx]
17:              end
18:            end
19:          end
20:        end      # end of "until" loop
21:        copy     # Return the sorted copy.
22:      end
23:    end
```

Do lines 8–18 seem repetitive? Then consider the alternative solution in Listing 14.8:

LISTING 14.8 Alternative Solution: `bubble-2.rb`

```
01:    class Array
02:      def mysort(&criterion)
03:        criterion = proc {|x,y| x<=>y} if not block_given?
04:        copy = self.dup
05:        all_done = false  # the bubblesort completion flag
06:        until all_done
07:          all_done = true
08:          (copy.size-1).times do |idx|
09:            if criterion.call(copy[idx], copy[idx+1]) == 1
10:              all_done = false
```

LISTING 14.8   Continued

```
11:                 copy[idx], copy[idx+1] = copy[idx+1], copy[idx]
12:             end
13:           end
14:       end    # end of "until" loop
15:       copy    # Return the sorted copy.
16:     end
17:   end
```

Look closely at line 3. `criterion` will initially appear as a `proc` object, but only if a block was given; otherwise we assign it a standard comparison `proc`. (Since criterion is `nil` whenever `block_given?` is false, here's another way to write line 2: `criterion ||= proc {|x,y| x<=>y}`.) In either case, it's invoked as a proc object, using `call` instead of `yield`, in line 9.

14

WEEK 3

Making It Work for You

15 Toward Habitable Interfaces

16 Putting It Together (Part I)

17 Ruby/Tk

18 Ruby/Gtk

19 Some Advanced Topics
    (That Aren't So Hard)

20 Working with the Web

21 Putting It Together (Part II)

WEEK 3

DAY 15

Toward Habitable Interfaces

> It's easy for my mind. I hope it's easy for yours too.
>
> —Matz (creator of Ruby), *on the* `comp.lang.ruby` *newsgroup*

The less a user is required to remember, the better. Remember that!

When building a class, you have to think about how it works, and you always
want to make sure it works well. When writing other code that uses that class,
on the other hand, you want to forget about the class's inner workings and
remember only its *interface*. That is, you remember only the method names
and what results they're supposed to accomplish. You assume a different role,
taking off a Class Builder hat and putting on a Class User hat. Since writing
object-oriented code on anything beyond the small scale often means creating
some new classes, it also involves occasionally changing hats—unless, perhaps, you belong to a team of programmers and have been assigned just part
of the work.

Today we're going to talk about making classes friendly to their users. The skills we've been acquiring up to now have made it possible to write code that works reliably, but today we're more concerned with ensuring that the interfaces make intuitive sense.

A class should be just as easy for anyone else to use as it is for the builder. This is a good guideline even if you're working by yourself, because once you've created a class and a little time has gone by, it can be hard to remember how it worked. You shouldn't ever have to rely on that knowledge. It is the interface that really matters. A well-designed interface allows you to move from one level of abstraction to another without having to deal with both together—in other words, it ensures that you need to wear only one hat at a time.

Interface Size and Intuitiveness

It's generally wise to keep the interfaces of new classes small whenever possible. Why? Because interfaces are the aspect of OO design that both class builders and class users have to worry about. A large interface ends up causing more work for everybody, gives everybody more to remember, and opens a wider door for bugs to slip through.

If there seem to be far too many methods in a new class, there are at least two ways to think about the problem.

On the one hand, an apparently excessive number of methods might indicate that the role of the class is poorly defined. Perhaps the class's job doesn't make all that much sense; it has been given too much or too little to do. There may be a better way to divide the labor up, redrawing the boundaries to make the interfaces naturally narrower. This is a difficult proposition, and we won't concern ourselves much with it here.

On the other hand, the class may be well defined, but the method names themselves may be poorly organized, requiring the class user to memorize a lot of idiosyncratic detail. In that case, the class designer should find ways to make them sensible in relation to each other.

Method names can be matched up across class boundaries. A method may have functionality that is analogous to that of another method in another class; we can name it after that other method, so that a user already familiar with that other class understands how to use it. If method names are chosen so that they make sense across the whole language, even a fairly large interface can feel comfortable and manageable.

Method names can also be grouped within a class. Several methods of the same class may work very differently but have some logical relationship that makes them suitable for combining under one name. The user calls that single method name, and suitable action is taken depending on the arguments given. This *method overloading* idea is a little different in Ruby if you've done it before in C++ or Java, but it's not very difficult.

15

An `IntegerMatrix` Class

Throughout this chapter we'll be building an `IntegerMatrix` class. Our matrices will hold numbers in rectangular grids of arbitrary sizes and allow certain kinds of math to be carried out on them.

It so happens that Ruby already comes with a sophisticated `Matrix` class. It lives in the matrix.rb module and is found by a script containing the line `require 'matrix'` or `load_'matrix.rb'`. Our `IntegerMatrix` will be much different, and will not pretend to be a functional approximation of `Matrix`.

Incidentally, there would be no name conflict if we called our class `Matrix` as well, so long as it was in a file that was *not* named `matrix.rb` and it was used only by scripts that didn't use the other kind of matrix.

Initialization

The first design choice is whether a matrix should be growable in the way that `Array` objects are. Remember that you can create an empty array and fill entries at arbitrary positions by assignment, so that, for instance, `ary=[]; ary[2]="X"` results in `ary` referring to the array `[nil, nil, "X"]`. It will be easier for us if we keep the matrix dimensions static, and all entries initially filled with zeros. But static dimensions need not be *fixed*—we want the user to be able to specify any number of rows and columns when creating a matrix. So the user[1] will be required always to specify dimensions, like this:

```
a = IntegerMatrix.new(3,4)
   # ... should yield a 3 row, 4 column matrix full of zeroes:
   #
   #  0 0 0 0
   #  0 0 0 0
   #  0 0 0 0
```

How shall we store the numbers? Recall that arrays can hold any kind of object including other arrays, and that a two-dimensional array can be implemented as an array containing other arrays. We'll have the "outer" array contain rows, each of which is a flat array of integers.

---

[1] *"User" means whatever entity (such as an object) invokes* `IntegerMatrix.new`*—not necessarily the flesh-and-blood critter at the keyboard, although it can be.*

The map method is pretty handy right now. Without it, code to construct an array of zeros might have to look like this:

```
def initialize(rows, cols)
  @rows, @cols = rows, cols  # we'll want to have these later
  @data = Array.new(rows)
  @data.each_index do |r|
    newrow = Array.new(cols)
    newrow.each_index {|c| newrow[c]=0}
    @data[r] = newrow
  end
end
```

We could have used the `Array.fill` method to avoid the `each_index` iterator calls. But better still, `map` enables us to condense the bulk of that logic—*make an array of* rows *things, each of which is an array of* cols *zeros*—into one line:.

```
def initialize(rows,cols)
  @rows, @cols = rows, cols
  @data = (0...rows).map{(0...cols).map{0}}
end
```

Wrap that in `class IntegerMatrix...end`, and we're under way.

Another very concise way to create the matrix takes advantage of the optional "default value" argument to `Array.new`, like this:

```
def initialize(rows,cols)
  @rows, @cols = rows, cols
  @data = Array.new(rows,Array.new(cols,0))
end
```

Still, using `map` is probably a little better in the interest of consistency, because mapping numeric ranges to create arrays is the more standard and generalizable technique. It's just as suitable for situations where you're not looking for a homogeneous result, as in the following examples:

```
(0..7).map{|n| (n+?0).chr * n}
#-> ["", "1", "22", "333", "4444", "55555", "666666", "7777777"]

(1...5).map{|x| (1...5).map{|y| x*y}}  # multiplcation table
#-> [[1, 2, 3, 4, 5],
#    [2, 4, 6, 8, 10],
#    [3, 6, 9, 12, 15],
#    [4, 8, 12, 16, 20],
#    [5, 10, 15, 20, 25]]
```

Storing and Retrieving Elements

How can we get data into our matrix and back out? It would be easy just to ask for an `attr_accessor` for `@data`, but that's not considerate to the user, who would have to know how @data was organized. Rather, we'd like the user to be able to access elements by *row, column* pairs, something like this:

```
mat = IntegerMatrix.new(2,2)
mat.put(0,1,514)
mat.get(0,1)        #-> 514
```

So we know how we want put and get to work; now we have to write the methods. To store something into the matrix, we find the inner array of @data according to the given row, and drop the value at the location within it according to the given column. Getting the information back out works exactly the same way. Here are working put and get method definitions.

```
class IntegerMatrix
  #...
  def put(row_index,col_index,value)
    @data[row_index][col_index] = value
  end
  def get(row_index,col_index)
    @data[row_index][col_index]
  end
```

While we're at it, wouldn't it be cool if we could support array-like indexing with square brackets, like this?

```
mat[1,1] = -6
mat[0,1]            #-> 514
mat[1,1]            #-> -6
```

Whaddaya know—we're in luck. [] and []= are legal method names. Drop two alias lines into the class definition, and *voila*, we've got it.

```
alias []= put
alias []  get
```

There's a point of safety to touch on here. We have decided to limit our matrix data to integers. Nothing is stopping the user from saying mat[0,0]="kaboom" and making a mess of things when the time comes to do some math, but we can teach put to look for such dangers and raise an exception sooner rather than later:

```
def put(row_index,col_index,value)
  raise TypeError "non-integer value in IntegerMatrix" unless
    value.is_a? Integer
  # ... fill in rest of method as before
```

There's no need to also fix up []= this way, since it's just an alias for put.

The Kernel.raise method can be called with just a descriptive string, in which case the type of exception raised is the generic RuntimeError, but in this case, we have been a little more precise and categorized our exception as one having to do with object types. The benefit of this comes when the caller wants to do different things to recover from different kinds of exceptions in a `begin...rescue...rescue...end` context, as we discussed on Day 6.

 **Note**

> Aliasing a method name actually makes a copy of the original method rather than just giving it a new name; this is why we alias a method after it's defined and not before. A consequence of this is that if a method is redefined after it is aliased, the alias refers to the old method rather than the new one. Some people like to use this property when experimenting with language extension: If you want to change the way a standard Ruby method works, make an alias of it first, then write a new method with the old name. The new method can call the aliased method if necessary.

Alternatively, we can sometimes get away with glossing over errors instead of complaining about them. A standard method named `to_i` converts other objects to integers. Most strings will make `to_i` return 0. It's safe to apply `to_i` to something that's already an integer (in which case nothing happens). If `to_i` finds that it can't make the required conversion, `IntegerMatrix#put` should still raise an exception. Here is another reasonable way to define the method:

```
def put(row_index,col_index,value)
  @data[row_index][col_index] = value.to_i
end
```

The `initialize`, `put`, and `get` methods provide the meat of the interface to `@data`. From here on out, even within other `IntegerMatrix` methods, we'll try to use those methods whenever possible rather than accessing `@data` directly. An instance method wanting to read the element at position *r,c* should say `self.get(r,c)` or `self[r,c]`, but not `@data[r][c]`. Although this approach might cost a little in performance, it will buy clarity. We're more concerned with getting the job done right, at least today, than with getting it done quickly.

Since `self` is the default receiver of method calls, `self.get(r,c)` can also be written as `get(r,c)`. We'll usually use the longer form in this chapter, making it clear exactly when we are referring to methods instead of local variables, but you can leave the `self` references out of your code if you like.

Accessing Dimensions

You noticed that in `initialize`, we stored the dimensions of the matrix in the instance variables `@rows` and `@cols`. Whenever those are needed later, they'll be readily accessible without making us examine `@data` for its length and the length of its elements.

The dimensions of a matrix should be read-only attributes, so we'll provide attribute readers for them. Just as with put and get, we'll generally use accessors (like self.row) rather than looking straight at the instance data. And although it's not strictly necessary, we'll provide a reader method that returns the dimensions together as a pair. That will make it easy later to determine whether two matrices have matching dimensions.

Listing 15.1 shows integermatrix.rb as it stands so far, including reader methods for rows, cols, and dimensions.

LISTING 15.1   integermatrix.rb

```
01:    class IntegerMatrix
02:      def initialize(rows,cols=1)
03:        @rows, @cols = rows, cols
04:        @data = (0...rows).map{ (0...cols).map {0}}
05:      end
06:
07:      attr_reader :rows, :cols
08:
09:      def dimensions
10:        [self.rows,self.cols]
11:      end
12:
13:      def get(rowidx,colidx)
14:        @data[rowidx][colidx]
15:      end
16:      alias [] get
17:
18:      def put(rowidx,colidx,value)
19:        raise TypeError "non-integer value in IntegerMatrix" unless
20:          value.is_a? Integer
21:        @data[rowidx][colidx]=value
22:      end
23:      alias []= put
24:    end
```

Viewing a Matrix as a Whole

If you load what we have so far into irb, you can create a matrix and immediately see all of its data.

```
irb(main):001:0> load 'integermatrix.rb'
true
irb(main):002:0> mat = IntegerMatrix.new(2,2)
#<IntegerMatrix:0x401e985c  @data=[[0, 0], [0, 0]], @cols=2, @rows=2>
```

We don't yet have a way to display matrices in rectangular form. All we have is what Ruby gave us without our asking: puts mat shows the class name and a cryptic-looking hex number, and p mat shows the same information we got back after creating mat. If a rectangular view were desired, the user would have to write the code to do it.

So our next task is to write a method returning a string that, when printed, lays out the matrix contents nicely. The method could be called display, or maybe rectangular_display, but for reasons we'll see shortly, the "correct" thing to call it is to_s.

```
def to_s
  (0...self.rows).map{|r|
    (0...self.cols).map{|c| "%5d"%self[r,c]}.join(" ")
  }.join("\n")
end
```

We already knew that to_s means to convert something to a string, but it seems less clear to say puts mat.to_s than puts mat.rectangular_display. So why use to_s? Because it's the method that automatically gets invoked when you attempt to print an object directly. In other words, all the user has to say is puts mat and the matrix will be printed in rectangular form. to_s isn't often called explicitly, but having it defined makes a class easier to use.

You use to_s to express the *default way of looking at an object*. You can always add more methods to show it in other ways, but since we know that a matrix is generally viewed in rectangular form, to_s should honor that convention.

Another special method for viewing objects is inspect. Its intent is slightly different from that of to_s, because it's not really intended for the users of a class but for you, the programmer. It typically gives more information than to_s, and does not always give it in a very pretty form. inspect is invoked when you print an object via the diagnostic method p. It's also used by irb when it displays objects.

A good diagnostic view of a matrix would probably be rectangular as well. We already have our to_s method working, so let's reuse it: inspect will invoke self.to_s and return its results along with the dimensions of the matrix and the class name. That's the same information we get from the default inspect, but in a tidier package.

```
def inspect
  "%dx%d %s\n%s" % [self.rows, self.cols, self.type, self.to_s]
end
```

Now we have two sensible views of IntegerMatrix objects, one for normal use and one for diagnostic use:

```
testm = IntegerMatrix.new(2,3)
testm[0,0]=68; testm[0,1]=94; testm[0,2]=-2
testm[1,0]=11; testm[1,1]=7;  testm[1,2]=50
```

```
puts testm
  # output:
        68      94      -2
        11       7      50

p testm
  # output:
    2x3 IntegerMatrix
        68      94      -2
        11       7      50
```

If we had wanted to, we could have stuck with a single view by simply making inspect an alias for to_s.

By the way, if you're thinking there should be a simpler way to populate the matrix with values than one element at a time, of course you're right. We'll get to that later today. Now that we've gone to the trouble of building this particular matrix, though, we can at least keep it around for some of the upcoming tests.

Providing Iterators

An IntegerMatrix is a container, and as such, it should provide iterators. We'll make three of them at first, because there are three obvious ways to iterate over a matrix: by row, by column, and by individual element.

Iteration by row is definitely the easiest to implement, because we know (at least when wearing the Class Builder hat) that @data is an array of rows. All IntegerMatrix#each_row will have to do is invoke each on @data, yielding back to the caller each row it sees.

```
Class IntegerMatrix
  def each_row
    @data.each {|row| yield row}
  end
end

testm.each_row {|r| p r}
#  output:
  [68, 94, -2]
  [11, 7, 50]
```

The each_column iterator is a little trickier, but we can handle it. We'll walk horizontally across the matrix, using map to build a different column array at every step:

```
Class IntegerMatrix
  def each_column
    self.cols.times do |colidx|
      yield(@data.map {|row| row[colidx]})
    end
  end
end
```

You might want to study that method, because, admittedly, it looks a little strange. It does the job though, as shown here:

```
testm.each_column {|c| p c}
#  output:
    [68, 11]
    [94, 7]
    [-2, 50]
```

The third iterator, each, is left for you as Exercise 2 at the end of today's lesson.

Doing the Math

There are several math operations that make sense on matrices. The four simplest are to add, subtract, multiply, or divide all elements by a single number. Here's an example of multiplying a matrix by a constant:

```
testm * 3   #->    204   282    -6
            #       33    21   150
```

To implement this kind of multiplication, we will want to define a method whose name is multiplied_by.[2] It should take one numeric argument, which is the factor to be multiplied by all elements. A more interesting question is what it should return. Clearly, it should give us back a matrix; but we have to be careful, because, just as 3×2 evaluates to 6 without affecting the sacred values of 3 or 2, multiplication of a matrix by a number should not affect that matrix. We don't want to change any values of self. In the following IntegerMatrix#multiplied_by method, notice the use of IntegerMatrix.new at the very top. This new matrix gets filled with the appropriate values, and is then returned at the end. As we wanted, self is undisturbed.

```
def multiplied_by(num)
  result = IntegerMatrix.new(self.rows,self.cols)
  self.rows.times do |r|
    self.cols.times do |c|
      result[r,c] = num * self[r,c]
    end
  end
  result
end
```

Next will be division. It would be pretty easy to implement a divided_by method by copying and pasting what we just wrote, changing the method name, and changing an asterisk to a forward slash. But what fun is that? Writing lots of redundant code is not the

---

[2]*I like all methods to have word names, which can then be aliased to operator symbols. But it doesn't have to be done that way; you can def *(factor) directly if you prefer. It's a personal matter that ultimately comes down to whatever helps you think clearly as you work.*

Ruby Way, even if good text editors support such bad habits. Instead, we should spend a little time deciding what's redundant and factoring it out.

Since almost all of the `multiplied_by` method could be used in other operations on our matrix, let's give it a more general name, and reuse it for all those operations. The only part that isn't redundant is the * operator itself, and since that's a piece of logic rather than a piece of data, this is starting to look like a job for an iterator. Here's how we would like to be able to use such an iterator (we'll call it `foo` for now—not a good name at all, but at least it's less of a mouthful than `plusminustimesordividedby`):

```
def plus(n)          self.foo {|x| x + n}  end
def minus(n)         self.foo {|x| x - n}  end
def multiplied_by(n) self.foo {|x| x * n}  end
def divided_by(n)    self.foo {|x| x / n}  end

alias +   plus
alias -   minus
alias *   multiplied_by
alias /   divided_by
```

There: four quick methods that will save a bunch of space. All we need to do now is create `foo` to breathe life into the rest of them. Have you come up with a better name than `foo` yet? Think: Haven't we seen an iterator that does something just like what we're asking of `foo`, but applied to arrays? Sure: it's map, also known as `collect`. Once we notice the connection, there's no reason to call our new iterator anything else (we sure weren't going to leave it as `foo`). Our map will do exactly what anyone familiar with `Array#map` would expect. Here it is:

```
def map
  result = IntegerMatrix.new(self.rows,self.cols)
  self.rows.times do |r|
    self.cols.times do |c|
      result[r,c] = yield(self[r,c])
    end
  end
  result
end
```

It might help you appreciate just how useful this is when someone asks, "While you're at it, could you implement a unary minus operator?" Snap your fingers and it's done.

```
class IntegerMatrix
  def negated() self.map {|x| -x} end
  alias -@ negated
end

-testm     #->    -68   -94    2
           #      -11    -7   -50
```

That funny symbol `-@` is Ruby's way of distinguishing a unary minus operator from the usual subtraction operator, which would appear as `-` in an `alias` statement.

Multipurpose Methods

We've made it possible to add a single number to every element of a matrix, but matrix addition can have another meaning, as illustrated in Figure 15.1.

FIGURE 15.1

Addition of two matrices.

$$\begin{bmatrix} 3 & 9 \\ 8 & 6 \\ 6 & 1 \end{bmatrix} + \begin{bmatrix} 5 & 7 \\ 2 & 3 \\ 6 & 1 \end{bmatrix} \rightarrow \begin{bmatrix} 8 & 16 \\ 10 & 9 \\ 12 & 2 \end{bmatrix}$$

A method to add c___ _____ __ _____ _____ ___ ____ ____ __ _____ __ _ _____ that we've already "used up" the method name `plus`, but we can remedy that soon. For now we'll just call it `plus_matrix` for lack of something better.

```
def plus_matrix(other)
  raise "Dimension mismatch" if
          other.dimensions != self.dimensions
  result = IntegerMatrix.new(self.rows,self.cols)
  self.rows.times do |r|
    self.cols.times do |c|
      result[r,c] = self[r,c] + other[r,c]
    end
  end
  result
end
```

For quick verification that plus_matrix works, let's see what happens when we add `testm` to itself:

```
testm.plus_matrix(testm)
 #->  2x3 IntegerMatrix
 #      136    188    -4
 #       22     14   100
```

Now to grapple with the naming issue. If we're going to make things easy for the users of our class, then two method names for addition in the interface are really one too many. The key to remedying the situation is to make `IntegerMatrix#plus` smart enough to tell the difference between one argument type and another. If its argument is a number, that number should be added into all elements of the result; if it's another matrix, each element should be added with the corresponding element of `self`.

You might remember the `Object#type` method that tells you what class an object belongs to. An `IntegerMatrix#plus` method laid out as follows might be good enough for our purposes today, but it leaves us open to accusations of short-sightedness.

```
def plus(z)
  if z.type == "IntegerMatrix"
    #... find the sum of the two matrices
  else
    #... add z to each element of the new array
  end
end
```

15

The reason this is short-sighted is that it doesn't allow for inheritance. Someday you or somebody else might create a new subclass of `IntegerMatrix`. Its plus method will immediately misbehave, because the `z.type` test will mistakenly return `false` for argu-ments that legitimately refer to matrices rather than numbers. The solution for this is pro-vided by `Object#is_a?`, which you saw in the definition of `IntegerMatrix#put` a little while ago. `is_a?` performs a more useful test based on inheritance, returning `true` if the argument matches the receiver object's class or any of its ancestor classes.

```
n = 4096
n.type == Fixnum  #->  true
n.type == Bignum  #->  false
n.type == Integer #->  false

n.is_a?(Fixnum)  #->  true
n.is_a?(Bignum)  #->  false
n.is_a?(Integer) #->  true
```

Note
Every class descends from `Object`, so `is_a?(Object)` can be expected always to return `true` unless a mischievous programmer has redefined `is_a?`. An alias for `is_a?` is `kind_of?`.

We don't have to rewrite `plus_matrix`, at least not yet—we can leave it where it is and call it from our new plus method. To take the name `plus_matrix` officially out of the user interface (where it will no be longer needed), we can make it `private`:

```
def plus(z)
  if z.is_a? IntegerMatrix
    self.plus_matrix(z)
  else
    self.map {|x| x+z}  # what the old plus method did
  end
end
private :plus_matrix
```

Now that we have a plus method that does two kinds of addition, we'll probably be wanting a more versatile minus method as well. That will mean coming up with a `minus_matrix` method that will end up looking . . . suspiciously . . . hmm . . . like `plus_matrix`.

I suppose you already know what's coming. It's time to refactor. `IntegerMatrix#combine` will be a general-purpose iterator for combining the matrices `self` and `other` into a new matrix, element by element, using any rule specified by the user. We can create it by slightly modifying `plus_matrix`:

```
def combine(other)
  raise "Dimension mismatch" if
              other.dimensions != self.dimensions
  result = IntegerMatrix.new(self.rows,self.cols)
  self.rows.times do |r|
    self.cols.times do |c|
      result[r,c] = yield(self[r,c],other[r,c])
    end
  end
  result
end
```

Armed with `combine`, we can knock `plus` and `minus` down to size, and we'll no longer need `plus_matrix`. Here are streamlined `plus` and `minus` methods:

```
def plus(x)
  if x.is_a? IntegerMatrix
    self.combine(x) {|e1,e2| e1+e2}
  else
    self.map {|e| e+x}
  end
end

def minus(x)
  if x.is_a? IntegerMatrix
    self.combine(x) {|e1,e2| e1-e2}
  else
    self.map {|e| e-x}
  end
end
```

A Versatile Constructor Using Default Values

A *constructor* is a method responsible for making a new object. In Ruby, just as in Java and C++, one class can have many constructors that make an object in different ways, which usually means they start with different kinds of information.

The standard constructor in Ruby is the class method `new`, which invokes the instance method `initialize`. We could write other class methods to be used instead of `new`, but today we'll be teaching `initialize` to do different things depending on the arguments it sees. An intelligent `initialize` can turn `new` into one rather talented constructor, which should behave as follows:

15

- If given a pair of numbers, make a matrix having those numbers as dimensions, and fill it with zeros. (We've already done this much.)
- If given three numbers, use the first two as dimensions and the third as the initial fill value.

Here are examples of the behavior we want:

```
IntegerMatrix.new(2,3)    #-> 0  0  0
                          #   0  0  0

IntegerMatrix.new(2,3,9) #-> 9  9  9
                          #   9  9  9
```

The following `IntegerMatrix#initialize` method definition is constructed so that the user must supply the first two arguments, but, since the third is associated with a default value, the user can omit it.

```
def initialize(rows,cols,value=0)
  @rows, @cols = rows, cols
  @data = (0...rows).map { (0...cols).map {value} }
end
```

Suppose we made `rows` and `cols` optional but made the user always specify the default value. Could it work? Well, not exactly in this form:

```
class IntegerMatrix
  def initialize(rows=2, cols=3, value)
    # ...

m = IntegerMatrix.new(6, 33)
```

Apparently 33 is intended to be the initial value of all elements of the matrix, but what about the 6? Is that for the rows, or is it for the columns? Should we use dimensions 6 × 3 or 2 × 6? To prevent this ambiguity, Ruby has a rule that optional arguments must always come last in the argument list.

A More Versatile Constructor

Now let's get really ambitious and teach `IntegerMatrix.new` two more ways to build a matrix.

- If given an `IntegerMatrix`, it should use it as a model to create the new matrix.
- If given an array of arrays, it should use that data to populate the new matrix.

The added behavior we want:

```
IntegerMatrix.new(testm)
   #->   68   94    2
   #     11    7   50
IntegerMatrix.new([[11,12], [13,14]])
   #->   11   12
   #     13   14
```

Things have become quite complicated. Now there might be one, two or three arguments, and the first argument no longer needs to be a number. Default values won't help us, but we can take all the arguments in as a single array and go from there. initialize will look at that array and delegate responsibility to some other method depending on what it finds. (See lines 9–37 of Listing 15.2.).

The user will always be constructing objects through new, so initialize isn't properly part of the interface. Ruby automatically makes initialize private. Since we've provided some helper methods for initialize that also shouldn't be part of the interface, we explicitly made those private too.

The important thing to notice is that although we went to a lot of trouble here and ended up with some complicated code, the complexity is *hidden inside the class implementation, behind a simple interface*. The user doesn't have to worry about what methods initialize relies on. IntegerMatrix.new just makes the right thing happen.

Listing 15.2 shows integermatrix.rb in a more complete state. You'll have a chance to enhance it still more in the exercises at the end of today's lesson.

LISTING 15.2   integermatrix.rb

```
001:   #
002:   # integermatrix.rb: the IntegerMatrix class
003:   #
004:
005:   class IntegerMatrix
006:     ##############################################
007:     # Initialization
008:     ##############################################
009:     def initialize(*args)
010:       if args.size==1
011:         if args[0].is_a? IntegerMatrix
012:           init_from_matrix(args[0])
013:         else
014:           init_from_array(args[0])
015:         end
016:       else
017:         init_without_data(*args)
```

LISTING 15.2   Continued

```
018:        end
019:      end
020:
021:      def init_from_matrix(m)
022:        @rows, @cols =  m.rows, m.cols
023:        @data = [];  m.each_row {|r| @data.push r.dup}
024:      end
025:
026:      def init_from_array(a)
027:        @rows, @cols = a.size, a[0].size
028:        @data = []
029:        a.each {|r| @data.push r.dup}
030:      end
031:
032:      def init_without_data(rows,cols,value=0)
033:        @rows, @cols = rows, cols
034:        @data = (0...rows).map { (0...cols).map {value} }
035:      end
036:
037:      private :init_from_matrix, :init_from_array, :init_without_data
038:
039:      attr_reader :rows, :cols
040:
041:      def dimensions
042:        [self.rows,self.cols]
043:      end
044:
045:      ################################################
046:      # Core interface: get, put
047:      ################################################
048:      def get(rowidx,colidx)
049:        @data[rowidx][colidx]
050:      end
051:      alias [] get
052:
053:      def put(rowidx,colidx,value)
054:        raise TypeError "non-integer value in IntegerMatrix" unless
055:          value.is_a? Integer
056:        @data[rowidx][colidx]=value
057:      end
058:      alias []= put
059:
060:      ################################################
061:      # Simple iterators
062:      ################################################
063:      def each_row
064:        @data.each {|row| yield row}
065:      end
```

continues

LISTING 15.2   Continued

```
066:
067:     def each_column
068:       self.cols.times do |colidx|
069:         yield(@data.map {|row| row[colidx]})
070:       end
071:     end
072:
073:     ##################################################
074:     # Iterators for creating new matrices
075:     ##################################################
076:     def map
077:       result = IntegerMatrix.new(self.rows,self.cols)
078:       self.rows.times do |r|
079:         self.cols.times do |c|
080:           result[r,c] = yield(self[r,c])
081:         end
082:       end
083:       result
084:     end
085:
086:     def combine(other)
087:       raise "Dimension mismatch" if
088:         other.dimensions != self.dimensions
089:       result = IntegerMatrix.new(self.rows,self.cols)
090:       self.rows.times do |r|
091:         self.cols.times do |c|
092:           result[r,c] = yield(self[r,c],other[r,c])
093:         end
094:       end
095:       result
096:     end
097:
098:     ##################################################
099:     # Math operations
100:     ##################################################
101:     def multiplied_by(n) self.map {|x| x*n} end
102:     def divided_by(n)    self.map {|x| x/n} end
103:     def plus(x)
104:       if x.is_a? IntegerMatrix
105:         self.combine(x) {|e1,e2| e1+e2}
106:       else
107:         self.map {|e| e+x}
108:       end
109:     end
110:     def minus(x)
111:       if x.is_a? IntegerMatrix
112:         self.combine(x) {|e1,e2| e1-e2}
113:       else
```

LISTING 15.2 Continued

```
114:            self.map {|e| e-x}
115:          end
116:        end
117:
118:        alias * multiplied_by
119:        alias / divided_by
120:        alias + plus
121:        alias - minus
122:
123:        #################################################
124:        # Conversion to string
125:        #################################################
126:        def to_s
127:          (0...self.rows).map{|r|
128:            (0...self.cols).map{|c| "%5d" % self[r,c]}.join(" ")
129:          }.join("\n")
130:        end
131:
132:        def inspect
133:          "%dx%d %s\n%s" %  [self.rows, self.cols, self.type, self.to_s]
134:        end
135:
136:      end
```

Summary

Our objective for today was to learn how to make a class easy to use. `IntegerMatrix`
turns out to have quite a lot of functionality, and perhaps we can't convincingly say we
succeeded in keeping its interface small. But we did make it quite intuitive, so that a user
would be able to do a lot of things right the first time even when guessing. Our constructor does a good job of setting up each new matrix based on the supplied information; the
basic mathematical operators all seem to do what they should; `to_s` and `inspect` make it
easy for the user to see what each `IntegerMatrix` object is made of.

We're in Week 3 now, the home stretch. Tomorrow is to be the first of two "putting it
together" sessions; that means that rather than introduce new topics, we'll be working
through two substantial projects together. You can think of them as in-class exercises,
with more detailed discussion than normally goes with the daily exercises. The second
of these sessions comes on Day 21. In between, we'll learn about graphic user interfaces, network services, and more of the stuff that makes knowing Ruby so useful in the
real world.

Exercises

1. Since we've written `IntegerMatrix#map`, should we try to write a `select` method, too? Why or why not?

2. Write the `IntegerMatrix#each` method that we omitted earlier. It should yield matrix elements one at a time, as in this example.

   ```
   testm
     #->    68    94     2
     #      11     7    50
   testm.each {|e| print -e," "}
     #output:    -68 -94 -2 -11 -7 -50
   ```

3. What should an `IntegerMatrix#find` method do? See if you can write one. *Hint:* You can model it after `IntegerMatrix#map`.

4. Write `IntegerMatrix#equal?` and alias it as `==`. It should take another `IntegerMatrix` as a parameter and return `true` if and only if it is identical to `self` both in its dimensions and its contents. *Hint:* A solution might resemble `IntegerMatrix#combine`.

5. Make `IntegerMatrix#multiplied_by` smart enough to do true matrix multiplication when it's given another matrix instead of a number. When multiplying a matrix with x rows and y columns by another with y rows and z columns, you get back a matrix with x rows and z columns. Element r,c in the resulting matrix is determined by multiplying each element in the rth row of the first matrix by the corresponding element in the cth column of the second, and adding those products up. (Consult any good algebra textbook for a much clearer explanation than this one!) Here's some test code to show the desired results:

   ```
   m1 = IntegerMatrix.new [[5,0,-2,1],[1,2,9,1]]
     #->  2x4 IntegerMatrix
     #         5    0    -2    1
     #         1    2     9    1

   m2 = IntegerMatrix.new [[-3,-2,2], [1,0,4], [0,0,6], [5,2,-9]]
     #->  4x3 IntegerMatrix
     #        -3    -2    2
     #         1     0    4
     #         0     0    6
     #         5     2   -9

   m1 * m2
     #->  2x3 IntegerMatrix
     #       -10    -8   -11
     #         4     0    55
   ```

   Hint: Instead of one big `multiplied_by` method, you might want to make a private `matrix_product` function and invoke it from `multiplied_by` when the argument is a matrix.

6. Create a two-dimensional `Vector` class. Each object will be a number pair, which you can think of as a horizontal and vertical displacement on a Cartesian graph. A vector has direction and length. See whether you can make your class support this test code:

```
v1 = Vector.new(3,4)          #-> (3.0,4.0)
v2 = Vector.new(12,-5)        #-> (12.0,-5.0)
v1 + v2                       #-> (15.0,-1.0)
v1 - v2                       #-> (-9.0,9.0)
-v1                           #-> (-3.0,-4.0)
v1.length                     #-> 5.0
v1.direction                  #-> "northeast"
v2.direction                  #-> "southeast"
(v1-v2).direction             #-> "southwest"
Vector.new(-15,0).direction   #-> "west"
```

Hint: Use the Pythagorean theorem to find the length of a vector (square *x* and *y*, add them together, then take the square root using `Math::sqrt`).

Answers

1. It's probably not a good idea. `Array#select` works by returning some elements and not others. That makes sense, because arrays can grow and shrink. But a matrix needs to be rectangular; eliminating some elements would have to change its size or shape. One way to solve that problem would be to replace rejected elements with `nil`s, but that would leave us with something that was no longer strictly an integer matrix. It's hard to think of a legitimate use for `IntegerMatrix#select`, anyway. Classes need not support every conceivable method.

2. The following solution accesses `@data` directly; as such, it's likely to perform well, but keep in mind that every time you write such a method, you commit yourself more firmly to the way the data is organized, and you just might make future maintenance of the class more difficult. (Notice that the `each_row` and `each_column` methods also share this characteristic.) Still, given the tradeoff, many programmers will opt for whatever gives better performance.

```
def each
  @data.flatten.each {|elt| yield elt}
end
```

Here are two alternative solutions that avoid referring to `@data` and so emphasize maintainability at the possible expense of speed. If you like, as a further exercise you can try rewriting `each_row` and `each_column` with the same goal in mind.

```
# Doing nested iteration over index pairs:
def each
  self.rows.times {|r| self.cols.times {|c| yield self[r,c]}}
end

# Slightly better, taking advantage of each_row:
def each
  each_row {|row| row.each {|elt| yield elt}}
end
```

3. Consider the behavior of Array#find. It suggests that IntegerMatrix#find should return indices: a *row, column* pair for the first element found that satisfies the given condition, or nil if none do. As hinted, it can be constructed like IntegerMatrix#map. The primary difference is that it needs to be prepared to return early, as soon as it finds an element that meets the user's critereon.

```
def find
  self.rows.times do |r|
    self.cols.times do |c|
      return r,c if yield self[r,c]
    end
  end
  nil # if we got here, all yields came back false
end
```

4. Like the find method, equal? should return as soon as it knows an answer.

```
def equal?(other)
  return false if self.dimensions != other.dimensions
  self.rows.times do |r|
    self.cols.times do |c|
      return false if self[r,c] != other[r,c]
    end
  end
  true  # if we got here, dimensions and all elements match
end
alias == equals
```

By the way, once you've defined ==, Ruby knows what != means without being told.

5. Here is the solution described in the hint. Because we previously had the * operator aliased to multiplied_by, * now becomes able to do this kind of matrix multiplication as well.

```
def multiplied_by(z)
  if z.is_a? IntegerMatrix
    self.matrix_product(z)
  else
    self.map {|e| e*z}
  end
end
```

15

```
def matrix_product(other)
  raise "Dimension mismatch" if self.cols != other.rows
  result = IntegerMatrix.new(self.rows, other.cols)
  self.rows.times do |r|
    other.cols.times do |c|
      sum = 0
      self.cols.times {|idx| sum += (self[r,idx]*other[idx,c])}
      result[r,c]=sum
    end
  end
  result
end
private :matrix_product
```

6. This was an opportunity to practice some of the tricks we learned in writing friendly methods for the `IntegerMatrix` class. Our solution in Listing 15.3 uses verbose names for the arithmetic functions and has operator symbols aliased to them, but you may prefer simply to define the methods with symbolic names.

LISTING 15.3 vector.rb

```
01:     class Vector
02:       def initialize(x, y)
03:         @x, @y = x,y
04:       end
05:       attr_reader :x, :y
06:
07:       def length      # from Pythagorus
08:         return Math::sqrt(@x*@x + @y*@y)
09:       end
10:       alias size length
11:
12:       def to_s
13:         "(%.1f,%.1f)" % [@x,@y]
14:       end
15:       alias inspect to_s
16:
17:       def plus(vec)        Vector.new(@x+vec.x, @y+vec.y)  end
18:       def minus(vec)       Vector.new(@x-vec.x, @y-vec.y)  end
19:       def multiplied_by(n) Vector.new(@x*n, @y*n)          end
20:       def divided_by(n)    Vector.new(@x/n, @y/n)          end
21:       def negated()        Vector.new(-@x, -@y)            end
22:       alias +  plus
23:       alias -  minus
24:       alias *  multiplied_by
25:       alias /  divided_by
26:       alias -@ negated
27:
28:       def direction
```

continues

LISTING 15.3   Continued

```
29:             if @y>0 and @x>0 then "northeast"
30:             elsif @y>0 and @x<0 then "northwest"
31:             elsif @y>0 then "north"
32:             elsif @y<0 and @x>0 then "southeast"
33:             elsif @y<0 and @x<0 then "southwest"
34:             elsif @y<0 then "south"
35:             elsif @x>0 then "east"
36:             elsif @x<0 then "west"
37:             else "none"
38:             end
39:         end
40:
41:         # A very terse alternative to the above:
42:         #
43:         # def direction
44:         #   d=["south","","north"][(@y<=>0)+1]+
                      ➥["west","","east"][(@x<=>0)+1]
45:         #   (d.empty?) ? "none" : d
46:         # end
47:
48:     end
```

We have provided for addition and subtraction with another vector, but not with an ordinary number. Do you think it seems reasonable, for instance, to have (1.5, -2.1) + 4.0 return the vector (5.5, 1.9)? If so, then as a further exercise, you might want to enhance Vector#plus and Vector#minus so they know what to do when they are given a number instead of another vector. Look again at lines 103–109 of Listing 15.2 if you need help getting started.

DAY 16

Putting It Together (Part I)

> He had been eight years upon a project for extracting sunbeams from cucumbers, which were to be put into vials hermetically sealed, and let out to warm the air in raw inclement summers.
>
> —Jonathan Swift, *Gulliver's Travels* (1726)

There is no single organizing topic today, and there will be no exercises at the end. Instead we'll work through two real-world projects together: one of them fun, the other more serious.

The fun project will help you cheat on a word puzzle from your newspaper. The serious project does some important Unix system administration work.

Anybody mind if we start with the fun one?

The Unjumbler

Scrambled words are hard for humans to deal with, though there are humans who have an uncanny knack for unscrambling them quickly. If you look at the scrambled word *clabena* and can unscramble it in your head in a few seconds, you're one of those lucky ones. Most of the rest of us would end up writing down lots of more or less random arrangements of the letters (canebal, neablac, acalenb, ...and so on) hoping that we stumble across one, say *balenca*, close enough to the answer to make us see it. When no such inspiration strikes, we have to try a lot of permutations—because there are, to be exact, *n*! of them for any *n*-letter word. For *clabena,* that's 7! = 5040.

The job is a little easier for a computer because it can spin out all the permutations without getting confused or tired. On the other hand, it never benefits from sudden inspirations. Also, unless it has a considerably more complicated program than we will write here, it will waste time on obviously unproductive paths, such as testing the 24 permutations starting with *aae* and the 120 starting with *cb*. Human sophistication and intuition might sometimes get you an answer faster, but when that fails, the script we are about to write will always get you there. Eventually.

A natural breakdown of the problem is first to generate all the permutations of the characters of a string and then to determine which of those permutations are words.

Getting the Permutations

Consider how you would rearrange the three-character string abc on paper.

```
abc, acb, bac, bca, cab, cba
```

The obvious logical approach is to take each letter, put it at the beginning, and combine it with all possible arrangements of the remaining letters before moving on. Easy enough when we have such a short string, but what if it's longer, such as abcde?

```
abcde
a....    ummm...
```

Hold on a minute. Leaving the a out front, we were about to figure out "all the permutations of the remaining letters," bcde. Doesn't that sound like we're dealing with a smaller version of the same problem we started with? Then this is a great candidate for recursion. We don't have to think about it so hard after all, because, like most recursive solutions, it is staring us in the face. We just have to go back and slightly formalize what we said a moment ago.

To find the permutations of a string, try each character at the front and attach it to all the permutations of the remaining characters. And what about when there are no remaining characters? That's the base case, and it can be expressed with happy simplicity: *A string of a single character has just one permutation, which is itself.* Listing 16.1 is a recursive function to return an array of all permutations of a string. For the sake of explanation, the listing has been made a little longer than it needs to be, but we'll tighten it up momentarily.

LISTING 16.1 A Function to Return All Permutations of a String

```
01:  def permutations( word )
02:     len = word.length
03:     if len > 1
04:        result = []
05:        len.times do |idx|
06:           front = word[idx,1]
07:           remaining_chars = word[0...idx]+word[idx+1..-1]
08:           perms_of_remaining = permutations(remaining_chars)
09:           recombined = perms_of_remaining.map{|w| front + w}
10:           result += recombined
11:        end
12:        result.uniq
13:     else
14:        [word]
15:     end
16:  end
```

Notice the use of ranges to specify substrings in line 7. We didn't mention this back on Day 3, because we learned about string indexing before having seen ranges, but it's nice to be able to use a range when you want to talk about "the rest of a string"—for instance, from position 4 to the end:

```
"CONFIDENTIAL"[4...-1]  #-> "IDENTIAL"
```

Otherwise we'd find ourselves needing to calculate the string length and subtract:

```
"CONFIDENTIAL"[4,"CONFIDENTIAL".length-4]  #->  "IDENTIAL"
```

The bulk of the permutations function is the if portion, lines 4 to 12, which takes care of the recursive case. result starts as an empty array and accumulates permutations for each possible first letter of word. Those letters are chosen from all possible indices of the string, which are the numbers given by len.times. The iterator block takes each index, assigns it to idx, and grabs a character at that position. This is actually a string one character long, expressed as word[idx,1].

Note

> Line 6 of Listing 16.1 could have been written as front=word[idx].chr. Remember, word[idx] returns a number (ASCII value) because Ruby has no Character class.

The variable remaining_chars in line 7 holds whatever is left from word once the front character has been extracted. To illustrate, suppose word is "abc". Then front should be "a" the first time through the iterator block, and remaining_chars should be "bc". When thinking about a recursive solution, we typically assume that it works properly on a smaller problem. So in line 8 we expect perms_of_remaining to receive an array of all possible arrangements of remaining_chars: ["bc", "cb"].

Look back at our strategy statement. . . . *Try each character at the front and attach it to all the permutations of the remaining characters.* We haven't done the attaching yet, and that's the job of line 9. map sticks the front character back onto each element of the array, so recombined becomes ["abc", "acb"].

Line 10 does a set union operation, putting all new permutations of the original string into the array result. Because that array started out empty in line 4, at this moment result contains ["abc", "acb"], making it identical to recombined.

Note

> If there are duplicate letters, some permutations will show up more than once, and we don't need that. We could use |= instead of += to avoid duplications, but applying uniq in line 12 gets rid of them as effectively (and, as it happens, more efficiently). By the way, if it's clearer to you, you can rewrite line 10 as result = result + recombined.

We've gone through the iterator block, lines 6–10, where front was "a". If we keep going and stop after the second pass through line 10, we observe the following values:

```
front                #-> "b"
remaining_chars      #-> "ac"
perms_of_remaining   #-> ["ac","ca"]
recombined           #-> ["bac", "bca"]
result               #-> ["abc","acb","bac","bca"].
```

By now you might see how permutations("abc") manages to return the right thing when it gets to line 11:

```
["abc", "acb", "bac", "bca", "cab", "cba"]
```

We're almost ready to tackle that second task of deciding which permutations are really words. Before we leave the permutations function, though, we'll give it a quick rewrite. The iterator block was constructed in several pieces so we'd have a way to look at intermediate stages along the way. But notice that remaining_chars gets looked at only once—immediately after being defined. If there's no reason to store those values (other than to help us think through the problem clearly, which is not a bad thing at all), they need not be assigned to a variable. Other temporary variables can be eliminated in the same way, as shown in Listing 16.2.

LISTING 16.2   The permutations Function, Rewritten

```
01:  def permutations( word )
02:    len = word.length
03:    if len > 1
04:      result = []
05:      len.times do |idx|
06:        result +=
07:          permutations(word[0...idx]+word[idx+1..-1]).
08:          map{|w| word[idx,1] + w}
09:      end
10:      result.map
11:    else
12:      [word]
13:    end
14:  end
```

Readability is, of course, a subjective thing. The longer version might make more sense to the beginner, but brevity sometimes breeds clarity. There's not a significant performance difference between them in this case. But does it still work? The following is a quick test.

```
print permutations("letho").join("   ")
```

```
# output:
letho   letoh   lehto   lehot   leoth   leoht   lteho   lteoh   ltheo
lthoe   ltoeh   ltohe   lheto   lheot   lhteo   lhtoe   lhoet   lhote
loeth   loeht   loteh   lothe   lohet   lohte   eltho   eltoh   elhto
elhot   eloth   eloht   etlho   etloh   ethlo   ethol   etolh   etohl
ehlto   ehlot   ehtlo   ehtol   eholt   ehotl   eolth   eolht   eotlh
eothl   eohlt   eohtl   tleho   tleoh   tlheo   tlhoe   tloeh   tlohe
telho   teloh   tehlo   tehol   teolh   teohl   thleo   thloe   thelo
theol   thole   thoel   toleh   tolhe   toelh   toehl   tohle   tohel
hleto   hleot   hlteo   hltoe   hloet   hlote   helto   helot   hetlo
hetol   heolt   heotl   htleo   htloe   htelo   hteol   htole   htoel
holet   holte   hoelt   hoetl   hotle   hotel   oleth   oleht   olteh
olthe   olhet   olhte   oelth   oelht   oetlh   oethl   oehlt   oehtl
otleh   otlhe   otelh   otehl   othle   othel   ohlet   ohlte   ohelt
ohetl   ohtle   ohtel
```

Because there are 5! = 120 permutations, we must have found them all (unless there are duplicates in there—you checked, right? Good. I won't bother).

Finding the Needles in the Haystack

Somewhere in the list of anagrams of *letho* in the preceding section, at least one legitimate English word is hiding. You might find it just by looking carefully, but it would be better if a Ruby script could find it for us. Otherwise, maybe the best we could do would be to store the output of permutations into a file, load that file into a word processor, and turn on automatic spell checking so that whatever didn't get highlighted on the screen must be a real word. But clearly, that's a less than optimal approach.

If you're running some flavor of Unix, you probably have a standalone spell checker installed. The best known of these is ispell. When invoked with the -l argument, ispell looks at its standard input and outputs a list of everything that isn't a word.

```
% echo "Come on Cec, gimme a dollar" | ispell -l
Cec
gimme
```

When a single token (we might as well have a name for those things that may or may not be words) is submitted to ispell, it produces output only if the token doesn't exist in the dictionary. So ispell makes it pretty simple to determine whether something *isn't* a word, whereas we're interested only in whether something *is*. Our first attempt at an is_word? function for Unix might test whether the output of ispell is empty. Suppose we try this (in fact, it *was* my first attempt):

```
def is_word?(token)
  `echo #{token} | ispell -l`.empty?
end
```

But it doesn't work; nothing seems to be recognized as a word.

```
is_word?("gimme")    #-> false
is_word?("dollar")   #-> false
```

Time to roll up sleeves and debug. For me, this often means breaking up the code so that I can look at intermediate values, but for this particular function it's simpler. The emptiness test can be temporarily commented out so that what gets returned is the output of ispell.

```
def is_word?(token)
  `echo #{token} | ispell -l`  #.empty?
end

is_word?("gimme")    #->  "gimme\n"
is_word?("dollar")   #->  "\n"
```

Mystery solved. ispell is giving us a line of text that always ends with a linefeed and so is never empty. A chomp, chop, or strip will fix that.

```
def is_word?(token)
  `echo #{token} | ispell -l`.chop.empty?
end

is_word?("gimme")    #->  false
is_word?("dollar")   #->  true
```

We're almost ready to incorporate is_word? into a complete unjumbling script. All that remains is securing input from the user. We could just use the first thing on the command line, ARGV[0]. But a friendlier user interface isn't hard to achieve. We should be able to do something like this:

```
% unjumble.rb lbdria
bridal
ribald
% unjumble.rb
enter a scrambled word: letho
hotel
```

In other words, the script should look for a token on the command line, and if it's not there, prompt the user and get it from the keyboard. An if...else...end will do the job nicely...

```
if ARGV.size > 0
  input_token = ARGV[0]
else
  print "Enter a scrambled word: "
  input_token = gets.chomp
end
```

...but the following more concise expression works just as well.

```
input_token =
  ARGV[0] || (print "Enter a word to descramble: "; gets.chomp)
```

Finished Product

Organized in such a way that the overall logic is plainly in view near the top, Listing 16.3 is a usable script. If you have ispell installed, this script will take a token either from the command line or from the user prompt and print out all the words into which the token can be rearranged, one per line.

LISTING 16.3 unjumble.rb

```
01:   #!/usr/bin/env ruby
02:
03:   # Un-jumbler script
04:   #
05:   # Accepts input from command line or from user
06:   # Prints all words that the input can be rearranged as
07:   #
08:   # Relies on ispell!
09:
10:
11:   def main
12:     input_token =
```

continues

LISTING 16.3   Continued

```
13:        ARGV[0] || (print "enter a scrambled word: "; gets.chomp)
14:      puts permutations(input_token).select{|w| is_word?(w)}
15:    end
16:
17:    def permutations(word)
18:      len = word.length
19:      if len > 1
20:        result = []
21:        len.times do |idx|
22:          result +=
23:            permutations(word[0...idx]+word[idx+1..-1]).
24:            map{|w| word[idx,1] + w}
25:        end
26:        result.uniq
27:      else
28:        [word]
29:      end
30:    end
31:
32:    def is_word?(s)
33:      `echo #{s} | ispell -l`.chop.empty?
34:    end
35:
36:    main
```

A Portable `is_word?` Function

That's all nice, but what if you're running Windows and don't have `ispell`? Or what if running `ispell` thousands of times (it has to run *n*! times when descrambling an *n*-letter word) is a big drag on your machine's performance? Then see whether you can acquire a dictionary file; that is, a simple text file containing real words, one per line:

```
a
ab
abaci
aback
...
```

Tip

Word lists are available on the Web, often for use in computerized word games. A Web search for "dictionary.dat" or "walled wallet" is likely to find something relevant.

If the dictionary file is available as `dictionary.dat`, our script can look there to decide whether something is a word:

```
def is_word?(token)
  dictionary = IO.readlines("dictionary.dat")
  dictionary.include?(token+"\n")
end
```

Substitute that for the original function, and you'll find that everything still works, but quite slowly. There is an unnecessary inefficiency in our design: The dictionary file must be loaded from disk over and over, once for each is_word? call. Machines usually provide some caching mechanism, but that can only help so much. Performance improves when we read the file in main to make sure it happens only once, strip off the linefeeds, and keep reminding is_word? about it. Notice that this time, we chop the newline characters off all the dictionary words, because it has to happen only once.

```
def main
  input_token =
    (ARGV[0] || (print "enter a scrambled word: "; gets)).chomp
  dict = IO.readlines("dictionary.dat").map{|w| w.chop}
  puts permutations(input_token).select{|w| is_word?(w,dict)}
end
#... the permutations function can go here ...
def is_word?(token,words)
  words.include? token
end
```

Some people would use a single global variable $words to avoid passing the words argument. It might not be very good style, but in short scripts you can usually get away with such shenanigans without causing grievous confusion.

A less modular approach is to dispense with the is_word? function altogether and say:

```
puts permutations(input_token).select{|w| dict.include?(w)}
```

At the other extreme, you might prefer to define a Dictionary class, and make it possible to initialize Dictionary objects using either a word file or an external program. Dictionary#is_word? would need to know how to do the right kind of test depending on the initialization.

Bailing Out Early

Suppose you don't care whether there are multiple answers; you want only one. Then the strategy of collecting all permutations first and testing them later seems wasteful. It might be better to generate one permutation, test it, generate the next, test that, and so on, stopping as soon as you find a real word.

What we can do is convert the permutations function into an iterator that yields to a word test every time it generates a new permutation. If a word is detected, the execution of the script can be stopped right away. Listing 16.4 shows how this might be done.

LISTING 16.4 `unjumble-once.rb`

```
01:  #!/usr/bin/env ruby
02:
03:  # Alternative unjumbler that quits as soon as it finds an answer
04:
05:  def main
06:    input_token =
07:      ARGV[0] || (print "enter a scrambled word: "; gets.chomp)
08:    permutations(input_token) {|s| (puts s; exit) if is_word?(s)}
09:  end
10:
11:  def permutations(from_word)
12:    if from_word.length > 1
13:      word = from_word
14:      begin
15:        word = word[1...-1] + word[0..0]
16:        permutations(word[1...-1]) {|rest| yield word[0..0] + rest}
17:      end until word == from_word
18:    else
19:      yield from_word
20:    end
21:  end
22:
23:  # Substitute the file-based version of is_word? if necessary.
24:  def is_word?(token)
25:    `echo #{token} | ispell -l`.chop.empty?
26:  end
27:
28:  main
```

To avoid the use of indices, this version rotates letters to the front of the string in line 15, recursively permuting the rest in line 16. As soon as a word test succeeds, the script is stopped in line 8. If, by dumb luck, one of the early permutations turns out to be a word, `unjumble-once.rb` can dramatically outperform `unjumble.rb`.

Resorting to Wizardry

The scripts we've written so far today perform slowly when given a long word to descramble. But using a dictionary file, it's possible to do better by alphabetizing the characters in the original word *and the dictionary words*. There is no recursion, and performance does not vary with the size of the input.

Listing 16.5 implements this strange strategy. We've left the script with a bargain-basement interface (the user must supply the token and dictionary filename on the command line); if you like, you can dress it up like the others.

LISTING 16.5   unjumble-magically.rb

```
01:   #!/usr/bin/env ruby
02:
03:   # Usage: unjumble-magically.rb token dictionary_filename
04:
05:   def char_sorted(str)  str.split('').sort.join  end
06:
07:   target = char_sorted(ARGV[0])
08:   File.foreach(ARGV[1]) do |w|
09:     w.chop!
10:     puts w if char_sorted(w) == target
11:   end
```

16

Like unjumble.rb in Listing 16.3, unjumble-magically.rb finds all legal words that can be made from the user's token. To stop as soon as the first is found, change line 10 of Listing 16.5 as follows:

```
10:       (puts w; exit) if char_sorted(w) == target
```

Notes on Language Enhancement

You will have noticed by now that no new classes were defined in our unjumbler project. So you might be asking, "Is this object-oriented programming or not?" Well, yes and no. Not all jobs require new classes, and the String and Array classes take care of enough of the basic work here that the logic sitting above them can be procedural. There's no pressing need for us to create, say, an UnscramblableString class. You need not fear the OO police. It is your inalienable right to use existing language tools without creating new ones.

However, whenever you come up with a cool idea that might be applicable down the road, it's worth asking yourself —*asking*, mind you—whether it would make sense to build that new capability into Ruby. It's a relatively easy task to take the code just written and use it to create a String#unscramble method. Then in the future, your scripts could say something like puts("poycim".unscramble), and out would pop "myopic". If you think that the majority of reasonable, right-thinking people would agree that self-unscrambling should be a basic capability of strings, you could agitate for it to be incorporated into standard Ruby. But always remember: The powers that be in the Ruby world are intent on keeping the language from growing out of hand. Most suggestions for enhancing the standard classes are politely, and quite wisely, turned aside. As this one should be!

Of course, there's nothing to prevent you from keeping your own enhancements around in some form that makes them easy for you to use later. A line like `require_'strange_string_methods'` might mean, for instance, *for the duration of this script, I hereby bestow upon Strings the power of unscrambling themselves.*

An Interactive Process Killer

Finally, we get to the serious work.

A variant of the next script is currently in use in a business setting. Here's the scenario: A central database server is consulted all day long by client machines throughout a workplace. The clients are running various versions of Windows, and the server is an old, underpowered, and overworked Unix machine. The client application running on the Windows workstations is interactive; it's possible for a user to walk away from a session without remembering to log out, and the server can handle only so many users at a time. So it's occasionally necessary for the system administrator to kick some users off the system.

But who gets kicked off is not an automatic choice dictated by inflexible policy. It's necessary to look at several factors and make a human decision. Where is the connection being made from? Who is on the other end? (Answering that question is made more difficult by the fact that many users are getting into the system using shared Unix account names.) Are they likely to be in the building? How long has the session been idle?

The `kill-slackers` script can be run whenever the server is overrun with users and has begun to sputter. It gathers information about database sessions in progress, sorts them by decreasing idle time, and presents information about each to the administrator with the option of killing the session, skipping to the next, or quitting the program.

A Little About the Unix Tools

To understand what we're about to do, it will be necessary to get familiar with some of the utilities that help a Unix administrator observe and control the system.

`who` produces a list of the current users with lots of extra information, depending on what command-line switches are used.

```
% who -Ru
hdata    pts/td   Aug 28 19:51  1:45  9469 (front04.vhosp.com)
hdata    pts/tg   Aug 28 19:29  .    14191 (accounts.vhosp.com)
root     pts/tc   Aug 28 19:59  .    14300 (busybody.vhosp.com)
hdata    pts/tw   Aug 28 11:22  0:02 12979 (front04.vhosp.com)
  ...
```

That `root` is you, the administrator. All other users are logged into the database server as user `hdata`. In this example, somebody seems to have two sessions running from the same remote terminal (`front04`). Session idle times are given in hours:minutes format, with a single dot meaning less than a minute and `old` meaning at least 24 hours. The first user on the list has been idle for the longest time: an hour and 45 minutes.

`ps` produces a list of running processes. Again, command line switches give you a great deal of latitude in deciding what extra information it should provide. Our particular server is running Hewlett Packard's HP-UX operating system. This means the `-e` switch ensures that all processes are displayed, and `-f` makes the report more verbose (without it, we wouldn't see the user account names, for instance).

```
% ps -ef
root    8137 81360 19:54:09 pts/te  0:00 ps -ef
hdata   7223 72220 19:51:38 pts/td  0:00 -sh
hdata   3382 33650 11:22:59 pts/tw  3:33 /hdata/app
hdata   7240 72230 19:51:39 pts/td  0:22 /hdata/app
hdata   3365 33640 11:22:58 pts/tw  0:00 -sh
...
```

The `-sh` processes are not of interest to us. `/hdata/app` is the name of the database application everybody is using, and in fact, in the script we'll filter the output of `ps` so that we see only the `/hdata/app` processes. The first two fields are important to us: the user account name and process ID (yes, the same sort of identifier you get back from a Ruby `fork` call).

`nmblookup` is part of the Samba suite of utilities commonly used to bridge the gap between the Unix and Microsoft networking worlds. When invoked with the `-A` switch and an Internet address, it looks for Windows networking information about the machine and user currently associated with that address. An `nmblookup` call from the Unix command line might look like this:

```
% nmblookup -A front04.vhosp.com
Looking up status of 192.168.50.53
received 4 names
        FRONT04         <00> -          M <ACTIVE>
        CLINIC          <00> - <GROUP>  M <ACTIVE>
        FRONT04         <03> -          M <ACTIVE>
        RECEPTION       <03> -          M <ACTIVE>
num_good_sends=0 num_good_receives=0
```

`kill` is something you've seen before in Ruby scripts, but it's also a standard Unix administration tool. Normally it sends a polite "terminate" signal to ask a process to do any necessary cleanup and exit, but when invoked with the `-9` (`SIGKILL`) switch, it kills the process forcefully and without warning. Sometimes an administrator will first send a `SIGTERM` to a process, wait a little while, then whack it hard if it hasn't gone down on its own. But we have faith that `/hdata/app` is well behaved, so our script will never use the heavy artillery.

Designing from the Top Down

Before starting to code a new script, it's often a good idea to write down in words what you want it to do.

Gather information for all database client sessions. Sort sessions by decreasing idle time, then present them in turn, each time giving the user (who is presumably the system administrator) the choice of killing, skipping, or quitting.

Here's high-level "pseudocode" that says about the same thing.

```
sessions = make a collection of "sessions" somehow
sessions.sort! { by decreasing idle time }
sessions.each do |session|
  print session info
  get input from user and either...
  quit if user says so
  kill session if user says so
end
```

Does that seem imprecise? Don't worry, it can be hammered into a working script if we can just figure out what we mean by *sessions*. Encapsulating them as objects of a new `Session` class will be a good start, if it gives us an interface to make creating, displaying, and killing them easy.

The tasks of creation and display can go in their customary places: `initialize` and `to_s`. That way we can make a session object with `Session.new` and display it using `print` or `puts`.

A few details in the top-level code can already be firmed up. Notice the reversal of `s1` and `s2` in the sort block (`sort` normally gives us things in increasing order).

```
sessions = make a collection of "sessions" somehow
# sessions.sort! {|s1,s2| s2.idle <=> s1.idle}
sessions.each do |s|
  puts s            # display session info
  print "\n Say 'k' to kill, 'q' to quit, or Enter to skip... "
  input = gets.upcase.chomp  # or gets.chomp.upcase, doesn't matter
  break if input == 'Q'
  s.kill if input == 'K'
end
```

Still missing are the definition of the `Session` class and the code to gather information from the operating system. Parts of the class definition can be knocked off fairly easily, so we'll do those first. We know that a session has certain characteristics including a process ID, user account, idle time, and terminal location. The process ID (let's call it

@process_id) is probably not needed except when a session is killed, and, because that will be done inside the `Session#kill` method, there seems no need to provide a @process_id accessor method.

```
class Session
  def initialize(still not sure what goes here)
    store values for @process_id, @user_id, etc.
  end
  def kill
    system("kill #{@process_id}")
  end
  def to_s
    return a descriptive string
  end
end
```

In this code we could have enclosed the call to the `kill` utility in backticks instead of using `system`, but then the user would not see the results on screen. We could also have used Ruby's `Process.kill(signal,id)` method instead of Unix's `kill` program.

To write #initialize and #to_s, we need to look again at our system tools. `ps` returns lines of output, which we get as a single string. Using `split("\n")` can put them into array form, with elements suitable for being gobbled up by a `Session` constructor. The same is true of `who`'s output. But there is no correspondence between the order of lines generated by one command and that from the other, and if we had arrays built from each, we couldn't neatly iterate over both at the same time. To keep things simple we will think in terms of `ps` at first, and work in the `who` later.

So, how can we create the `Session` objects?

```
ps_output = `ps -ef | grep /hdata/app`.split("\n")
ps_output.each {|line| make a Session object from the line}
```

That's close, but it won't give us an *array* of `Session` objects. There's no way to save references to all those new objects; we would end up losing them through automatic garbage collection. Because ps_output is already an array, and we intend to construct another array from it, `map` is a better choice than `each`:

```
sessions = `ps -ef | grep /hdata/app`.split("\n").
             map {|line| Session.new(line)}
```

initialize and to_s can be written next. `initialize` needs to be taught what to do with a line of ps output. The fields are separated by whitespace, so a `split` with no arguments will yield an array of individual fields. The interesting ones will be stored in instance variables.

```
class Session
  def initialize(ps_line)
    tokens = ps_line.split
    @user_id = tokens[0]
    @process_id = tokens[1]
  end
  def to_s
    "User: #{@user_id}\n"
  end
end
```

These elements can be combined into a script (with sorting commented out because we haven't done anything with session idle times). But, because people are sharing Unix accounts, we wouldn't really be able to tell whose sessions we would be killing. So the who and nmblookup information needs to be worked in now.

The finished script is shown in Listing 16.6. It invokes ps and who at the very beginning, and does an individual nmblookup call for each session during initialize. Notice that idle time is given to us in a string form that is useless for sorting, so the idle attribute reader returns a number.

Note

Here we do the conversion of idle time from string to numeric form in Session#idle. It would work just as well to do it in Session#initialize, although it would affect the appearance of the output of to_s.

LISTING 16.6   kill-slackers

```
01:   #!/usr/local/bin/ruby
02:
03:   # kill-slackers
04:   #
05:   # Gather information about database application clients,
06:   # sort sessions in order of decreasing idle time,
07:   # present them to be killed at admin's whim.
08:
09:   def main
10:     who_lines = `who -Ru`.split("\n")
11:     sessions = `ps -ef| grep /hdata/app`.split("\n").
12:             map {|line| Session.new(line,who_lines)}
13:     sessions.sort! {|s1,s2| s2.idle <=> s1.idle}
14:     sessions.each do |s|
15:       puts s          # display session info
16:       print "\n Say 'k' to kill, 'q' to quit, or Enter to skip... "
17:       input = gets.upcase.chomp
18:       break if input == 'Q'
19:       s.kill if input == 'K'
```

LISTING 16.6 Continued

```
20:      end
21:    end
22:
23:    class Session
24:      def initialize(ps_line,who_lines)
25:        tokens = ps_line.split
26:        @user_id = tokens[0]
27:        @process_id = tokens[1]
28:
29:        # Get extra info from "who", if a matching line exists.
30:        tty = tokens[5]
31:        who_line = who_lines.find {|l| (l.split)[1] == tty}
32:        if who_line.nil?
33:          @ip = @samba_info = @idle ="N/A"
34:        else
35:          who_tokens = who_line.split
36:          @idle = who_tokens[5]
37:          @ip = who_tokens[7]
38:          s_inf = `nmblookup -A #{@ip}`.split("\n")
39:          s_inf = s_inf[2..-2]  if s_inf.size>3   # discard header/footer
40:          @samba_info = s_inf.join("\n")
41:        end
42:      end
43:
44:      def idle  # return number of minutes idle
45:        case @idle
46:        when /(\d+):(\d+)/
47:          ($1.to_i)*60 + ($2.to_i)  # specific time was given
48:        when /old/i
49:          24*60                      # at least one day
50:        else
51:          0                          # under one minute
52:        end
53:      end
54:
55:      def kill
56:        system("kill #{@process_id}")
57:      end
58:
59:      def to_s
60:        "\n User: %s  Idle: %s  Address: %s\n Samba info:\n%s" %
61:          [@user_id, @idle, @ip, @samba_info]
62:      end
63:    end
64:
65:    main
```

Figure 16.1 shows `kill-slackers` in action.

```
K  main server                                                    . □ ✕
[ADMIN] /ruby-scripts::>ruby kill-slackers

User: hdata   Idle: 2:27  Address: 192.168.58.232
Samba info:
    FRONT06          <00> -            M <ACTIVE>
    CLINIC           <00> - <GROUP> M <ACTIVE>
    MARTHA_J         <03> -            M <ACTIVE>

Say 'k' to kill, 'q' to quit, or Enter to skip... []
```

Summary

Relax, there's no homework today. But the scripts in this chapter might serve as jumping-off points for new projects. One idea you might consider is a crossword puzzle assistant that uses `ispell` (or a dictionary file) to find possible completions for words.

```
% ruby xword-assist.rb r_bbl_
rabble
rubble
```

Like many system administration scripts, `kill-slackers` was built to do a specific job in a specific environment; this will also prevent you from testing it directly. If you want to adapt it for another use, be sure to examine the raw output of your system's `ps` and `who` commands closely and make any necessary adjustments. You might find the `w` command useful in FreeBSD, or `who` with the `-i` and `-l` flags in Linux.

If system administration work strikes you as a little dry, then things are about to look up for you. In the next two days, we'll be learning how to give our Ruby scripts attractive graphical user interfaces.

WEEK 3

DAY 17

Ruby/Tk

Tell me where is fancy bred,

Or in the heart or in the head?

How begot, how nourished?

Reply, reply.

It is engender'd in the eyes . . .

—William Shakespeare, *The Merchant of Venice,* Act III, Scene II

Thirty years ago, people normally used command-line interfaces if they interacted with computers in "real time" at all. That type of interface is less common today with the ready availability of high-resolution graphics and the mouse. Every modern operating system has a *graphical user interface* (GUI), and the average computer user has come to take this for granted.

Of course, what makes life easier for the user often makes life harder for the programmer. A GUI-based application is harder to code because it is so highly presentation oriented. The programmer has to worry about the types of controls used; their width and height; their placement onscreen; their colors; their resizability; and so on.

Think for a moment about the typical windowed application. It generally is resizable by the user, and the components on the screen expand, contract, and rearrange themselves as needed. There are usually little icons that handle minimizing, maximizing, and closing the application. There is usually a menu bar, a toolbar, or both, and the icons may have helpful tips that are displayed when the mouse hovers over them. All these things could be tediously coded by hand every time by the application programmer, but the whole world of GUI coding is the search for an easy, flexible way to do these kinds of tasks.

From a user's perspective, GUI applications all behave in similar ways. You might think that they were similar internally as well, but you'd be mistaken. It's difficult to appreciate how one windowing system differs from another until you try working with them as a programmer. The problem domain is complex, and people do not agree on how to solve the problems (or even how to think about them).

But there is certainly some common terminology used among most or all of them. Let's look at some of that now.

Any item that can be viewed or manipulated is called a *widget* in the Tk world; similar terms are *control* and *component*. An example of a widget might be a pushbutton, a check box (also called a check button), or a radio button. A list box, from which one item (or sometimes more than one) can be selected, is another common example. Any windowing system is going to support all of these widgets, in addition to others such as text entry fields (single-line and multiline), menus, and so on.

A self-contained rectangular area is called a *window*, of course. There is usually some concept of a *top-level* (or *root*) window; this may contain widgets or may contain smaller containers nested arbitrarily. An application may be divided into *panes,* or it can have more than one window; sometimes we use the terms *single-document interface* (SDI) and *multiple-document interface* (MDI).

If a window or dialog box grabs the focus and holds onto it, it is said to be *modal;* you can't switch to another window because of the state or "mode" you're in. If it allows the user to switch elsewhere and return later, it is said to be *nonmodal.*

Nearly every GUI system has the concept of an *event loop*. This is effectively an infinite loop in which the system monitors certain events, such as key presses, mouse movements, and mouse clicks. When such an event occurs (and a widget is the target of the action), the appropriate piece of application code is called. This calls for a certain amount of "inside-out" thinking. Programmers are accustomed to managing their own control flow, but event loops necessitate a "don't-call-us-we'll-call-you" way of coding.

There is other common terminology we could cover, but we'll let this be enough. Much of it you already know, and much of it is intuitive, especially once you see it in context.

What Is Tk?

Tk is a "graphic toolkit," something that lets your Ruby programs interact with the user by means of windows, dialogs, buttons, drop-down menus, and the rest of the paraphernalia we all associate with user-friendly applications.

Before trying to understand why Ruby/Tk works the way it does, you should become aware of a little bit of history, because Tk was not originally written for Ruby. The story of Tk starts with a scripting language named Tcl ("Tool Command Language"), which was created by John Ousterhout in 1988. Tk was created to lend GUI functionality to Tcl.

For years, it was most common to hear Tcl and Tk mentioned together, even written Tcl/Tk almost as if they were one thing. But they are really separate from each other, so Tk can be used with other languages besides Tcl. Programmers have written *binding code* that interfaces it with other languages. You don't have to know Tcl in order to use Tk, as long as someone has created Tk bindings for the language you are using. Ruby comes supplied with Tk bindings, and as of now at least, Tk is the *de facto* standard graphic toolkit for Ruby.

Tk has some strong points. It is relatively full-featured, with a rich set of widgets. It is implemented on many different platforms, including the Windows and Unix families. It has been around awhile, so it is mature and stable; this means that it is well documented by books and has an established user community.

Tk's faults are debatable. Arguably it is not well suited for object-oriented coding. In addition, its complexity can be a little daunting (although, as you'll see, you need not understand every aspect of it just to create usable applications).

But it's time now to look at the code. Let's start with the obligatory "Hello, world" application, followed by a little discussion.

Our First Tk Application

The Ruby/Tk binding code lives in a file named `tk.rb` somewhere in the load path. We need to `require` this file in any Ruby script that will use the Tk toolkit.

Listing 17.1 is our first Tk script.

LISTING **17.1**   A "Hello, World" Application in Ruby/Tk

```
01:    #!/usr/bin/env ruby
02:
03:    require 'tk'
04:
05:    root = TkRoot.new { title "Our First Tk App" }
06:    label = TkLabel.new(root) do
07:      text "Hello, world!"
08:      pack("padx" => 90)
09:    end
10:    Tk.mainloop
```

Figure 17.1 shows how this program appears on the screen when it's run. (Note that this screenshot and all of the others in this chapter were produced on a Microsoft Windows platform. On other platforms the results may look different, but not significantly so.)

FIGURE **17.1**

The "Hello, world!"
window.

It's not very impressive to look at—there is not much for the user to see or do, at least at first glance—but there's a lot going on behind the scenes. It responds to mouse clicks as you would expect. You can minimize, maximize, or close this application. You can grab the edge or the corner and resize it at will. The `title` is displayed on the title bar next to the Tk logo. All of this was done in just a few lines of Ruby code, because Tk is handling the details for you and making reasonable assumptions about default behavior.

Now let's dissect the script itself. After the necessary `require`, all of Tk is at our disposal. In line 5, we create a root window, which is an instance of the `TkRoot` class. Notice that most widgets in Ruby/Tk have classes that are named with the widget name prefaced by Tk—`TkRoot`, `TkLabel`, `TkButton`, `TkMenu`, and so on.

As you'd expect, `new` returns an instance of the class, and we save it in the `root` variable. Such return values need not always be saved; we do it here so that we can pass it into the `TkLabel` constructor. That is good form, but not strictly necessary. Tk knows without being told that any widgets we will create later will be contained by the root.

You can have only one `TkRoot` object in an application. However, that doesn't mean you are limited to doing everything in one window. It's possible to create as many windows as you want via the `TkToplevel` class, which you'll see later today—but let's not get ahead of ourselves just yet.

What's going on with this `new` call, anyway? Notice that we are passing a block in when we create the object. This means that the `initialize` method for the `TkRoot` class is defined to take a block and evaluate it (in addition to any other parameters, although none are used here). So far, so good.

What's important to understand is that behind the scenes, in `initialize`, we're doing an `instance_eval` when we create this object. The block that is passed in is evaluated not in its own context but in the context of the object being created. So the `title` method, which appears to be called "without a receiver" in line 5, is really called *with* a receiver—that is, the newly created object. This trick is frequently used when we have a lot to do in creating an object, as an alternative to complicated expressions or lengthy parameter lists. The same trick is used again when the `do...end` block containing lines 7 and 8 is passed into the `TkLabel.new` method.

A `label` in Tk is what you would guess it is. It's simply a piece of static text that cannot be manipulated by the GUI user. (Actually, it isn't really static, because it can be changed or manipulated by the program.) The `text` method that we call in line 7 defines the contents of the label, which can be one line or multiple lines of text.

In this bare-bones example, we're not worried about details such as the *justification* or alignment of the text, the colors, or the *font* or typeface. These and other details are controllable, as you will see.

What is this `pack` method that we're calling? It looks unimportant, but it is absolutely crucial that it be called. Leave it out, and the widget will never be displayed!

The purpose of `pack` is to place a widget at the proper location in its container. There are numerous options available; Listing 17.1 uses only one (`"padx"` on line 8), which specifies a number of pixels to pad in the *x* direction (or horizontally). In this particular case, we specified this horizontal padding only so that the title bar would be wide enough to show the entire title, "Our First Tk App."

The `pack` method really takes only one parameter, which is a hash. Ruby lets us omit the braces when a hash is passed into a method as the last conventional parameter. This looks deceptively like a "named parameter" scheme (like Python's keyword parameters), but it isn't that at all. We'll talk in a few moments about the various options that can be used here.

Finally, line 10 is a call to the `Tk.mainloop` method. This starts the event loop mentioned previously. The loop does not terminate until the application itself is terminated—in this case, by the user clicking the closer icon usually found in the upper right corner of the application window.

17

We should mention that there is another way to initialize most of the objects in Tk. The "block method" that you've just seen can also be replaced with a hash, making it look like the call to `pack`. For example, this code fragment behaves exactly like Listing 17.1:

```
require 'tk'

root = TkRoot.new
root.title "Our First Tk App"
label = TkLabel.new(root, "text" => "Hello, world!")
label.pack("padx" => 90)
Tk.mainloop
```

This is confusing in some ways. First, look at the `TkLabel.new` call. We see that we have passed in a hash as a parameter rather than a block, and the hash key `"text"` has replaced the actual call of the text method. So that's not so bad after all.

But what about the `pack` call? We can't stuff it into the hash, because the Ruby/Tk binding simply isn't designed to allow it. We have to call the public instance method separately afterward.

What about the `TkRoot.new` call? Shouldn't we be able to pass in a hash here? We thought so, too; but it isn't supported. Call it a bug or a feature; either way, we can't do it. On the other hand, `pack` itself can take only a hash, not a block. There may be good design reasons for this, but I am unaware of them.

To summarize: If you find that you like your Ruby/Tk code in the hash style, you can write most of it that way. You may have to do a little experimentation to find out exactly what syntax variations are permitted. But I don't recommend the hash style personally, and I generally stick with block style in this chapter.

As a minor variation, it's certainly possible to use the block style and still put as much code as possible on a single line. So this is permitted:

```
TkLabel.new(root) {text "Hi!"; pack("padx" => 90)}
```

We won't do much of this in today's examples either, but it's purely a matter of taste.

Geometry Managers

A *geometry manager* helps you place the widgets in the proper locations within their containers onscreen. (If you are a Java programmer, you are more familiar with the term *layout manager*.) This job is more complex than it sounds, because of variations in widget size and shape, text justification, alignment, and so on. It is complicated further by the fact that the calculations must be performed again if the window is resized.

Every GUI system has some kind of geometry management, and there often is more than one kind. Tk, in fact, has three: `grid`, `place`, and `pack` (which you've seen briefly).

The `grid` method views the window as being divided into rows and columns, like a table or a spreadsheet. It is roughly analogous to Java's `GridBagLayout`. Components may span rows or columns or both. They may expand to fill the cell horizontally, vertically, or both; and they may "stick to" one side of the cell. Cells may vary in size and may be empty. This technique is powerful and sophisticated, but it is also more difficult to work with than `pack`. We won't cover it here.

The `place` method is perhaps the most tedious and inflexible to use. It involves actually specifying the precise locations (pixel coordinates) for each component. We won't cover it here, either.

The `pack` method offers the best mix of flexibility and convenience for the beginner, and we'll use it throughout the day. Although it is theoretically possible to mix different geometry managers in your code, I discourage this practice unless you really know what you're doing.

So let's look a little more deeply at how `pack` works. Tk has the concept of an *allocation rectangle*—an area in which a widget "lives" onscreen.

The `side` option may take one of the values `top`, `bottom`, `left`, or `right`. (The option and the values are all represented in code as character strings; we're omitting the quotation marks for readability, here and elsewhere.) This option governs where in the container the allocation rectangle is placed. The default is `top`.

The `anchor` option may take the value `center` or the "compass point" values (`n`, `ne`, `e`, `se`, `s`, `sw`, `w`, `nw`). This governs where in the allocation rectangle the widget is placed.

The `fill` option governs how the widget fills its allocation rectangle. The default value is `none`; other values are `x`, `y`, and `both`. An `x` value tells a widget to stretch horizontally to fill available space, a `y` makes it stretch vertically, and `both` makes it completely cover the available space.

The `expand` option governs whether the allocation rectangle fills the remaining space in the container. Legal values are `0` (default) and `1`; these are anachronistic holdovers from the customary coding of `false` as `0` and `true` as `1` in some languages.

The `padx` and `pady` options define "padding" values (like margins) for a widget. These values are specified in pixels by default; you can specify distances in inches, points, millimeters, or centimeters by converting to a string and appending the appropriate character: `i`, `p`, `m`, or `c`.

Widgets are normally packed in the order in which they are created. You can use `before` and `after` to change this order and make the ordering explicit.

There are other options for `pack`, but the ones just mentioned are the most commonly used. To get a real feel for how they work, you can read existing code. To get a better feel, there is no substitute for trying them out.

For more complex layout problems, it is possible to nest containers. A frame (`TkFrame`) works well for this purpose. Nesting allows flexible placement of widgets while still choosing `pack` over `grid`. You'll see this in our next example.

Entry Widgets and Buttons

Let's look at a slightly more sophisticated script. Suppose we want to take a pair of phrases and determine whether they are *anagrams* of each other—that is, whether the letters of one phrase can be rearranged to form the other phrase, ignoring spaces and punctuation.

The algorithm for determining whether two strings are anagrams is quite easy, so we'll leave that aside for now and concentrate on the graphic interface. We obviously need two text entry fields, and for these we'll use `TkEntry` widgets. Each will be labeled suitably with a `TkLabel` widget. Finally we'll use a `TkVariable` to associate a Ruby variable with a text field, although this is more of an implementation detail than a matter of appearance.

You're not supposed to understand all of this yet. Don't worry; the code will make everything clear.

To keep things fairly simple, let's also use a label for displaying results. This illustrates how a label's text can be changed during program execution.

We'll want three buttons along the bottom of the window: a Test button to test the phrases to find whether they are anagrams; a Clear button to clear the input fields and the result; and an Exit button to simply exit the program.

Let's craft the window to contain four rows: the first phrase, the second phrase, the output, and the buttons. Each of these is represented as a frame, and the four frames are packed from top to bottom in the window. Within each frame, we can pack any way we want, but conventionally this is done from left to right.

The code is shown in Listing 17.2. You might want to test and study it a little before reading the discussion that follows it.

Figure 17.2 shows a positive response from our application after the Test button has been clicked.

FIGURE 17.2

Correctly identifying a pair of anagrams.

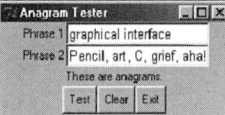

LISTING 17.2 Anagram Tester

```
01:    require "tk"
02:
03:    def transform(str)
04:      str.delete!("^A-Za-z")
05:      str.downcase!
06:      str.split("").sort.join
07:    end
08:
09:    def test_phrases(v1, v2, lab)
10:      if transform(v1.value) == transform(v2.value)
11:        lab.configure("text" => "These are anagrams." )
12:      else
13:        lab.configure("text" => "These are NOT anagrams." )
14:      end
15:    end
16:
17:    def clear_all(e1, v1, v2, lab)
18:      v1.value = ""
19:      v2.value = ""
20:      lab.configure("text" => "")
21:      e1.focus
22:    end
23:
24:    root = TkRoot.new() { title "Anagram Tester" }
25:
26:    row1 = TkFrame.new(root)
27:    row2 = TkFrame.new(root)
28:    row3 = TkFrame.new(root)
29:    row4 = TkFrame.new(root)
30:
31:    var1 = TkVariable.new
32:    var2 = TkVariable.new
33:
34:    lab1 = TkLabel.new(row1) do
35:      text "Phrase 1"
36:      pack("side" => "left")
37:    end
38:    ent1 = TkEntry.new(row1) do
39:      textvariable var1
40:      pack
41:    end
42:
```

17

continues

LISTING 17.2   Continued

```
43:    lab2 = TkLabel.new(row2) do
44:      text "Phrase 2"
45:      pack("side" => "left")
46:    end
47:    ent2 = TkEntry.new(row2) do
48:      textvariable var2
49:      pack
50:    end
51:
52:    labResult = TkLabel.new(row3) do
53:      text " "
54:      pack
55:    end
56:
57:    btnTest = TkButton.new(row4) do
58:      text "Test"
59:      command { test_phrases(var1,var2,labResult) }
60:      pack("side"=>"left")
61:    end
62:    btnClear = TkButton.new(row4) do
63:      text "Clear"
64:      command { clear_all(ent1,var1,var2,labResult) }
65:      pack("side"=>"left")
66:    end
67:    btnExit = TkButton.new(row4) do
68:      text "Exit"
69:      command { exit }   # Just exits
70:      pack
71:    end
72:
73:    row1.pack
74:    row2.pack
75:    row3.pack
76:    row4.pack("side"=>"bottom")
77:
78:    Tk.mainloop
```

After setting up three utility functions in lines 3–22, we define a root in line 24 and then give it four frames in lines 26–29. Since side defaults to top, the rows will be packed from top to bottom. For the first row, we place a label (lines 34–37) and an entry widget (lines 38–41); we associate a TkVariable with the entry widget (line 39) so that we can easily get and set the value of the text field. The construction of the second row in lines 43–50 is much the same.

For the third row, we define a label with a blank value (line 53). This is where we're going to put the "yes or no" result of our computation. In lines 57–71, we add the buttons for the fourth and final row and define their actions. The `command` method takes a block and internally stores it as a `proc` object. This block is invoked when the corresponding button is clicked and released.

For the Exit button, we simply call the `exit` method. For the Test and Clear buttons, we call code of our own—the `test_phrases` and `clear_all` methods that we had defined earlier in the script.

Any information we want to access or manipulate must in general be passed into these methods. A block in Ruby is not merely a chunk of code, but something special that computer linguists call a *closure,* meaning it remembers the context in which it was called and can access the variables that were defined in that context. For example, the variable `var1` refers to the local variable from the context in which the block was created. The `test_phrases` method could not have accessed this variable directly; we had to pass it in.

We could have defined a class that would encapsulate the `test_phrases` and `clear_all` methods and many of our local variables as well. In a small example like this one, that might be overkill. In a larger context, it would probably be the way to go. For one thing, if the methods were encapsulated, we would not have to pass so many parameters.

How does `test_phrases` work? To begin with, a `TkVariable` has an accessor called `value`, which can be used to `get` and `set` the value associated with a widget. Because `var1` is tied to the `ent1` entry widget, `var1.value` will refer to the contents of that field.

So in `test_phrases`, we start by retrieving the values of these two phrases. Since we're ignoring spaces and punctuation, we delete everything that isn't a letter of the alphabet. (We're working with a copy of the string, so what we do has no effect on the original; the string that appears on the screen is unchanged.) The special caret notation (`^`) for the `delete` method indicates character class negation, just as in regular expressions. Then we switch everything to lowercase using `String#downcase` in preparation for an easy case-insensitive comparison.

At this point, we want to sort the letters in the string, because sorting the letters makes anagrams into identical strings. There is no built-in sort method for strings, but we know that there is one for arrays, so we use a simple trick. We convert to an array via `String#split` with an empty string as an argument, sort that array, then convert it back to a string using the `join` method.

Now we compare the resulting strings. If they're identical, the original strings must have been anagrams. We use the "output label" that was passed in as a parameter and call its `configure` method, which allows us to change a value or setting at runtime. Here we are setting the text attribute for this label to an appropriate message.

What about the `clear_all` method? It's a little easier to understand, but it still introduces some important concepts.

The two `TkVariable` objects (tied to the entry fields) are passed in as with the `test_phrases` method, but here we're actually changing them via the `value` accessor. We're setting them to `null` strings, and because these variables are tied directly to the widgets, these changes are reflected onscreen immediately.

We also call `configure` on the output label again. Here we set the text to a `null` string so that the field is made effectively invisible.

Finally, we have a third parameter passed into this method. The parameter `e1` refers to the same object as `ent1` in the outer scope (the first text entry field). We do this so that we can call the `focus` method on this widget, giving it the focus and placing the text cursor there.

As with every script in this book, you should feel free to play around with it. Try changing things and figure out what is essential, what improves it, and what breaks it and why.

Some Other Widgets

There are many other standard widgets available for your use. Let's look at a few of the most common ones.

A *check button,* also called a *check box,* is represented by the `TkCheckbutton` class. This is used when a specific user choice can have two states (essentially "on" and "off"). It is usually represented onscreen by a square box that may be checked or unchecked.

A *radio button* (`TkRadiobutton`) is analogous to the tuning preset buttons on a car radio; only one can be selected at a time. This is used when there is a small, fixed number of mutually exclusive choices available. A radio button usually appears as a circular "box" that may or may not be filled in. Check boxes are independent of each other, but radio buttons typically belong to a group representing mutually exclusive choices.

A *list box* (`TkListbox`) is similar in some ways to a set of check boxes or radio buttons; it allows the user to select and deselect choices from a list. It is used when there is a greater number of choices to choose from or when these are likely to change at runtime or in the life cycle of the program. A list box may be set up so that only one choice can be made (like a radio button) or multiple choices (like a set of checkboxes).

The scrollbar widget (`TkScrollbar`) is useless by itself, but it comes in very handy in conjunction with other widgets. It is used to make other widgets "scrollable" (horizontally, vertically, or both) when they are too large to fit in a reasonable area on the screen. The next example uses a scrollbar with a listbox.

Let's examine a little application that illustrates the use of all of the widget types that were just introduced. Imagine that this application is gathering personal information from a user who is subscribing to some magazine or service or participating in some kind of marketing survey. (After Day 20, you might consider doing something similar to this as a Web-based application!)

We want to know several pieces of information such as the person's age range, gender, nation of residence, and hobbies. We also want to know whether the person wants to receive an e-mailed newsletter.

How can we represent these data items? If we can content ourselves with storing ranges of ages rather than exact numbers, we can use a set of radio buttons for that purpose. As far as gender is concerned, radio buttons are natural here also.

But there are many nations in the world. We don't want to make the user type in the country name, but we also don't want to list them all visually, because that would consume a lot of screen real estate. A list box is perfect here, especially since the list of countries we track may change over time. We won't mess around with issues of dual citizenship; each person will be considered as being from just one country, and this list box should not allow multiple entries to be selectable at the same time.

The list of hobbies may also change and may be too large to display as a set of check boxes or radio buttons. This list box should allow multiple choices, because a person may have any number of hobbies.

A simple "yes-no" question is best implemented as a check box. We'll use this technique for the newsletter option.

To clarify how it works, the application prints out little messages to the console. This is not a real-world technique, since in a real application we probably wouldn't even want a console around.

Figure 17.3 shows the application in use. The survey application code is in Listing 17.3.

FIGURE 17.3

A simple survey application.

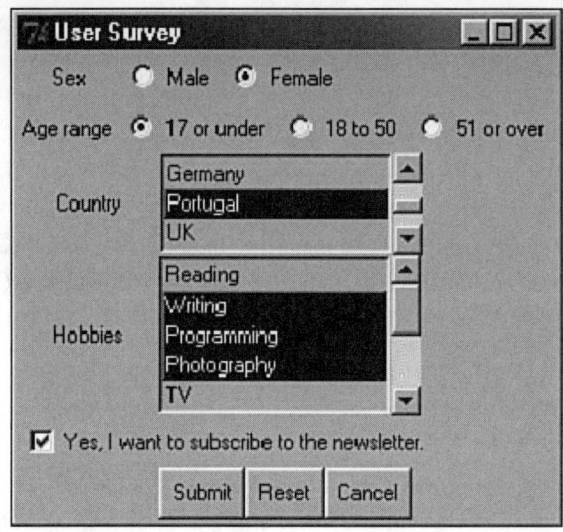

LISTING 17.3   A Simple Survey

```
001:    #!/usr/bin/env ruby
002:
003:    require "tk"
004:
005:    root = TkRoot.new() { title "User Survey" }
006:
007:    gender_frame = TkFrame.new(root)
008:    age_frame = TkFrame.new(root)
009:    nation_frame = TkFrame.new(root)
010:    hobby_frame = TkFrame.new(root)
011:    yes_no_frame = TkFrame.new(root)
012:    submit_frame = TkFrame.new(root)
013:
014:    lab_age = TkLabel.new(age_frame) do
015:      text "Age range"
016:      pack("side"=>"left")
017:    end
018:
019:    lab_gender = TkLabel.new(gender_frame) do
020:      text "Gender"
021:      pack("side"=>"left","padx"=>16)
022:    end
023:
024:    lab_nation = TkLabel.new(nation_frame) do
025:      text "Country"
026:      pack("side"=>"left","padx"=>18)
```

LISTING 17.3 Continued

```
027:    end
028:
029:    lab_hobby = TkLabel.new(hobby_frame) do
030:      text "Hobbies"
031:      pack("side"=>"left","padx"=>16)
032:    end
033:
034:    gender = TkVariable.new
035:    gender.value = "M"
036:
037:    age = TkVariable.new
038:    age.value = 0..17
039:
040:    newsletter = TkVariable.new
041:    newsletter.value = 1
042:
043:    b_male = TkRadioButton.new(gender_frame) do
044:      variable gender
045:      text "Male"
046:      value "M"
047:      command { puts "Gender = #{gender.value}" }
048:      pack("side"=>"left")
049:    end
050:
051:    b_female = TkRadioButton.new(gender_frame) do
052;      variable gender
053:      text "Female"
054:      value "F"
055:      command { puts "Gender = #{gender.value}" }
056:      pack("side"=>"left")
057:    end
058:
059:    b_age_017 = TkRadioButton.new(age_frame) do
060:      variable age
061:      text "17 or under"
062:      value 0..17
063:      command { puts "Age = #{age.value}" }
064:      pack("side"=>"left")
065:    end
066:
067:    b_age_1850 = TkRadioButton.new(age_frame) do
068:      variable age
069:      text "18 to 50"
070:      value 18..50
071:      command { puts "Age = #{age.value}" }
072:      pack("side"=>"left")
073:    end
074:
```

17

continues

LISTING 17.3 Continued

```
075: b_age_51_plus = TkRadioButton.new(age_frame) do
076:   variable age
077:   text "51 or over"
078:   value 51..120
079:   command { puts "Age = #{age.value}" }
080:   pack("side"=>"left")
081: end
082:
083: nations = %w[ Albania Argentina France Germany
084:               Portugal UK USA Uzbekistan ]
085: nation_list = TkListbox.new(nation_frame, "height"=>3,
086:                             "selectmode"=>"single",
087:                             "exportselection"=>0)
088: nation_list.insert("end", *nations)
089: nation_scroll = TkScrollbar.new(nation_frame) do
090:   command { |args| nation_list.yview *args }
091:   pack("side" => "right", "fill" => "y")
092: end
093: nation_list.yscrollcommand {|y0,yn| nation_scroll.set(y0,yn)}
094: nation_list.pack
095:
096: hobbies = %w[ Reading Writing Programming Photography
097:               TV Movies Concerts Theater Opera Ballet ]
098: hobby_list = TkListbox.new(hobby_frame,"height"=>5,
099:                            "selectmode"=>"multiple",
100:                            "exportselection"=>0)
101: hobby_list.insert("end", *hobbies)
102:
103: hobby_scroll = TkScrollbar.new(hobby_frame) do
104:   command { |args| hobby_list.yview *args }
105:   pack("side" => "right", "fill" => "y")
106: end
107: hobby_list.yscrollcommand {|y0,yn| hobby_scroll.set(y0,yn)}
108: hobby_list.pack
109:
110: subscribeBox = TkCheckButton.new(yes_no_frame) do
111:   variable newsletter
112:   text "Yes, I want to subscribe to the newsletter."
113:   command { puts "Subscribe = #{newsletter.value}" }
114:   pack("side"=>"left")
115: end
116:
117: submit_button = TkButton.new(submit_frame) do
118:   text "Submit"
119:   command do
120:     popup = TkToplevel.new() { title "Your data..."}
121:     TkLabel.new(popup) do
122:       your_gender = (gender.value=="M") ? "man" : "woman"
```

LISTING 17.3 Continued

```
123:              your_age = case age.value
124:                when "0..17"          # Notice that these ranges
125:                  "under 18"          # must be expressed as
126:                when "18..50"         # strings, because that's
127:                  "between 18 and 50" # how the TkVariable stores
128:                when "51..120"        # them.
129:                  "over 50"
130:                end
131:
132:              your_nation =
133:          if (idx=nation_list.curselection[0]).nil?
134:            "an unspecified nation"
135:          else
136:            nations[idx]
137:          end
138:              hobby_array = hobby_list.curselection
139:              your_hobbies =
140:                if hobby_array != []
141:                  hobby_array.map {|x| ' '*24 + hobbies[x]}
142:                else
143:                  [' '*24 + "None specified."]
144:                end
145:
146:              notsub = newsletter.value.to_i == 1 ? "" : " not"
147:              text <<-EOS + your_hobbies.join("\n")
148:              Our records now show:
149:
150:                You are a #{your_gender} from #{your_nation},
151:              and you are #{your_age} years of age.
152:              You are#{notsub} subscribing to the newsletter.
153:              Your hobbies are:
154:          EOS
155:              justify "left"
156:              pack("pady"=>10)
157:            end
158:            TkButton.new(popup) { text "OK"; command {exit}; pack }
159:            submit_button.state "disabled"
160:          end
161:        pack("side"=>"left")
162:      end
163:
164:      reset_button = TkButton.new(submit_frame) do
165:        text "Reset"
166:        command do
167:          age.value = 0..17
168:          gender.value = "M"
169:          newsletter.value = 1
170:          b_male.focus
```

continues

LISTING 17.3   Continued

```
171:       end
172:       pack("side"=>"left")
173:    end
174:
175:    cancel_button = TkButton.new(submit_frame) do
176:       text "Cancel"
177:       command {exit}
178:       pack
179:    end
180:
181:    gender_frame.pack("anchor"=>"w")
182:    age_frame.pack("anchor"=>"w")
183:    nation_frame.pack("anchor"=>"w")
184:    hobby_frame.pack("anchor"=>"w")
185:    yes_no_frame.pack("anchor"=>"w")
186:    submit_frame.pack
187:
188:    Tk.mainloop
```

When the Submit button is clicked, the user is given a summary of the data input (see Figure 17.4).

FIGURE 17.4

The survey summary window.

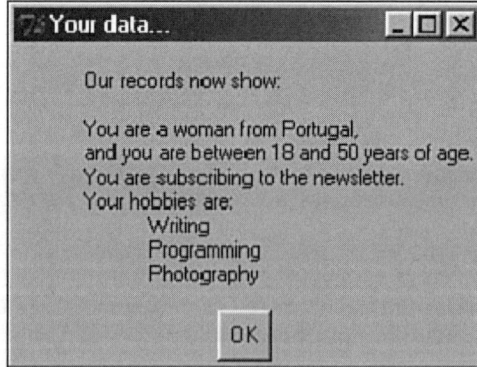

Now let's look at the details of how it works. We start by creating a root window and a series of frames (much as in our previous example) in lines 5–12. Since side has a default value of top, these frames stack vertically when we do a pack with no parameters.

In lines 19–32 we create a series of labels and pack them on the left-hand side of their respective frames. The yes_no_frame does not need a label, because it will be given a check box in lines 110–115, and a check box already has a piece of text associated with it.

The bottom-most frame, `submit_frame`, contains three buttons. These are defined in lines 117–179. That's quite a lot of code. Most of it, lines 118–160, defines what happens when the user clicks the *Submit* button.

We assign variable names to the labels as we create them, but this is not really necessary; it is convenient only in case we have to refer to that label later in the code. In this case, they are not actually needed at all.

When we `pack` the labels, we sometimes use the `padx` option, which simply pads a certain number of pixels horizontally so that you can fine-tune the layout of the window.

We create a `TkVariable` named `gender` in line 34. Later, when we create a pair of radio buttons in lines 43–57, we associate this variable with each of them. Since we initialize the variable to `"M"`—the value associated with the `b_male` button—this corresponding button will be initially selected. The command associated with the button does nothing but print a message on the console. (This was done for illustration only; command line 47 could have been omitted, since the value is still captured in the `gender` variable and is recovered in line 122.)

In lines 37–38 and 59–81 we go through similar steps for the "age range" section, creating three radio buttons, each one associated with a range of ages (corresponding nicely to a `Range` object) and all three associated with the same `TkVariable`, which we named `age`.

For both these sets of radio buttons, we `pack left`. This lays the buttons out in a single row. If you wanted to lay them out vertically, you could use `pack` with no options (defaulting to `top`); then you might want to create another nested frame so that the label could still be to the left of them all.

For the nationality, in lines 83–88 we create a list box named `nation_list` inside the appropriate frame, giving it a height of 3, meaning that three values will be visible at a time. The `exportselection` option in line 87 must be set to `0` to prevent the selections of the `nation_list` and `hobby_list` boxes from being treated as logical alternatives. If you change its value from `0` to `1` here and in line 100, you'll find that whenever you click within one list box, the other loses its selections.

The `selectmode` option in line 86 has a default value of `browse`, which is similar to `single`; both these modes allow only a single item to be selected. The values `extended` and `multiple` allow the selection of more than one item at a time.

Since we're assuming that no one comes from more than one country, we use `single` for the selection mode here.

After creating the list box, we populate it in line 88 using the `insert` method. Its first parameter is an index. The string `end` is a special index (and there are others we won't go into here). Following this index is either one parameter that is an array of items or (as in this case) a list of items as separate parameters.

At this point, we see a brand new widget: the scrollbar (`TkScrollbar`). This, as you might guess, enables us to attach a scrollbar to some other widget (in this case, a list box). A widget may have horizontal scrollbars, vertical scrollbars, or both; they may be placed arbitrarily in relation to the scrolled widget.

In this case, we are concerned only with scrolling vertically, so we place a vertical scrollbar on the right-hand side of the list box.

There is two-way communication between the scrollbar and the list box. If the user moves the scrollbar, that action is passed to the list box; and if the user moves around in the list box (for example, with the keyboard), that information is passed back to the scrollbar, which then updates its position.

The `yscrollcommand` method ties the receiving widget (the list box) to the scrollbar so that the scrollbar will be updated. The `yview` method of the scrollbar is used to update the contents of the list box when the scrollbar is moved. The `set` method takes the beginning and ending item numbers as parameters. If you want to really understand this, there is no substitute for looking at the code and playing with it.

We create three buttons: *Submit*, *Reset*, and *Cancel*. The *Submit* button will display a summary of the data collected; the *Reset* button will reset each widget to its default value. The *Cancel* button exits the application.

This example uses a `TkTopLevel` widget, which is simply a window at the same level as the root. The results are displayed in the new window; we give it a button so that we can close it (and the rest of the application with it). This example is comfortably nonmodal, so we can switch between these windows at will. We therefore have to consider the effects on the new window if the user switches to the other window and makes a change. In this example, when we display the results in the new window, we also disable the Submit button in the original window so that it cannot be clicked a second time. We will explore alternative behaviors in today's Exercise 5.

In the list box code, notice the use of the `curselection` method, which tells us what items the user has selected from the list. This method returns an array of list indices; since we want the actual data, we `map` the result into a new array.

More Complex Coding

Widgets have more attributes than we've mentioned yet. We'll look at some of the others now, and we'll also talk about some other kinds of Tk widgets.

Many attributes (for example, width and height) are common to all or nearly all widgets. When in doubt, consult a reference or simply try an experiment. A few recommended Tk references are listed at the end of this chapter.

Any widget dealing with text (such as TkLabel or TkEntry) will have such options as foreground, background, and font. The colors can be specified as six-digit hex values preceded by a pound sign; there is also a limited set of names defined for colors ("red", for example, is the same as "#FF0000"). A font string consists of (at most) three parts: a font name (in braces if it is more than one word); a type size in points; and a style (optionally in braces). Thus "{Arial Condensed} 12 {bold italic}" is a valid font string.

When using an option such as width, note that its units sometimes are in screen units (such as pixels) and sometimes not. For example, we specify the width of a frame in screen units, but we specify the width of an entry widget in characters.

It's important to understand the configure and cget methods. The cget method enables you to retrieve the value of any option associated with a widget, whereas configure enables you to actually change that value.

There are several other standard Tk widgets besides the ones we've covered. We'll mention just a few others here.

The TkPhotoImage widget is useful for displaying pictures in various image formats. Besides the obvious uses (such as in picture viewers), this widget can also be used to decorate a button instead of using simple text. To do this, use the image option of TkButton rather than the text option.

The TkMenu widget allows the creation of full-featured menus (popup, toolbar, and so on). Any serious application is likely to need a menu of some kind.

The TkText widget is a highly sophisticated multiline text entry field. If you ever need to embed a complete editor in an application, this widget has almost everything you would need from an interface standpoint.

The TkCanvas widget is useful for drawing arbitrary pictures (lines, curves, polygons, and so on). Its contents can easily be saved as a PostScript document or in other formats.

17

Summary

I hope you've found this quick tour of Ruby/Tk useful.

When you have a computing task to do, Ruby typically makes the logical work pretty easy, but building a graphical interface around it can still be a lot of work and can make the script grow large and unwieldy. Is it worth the trouble? Keep in mind that if you do your job well, the end user will appreciate your effort. Perhaps paradoxically, if you do your job *very* well, the user won't have to think about the interface much and may as a result give no thought to how much you must have slaved over it! But this is, unquestionably, a Good Thing when it happens.

Tk is significantly older than Ruby. The Ruby/Tk bindings are based on some fairly old thinking, and you can take that any way you like. You might think of "old" as "worn and outdated" or "time-honored." To be fair, both outlooks hold some validity, and this is no coincidence. Tk is both frustrating and valuable for a single reason: It has been pieced together over a long period of time. It's a little clunky and doesn't lend itself well to modular organization, but it contains everything you need, and a lot of documentation and resources are out there to be consulted. There are many good programmers who know Tk, not only in Ruby, but in just about every computer language that is in use; whenever you get stuck, you don't have to look around long to find answers or useful clues.

Tk Resources

As of this writing, there are not yet any substantial Ruby/Tk reference materials available. However, the following books can help you learn about Tk itself:

- *Tcl & The TK Toolkit* by John K. Ousterhout (Addison-Wesley, 1994)
- *Sams Teach Yourself Tcl/Tk in 24 Hours* by Venkat Sastry and Lakshmi Sastry (Sams Publishing, 1999)

Good online references for Tk and Perl/Tk may be found at

- http://www-pool.math.tu-berlin.de/doc/PerlTk/
- http://www.lns.cornell.edu/~pvhp/ptk/doc/

The same information exists at various other sites around the world. There is enough similarity in the bindings that many people have been able to progress rapidly with their Ruby/Tk skills by consulting the plentiful Perl-specific documentation after learning the Ruby/Tk fundamentals.

Tomorrow we'll look at Gtk, another of several graphic toolkits you can use with Ruby scripts. It's younger than Tk and a little less complete, but you are likely to find that the Ruby/Gtk binding code feels a bit more elegant, more direct, more intuitive, and. . . well, just a little more Rubyish than Ruby/Tk.

Exercises

1. What is wrong with this code fragment?

```
name = "No default"
nameField = TkEntry.new(root) do
  textvariable name
  pack
end
```

2. Write a "color picker" that will display a rectangle filled with any specified color. Let the user control this by entering color names or hex color values (like #ffc055) into a text field and pressing a button. (*Hint:* Use a TkFrame for the colored region; use the `configure` method with the `"background"` option to control the frame's color.)

3. In a similar vein to the color picker, write a "text style" picker. Display a label based on choices that the user inputs. Select the font (typeface) by means of a text entry field.

   Use radio buttons to select between three backgrounds (white, gray, and black) and three foregrounds (red, green, and blue). Use a pair of checkboxes for boldface and italic options. Add a "display" button (needed only when the font name is changed in the entry field).

4. What is wrong with this code fragment?

```
require "tk"
root = TkRoot.new { title "My App" }
frame = TkFrame.new(root)
b1 = TkButton.new(frame) { text "Exit"; command {exit}; pack}
b2 = TkButton.new(frame) { text "Quit"; command {exit}; pack}
b3 = TkButton.new(frame) { text "Bye!"; command {exit}; pack}
Tk.mainloop
```

5. The behavior of our survey script (Listing 17.3) seems a little unforgiving. Wouldn't it be nicer if the user could click the Submit button, review the summary of choices, go back and make changes, and Submit again? After all, what's a summary window for but to give the user a chance to verify input?

   Before we can accomplish this, we need to think about how we destroy windows in Ruby/Tk. In a single-window application, we can usually get away with binding an event—say, the clicking of some button—to an `exit` command. But a `TkObject#destroy` method is also available; this gives us some flexibility when we are dealing with more than one window at a time. The `destroy` method is inherited by all Tk objects, including windows and buttons.

   Experiment with lines 158–159 of Listing 17.3. See whether you can use `TkObject#destroy` to allow the user to submit survey results repeatedly. Make sure that the program exits only when Cancel is clicked in the main window.

6. Design a simple two-function or four-function calculator interface, using a label for the result and button widgets for the numbers and operators. As an additional exercise, make it functional. Two solutions will be provided.

Answers

1. The name variable should refer to a TkVariable object, not just a simple string.

2. One solution is given in Listing 17.4. To be friendly to the user, we've made it so that hex values can be entered without the pound sign. Keep in mind that such niceties are not always appreciated and can get in the way; for example, if there happens to be a color name made up of exactly six letters all in the "A" to "F" range (I'm sure there isn't one, but who knows, maybe someday "facade" will be an officially recognized Tk color), then lines 37–39 will prevent the user from specifying that color by name.

LISTING **17.4**   A Color Picker

```
01:    #!/usr/bin/env ruby
02:
03:    require "tk"
04:
05:    root = TkRoot.new do
06:      title "Color picker"
07:      background "gray"
08:    end
09:
10:    c_frame = TkFrame.new(root) { width 200; height 80; pack }
11:
12:    err = TkLabel.new(root) do
13:      text "Color name or hex value:"
14:      background "gray"
15:      pack("pady"=>10)
16:    end
17:
18:    var = TkVariable.new
19:    entry = TkEntry.new(root) do
20:      width 10
21:      textvariable var
22:      pack
23:    end
24:
25:    err = TkLabel.new(root) do
26:      text ""
27:      background "gray"
28:      foreground "red"
29:      pack
30:    end
```

LISTING 17.4 Continued

```
31:
32:     disp = TkButton.new(root) do
33:       text "Display"
34:       command do
35:         err.configure("text"=>"")
36:         color = var.value                # Assume it's a name
37:         if color =~ /^[0-9a-fA-F]{6}$/   # Prepend # if hex
38:           color = "#" + color
39:         end
40:         begin
41:           c_frame.configure("background"=>"#{color}")
42:         rescue => except
43:           err.configure("text"=>except)
44:         end
45:       end
46:       pack
47:     end
48:
49:     Tk.mainloop
```

17

3. The solution in Listing 17.5 exhibits behavior similar to the solution given for
   Exercise 2. But if you look around for good places to insert copies of line 130
   (such as between lines 57 and 58), you can make the display update automatically
   whenever one of the radio buttons is clicked.

LISTING 17.5 A Text Style Picker

```
001:   #!/usr/bin/env ruby
002:
003:   require "tk"
004:
005:   root = TkRoot.new do
006:     title "Text style picker"
007:   end
008:
009:   tlab = TkLabel.new(root) do
010:     text "ABC abc 123"
011:     font "Arial 18"      # Reasonable default
012:     background "white"
013:     foreground "red"
014:     pack
015:   end
016:
017:   fg_frame = TkFrame.new(root)
018:   bg_frame = TkFrame.new(root)
019:
```

continues

LISTING **17.5**   Continued

```
020:    TkLabel.new(bg_frame) do
021:      text "Background"
022:      pack("side"=>"left")
023:    end
024:
025:    bg = TkVariable.new      # Background color
026:    bg.value = "white"
027:    fg = TkVariable.new      # Foreground color
028:    fg.value = "red"
029:    font = TkVariable.new    # Font
030:    font.value = "Arial"
031:    btext = TkVariable.new   # Bold text
032:    itext = TkVariable.new   # Italic text
033:
034:    err = TkLabel.new(root) do
035:      text ""
036:      foreground "red"
037:      pack
038:    end
039:
040:    # adjust_text is a proc so that (as a closure) it can
041:    # have access to the variables it needs.
042:
043:    adjust_text = proc do
044:      fontstr = "{#{font.value}} #{size} " +
045:                btext.value + " " + itext.value
046:      begin
047:        tlab.configure("font"=>fontstr)
048:        tlab.configure("background"=>bg.value, "foreground"=>fg.value)
049:      rescue => except
050:        err.configure("text"=>except)
051:      end
052:    end
053:
054:    bg_white = TkRadioButton.new(bg_frame) do
055:      variable bg
056:      text "White"
057:      value "white"
058:      pack("side"=>"left")
059:    end
060:
061:    bg_gray = TkRadioButton.new(bg_frame) do
062:      variable bg
063:      text "Gray"064      value "gray"
065:      pack("side"=>"left")
066:    end
067:
068:    bg_black = TkRadioButton.new(bg_frame) do
069:      variable bg
070:      text "Black"
```

LISTING 17.5 Continued

```
071:        value "black"
072:        pack("side"=>"left")
073:      end
074:
075:      TkLabel.new(fg_frame) do
076:        text "Foreground"
077:        pack("side"=>"left")
078:      end
079:
080:      fg_red = TkRadioButton.new(fg_frame) do
081:        variable fg
082:        text "Red"
083:        value "red"
084:        pack("side"=>"left")
085:      end
086:
087:      fg_green = TkRadioButton.new(fg_frame) do
088:        variable fg
089:        text "Green"
090:        value "green"
091:        pack("side"=>"left")
092:      end
093:
094:      fg_blue = TkRadioButton.new(fg_frame) do
095:        variable fg
096:        text "Blue"
097:        value "blue"
098:        pack("side"=>"left")
099:      end
100:
101:      bg_frame.pack
102:      fg_frame.pack
103:
104:      entry = TkEntry.new(root) do
105:        width 9
106:        textvariable font
107:        pack
108:      end
109:
110:      size = 18   # Fixed in this example
111:
112:      bold = TkCheckButton.new(root) do
113:        text "Bold"
114:        variable btext
115:        onvalue "bold"
116:        offvalue ""
117:        pack
118:      end
119:
```

17

continues

LISTING **17.5**   Continued

```
120:      italic = TkCheckButton.new(root) do
121:        text "Italic"
122:        variable itext
123:        onvalue "italic"
124:        offvalue ""
125:        pack
126:      end
127:
128:      disp = TkButton.new(root) do
129:        text "Display"
130:        command { adjust_text.call }
131:        pack
132:      end
133:
134:      Tk.mainloop
```

4. The frame named `frame` is never packed, so its contents are never displayed.

5. We need to change the `command` block in line 158. Rather than exit the program, we will make it destroy the new popup window so the user is looking at the main window again. Line 159 can then be removed or commented out. So the solution is quite simple:

```
158:      TkButton.new(popup) { text "OK"; command {popup.destroy}; pack }
159:      #submit_button.state "disabled"
```

An even better goal would be to require a check of whether a popup window already exists, and if so, to update that window instead of creating a new one. We'll leave that solution up to the ambitious reader.

6. Both of these solutions provide a minimal implementation of calculator functionality; you are encouraged to tinker with them. The first is given in Listing 17.6. It knows only how to add and subtract.

LISTING **17.6**   Two-Function Calculator

```
001:      #!/usr/bin/env ruby
002:
003:      require "tk"
004:
005:      op1 = "0"
006:      newnum = [nil]
007:      op2 = opr = nil   # Needed in blocks below.
008:
009:      def digit(display,newnum)
010:        if newnum[0]
```

Listing 17.6   Continued

```
011:        display.configure("text"=>"0")
012:        newnum[0] = false
013:      end
014:      myval = self.cget("text")
015:      disp = display.cget("text")
016:      return if disp == "0" and myval == "0"
017:      if disp == "0"
018:        display.configure("text"=>myval)
019:      else
020:        display.configure("text"=>(disp+myval))
021:      end
022:      display.configure("justify"=>"right")
023:    end
024:
025:    root = TkRoot.new do
026:      title "Two-function calculator"
027:      background "gray"
028:    end
029:
030:    display = TkLabel.new(root) do
031:      text "0"
032:      width 10
033:      border 3
034:      justify "right"
035:      background "white"
036:      pack
037:    end
038:
039:    button_frame = TkFrame.new(root) { pack }
040:    num_frame = TkFrame.new(button_frame) { pack("side"=>"left") }
041:    op_frame = TkFrame.new(button_frame) { pack }
042:
043:    b789_frame = TkFrame.new(num_frame) { pack }
044:    b456_frame = TkFrame.new(num_frame) { pack }
045:    b123_frame = TkFrame.new(num_frame) { pack }
046:    b0_frame = TkFrame.new(num_frame) { pack }
047:
048:    num_btn_options = { "height" => 1, "width" => 1,
049:                        "background" => "white",
050:                        "foreground" => "black"}
051:    op_btn_options = num_btn_options.dup
052:    op_btn_options.update("background"=>"blue",
053:                          "foreground"=>"white")
054:    eq_btn_options = op_btn_options.dup
055:    eq_btn_options.update("background"=>"darkgreen")
056:    clr_btn_options = op_btn_options.dup
057:    clr_btn_options.update("background"=>"red")
058:
059:    # Note: command HAS to be specified in the block,
```

17

continues

LISTING **17.6**   Continued

```
060:     # not in the hash, because we call the digit method
061:     # (which references self and thus requires instance_eval).
062:
063:     numbers = []
064:
065:     for num in "0".."9" do
066:       frame = case num
067:         when "0" then b0_frame
068:         when "1".."3" then b123_frame
069:         when "4".."6" then b456_frame
070:         when "7".."9" then b789_frame
071:       end
072:       numbers << TkButton.new(frame,num_btn_options) do
073:         text num
074:         command { digit(display,newnum) }
075:         pack("side"=>"left")
076:       end
077:     end
078:
079:     b_plus = TkButton.new(op_frame,op_btn_options) do
080:       text "+"
081:       command do
082:         op1 = display.cget("text")
083:         opr = "+"
084:         newnum = [true]
085:       end
086:       pack
087:     end
088:     b_minus = TkButton.new(op_frame,op_btn_options) do
089:       text "-"
090:       command do
091:         op1 = display.cget("text")
092:         opr = "-"
093:         newnum = [true]
094:       end
095:       pack
096:     end
097:     b_equal = TkButton.new(op_frame,eq_btn_options) do
098:       text "="
099:       command do
100:         op2 = display.cget("text")
101:         result = eval("#{op1}#{opr}#{op2}").to_s
102:         display.configure("text"=>result)
103:       end
104:       pack
105:     end
106:     b_clear = TkButton.new(op_frame,clr_btn_options) do
107:       text "C"
108:       command { display.configure("text"=>"0") }
```

LISTING 17.6   Continued

```
109:        pack
110:      end
111:
112:      Tk.mainloop
```

Listing 17.7 implements a four-function calculator. The code is written in a different style and demonstrates that even though Tk code traditionally tends to be procedural in character, it can be crafted in such a way as to take advantage of Ruby's object-oriented features.

LISTING 17.7   A Four-Function Calculator

17

```
001:    #!/usr/bin/env ruby
002:
003:    require "tk"
004:
005:    class Calculator < TkRoot
006:
007:      class Digit < TkButton
008:        def initialize(calc, frame, digit)
009:          super(frame, "text" => digit.to_s)
010:          pack "side" => "left"
011:          background "navyblue"
012:          foreground "white"
013:          command proc { calc.handle_digit(digit) }
014:        end
015:      end
016:
017:      class Button < TkButton
018:        def initialize(calc, frame, label, function)
019:          super(frame, "text" => label)
020:          background "darkgreen"
021:          foreground "white"
022:          pack
023:          command proc { calc.handle_button(function) }
024:        end
025:      end
026:
027:      class ClearButton < TkButton
028:        def initialize(calc, frame)
029:          super(frame, "text" => "Clear")
030:          background "darkgreen"
031:          foreground "white"
032:          pack
033:          command proc { calc.clear }
034:        end
```

continues

LISTING 17.7 Continued

```
035:      end
036:
037:      def initialize
038:        title "Calculator"
039:        number_frame  = TkFrame.new(self) { pack "side" => "left"  }
040:        @button_frame = TkFrame.new(self) { pack "side" => "right" }
041:        @display = TkLabel.new(number_frame) do
042:          text "0"
043:          border 3
044:          justify 'right'
045:          background "darkslategrey"
046:          foreground "lightgoldenrod"
047:          pack "side" => "top", "expand" => "yes", "fill" => "x"
048:        end
049:        @number_rows = []
050:        4.times do
051:          @number_rows.push(TkFrame.new(number_frame) do
052:                            pack "expand"=>"yes", "fill"=>"x"
053:                          end)
054:        end
055:
056:        ClearButton.new(self, @number_rows[3]) do
057:          background "darkslategrey"
058:          foreground "yellow4"
059:          pack "side" => "left", "expand" => "yes", "fill" => "both"
060:        end
061:
062:        clear
063:      end
064:
065:      def clear
066:        @accumulator = @current_value = 0
067:        @pending_function = nil
068:        @display.configure("text" => "0")
069:      end
070:
071:      def add_digit(digit)
072:        frame = (9 - digit)/3
073:        Digit.new(self, @number_rows[frame], digit)
074:      end
075:
076:      def add_button(label, &fn)
077:        Button.new(self, @button_frame, label, fn)
078:      end
079:
080:      def run
081:        (0..9).each {|d| add_digit(d)}
082:        add_button("+") {|a,b| a+b}
083:        add_button("-") {|a,b| a-b}
```

LISTING 17.7   Continued

```
084:        add_button("*") {|a,b| a*b}
085:        add_button("/") {|a,b| a/b}
086:        add_button("=") {|a,b| a}
087:        Tk.mainloop
088:      end
089:
090:      # action handlers
091:
092:      def handle_digit(digit)
093:        if @clear_next_time
094:          @current_value = 0
095:          @clear_next_time = false
096:        end
097:        @current_value = @current_value * 10 + digit
098:        @display.configure("text" => @current_value.to_s)
099:      end
100:
101:      def handle_button(function)
102:        if @pending_function
103:          @accumulator = @pending_function.call(@accumulator,
104:                                                @current_value)
105:        else
106:          @accumulator = @current_value
107:        end
108:        @pending_function = function
109:        @display.configure("text" => @accumulator.to_s)
110:        @clear_next_time = true
111:      end
112:
113:    end
114:
115:    calc = Calculator.new
116:    calc.run
```

17

DAY 18

Ruby/Gtk

> A thing of beauty is a joy forever.
>
> —John Keats, *Endymion* (1818)

If you have never wondered whether the modern world's use of acronyms is getting out of hand, consider the following.

Gtk stands for the *GIMP Tool Kit.*

GIMP stands for the *GNU Image Manipulation Program.*

GNU stands for *GNU's Not Unix,* a recursive acronym that you can go on expanding forever without ever discovering the meaning of the *G*.

Don't worry; you don't have to be a GIMP user, or a GNU diehard, to use Gtk. It's just a spiffy general-purpose graphic toolkit for programmers. It works in Unix and Windows environments, and it interfaces nicely with Ruby. It's not considered a finished product just yet, especially for Windows, but it is still functional enough to let us build some solid and attractive interfaces for Ruby programs.

Ruby/Gtk is not yet officially part of the Ruby distribution, so you need to take a little time to set it up before you can use it. Fortunately, it's freely available, and installation is not difficult.

Why would you bother with installing and learning Ruby/Gtk at all, when Tk is an established standard? One reason is that compared to Tk, Gtk has a more polished and professional look. Also, as you are about to see, it is often easier to work with.

We won't get into any deep discussion about the nature of graphical user interfaces (GUI) today, since that was pretty well hashed out on Day 17. Nor will we attempt to cover all (or even most) of the Gtk widget set; that material could fill an entire book or more. Today's objectives are to get a feel for Gtk, learn some organizational conventions, write a few short scripts and one substantial project, and learn where to go to learn more.

Screen captures from today's examples are taken from Unix sessions, but all of the scripts will work on Windows too. Some of them require version 0.26 or newer of Ruby/Gtk.

Installation under Unix

A working Ruby/Gtk installation requires the Ruby interpreter on one side, Gtk graphics libraries on the other, and some binding code that makes them work together. Strictly speaking, that binding code is what we mean when we talk about Ruby/Gtk.

Most Linux and BSD distributions now come with the Gtk libraries preinstalled, so we will assume you already have them. Also, you must have taken care of installing the Ruby interpreter a while ago (otherwise, reading the rest of the book up to now must have been a rather detached experience for you). So Ruby/Gtk is the piece you need.

First, acquire Ruby/Gtk from the Web; you can download it from `http://www.ruby-lang.org/~slagell/gtk/`. Once you have it, unzip and untar the package, and then change into the new directory that was just created. For Ruby/Gtk version 0.26, this might be done as follows (adjust directory and file names as necessary):

```
% gunzip ruby-gtk-0.26.tar.gz
% tar xf ruby-gtk-0.26.tar
% cd ruby-gtk-0.26
```

Compiling a Ruby extension is a little like compiling the Ruby interpreter itself, as well as almost any other Unix program (this would be a good time to read Appendix B if the general process is unfamiliar to you). The main difference is that a Ruby script is substituted for the "configure" step in the usual "configure, make, make install" sequence.

```
% ruby extconf.rb
% make
% su
   (you are prompted for the root password)
# make install
# logout
% ruby -e 'require "gtk"; p Gtk::VERSION'
```

If all went well in the installation, the last command should display the major, minor, and micro version numbers of your Gtk installation as an array, for example, [1, 2, 10].

Installation under Windows

If you originally installed Ruby from the "one-click" installer mentioned in Appendix B, then you already have the Ruby/Gtk binding code in precompiled form, so what remains is to acquire the Gtk libraries. The files are available at http://www.ruby-lang.org/~slagell/gtk/. Read the recommendations there and select a download that is compatible with your version of Ruby and Ruby/Gtk.

The Gtk libraries usually come as a zipped set of .dll files. These need to be placed where the Ruby interpreter can find them. One safe location is in the same directory with the ruby.exe and rubyw.exe files, assuming that directory was made part of the system path during the original installation; in a Cygwin-based installation, for example, this is likely to be something like C:\RUBY\USR\LOCAL\BIN\.

However, you may now or in the future have other uses for Gtk than just your Ruby scripts. To ensure the system-wide availability of Gtk, cloister its .dll files with your other system libraries. Those libraries are stored in a directory named System that is inside the directory that is specified by the %windir% environment variable. Consult %windir% in a command window; the following command will give the library location directly:

```
C:> echo %windir%\SYSTEM
C:\WINDOWS\SYSTEM
```

Often the directory is C:\WINDOWS\SYSTEM, C:\WINDOWS.000\SYSTEM, or C:\WINNT\SYSTEM. Copy the Ruby/Gtk .dll files there, and you're good to go.

18

Tip

> Recall that two Ruby interpreters are supplied for Microsoft Windows. ruby.exe is the usual console-based interpreter that has standard input and output streams, whereas rubyw.exe lacks those streams. We recommend using ruby.exe for developing and testing the examples in this chapter, so that error and debugging information is visible. Once a GUI-based Ruby script seems stable, you can start running it with rubyw.exe.
>
> We've been naming our Ruby scripts with the .rb file extension. Another convention is that Ruby GUI scripts may be named with the .rbw extension, at least in a Windows environment. If the proper file association has been established, then .rbw files can be double-clicked from the desktop, effectively feeding them straight to the rubyw.exe interpreter without a command window appearing. That association is normally an automatic feature of a Ruby installation, but if you open My Computer and select Tools. . . Folder Options. . . File Types, you can edit all file associations manually.

First Ruby/Gtk Scripts

The simplest Ruby/Gtk scripts tend to look quite a bit like their Ruby/Tk counterparts. You require the toolkit, then define the windows, widgets, and functions that make up the logic of your program, and finally invoke an event loop. A minimal Ruby/Gtk application is shown in Listing 18.1.

LISTING 18.1 minimal_1.rb

```
01:    #!/usr/bin/env ruby
02:
03:    require 'gtk'
04:
05:    win = Gtk::Window.new
06:    win.set_title('First Ruby/Gtk application')
07:    win.signal_connect('destroy') {exit}
08:    win.show_all
09:
10:    Gtk::main
11:    puts 'All done.'
```

When you run minimal_1.rb, an empty window appears. You can close the window by clicking the closer widget (depending on the window manager in use, typically a box, marked with an X, in the upper right corner of the window).

Now that you have learned about Ruby/Tk, several lines of the script probably make immediate sense to you. Line 5 creates a window, line 6 gives it a caption for its title bar, and line 8 makes it visible. Line 10 corresponds to Tk::mainloop.

Lines 7 and 11 remain to be explained.

To make sense of the `Gtk::Window#signal_connect` call in line 7, we need to understand that all actions in a Ruby/Gtk program are coordinated using signals that correspond to events. When the window is being closed, it receives a message telling it so; we associate the reception of that signal with a block that causes the main program to exit.

Still, using `exit` to nuke the whole program is not always the best approach. You may have noticed that line 11 never gets executed in our example; when control reaches line 10, the `Gtk::main` loop keeps control until the window gets its *destroy* signal, and then the show's over. We can buy more flexibility by invoking `Gtk::main_quit`. Try substituting this for line 7:

```
07:   win.signal_connect('destroy') {Gtk::main_quit}
```

Run the script again, and the goodbye message from line 11 appears as soon as the window gets closed. We see now that `Gtk::main` is not the end of the story, because the `Gtk::main_quit` method causes it to fall through. This makes it possible to write scripts that use a graphic interface for just an initial information-gathering phase, shifting into a more conventional mode once the user has made his or her demands clear. It also allows for the possibility of another GUI session, with its own `Gtk::main` call, being started later by the same script.

Before proceeding to discuss Gtk geometry and widgets, here's one other useful observation. If we pair the `require 'gtk'` statement with `include Gtk`, we can avoid some clutter by omitting the mention of `Gtk::` before lots of references to objects and methods. We can say `Window` instead of `Gtk::Window`, `Button` instead of `Gtk::Button`, `main` instead of `Gtk::main`, and so on.

In Listing 18.2 we add a button to the window and have a little fun with it.

LISTING 18.2 `minimal_2.rb`

```
01:   #!/usr/bin/env ruby
02:
03:   require 'gtk'; include Gtk
04:
05:   win = Window.new
06:   win.signal_connect('destroy') {main_quit}
07:
08:   btn = Button.new('Click me, please.')
09:   win.add btn
10:
11:   first_click = true
12:   btn.signal_connect('clicked') do
```

continues

18

LISTING 18.2 Continued

```
13:        if first_click
14:          btn.child.set_text('Thanks!')
15:          first_click = false
16:        else
17:          main_quit
18:        end
19:      end
20:
21:      win.show_all
22:      main
```

You got some experience with windows and buttons yesterday, so the structure and behavior of this example should seem fairly familiar. As you'll see shortly, adding a widget in Gtk is something like packing it in Tk. The only tricky part is line 14, which changes the text in the button, but the explanation for that will come soon.

Simple Widget Layout

You learned yesterday about the idea of packing in Ruby/Tk. A widget needs to be packed before it can be seen, and the way a thing is packed determines its location within its parent.

The process is slightly different in Ruby/Gtk. Placement and visibility are achieved separately. Making things visible is very simple, because you can wait until everything in the window is set up, then invoke Gtk::Window#show_all. Placement is mostly a matter of understanding the roles of the Gtk::Bin, Gtk::Box, and Gtk::Table classes, so let's look at them next.

Bin Containers

A Bin is a special kind of container that has room for only one occupant. Descendant classes of Gtk::Bin include Gtk::Window and Gtk::Button. The Gtk::Bin#child method provides access to whatever that single occupant is. When you create a Button, its child is usually a Label, which has a set_string method; thus, to change the text of a button, it is necessary to refer to the child, as we did in line 14 of Listing 18.2.

You cannot add two widgets to the same Window directly, because the Window has no concept of how to organize its contents. You must add some other, more versatile kind of container and then put the widgets there. The kind of container you choose determines how the inner widgets can be arranged.

Box Containers

We never instantiate the Box class directly; instead we choose one of its subclasses, HBox or VBox, according to our needs. As you might have already guessed, H and V stand for horizontal and vertical. An HBox is an invisible container into which widgets may be added from left to right. When a new widget is added to an HBox, there is no need to "pack" it to a side; the left side is always assumed. Similarly, widgets go into a VBox from top to bottom.

Of course most windows containing more than a couple of widgets are too complex to be accommodated by a single HBox or VBox, but it's usually not hard to break up such a layout into one-dimensional components. For example, recall our anagram test program from yesterday (Listing 17.2). There, we created four frames that were stacked vertically, and each frame in turn contained some elements arranged horizontally. In Ruby/Gtk, we would accomplish the same thing by creating a single VBox, putting four HBoxes into it, and then placing the individual widgets into their respective HBoxes. Listing 18.3 is a Ruby/Gtk implementation of yesterday's anagram tester.

LISTING 18.3   Anagram Tester

```
01:     #!/usr/bin/env ruby
02:
03:     # Ruby/Gtk version of the anagram tester.
04:
05:     require 'gtk' ; include Gtk
06:
07:     # Create a main window with one vertical box.
08:     window = Window.new
09:     window.set_title 'Gtk Anagram Test'
10:     window.border_width 10
11:     window.signal_connect('destroy') {main_quit}
12:     window.add(vb = VBox.new)
13:
14:     # Put some horizontal boxes in the vbox.
15:     vb.add(phrase1box = HBox.new(false,10))
16:     vb.add(phrase2box = HBox.new(false,10))
17:     vb.add(resultbox = HBox.new(true,10))
18:     vb.add(buttonbox = HBox.new(true,10))
19:
20:     # Add the visible widgets to the hboxes.
21:     phrase1box.add(Label.new("Phrase 1"))
22:     phrase1box.add(e1 = Entry.new)
23:     phrase2box.add(Label.new("Phrase 2"))
24:     phrase2box.add(e2 = Entry.new)
```

18

continues

LISTING 18.3   Continued

```
25:     resultbox.border_width 4
26:     resultbox.add(l_result = Label.new(''))
27:     buttonbox.add(b_test  = Button.new('Test'))
28:     buttonbox.add(b_clear = Button.new('Clear'))
29:     buttonbox.add(b_quit  = Button.new('Quit'))
30:
31:     # Say what should happen when the buttons get clicked.
32:     b_quit.signal_connect('clicked') do
33:       main_quit
34:     end
35:     b_clear.signal_connect('clicked') do
36:       [e1, e2, l_result].each {|widget| widget.set_text('')}
37:       e1.grab_focus
38:     end
39:     b_test.signal_connect('clicked') do
40:       if are_anagrams?(e1.get_text, e2.get_text)
41:         l_result.set_text("These are anagrams.")
42:       else
43:         l_result.set_text("These are NOT anagrams.")
44:       end
45:       b_clear.grab_focus
46:     end
47:
48:     # Set up an anagram test that returns a Boolean.
49:     def are_anagrams?(s1, s2)
50:       chars1, chars2 = [s1,s2].map do |str|
51:         str.delete("^A-Za-z").downcase.split('').sort.join
52:       end
53:       return (chars1 == chars2)
54:     end
55:
56:     # Place the cursor and interact with the user.
57:     e1.grab_focus
58:     window.show_all
59:
60:     main  # it's not a method of ours, but Gtk::main
```

The Ruby/Gtk version turns out to be slightly shorter than the original, partly because we are using a more compact style and partly because Gtk's design is better suited to an object-oriented environment. Notice, for example, the lack of any TextVariable objects. A text entry object can be asked directly about its text content, using Gtk::Entry#get_text. Figure 18.1 shows the window produced by this script.

FIGURE **18.1**

*Anagram tester imple-
mented using Ruby/Gtk
in Listing 18.3.*

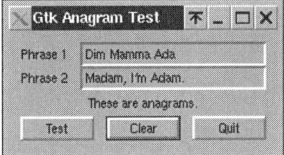

Look closely at lines 12 and 15–18. Each of these lines creates, names, and positions a
new widget. For the purpose of explanation, line 18 can be broken up into four separate
lines as follows:

```
buttonbox = HBox.new
buttonbox.set_homogeneous(true)
buttonbox.set_spacing(10)
vb.add(buttonbox)
```

Most Gtk objects have a great many characteristics that can be manipulated. If you want
to know everything that can be done with an HBox, you can consult Gtk reference materials, or you can look at the value of Gtk::HBox.instance_methods.sort (perhaps in an
irb session, being sure to issue require 'gtk' as the first command) for a quick list.
Most of the method names are pretty close to self-explanatory, but there's no need to
learn all of them before starting to write Ruby/Gtk scripts. Stick close to the defaults,
and look up what you don't know only when new needs arise. The new methods for most
Ruby/Gtk classes accept parameters allowing you to control the characteristics that most
often really need to be changed.

Getting back to our example, the set_spacing parameter enforces some amount of
separation—ten pixels in this case—between whatever elements will later be added to
the box. The separation does not extend vertically for an HBox, nor horizontally for a
VBox. If what you want is extra space extending in all directions around the box, you can
use the border_width method, as in line 25, where the result label is given some extra
padding to improve readability.

The set_homogeneous parameter indicates whether all elements in the box will be made
the same size. We set this to true for the button box and false for the text entry boxes
(the setting has no effect when applied to the result box, which has one lonely resident).
So our buttons are kept a uniform size, but the labels next to the text entry regions are
allowed to remain relatively small.

Here are two experiments you can try to help you understand homogeneity. First, change
false to true in lines 15 and 16, and notice what it does to the appearance of the window.
You see that the "Phrase 1" and "Phrase 2" labels are made unnecessarily large to match the
width of the text entry widgets. Second, comment out line 25, and change line 12 to:

```
12:    window.add(vb = VBox.new(true))
```

18

Since this ensures that the four horizontal boxes will be of uniform size, it becomes unnecessary to give extra padding to the result box.

Why do we create and attach widgets in the condensed form of lines 15–18 instead of spelling everything out? Well, it's hard for many of us to spell homogeneous correctly all the time, for one thing. But the main reason is simply that it's desirable to keep GUI code compact when possible. A problem with the typical GUI project is sheer length, and most of that length is tied up in verbose widget code having little to do with the real logic of the program. Any way to avoid that bloat is worth looking into.

Not convinced? Look at line 18 again. Although it may look dense, it corresponds to a straightforward natural-language sentence: *Add to this box a horizontal box, named "buttonbox," for holding uniformly sized widgets 10 pixels apart.* That sounds enough like one unit of work that it is permissible to code it on one line.

If being forced to add widgets in left-to-right and top-to-bottom order offends your sense of personal liberty, you can use the pack_start and pack_end methods instead of add. These allow you to work from either end of a box. They also accept three extra parameters to give you some more control. These are referred to as *expand, fill*, and *padding*. When *expand* is set to true, widgets are spread out so that all space in the container gets allocated; otherwise they collect at the ends. The *fill* parameter decides whether expansion is applied within or between widgets; it has no effect when *expand* is false. Finally, *padding* is a number of extra pixels to be placed between widgets. Listing 18.4 and Figure 18.2 demonstrate some effects of these extra arguments.

LISTING 18.4   Illustration of Packing Options

```
01:    #!/usr/bin/env ruby
02:
03:    require 'gtk'; include Gtk
04:
05:    def newrow(exp, fill, pad)
06:      h = HBox.new
07:      [ "expand=#{exp}, fill=#{fill}, pad=#{pad}",
08:        '1', '2', '3' ].each do |msg|
09:        h.pack_end(Button.new(msg),exp,fill,pad)
10:      end
11:      h
12:    end
13:
14:    window = Window.new
15:    window.set_title('Test of packing options')
16:    window.signal_connect('destroy') {main_quit}
17:    window.set_default_size(350,100)
18:
```

LISTING 18.4 Continued

```
19:    window.add(vb=VBox.new)
20:    vb.add(newrow(false,false,0))
21:    vb.add(newrow(true,false,0))
22:    vb.add(newrow(true,true,0))
23:    vb.add(newrow(true,true,5))
24:
25:    window.show_all
26:    main
```

FIGURE 18.2

*Effects of packing
options in Listing 18.4.*

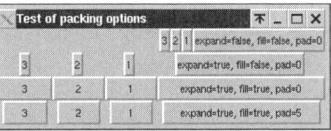

When you simply add a widget to a container, you are essentially calling pack_start
with *expand* and *fill* both set to true and *padding* set to 0.

Table Containers

A Table lets you arrange a group of widgets in rows and columns. Like a Box, it can be
set up to hold widgets of identical or different sizes and shapes; however, it requires
knowledge in advance about how many widgets it will be asked to hold.

There is no assumption about the order in which table cells will be populated, so instead of a simple add method, we have an attach method that needs to be told exactly
where each widget will go. Also, a widget may occupy any rectangular region of a
table, not just one cell. Table#attach, not surprisingly, takes more arguments than
Hbox#add does:

```
table.attach(widget, left, right, top, bottom)
```

There are two things to watch out for here. First, the order of the coordinates is inconsistent with Table.new, in which the number of rows comes before the number of columns.
Second, the *right* and *bottom* coordinates correspond not to the last position occupied by
the widget but to the next position *not* occupied by the widget. Thus, a widget that will
occupy columns 0 through 3 and rows 2 through 4 would be attached using the coordinates 0, 4, 2, 5.

By the way, what we are calling a "widget" may in fact be a container, such as a VBox or
another Table. It's fine to use boxes inside tables, and vice versa.

We'll cook up an example of a table layout in the next section.

18

Modular Design for Multiple Windows

Most GUI programs will work with more than one window. When you're used to tradi-tional text-based programming, it can be a little tricky to get your head around the logic of making windows come and go in an event-driven environment, but if you organize your code using the trick you are about to learn, it should begin to make perfect sense.

Window Subclasses and Test Code

When designing a window, we never write code to create a `Gtk::Window` directly; instead we write a subclass of `Gtk::Window` and instantiate that subclass. (The same idea applies when working with other Gtk classes, as you'll see.) This involves just a little extra over-head, compared to what we've been doing. Each new class will go in a file that looks something like this one:

```
require 'gtk'; include Gtk

class MyWindowClass < Window
  def initialize
    super()
    # define window's widgets and behavior here
    show_all
  end
end

if $0 == __FILE__
  # TEST CODE FOR THIS WINDOW CLASS
  w = MyWindowClass.new
  w.signal_connect('destroy') {main_quit}
  main
end
```

We have not yet discussed the global variable `$0`. It refers to the filename of the primary script that the interpreter was asked to run. `__FILE__` refers instead to "this" file, the file within which the reference appears. This scheme enables us to test new window types in isolation easily. If we create a file in the foregoing style and run it directly, the test code runs, and we can see how an instance of our new kind of window behaves; but if we instead `load` or `require` this file from another Ruby script, the test code does not run, because `$0` refers to the other script.

A Table Window

Listing 18.5 incorporates this design idea into a window class that demonstrates a table layout.

LISTING 18.5   Table Layout Example (`analyzer.rb`)

```
01:  #!/usr/bin/env ruby
02:
03:  require 'gtk'; include Gtk
04:
05:  class TextAnalyzer < Window
06:    def initialize
07:      super()
08:
09:      # Create table and attach widgets to it.
10:      add(t = Table.new(2,4,true))
11:      t.border_width 5
12:      t.set_row_spacings 10
13:      t.set_col_spacings 10
14:      t.attach(Label.new('Enter a string: '),0,1,0,1)
15:      t.attach((entry = Entry.new), 1,4,0,1)
16:      t.attach((b_quit = Button.new('Exit')),0,1,1,2)
17:      t.attach((b_calc = Button.new('Analyze')),1,2,1,2)
18:      t.attach((result = Label.new('')),2,4,1,2)
19:
20:      b_calc.signal_connect('clicked') do
21:        result.set_text(analysis(entry.get_text))
22:        entry.grab_focus
23:      end
24:
25:      b_quit.signal_connect('clicked') {destroy}
26:
27:      entry.grab_focus
28:      show_all
29:    end
30:
31:    private
32:    def analysis(str)
33:      "%d words, %d characters" %
34:        [str.strip.split.length, str.length]
35:    end
36:  end
37:
38:  if $0 == __FILE__
39:    ta = TextAnalyzer.new
40:    ta.set_title 'Text analyzer'
41:    ta.signal_connect('destroy') {main_quit}
42:    main
43:  end
```

18

In this example, a homogeneous four-column layout was chosen just to get the widths right. The resulting window is shown in Figure 18.3. Since it doesn't exactly look like a table, you might want to experiment to help you understand the layout: Change the homogeneity flag to `false` in line 10, or narrow the table to three columns, making the corresponding adjustments to the `attach` calls in lines 15 and 18.

FIGURE **18.3**

Text analyzer with column layout.

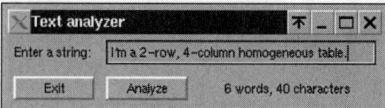

However, the example could have as effectively been implemented with `Box` containers, and in today's exercise 1 you're asked to rewrite it that way. The classic introductory example of table layout is a calculator program, because the keys look nice in a grid. Rather than provide a calculator here, I refer you to the one in the Ruby/Gtk Web tutorial at `http://www.ruby-lang.org/gtk/en/tutorial/`.

An Application Split into Two Files

The test code area at the bottom of Listing 18.5 is responsible for making an instance of the new class, linking its destruction to a `Gtk::main_quit` call, and invoking `Gtk::main`. Whenever the file is invoked as part of a larger program, none of those tasks is necessary, and indeed the test code needs to be prevented from running. To see what impact this has on modular design, save Listing 18.6 and run it from the directory in which you saved Listing 18.5.

LISTING 18.6   A Script to Call `analyzer.rb`

```
01:   #!/usr/bin/env ruby
02:
03:   require 'gtk'; include Gtk
04:   require 'analyzer'
05:
06:   class TextAnalyzerCaller < Dialog
07:     def initialize
08:       super
09:       vbox.add(Label.new('This is a Gtk::Dialog instance.'))
10:       action_area.add(b_test = Button.new('New window'))
11:       b_test.signal_connect('clicked') do
12:         TextAnalyzer.new
13:       end
14:       action_area.add(b_quit = Button.new('Quit'))
15:       b_quit.signal_connect('clicked') do
16:         destroy # think: *what* exactly is destroyed?
17:       end
18:       show_all
19:     end
20:   end
```

LISTING 18.6 Continued

```
21:
22:  if $0 == __FILE__
23:    ta = TextAnalyzerCaller.new
24:    ta.signal_connect('destroy') {main_quit}
25:    main
26:  end
```

Gtk::Dialog is a subclass of Gtk::Window, making our TextAnalyzerCaller class, in turn, a Window descendant. Each Dialog instance is based on a top-level window. It eases the creation of dialog boxes slightly by providing a prefabricated HBox (named action_area) for buttons and a VBox (named vbox) for everything else. Our dialog in Listing 18.6 has a label in vbox and two buttons in action_area. In a few moments we will design a Dialog subclass that allows for an even more streamlined creation of certain simple dialogs.

Clicking the "New window" button in the dialog box produced by the code in Listing 18.6 causes a text analysis window to be displayed. After exiting from that window, you can click the button again and get another one.

Modal Dialogs

When you run the script in Listing 18.6, you can click "New window" over and over without closing the new windows that appear, resulting in many TextAnalyzer instances visible at the same time. Sometimes such behavior is desirable, but you might prefer to disallow duplicates. If we mark the TextAnalyzer window as *modal*, the user is forced to deal with it before any other windows in the program will be allowed to respond to events. Change line 8 of Listing 18.5 to

```
08:      set_modal(true)
```

and run Listing 18.6 again. You'll find it impossible to open more than one analysis window at a time.

The MessageBox Class

One thing currently lacking in standard Ruby/Gtk is a class for popping up simple message boxes and giving the user an appropriate list of responses (for example, Yes/No, OK/Cancel, or Yes/No/Cancel). When creating a message box, we shouldn't have to

18

think about creating widgets and connecting signals: It should be sufficient for the programmer to provide the message text, plus a list of strings (and, optionally, actions) to be assigned to buttons.

Listing 18.7 defines a MessageBox class that descends from Gtk::Dialog. You can run it by itself to test it; we'll incorporate it into a larger project later today and also use it for Exercise 3.

LISTING 18.7　messagebox.rb

```ruby
01:    #!/usr/bin/env ruby
02:
03:    require 'gtk'; include Gtk
04:
05:    # To create a MessageBox, supply message text and an array
06:    # of button specifications.
07:    #
08:    #   MessageBox.new( message,
09:    #     [ [buttontext, proc, default],
10:    #       [buttontext, proc, default], ... ] )
11:    #
12:
13:    # "proc" is a proc object that will be called if the
14:    # button is clicked. "default" is a flag which, when
15:    # set to true, allows the user to choose the button by
16:    # pressing "Enter" on the keyboard. Both are optional.
17:
18:    class MessageBox < Dialog
19:      def initialize(message,btns)
20:        super()
21:        vbox.pack_start(Label.new(message),true,true,10)
22:        btns.each do |text,action,dflt|
23:          action_area.add(b=Button.new(text))
24:          b.signal_connect('clicked') do
25:            action.call unless action.nil?
26:            destroy
27:          end
28:          if dflt
29:            b.set_flags(Widget::CAN_DEFAULT)
30:            b.grab_default
31:          end
32:        end
33:        set_modal true
34:        show_all
35:      end
36:    end
37:
38:    if $0 == __FILE__
39:      q = MessageBox.new("Are we having fun?",
```

LISTING 18.7   Continued

```
40:              [ ["Yes", proc {puts "yes"}, true],
41:                ["No", proc {puts "no"}],
42:                ["Cancel"] ])
43:      q.set_title 'message box test'
44:      q.signal_connect('destroy') {main_quit}
45:      main
46:   end
```

The `grab_default` method behaves similarly to `grab_focus`, which we've seen before, but there are some differences. It provides a more striking visual highlight, and it allows the button to be selected with the Enter key. It also usually requires the button to be explicitly marked as eligible to hold default status. If we leave out line 29, line 30 generates an error.

Figure 18.4 shows the results of Listing 18.7.

FIGURE 18.4

Simple dialog produced by `messagebox.rb`.

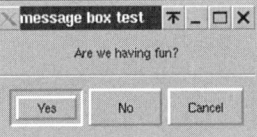

More Widget Types

As mentioned earlier, this chapter does not attempt to document every feature of Gtk or Ruby/Gtk, but there are several other fundamental Gtk classes that you are likely to find useful, and we would be remiss not to mention them. They will be introduced in the following four sample scripts.

Sample 1: `CheckButton` and `RadioButton`

Listing 18.8 lets the user configure a burger for lunch.

LISTING 18.8   The Burger Stand

```
01:   #!/usr/bin/env ruby
02:
03:   require 'gtk'; include Gtk
04:
05:   class BurgerSelector < Window
06:     def initialize
07:       super()
```

continues

LISTING **18.8** Continued

```
08:        add(vb = VBox.new)
09:        vb.add(hb = HBox.new)
10:
11:        hb.add(meats = VBox.new)
12:        meats.add(rb_beef = RadioButton.new(nil,'Beef'))
13:        meats.add(rb_turkey = RadioButton.new(rb_beef,'Turkey'))
14:        meats.add(rb_soy = RadioButton.new(rb_turkey,'Soy'))
15:        rb_soy.active = true
16:
17:        hb.add(extras = VBox.new)
18:        extras.add(cb_lettuce = CheckButton.new('Lettuce'))
19:        extras.add(cb_onion = CheckButton.new('Onion'))
20:        extras.add(cb_tomato = CheckButton.new('Tomato'))
21:
22:        vb.add(buttons = HBox.new)
23:        buttons.add(b_order = Button.new('Order'))
24:        buttons.add(b_quit = Button.new('Quit'))
25:
26:        vb.add(results = HBox.new)
27:        results.add(l_results = Label.new(' '*70))
28:
29:        b_quit.signal_connect('clicked') {destroy}
30:        b_order.signal_connect('clicked') do
31:          order = if rb_beef.active? then "Beef"
32:                  elsif rb_turkey.active? then "Turkey"
33:                  else "Soy"
34:                  end
35:          order += ", lettuce" if cb_lettuce.active?
36:          order += ", onion" if cb_onion.active?
37:          order += ", tomato" if cb_tomato.active?
38:          l_results.set_text order
39:        end
40:
41:        show_all
42:      end
43:    end
44:
45:    if $0 == __FILE__
46:      window = BurgerSelector.new
47:      window.set_title 'Burger stand'
48:      window.signal_connect('destroy') {main_quit}
49:      main
50:    end
```

The results of this script are shown in Figure 18.5. In addition to the standard buttons shown near the bottom of the window, we now have check boxes and radio buttons. These are not associated with actions directly. Rather, they are queried for their state in lines 35–37.

FIGURE 18.5

Electronic "menu" of the Burger Stand.

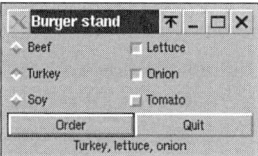

Check boxes and radio buttons have the property of being active or inactive. Some people might think of "active" as meaning "responsive" (we'll pursue this idea in Exercise 4), but what we are really talking about is whether the widget is visibly selected, generally as a result of user interaction. The active? method returns true or false to reflect that state. It can also be manipulated under program control, via the active= method as in line 15, or the set_active method (for instance, set_active(false) and active=false have the same effect).

Each radio button belongs to a group, within which no more than one member is allowed to be active at a time. The activation of any one automatically deactivates the others. Grouping radio buttons is done by linking them as if in a chain, as shown in lines 12–14. The first button is linked to nil, and each button added to the group is linked to the previous one.

The behavior of a check box is simpler. When clicked, it alternates between active and inactive states without affecting anything else.

You are allowed to associate blocks with radio buttons and check boxes via signal_connect('clicked'), although it is usually unnecessary to do so. Since such a block will execute even when a button is being deactivated (in the case of a check box), the block might need to check the widget's state before proceeding:

```
cb_onion.signal_connect('clicked') do
  if cb_onion.active?
    MessageBox.new(
        "I hope you don't have a date tonight!",
        [["Leave me alone!"]])
  end
end
```

If you saved messagebox.rb from Listing 18.7, try inserting the preceding code fragment between lines 20 and 21 of Listing 18.8. Also be sure to require 'messagebox' somewhere near the top of Listing 18.8. Now your mother will help you run your burger stand.

Sample 2: `AccelGroup`, `ToggleButton`, and `HSeparator`

Listing 18.9 displays a toggle button that is selectable either by clicking or by pressing the F5 function key. The state of the toggle button controls the contents of a label just below it.

LISTING 18.9 Keyboard Accelerator Example

```ruby
01:    #!/usr/bin/env ruby
02:
03:    require 'gtk' ; include Gtk
04:
05:    class AccelTest < Window
06:      def initialize
07:        super()
08:        add(vb = VBox.new(false,5))
09:        vb.border_width(5)
10:        vb.add(tb = ToggleButton.new('Click me or press F5'))
11:        vb.add(state = Label.new('INACTIVE'))
12:        vb.add(HSeparator.new)
13:        vb.add(b_quit = Button.new('Quit'))
14:        b_quit.signal_connect('clicked') {destroy}
15:
16:        # Associate the F5 key with the toggle button.
17:        (ag = AccelGroup.new).attach(self)
18:        tb.add_accelerator('clicked', ag, Gdk::GDK_F5, 0, 0)
19:
20:        # Link the state label to the toggle button.
21:        tb.signal_connect('clicked') do
22:          state.set_text(tb.active ? 'ACTIVE' : 'INACTIVE')
23:        end
24:
25:        show_all
26:      end
27:    end
28:
29:    if $0 == __FILE__
30:      w = AccelTest.new
31:      w.set_title 'Toggle test'
32:      w.signal_connect('destroy') {main_quit}
33:      main
34:    end
```

The resulting window is shown in Figure 18.6. An `HSeparator` object, such as the one created in line 12, draws a horizontal line for visibly separating different regions of a `VBox`. Similarly, you can use `VSeparator` objects to break up an `HBox`.

FIGURE **18.6**

*Dialog with a keyboard
accelerator.*

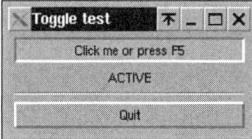

FIGURE **18.6**

*Dialog with a keyboard
accelerator.*

A toggle button is nothing shocking. It's logically like a check box, so it alternates between active and inactive states when clicked, but it looks just like an ordinary button.

What is really new here is the ability to "click" on something by pressing a key chosen arbitrarily by the programmer. Power users are not always very fond of mice. They find they can work much faster if they can keep their hands on the keyboard; hence the term *accelerators* for keyboard equivalents to mouse actions.

Associating a widget with a keypress cannot be done directly. You have to go through the slightly awkward business of defining an accelerator "group" and attaching it to the window containing the widget in question, as in line 17.

The mention of "Gdk" in line 18 looks like a typo, but in fact it refers to the GIMP Drawing Kit, a lower, more system-dependent layer that Gtk relies on. We haven't mentioned it before, because we seldom have to deal with it, but some constants, such as GDK_F5, will be found there. You can think of key specifications as introducing a system dependency, because not all computers can be counted on to have exactly the same keys or key layouts.

More than one accelerator key can be associated with a widget. If you insert the following as line 19, the toggle button becomes responsive to Ctrl+T in addition to F5:

```
tb.add_accelerator('clicked', ag, Gdk::GDK_T, Gdk::CONTROL_MASK, 0)
```

We'll be doing a little more with keyboard accelerators before the day is through.

Sample 3: `Text`

The `Gtk::Text` widget is a self-contained text editor that's quite simple to drop into an application. It supports word wrap, copy/cut/paste, and a variety of keyboard shortcuts. It does not support mixed fonts or text highlighting, but those bits of finery are expected to appear in a future incarnation of Gtk.

In Listing 18.10 we create a text editor that the user can type into. When the editor is closed, the contents of the editor widget appear in the console window. Lines 8 and 9 were left blank for future enhancement; you won't have to wait long to see why.

18

Listing 18.10   Text Widget

```
01:    #!/usr/bin/env ruby
02:
03:    require 'gtk'; include Gtk
04:
05:    class TextEditor < Window
06:      def initialize
07:        super
08:
09:
10:        add(@text = Text.new)
11:        @text.set_editable(true)
12:        @text.set_word_wrap(true)
13:        @text.grab_focus
14:        show_all
15:      end
16:      def contents
17:        @text.get_chars(0,@text.get_length)
18:      end
19:    end
20:
21:    if $0 == __FILE__
22:      te = TextEditor.new
23:      te.set_title 'Text test'
24:      te.signal_connect('destroy') do
25:        puts te.contents
26:        main_quit
27:      end
28:      main
29:    end
```

We have made @text an instance variable so that it will be accessible from the TextEditor#contents method.

Figure 18.7 shows a famous speech being typed into our editor. If you start composing your autobiography in this editor, you'll find that there seems to be no limit to the amount of text it can hold. Unfortunately, there are no scroll bars to help you find your way around either, and that gets disorienting before long.

Figure 18.7

A Text *widget without scrollbars.*

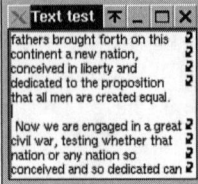

Since the `Text` widget already supports basic editing operations, we don't have to write the logic for them. The familiar Ctrl+X, Ctrl+C, and Ctrl+V keyboard shortcuts already work. The user can move the cursor around with the arrow keys and the Home, End, PageUp, and PageDn keys and can hold down the Shift key while moving the cursor to select a range of text.

The Text widget doesn't supply scrollbars by itself, but Gtk offers a more general solution for widgets whose contents grow beyond the physical space available to them. Read on. . . .

Sample 4: `ScrollableWindow`

Giving scrollbars to a Text widget is very easy in Gtk. Enclose the widget in a `ScrollableWindow`, specify *policies* (which will be explained in a moment), and you're done. Change lines 8–10 of Listing 18.10 as follows, and our text editor gets a working vertical scrollbar.

```
08:     add(sw = ScrolledWindow.new)
09:     sw.set_policy(POLICY_NEVER,POLICY_ALWAYS)
10:     sw.add(@text = Text.new)
```

The `ScrolledWindow#set_policy` method lets you decide which scrollbar(s) to display and when. The two arguments refer to the horizontal and vertical scrollbars respectively, so (`POLICY_NEVER,POLICY_ALWAYS`) means our editor has only a vertical scrollbar.

The other possible policy is `POLICY_AUTOMATIC`, which means a scrollbar should be displayed only if the contents warrant it. Had we used `POLICY_AUTOMATIC`, no scrollbars would have been visible at first, but a vertical scrollbar would have appeared when we had typed enough to fill all the visible lines. No horizontal scrollbar would have appeared in this case, because the wrapping logic of the `Text` widget splits long lines with the curved-arrow character so that there is never a horizontal overflow.

A `ScrolledWindow` is a `Bin`, meaning it can hold just one thing. As you know by now, no real limitation is implied by that fact. `Text` is considered a "scrollable widget," meaning it can be enclosed in a `ScrollableWindow` with no complications. Scrolling some other things, like tables, involves a little more work; we won't get into that topic here, but if you find it necessary, start by looking up "viewports" in any Gtk reference.

A Full Ruby/Gtk Application

In today's final example we'll bring together some of the Gtk features we have just learned about and will add a few new ones. The goal is to build a more versatile text editor around a `Gtk::Text` widget, giving it drop-down menus, global search and replace, and the ability to load and save files. There will be three classes in separate files, but one of those files, `messagebox.rb`, we have already written.

18

The top-level editor class is given in Listing 18.11.

LISTING 18.11 editor.rb

```ruby
001:    #!/usr/bin/env ruby
002:
003:    require 'gtk'; include Gtk
004:    require 'findbox'
005:    require 'messagebox'
006:
007:    class Editor < Window
008:      def initialize(initial_filename = nil)
009:
010:        super()
011:        (ag = AccelGroup.new).attach(self)
012:
013:        # Create the main text window.
014:        set_title('Simple editor')
015:        set_default_size(400,400)
016:        add(frame = VBox.new(false))
017:
018:        # Create drop-down menus using an item factory.
019:        items = [
020:          ['/F_ile', nil,
021:            ItemFactory::BRANCH],
022:          ['/F_ile/_Open', '<control>O',
023:           ItemFactory::ITEM, proc{do_open}],
024:          ['/F_ile/_Save', '<control>S',
025:            ItemFactory::ITEM, proc{do_save}],
026:          ['/F_ile/sep1', nil,
027:            ItemFactory::SEPARATOR],
028:          ['/F_ile/_Quit', '<control>Q',
029:            ItemFactory::ITEM, proc{do_exit}],
030:          ['/_Edit', nil,
031:            ItemFactory::BRANCH],
032:          ['/_Edit/_Search', '<control>S',
033:            ItemFactory::ITEM, proc{do_search}]
034:        ]
035:
036:        factory = ItemFactory.new(ItemFactory::TYPE_MENU_BAR, '<main>', ag)
037:        factory.create_items(items)
038:      frame.pack_start(factory.get_widget('<main>'), false, false, 2)
039:
040:        # Create the text area in a scrolled window.
041:        frame.add(sw = ScrolledWindow.new)
042:        sw.add(@textbox = Text.new)
043:        @textbox.set_editable true
044:        sw.set_policy(POLICY_NEVER,POLICY_ALWAYS)
045:        @textbox.set_word_wrap true
046:
```

LISTING 18.11 Continued

```
047:        # Load initial file, if given, and we're ready to roll.
048:        load_file(initial_filename) if initial_filename
049:        @textbox.grab_focus
050:        show_all
051:      end
052:
053:      def do_exit # What enhancements could be added here?
054:        destroy
055:      end
056:
057:      private
058:      def do_open
059:        fs = FileSelection.new('load file')
060:        fs.cancel_button.signal_connect('clicked') {fs.destroy}
061:        fs.ok_button.signal_connect('clicked') do
062:          load_file(fs.get_filename)
063:          fs.destroy
064:        end
065:        fs.set_modal(true)
066:        fs.show_all
067:      end
068:
069:      def load_file(filename)
070:        begin
071:          clear_all
072:          @textbox.insert_text(File.open(filename,'r').read,0)
073:        rescue
074:          MessageBox.new($!,[['Cancel']])
075:        end
076:      end
077:
078:      def do_save
079:        fs = FileSelection.new('save file')
080:        fs.cancel_button.signal_connect('clicked') {fs.destroy}
081:        fs.ok_button.signal_connect('clicked') do
082:          begin
083:            File.open(fs.get_filename,'w') {|f| f.write(all_text)}
084:            fs.destroy
085:          rescue
086:            MessageBox.new($!,[['Cancel']])
087:          end
088:        end
089:        fs.set_modal(true)
090:        fs.show_all
091:      end
092:
093:      def do_search
```

18

continues

LISTING 18.11   Continued

```
094:        fb = FindBox.new
095:        fb.find_btn.signal_connect('clicked') do
096:          newpos = find_next(fb.find.get_text)
097:          @textbox.set_position newpos if newpos
098:          fb.destroy
099:        end
100:        fb.one_btn.signal_connect('clicked') do
101:          replace_one(fb.find.get_text, fb.replace.get_text)
102:          fb.destroy
103:        end
104:        fb.all_btn.signal_connect('clicked') do
105:          replace_all(fb.find.get_text, fb.replace.get_text)
106:          fb.destroy
107:        end
108:      end
109:
110:
111:      def find_next(old_text)
112:        all_text.index(old_text, @textbox.position+1)
113:      end
114:
115:      def replace_all(old_text, new_text)
116:        while replace_one(old_text, new_text)
117:        end
118:      end
119:
120:      def replace_one(old_text, new_text)
121:        # return value: true iff replace was successful
122:        if (where=find_next(old_text))
123:          @textbox.set_position where    # physical cursor
124:          @textbox.set_point where       # logical cursor
125:          @textbox.forward_delete(old_text.length)
126:          @textbox.insert_text(new_text, where)
127:          @textbox.set_position(where+new_text.length)
128:          true
129:        else
130:          false
131:        end
132:      end
133:
134:      def clear_all
135:        @textbox.set_position 0
136:        @textbox.forward_delete(@textbox.get_length)
137:      end
138:
139:      def all_text
140:        @textbox.get_chars(0,@textbox.get_length)
141:      end
142:
```

LISTING 18.11   Continued

```
143:    end
144:
145:    if __FILE__ == $0
146:      # Create an editor and pass it a filename, if
147:      # the user supplied one. How could this be improved?
148:      w = Editor.new(ARGV[0])
149:      w.signal_connect('destroy') {w.do_exit}
150:      main
151:    end
```

The editor is almost ready to run, although we don't yet have the findbox.rb file
referred to in line 4. To test Listing 18.11 right now, comment out lines 4 and 32–33 to
disable search and replace operations temporarily.

You should find most of the code in lines 1–50 intelligible based on what we have learned
so far, except for the "item factory" references in lines 18–38. The process of building a
menu is fairly complex, involving the construction of a logical hierarchy of choices, definition of key assignments (two separate sets—one that applies when a menu is in a
dropped-down state and another that applies the rest of the time), and the underlining of
certain characters in the menus. We won't bother to go through such a construction step-
by-step, although that would be possible. There is no good reason for us to do it the hard
way, because Gtk's item factories condense the whole enterprise into a few lines.

Each element of the items array, defined starting at line 19, contains a menu path (the
sequence of words the user clicks on while navigating there), a global accelerator key
that is applicable when no menus are dropped, a "type" name, and optionally a procedure
to be executed when the item is invoked from the menu. The "type" we care most about
is ItemFactory::ITEM, which creates an ordinary menu entry as opposed to a separator
or hierarchical heading.

Look at lines 24–25. The <control>S shortcut means that when no menus are dropped
down, pressing Ctrl+S will have the same effect as selecting File, Save from the menu. But
we said before that there was another way to use the keyboard to the same effect. Pressing
Alt+I will drop the File menu, after which pressing the S key by itself selects the menu item.
These are specified by inserting underscores before the relevant characters of /File/Save.
The underscores are interpreted during the ItemFactory#create_items call in line 37. They
have the effect of both visibly underlining the accelerator characters and binding the corresponding keys to the menu.

18

> **Note**   Why do we assign Alt+I to the File dropdown, instead of the more traditional Alt+F? Alt+F happens to be one of the built-in accelerators of the `Gtk::Text` widget. It moves the cursor forward to the next word.

Everything from line 57 down is marked `private` because it is not to be called from outside. It shouldn't be surprising that our `Editor` should have such a small public interface; this is true of many GUI objects, because their lot in life—rather like our own, when you think about it—is to get initialized and then respond to events.

The `do_open` and `do_save` methods refer to some methods supplied with the `Gtk::FileSelection` class. A file selector is a special window that displays directory and file information and lets the user navigate the file system before selecting an existing file or typing in a new one. We don't have to worry about how it works; all we need to know is how to attach our own meanings to the OK and Cancel buttons (see lines 80–81 in `do_save`) and how to retrieve the filename the user selected (line 83).

Notice that we have made the file selector modal (line 89), rendering the editor window unresponsive until the selector window is destroyed. The way we have set this up in line 84 within a `begin...rescue...end` structure ensures that if the user chooses a bad save destination, the selector window stays open to invite another attempt. The file selector window does not close until the save succeeds or the user explicitly cancels the operation.

The `do_exit` method could be improved by adding code to check whether the text was altered after the last save, and if so, warn the user about it. We won't make that enhancement here, but you can experiment with it if you like. How could you tell whether the text had changed since the last save?

Now let's see about taking advantage of all that search/replace logic in lines 93–132. You might notice that the invocation and use of a `FindBox` object is fairly similar to what we discussed regarding the `FileSelection` object just now: Instantiate the window, attach callback code to some of its widgets, and that's about all. A `FindBox` will look like Figure 18.8.

FIGURE 18.8

Appearance of a FindBox object.

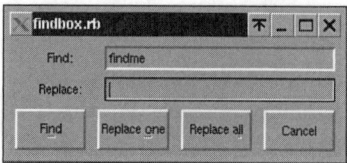

We're about to look at the `FindBox` class code, but first go back and examine the `Editor#do_search` method, lines 93–108 of Listing 18.11, which shows what the public interface of `FindBox` should be. There should be five accessible widgets: two text entry fields (one for search text, another for replacement text) and three buttons (Find Next, Replace One, Replace All). A Cancel button will be defined, but the caller, `Editor#do_search` in this case, needn't know anything about it; the `FindBox` class should handle that button internally by simply destroying its window, invoking no callback functions. Armed with this understanding, we're ready for Listing 18.12.

LISTING 18.12 `findbox.rb`

```
01:    require 'gtk'; include Gtk
02:
03:    class FindBox < Window
04:      def initialize(initial_find = '', initial_replace = '')
05:        super()
06:        (ag = AccelGroup.new).attach(self)
07:
08:        border_width 5
09:        set_default_size 200,100
10:        set_modal true
11:        add(main_frame=VBox.new(false,4))
12:
13:        main_frame.add(tbl = Table.new(2,2,false))
14:        tbl.attach(Label.new('Find:'), 0,1,0,1)
15:        tbl.attach((@find=Entry.new), 1,2,0,1)
16:        tbl.attach(Label.new('Replace:'), 0,1,1,2)
17:        tbl.attach((@replace=Entry.new), 1,2,1,2)
18:
19:        @find.set_text(initial_find)
20:        @replace.set_text(initial_replace)
21:
22:        main_frame.add(frame=HBox.new(true,10))
23:        frame.add(@find_btn = Button.new('Fi_nd'))
24:        frame.add(@one_btn = Button.new('Replace _one'))
25:        frame.add(@all_btn = Button.new('Replace a_ll'))
26:        frame.add(cancel_btn = Button.new('Cancel'))
27:
28:        @find_btn.add_accelerator('clicked', ag,
29:          @find_btn.child.parse_uline('Fi_nd'),
30:          Gdk::CONTROL_MASK, 0)
31:        @one_btn.add_accelerator('clicked', ag,
32:          @one_btn.child.parse_uline('Replace _one'),
33:          Gdk::CONTROL_MASK, 0)
34:        @all_btn.add_accelerator('clicked', ag,
35:          @all_btn.child.parse_uline('Replace a_ll'),
36:          Gdk::CONTROL_MASK, 0)
```

18

continues

LISTING 18.12　Continued

```
37:          cancel_btn.add_accelerator('clicked', ag,
38:            Gdk::GDK_Escape,
39:            0, 0)
40:
41:          cancel_btn.signal_connect('clicked') {destroy}
42:
43:          @find.grab_focus
44:          show_all
45:        end
46:
47:        # Make the widgets accessible to the caller, so
48:        # signals can be connected to them, and info
49:        # extracted from them.
50:        attr_reader :find_btn, :one_btn, :all_btn
51:        attr_reader :find, :replace
52:
53:      end
54:
55:      # test code
56:      if __FILE__ == $0
57:        f = FindBox.new("findme")
58:        f.find_btn.signal_connect('clicked') do
59:          puts f.find.get_text
60:          f.destroy; main_quit
61:        end
62:        f.one_btn.signal_connect('clicked') do
63:          puts f.find.get_text
64:          puts f.replace.get_text
65:          f.destroy; main_quit
66:        end
67:        f.all_btn.signal_connect('clicked') do
68:          puts 'replace all:'
69:          puts f.find.get_text
70:          puts f.replace.get_text
71:          f.destroy; main_quit
72:        end
73:        main
74:      end
```

As has been our custom, we append some test code (lines 55–74) so that we can debug the FindBox class by itself. Once satisfied that it behaves the way we want, we can delete those lines.

The keyboard accelerators for FindBox are created without recourse to an item factory. As with the drop-down menus, we give the user hints about the accelerator keys by underlining them in the button labels. In lines 29, 32, and 35, Gtk::Label#parse_uline takes care of the underlining and returns the correct keycodes for the accelerators so that we don't have to refer to the correponding Gdk constants. We have associated all three accelerators with the Control key (see lines 30, 33, and 36); for example, when the FindBox window is open, the user can Replace All by pressing Ctrl+L.

To test the editor, check that all three files (from Listings 18.7, 18.11, and 18.12) have been saved in the same directory, and then run the top-level editor.rb script. The results are shown in Figure 18.9.

FIGURE 18.9

Our text editor.

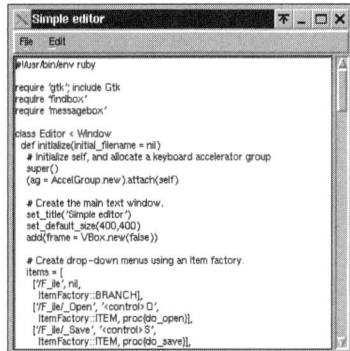

This editor, while quite versatile considering the small amount of code it is built from, is just a start; many improvements are possible, and some will be discussed in today's exercises. (To paraphrase Ecclesiastes 12:12, "Of making text editors there is no end.")

Summary

We've devoted two days to learning about two of the more popular GUI toolkits that can be used with Ruby. There are others that you may like as well or better, such as FXRuby, based on the cross-platform FOX toolkit family, and Ruby/Qt, based on the windowing system that underlines the popular KDE desktop environment for Unix. Both of these also have Windows versions, and Fox in particular seems to be gaining popularity quickly within the Ruby community.

Currently, no complete English language translation of the Ruby/Gtk documentation exists, but work on it is progressing, and information on Gtk itself is plentiful on the Web. Look at http://www.gtk.org for C-based documentation, or search the Web or Usenet for some of the many Perl/Gtk examples that exist there. Most Perl/Gtk code can be translated with some small effort to Ruby/Gtk.

One way or another, there is plenty to learn. Today's introduction hardly scratches the surface. It's possible to do all kinds of fun things with text styles and colors, define icon

18

images for buttons and other widgets by importing .xpm graphic files directly into your source code, and much more. The flagship application for Gtk is the GIMP, the free image manipulation application for which it was written in the first place; getting to know the GIMP will show you many of Gtk's most impressive capabilities, but since the GIMP is written in C, its source code may not be all that helpful to many readers of this book. Of greater interest are the enlightening example scripts that you will find packaged with Ruby/Gtk itself. They are written in a style somewhat different from the examples in this chapter, but you should still be able to gain a lot from them based on what you have learned today.

Tomorrow we delve into the design and creation of network services. Because it involves sockets and threads, both of which present some difficulties when working in a lower-level language like C, this used to be the private domain of computer science wizards; but you'll find that Ruby makes it a surprisingly approachable topic.

Exercises

1. Rewrite Listing 18.5 using HBoxes and VBoxes instead of tables.

2. If you saved the following code as tersegtk.rb, what would be the effect of inserting require 'tersegtk' at the top of a Ruby/Gtk script?

```ruby
module Gtk
  class Button
    def when_clicked(&action)
      signal_connect('clicked', &action)
    end
  end

  class Window
    def when_destroyed(&action)
      signal_connect('destroy', &action)
    end
  end
end
```

3. Why do we need parentheses in the super call of MessageBox#initialize (Listing 18.7, line 20)? Try removing them. Can you make sense of the error message?

4. Suppose your burger stand (see Listing 18.8) is stocked with leaf lettuce and iceberg lettuce. Customers who want lettuce on their burgers may choose either kind, but not both. How could you change the script to reflect this? There is more than one reasonable solution.

5. If the user supplies our text editor with several filenames on the command line, we really ought to open as many windows as necessary, loading one file into each. Change Listing 18.11 to support this feature.

6. In an attempt to demonstrate our awesome power of foresight, we've provided for two optional arguments to `FindBox#initialize`, although our editor doesn't yet take advantage of them. These make it possible for the caller to preload the text entry fields with default values. Add the appropriate logic to the editor so that strings are remembered from one search to the next.

Answers

1. Substitute something like this for lines 9–18 of Listing 18.5:

```
add(vb = VBox.new(true,5))
vb.add(h1 = HBox.new(false,5))
h1.add(Label.new('Enter a string: '))
h1.add(entry = Entry.new)

vb.add(h2 = HBox.new(false,5))
h2.add(b_quit = Button.new('Exit'))
h2.add(b_calc = Button.new('Analyze'))
h2.add(result = Label.new(''))
```

The window will not start out quite as wide as before. The user can manually resize the window, or you can name a default size via `Gtk::Window#set_default_size` as we did in Listing 18.4, line 17.

2. C/C++ veterans often miss the ability to define macros when they begin working in other languages. This is a frequent complaint from people just being introduced to Java, for instance. In Ruby, you can get something like macro functionality by extending existing classes. Here we've created a `tersegtk` module to reduce the repetitive work of coding actions for button clicks, particularly when there are many buttons to deal with. It extends `Gtk::Button` so that a programmer can say something like this:

```
b1.when_clicked {proc_b1}
b2.when_clicked {proc_b2}
b3.when_clicked {proc_b3}
b4.when_clicked {proc_b4}
```

instead of this:

```
b1.signal_connect('clicked') {proc_b1}
b2.signal_connect('clicked') {proc_b2}
b3.signal_connect('clicked') {proc_b3}
b4.signal_connect('clicked') {proc_b4}
```

A little less usefully, the module also extends `Gtk::Window` to allow this:

```
w.when_destroyed {main_quit}
```

18

instead of this:

```
w.signal_connect('destroy') {main_quit}
```

You might remember from Day 14 that the ampersand character (&) allows an itera-tor block to be passed as an ordinary method argument. Here we use it to transpar-ently invoke one iterator method from another.

Macro-style extensions such as tersegtk.rb are seldom employed in Ruby, how-ever. Even if they make your scripts more readable to you, the space savings that result tend to be small. A more important concern is that other Ruby programmers who are not familiar with your private extensions may not appreciate them when your code passes into their hands for maintenance.

3. Here is the error message:

```
messagebox.rb:20:in `initialize': wrong # of arguments(2 for 0)
(ArgumentError)
        from q3.rb:20:in `initialize'
        from q3.rb:39:in `new'
        from q3.rb:39
```

Invoking super with no argument list has the effect of relaying the caller's argu-ments verbatim to the superclass method, but the arguments that go to MessageBox#initialize mean nothing to Gtk::Dialog#initialize. Normally a Dialog is initialized with no arguments, and the parentheses in the super() call indicate that we really want to pass an empty argument list.

4. The preferred way to make the two kinds of lettuce mutually exclusive is to bind actions to the clicked message for their buttons so that each is able to deactivates the other. This makes them act almost like a little radio button group. Try replacing line 18 of Listing 18.8 with this:

```
extras.add(cb_ilet = CheckButton.new('Iceberg Lettuce'))
extras.add(cb_llet = CheckButton.new('Leaf Lettuce'))
cb_ilet.signal_connect('clicked') do
  cb_llet.active = false if cb_ilet.active?
end
cb_llet.signal_connect('clicked') do
  cb_ilet.active = false if cb_llet.active?
end
```

How is this different from the behavior of real radio buttons? The assumption behind radio buttons is that *exactly one* should be active at a time; once one button is active, there is no way to deactivate it directly without activating another. Our approach allows the user to click a lettuce type and then reconsider, deciding not to order any lettuce after all.

A second and less elegant solution is to allow the user to select both lettuce types temporarily, but cause that combination to disallow the order. Replace line 18 of the original script with this:

```
extras.add(cb_ilet = CheckButton.new('Iceberg Lettuce'))
extras.add(cb_llet = CheckButton.new('Leaf Lettuce'))
```

and insert this just before show_all, which originally was line 41 (the location is not crucial, but it must go somewhere after the point where b_order gets defined):

```
cb_ilet.signal_connect('clicked') do
  b_order.set_sensitive(
    !(cb_ilet.active? and cb_llet.active?))
end
cb_llet.signal_connect('clicked') do
  b_order.set_sensitive(
    !(cb_ilet.active? and cb_llet.active?))
end
```

This ensures that no burger can be ordered with both kinds of lettuce, but it can be confusing and inconsiderate to the user. Not everybody will immediately see the connection between the two lettuce buttons being selected and the Order button becoming disabled. Extra feedback, perhaps in the form of a label to display messages like "Sorry, you can't have both kinds of lettuce" at the appropriate times, would help.

A third solution keeps a single lettuce button in the extra ingredients list, as in the original script, and adds a pair of radio buttons off to the side so that if the main lettuce button is active when the Order button is pressed, the state of the radio buttons indicates which type of lettuce should go on the burger. The extra radio buttons result in a more cluttered dialog, but they also make your lettuce policy clearer to the user. I leave the coding of this last solution up to you.

5. Replace lines 145–151 of Listing 18.11 with the following:

```
if __FILE__ == $0
  def start_editor(filename)
    w = Editor.new(filename)
    w.signal_connect('destroy') {w.do_exit}
  end

  if ARGV.length > 0
    ARGV.each {|f| start_editor(f)}
  else
    start_editor(nil)
  end
  main
end
```

18

This will open windows for all filenames given on the command line, but there is some extra work to do if we really want a well-behaved editor supporting multiple windows. Notice that when the user closes one window, they all go away. This is because we bound the "destroy" message of each window to main_quit in line 54. Omitting that binding lets one window close without disturbing the others, but then we seem to lose the ability to exit the program; the main loop keeps running even after all the windows have gone. So the next step might be to keep track of the open windows, say, in a hash; the destruction of a window would be bound to a procedure that deletes its entry in the hash and invokes main_quit when the hash becomes empty.

Come to think of it, we would also probably end up wanting to add "New" and "Close" command to the drop-down menus. The fun just goes on and on, doesn't it?

6. The changes can be confined to the Editor#do_search method:

```
def do_search
  @search ||= ''
  @replace ||= ''
  fb = FindBox.new(@search,@replace)
  fb.find_btn.signal_connect('clicked') do
    @search = fb.find.get_text
    @replace = fb.replace.get_text
    newpos = find_next(@search)
    @textbox.set_position newpos if newpos
    fb.destroy
  end
  fb.one_btn.signal_connect('clicked') do
    @search = fb.find.get_text
    @replace = fb.replace.get_text
    replace_one(@search, @replace)
    fb.destroy
  end
  fb.all_btn.signal_connect('clicked') do
    @search = fb.find.get_text
    @replace = fb.replace.get_text
    replace_all(@search, @replace)
    fb.destroy
  end
end
```

A variable assignment using ||=, as we have seen before, has an effect only when the variable starts out as nil. In this case, @search and @replace are assigned empty strings the first time do_search is called, but retain their old values for all subsequent calls. Alternatively, these lines could be changed to ordinary assignments and moved to the beginning of the initialize method. If we did this, the instance variables would always be valid, and we might find it easier to write a "repeat last search" function sometime.

We end this day with some words of caution. Observe that our last solution contains some identical assignments to the new @search and @replace instance variables. Refactoring might make the script a little more maintainable, but there is no grievous harm in this redundancy, and any refactoring in a GUI script has to be done carefully while you're getting the hang of it. A first attempt might involve moving the assignments to the bottom of do_search, something like this:

```ruby
def do_search
  @search ||= ''
  @replace ||= ''
  fb = FindBox.new(@search,@replace)
  fb.find_btn.signal_connect('clicked') do
    newpos = find_next(fb.find.get_text)
    @textbox.set_position newpos if newpos
    fb.destroy
  end
  fb.one_btn.signal_connect('clicked') do
    replace_one(fb.find.get_text, fb.replace.get_text)
    fb.destroy
  end
  fb.all_btn.signal_connect('clicked') do
    replace_many(fb.find.get_text, fb.replace.get_text)
    fb.destroy
  end
  @search = fb.find.get_text          # ????
  @replace = fb.replace.get_text
end
```

Intuitively, this looks about right, but it fails because program flow disrespects our intuition. We've spent most of our time writing scripts that do what we want in a sequence that we control, but GUI code is event-driven, so we need new intuitions.

The three do...end blocks handle three alternative events, inviting the unwary to treat them like an if...elsif...elsif...end construction, as we did just now. They are not, however, mutually exclusive in the immediate sense: When the do_search method is invoked, *all* of the signal_connect calls run, in order, setting up callbacks that will be used in the future if at all. In fact, do_search is finished executing before the user even begins interacting with the FindBox window, so the instance variables get their new assignments prematurely; we didn't want those assignments to happen until after the user clicked a button.

So is it impossible to refactor this? No, the redundant lines could be moved to a function that is then called by the callbacks, but it might be more trouble than it's worth in this particular case.

18

DAY 19

Some Advanced Topics (That Aren't So Hard)

I'd discovered, after a lot of extreme apprehension about what spoons to use, that if you do something incorrect at table with a certain arrogance, as if you knew perfectly well you were doing it properly, you can get away with it. . .

—Sylvia Plath, *The Bell Jar*

Today we rush into the realm of network services, where angels fear to tread.

You've already seen objects of the `IO` class and its descendants; they're just all those things that can be read from and written to. Once we have opened an IO object, whatever it is, communication works through a consistent and familiar interface: `read/write`, `gets/puts/print`, `each/each_line`, and so on.

Until now all the IO objects we've encountered have been local: a keyboard, a screen, a file, a pipe, or a process running on the same machine. As we are about to see, *sockets* make it possible to communicate with IO objects anywhere in the world without breaking a sweat.

We'll also learn about *threading,* a slick way to split your personality and carry on a lot of conversations at the same time (without having to fork off new processes as we did on Day 13).

Sockets

Almost every desktop computer in existence now implements a protocol whereby numbered *ports* can be opened to the outside world. Most of the low-numbered ports have consistent assignments. For instance, port 80 is generally used to accept Web browser connections, and 25 and 110 are used for e-mail delivery and retrieval, respectively. Microsoft Windows does the bulk of its networking on ports 137, 138, and 139.

Note On Unix, look at the /etc/services file for an extensive list of network services and the port numbers associated with them.

A port is useless until it is associated with a *socket*, since a port is hardly anything more than a number, and a socket is a real IO object. Sockets are the means by which your Ruby scripts talk to the world.

There are two kinds of sockets: one working on the *post office* principle and the other working on the *phone company* principle. Sending information through a UDP socket is like dropping postcards into a mailbox; the postal service is generally reliable, but it's possible for items to be lost in the mail or to arrive in a different order than sent, without the sender knowing about it. Using a TCP socket is more like talking on a telephone. Just as you dial a phone to create a connection, converse for a while with the party at the other end, and then hang up, a TCP connection is established for the duration of a data exchange and then closed.

Of the two socket types, we are more interested in TCP.

Note Like the great majority of TLAs (three-letter acronyms), what UDP and TCP stand for is largely forgotten and is not very important anyway. In case you just have to know, they are the User Datagram Protocol and the Transmission Control Protocol.

"Hello, World" Using TCP

To test this pair of scripts, open two terminal windows. Start get_via_TCP.rb (Listing 19.2) in one window before starting send_via_tcp.rb (Listing 19.1) in the other. They will exit together.

LISTING 19.1 send_via_TCP.rb

```
01:    #!/usr/bin/env ruby
02:
03:    # send_via_TCP.rb:
04:
05:    # Sends a line of text, to be received by
06:    # the get_via_TCP.rb script
07:
08:    require 'socket'
09:
10:    port = 10000
11:
12:    sock = TCPSocket.new("localhost", port)
13:    sock.puts "Hello, world."
14:    sock.close
```

LISTING 19.2 get_via_TCP.rb

```
01:    #!/usr/bin/env ruby
02:
03:    # get_via_TCP.rb:
04:
05:    # Receives a line of text through
06:    # a TCP socket, and prints it
07:
08:    require 'socket'
09:
10:    port = 10000
11:
12:    listener = TCPServer.new(port)
13:
14:    sock = listener.accept
15:    input = sock.gets
16:    sock.close
17:
18:    print "Message received: #{input}\n"

       # output of get_via_TCP.rb:
       Message received: Hello, world.
```

19

We chose port 10000 arbitrarily, but another could have been used so long as the scripts agreed about it. Generally speaking, the lowest 1024 ports should not be tampered with, but that's not much of a problem, because they are numbered all the way up to 65535.

send_via_TCP.rb is fairly simple and familiar. We could have substituted File.new("textfile","w") for TCPSocket.new("localhost", port) in line 12 of Listing 19.1 and written a file to disk instead of sending a message to the other window.

get_via_TCP.rb is more interesting. The receiving socket is not opened directly, because get_via_TCP.rb does not know in advance when or from where the incoming connection will be made. Its first duty is to sit next to the phone, as it were, and wait. The TCPServer object makes a port available to the outside world, then patiently listens, via the accept method, for an incoming connection (phone call). When accept returns, somebody has requested a connection (dialed our number), so there is finally a socket to read and write to (we've picked up the phone).

It is important that get_via_TCP.rb should be the first to start running. Somebody has to be listening for the phone to ring, because the caller expects it to be picked up right away. If send_via_TCP.rb tries to connect to a port where nobody is listening, then TCPSocket.new in line 12 of Listing 19.1 will raise an exception. This is a fundamental difference between TCP and UDP, which would instead fail silently.

send_via_TCP.rb refers to *localhost*. That's because our test doesn't yet extend to the outside world. But it's not hard to run the example on two separate machines. Just edit send_via_TCP.rb so that it contains the location of the receiving machine, which can be either a numeric address like "10.0.1.4" or a symbolic name like "wookie.yale.edu".

get_via_TCP.rb indicates which port it will be listening on in line 12 of Listing 19.2. It does not specify the address of the other party, for the simple reason that it cannot know ahead of time who will be calling. Once the connection is made, the receiver can invoke the peeraddr method on sock; it's like a Caller ID service for sockets.

```
14   sock = listener.accept; p sock.peeraddr
   # typical output:
   ["AF_INET", 3900, "somewhere.foo.org", "192.168.1.6"]
```

"Hello, World" Using UDP

Here we demonstrate the passing of information using the "post office" model, using UDP. Start get_via_UDP.rb (Listing 19.4) in one window before starting send_via_TCP.rb (Listing 19.3) in another.

LISTING 19.3   `send_via_UDP.rb`

```
01    #!/usr/bin/env ruby
02:
03:   # send_via_UDP.rb:
04:   # Sends a line of text, which we hope will
05:   # be received by the get_via_UDP.rb script
06:
07:   require 'socket'
08:
09:   port = 10001
10:
11:   UDPSocket.new.send("Hello, world.",0,'localhost',port)
```

LISTING 19.4   `get_via_UDP.rb`

```
01    #!/usr/bin/env ruby
02:
03:   # get_via_UDP.rb:
04:   # Receives a line of text through
05:   # a UDP socket and prints it
06:
07:   require 'socket'
08:
09:   port = 10001
10:
11:   sock = UDPSocket.new
12:   sock.bind("localhost",port)
13:
14:   msg = sock.recvfrom(80)  # 80 is maximum message length
15:   puts "message from #{msg[1][2]} on port #{msg[1][1]}: '#{msg[0]}'"
    # output of get_via_UDP.rb:
    message from localhost on port 1035: Hello, world.
```

19

UDP makes things simple for the sender of a message, because no connection has to be established. It's like tying a message and destination address to a pigeon's leg, watching it fly away, and then forgetting about it. If delivery is unsuccessful, there is no error (try running send_via_UDP by itself to verify this); in fact, there is never any kind of feedback to the sender, unless the other party happens to send an explicit return message.

Things look a little strange on the receiving end. The return value of the recvfrom method is a two-element array, which we tear apart clumsily in line 15 of Listing 19.4. The first element is the message received, and the second is another array with information about the sender: protocol family, remote port number, name of host, and IP address of host. This is awkward, and the fact that no standard Datagram class exists reflects how infrequently UDP is really used. (Today's Exercise 1 gives you a chance to remedy that situation.)

UDP is less reliable than TCP, but it also requires little overhead processing. In some situations where 100% correct reception of the information is not crucial, such as voice or video communication, it can be the better choice.

A TCP Chat Session

An extended conversation can be conducted once sockets are open at each end. Here's a simple way to implement an online chat session between two individuals anywhere in the world. As before, there are two scripts. chat_listen.rb (Listing 19.6) must be run first so it can listen for the incoming connection from chat_initiate.rb (Listing 19.5).

LISTING 19.5 chat_initiate.rb

```
01    #!/usr/bin/env ruby
02:
03:   # chat_initiate.rb:
04:   # "Dial the phone", and carry on a conversation
05:   # with the chat_listen script.
06:
07:   require 'socket'
08:
09:   port = 10002
10:
11:   session = TCPSocket.new("localhost", port)
12:
13:   begin
14:     loop do
15:       inmsg = session.gets
16:       print ">> ",inmsg
17:
18:       outmsg = STDIN.gets;   break if outmsg.nil?
19:       session.puts outmsg
20:     end
21:   ensure
22:     session.close
23:   end
```

LISTING 19.6 chat_listen.rb

```
01    #!/usr/bin/env ruby
02:
03:   # chat_listen.rb:
04:   # "Answer the phone", and carry on a conversation with
05:   # the caller (who is, presumably, chat_initiate.rb)
06:
07:   require 'socket'
08:
09:   port = 10002
10:
```

LISTING 19.6　Continued

```
11:    listener = TCPServer.new(port)
12:    session = listener.accept
13:    listener.close
14:
15:    session.puts "Start talking.  It's your nickel."
16:
17:    begin
18:      loop do
19:        inmsg = session.gets
20:        print ">> ",inmsg
21:
22:        outmsg = STDIN.gets;  break if outmsg.nil?
23:        session.print outmsg
24:      end
25:    ensure
26:      session.close
27:    end
```

Quitting is a slight problem. Somebody has to break out of the program by pressing an end-of-file key (usually Ctrl + D or F6). If one user exits and the other tries to send a message, a "broken pipe" exception gets raised, but no harm is done. We've ensured that the sockets will get closed properly in any case.

The more serious limitation is that conversation has to follow a strict order, with participants alternating messages. It will take some thought before we can support a natural conversation, where either party is allowed to speak at any time.

Notice that we close the `listener` object as soon as it gives us a socket. This is necessary because we intend to accommodate only one conversation, whereas a `TCPServer` is happy to keep opening new sockets when it hears more users trying to connect to the same port. That's nice if what you are writing is a server that will be in heavy use. Suppose you are providing something like an FTP service, from which the general public can download files. If one user is retrieving a long file, you don't want everybody else to get connection errors. Rather, you should accept those connections and get on with business, taking care of the requests as soon as possible.

A Simple Web Server

Web servers are, at heart, glorified file servers. They listen for TCP connections, take requests for files, and reply by sending the appropriate file contents. There's more to it than that, but not much more; rendering of HTML code into attractive pages is a job not for the server but for the browser at the user's end. Writing a browser would be a big job, but we can throw together a functional Web server in a few dozen lines of code.

Our server won't implement the entire HTTP (Hypertext Transfer Protocol). It will be just smart enough to serve conventional Web pages and take care of one important security precaution. A client who makes a connection will be expected to request a document by transmitting a line in this form:

```
GET filename HTTP version
```

where the *filename* is absolute (starting with a forward slash) and the protocol version, usually 1.0 or 1.1, is ignored. We'll reply with this, which any browser should understand:

```
HTTP/1.1 200/OK
Content-type: text/html

... contents of file ...
```

Before processing any request, our server will prepend a dot to the filename, ensuring that the current working directory is used. For example, if the web server script is running in /home/www, and a request is made for /index.html, then the server will try to send back the contents of ./index.html, which is really /home/www/index.html.

The one security precaution we take is this: Any file request containing two dots together (..) is rejected. Otherwise the normal course of action is to move upward in the directory tree, which is dangerous because it allows anybody in the world to look at private information. For instance, GET /../../../etc/passwd might divulge a list of user accounts on the host machine. Only files in the working directory of the server script and its subdirectories should be accessible to outsiders.

Just as we did yesterday, let's build from the top down, starting with a main function:

```
def main
  listener = TCPServer.new("localhost", (ARGV[0] || 80).to_i)
  loop do
    sock = listener.accept
    get the user reqeust
    process the user request
    sock.close
  end
end
```

This expresses the basic logic of the server. A port number is taken from the command line, defaulting to 80 (the standard web port) if the user didn't specify one. If you find that the server fails to work on port 80, it is probably either because you already have a Web server running there or because you are logged in as a nonprivileged user; services that use low-numbered ports need special permission to do so. Rather than logging on as root and trying again, be safe and specify a different port.

The listener will provide a new socket each time somebody asks for a file, and the socket will be where we find that request. After processing the request, we close the socket and go back to wait for the listener to give us another one. That sounds like a reasonable plan; next we must decide how to "get the user request" and "process the user request."

The client's browser is likely to send several lines to us. The GET line, which conventionally comes first, is the only one we care about. But we shouldn't just read one line and stop; some browsers don't mind that, but others will hang if we fail to read the entire request. So maybe we should iterate over all input lines in such a way that at the end, a variable req will refer to the requested filename (or nil if no GET line was encountered):

```
req = nil
session.each do |line|
  if line =~ /^GET (.+) HTTP/
    req = $1
  end
end
```

Watch it—there's a mistake here. HTTP specifies that the request must end with a blank line, but we are trying to read to the end of available input. The only way to be sure there is no more input is by the socket getting closed from the other end, and the client won't do that before getting its precious Web page from us. So client and server fall into a deadlock situation, with each waiting for the other to do something. One cure for this is to read input in a while or until loop that looks for the right exit condition:

```
req = nil
until (line=session.gets).strip.empty?
  if line =~ /^GET (.+) HTTP/
    req = $1
  end
end
```

Or you might prefer to apply a minor fix, just a little "duct tape," to what we had:

```
req = nil
session.each do |line|
  if line =~ /^GET (.+) HTTP/
    req = $1
  end
  break if line.strip.empty?
end
```

If there was no GET line, then the request was bad and we ought to return an error page. Otherwise we will try to honor the request. In either case, our reply is printed to the socket.

```
if req
  session.puts error_page("eh?", "I didn't understand that.")
else
  session.puts http_file("." + $1)
end
```

19

We need two functions to make the server complete, but before writing them, let's settle on a simplifying design choice: Every page served, regardless of whether it came from a file or from an error message, will have the same header information. We can make that a constant string.

```
Header = "HTTP/1.1 200/OK\nContent-type: text/html\r\n\r\n"
```

The error_page function will wrap information about some error in some HTML code to make it a proper page. This is not quite ideal behavior, but it's enough to provide feedback to whoever is out there browsing.

```
def error_page(title,message)
  Header +  "<html><head><title>#{title}</title></head>\n" +
            "<body><b>Error:</b> #{message}</body></html>\n"
end
```

The http_file function will return file contents verbatim, as a string. We are assuming that the file contains an HTML Web page rather than plain text or something else, but a more sophisticated server would check the filename, or perhaps even its contents, to verify the fact. A first draft of the function might look like this:

```
def http_file(filename)
  f = File.open(filename,"r")
  contents = f.read
  f.close
  return (Header + contents)
end
```

Or like this:

```
def http_file(filename)
  File.open(filename,"r") {|f| contents = f.read}
  return (Header + contents)
end
```

In Ruby 1.7 or later, it can be reduced to this:

```
def http_file(filename)
  contents = File.read(filename)
  return (Header + contents)
end
```

What http_file still needs is robustness. Any number of things can go wrong. Suppose the request was for a nonexistent file, for a file that the server lacks permission to read, or for a directory. Rather than write tests for all possible problems, we can wrap most of the function in begin...rescue...end, and cleverly (or is it lazily?) exploit Ruby's own error information from the global variable $! to make any error page we eventually create more informative. Add a little pattern-matching code to disallow names containing "..", and we're done. Listing 19.7 is a working server:

LISTING 19.7   looping-webserver.rb

```ruby
01:  #!/usr/bin/env ruby
02:
03:  # looping-webserver.rb:
04:  # Serves no more than one client at a time.
05:
06:  require 'socket'
07:
08:  def main
09:    listener = TCPServer.new("localhost", (ARGV[0]||80).to_i)
10:    loop do
11:      session = listener.accept
12:
13:      # Get a request from the client
14:      req = nil
15:      session.each do |line|
16:        if line =~ /^GET (.+) HTTP/
17:          req = $1
18:        end
19:        break if line.strip.empty?
20:      end
21:
22:      # Honor the request if possible
23:      if req
24:        session.puts http_file("." + req)
25:      else
26:        session.puts error_page("eh?", "I didn't understand that.")
27:      end
28:
29:      session.close
30:    end
31:  end
32:
33:  Header = "HTTP/1.1 200/OK\nContent-type: text/html\r\n\r\n"
34:
35:  def error_page(title,message)
36:    Header +
37:      "<html><head><title>#{title}</title></head>\n" +
38:      "<body><b>Error:</b> #{message}</body></html>\n"
39:  end
40:
41:  def http_file(filename)
42:    if filename =~ /\.\./
43:      return error_page 'Bad Request', '".." in URL not allowed'
44:    else
45:      begin
46:        f = File.open(filename,"r")
47:        contents = f.read
48:        f.close
49:        Header + contents
```

continues

LISTING 19.7 Continued

```
50:        rescue
51:          error_page 'File Error', $!.to_s.gsub(/\n/, "<br>")
52:        end
53:    end
54:  end
55:
56:  main
```

Supporting Concurrent Sessions

Our looping Web server does its job correctly—as long as we don't ask it to do anything fancy—but it's still a poor performer. Clients experience unnecessary delays under some circumstances, such as when a page is being transmitted and runs into network congestion somewhere along the line; for instance, since TCP is being used, line 24 of Listing 19.7 cannot return until it knows whether it has succeeded. While a session is idly waiting to hear about distant events, another client is probably going to ask for a Web page. The new client really should be served right away, but it doesn't happen.

In the old days, the only way to deal with the problem would be to fork a new process whenever a new client connected, so that the listener could go on to accepting more connections without delay:

```
loop do
  sock = listener.accept
  fork do
    get the reqeust
    process the request
    sock.close
  end
  sock.close    # parent doesn't need this
end
```

Why does the socket seem to get closed twice? The reason is that there are two of them after the fork. The parent won't be using its copy of the socket, so it closes it right away and goes back to listening for more connections. The child keeps its copy open long enough to help a client, then closes it.

The accumulation of zombies complicates this solution, because the server gives birth to many children but never waits for any of them. As a result, the operating system has increasing trouble keeping track of processes, and eventually something has to break.

Fortunately, every time a child runs its course and exits, its parent receives a special signal labeled SIGCHLD. To keep the population from getting out of hand, we can trap that signal with a block that does a wait on a single process.

Unfortunately, wait waits for *all* child processes to stop. That would disable the listener object while requests were outstanding, defeating the purpose of supporting concurrent sessions in the first place. What's more, waitpid waits for one process, but we have to give it a process ID, and the SIGCHLD signal doesn't give us that information. There is another wait variant that we haven't seen yet, however. The rather unimaginatively named wait2 waits for and properly disposes of exactly one process at a time. We arrange things so that wait2 is invoked only in response to a SIGCHLD signal, and therefore it is guaranteed always to find one zombie out there ripe for the picking.

Listing 19.8 is an improved Web server that forks off a separate process for each client, allowing new requests to be honored even if old ones are stuck in traffic.

LISTING 19.8   forked-webserver.rb

```
01:   #!/usr/bin/env ruby
02:
03:   # forked-webserver.rb:
04:   # Serves multiple clients simultaneously.
05:
06:   require 'socket'
07:
08:   def main
09:     listener = TCPServer.new("localhost", (ARGV[0]||80).to_i)
10:
11:     trap 'SIGCHLD', 'Process.wait2'
12:
13:     loop do
14:       session = listener.accept
15:       fork do
16:
17:         # Get a request from the client
18:         req = nil
19:         session.each do |line|
20:           if line =~ /^GET (.+) HTTP/
21:             req = $1
22:           end
23:           break if line.strip.empty?
24:         end
25:
26:         # Honor the request if possible
27:         if req
28:           session.puts http_file("." + req)
29:         else
30:           session.puts error_page("eh?", "I didn't understand that.")
31:         end
32:
33:         session.close
34:       end
```

19

continues

LISTING 19.8 Continued

```
35:       session.close  # this is the parent's copy of the socket
36:     end
37:   end
38:   # Remainder of script is same as Listing 19.7, lines 33 onward.
```

Threads

Programming with concurrent processes is an old and well-understood practice, but it is rapidly falling out of favor, because a more efficient technique has been developed in recent years.

Remember that when a process undergoes a `fork`, it creates a copy of itself. Surely that's overkill, though. When you're reading a truly fascinating book and the telephone rings, you don't clone yourself so there can be one of you attending to the phone and the other attending to your reading. Instead you put your finger on the page so as not to lose your place, reach over with the other hand to grab the phone, and chatter politely (*mm hmm, mm hmm*), glancing back down at the book every chance you get. See how much reading you can still get done? And if your caller isn't listening too closely either, you might not get caught being rude.

The point is this: Whereas reproducing something into multiple copies will tend to eat up significant space (and time too, as it turns out), splitting just your attention isn't such a big deal. It just means that you add a new task to a list you keep in the back of your head, putting one task aside now and then to pick up another. The name for this technique is *threading*. Each task is a thread; think of the phone call as a new *thread of conversation,* if it helps you remember. Just as with forked processes, several threads can do their work overlapped in time—that is, apparently simultaneously.

 Note
> The space penalty for duplicating processes can be more pronounced in an interpreted language like Ruby, because as far as the operating system is concerned, the process is larger than just your script. The language interpreter's data ends up getting cloned, too.

At a quick glance, threaded code looks quite a bit like forked code. But having all the threads launched by a script remain part of the same process leads to some practical differences. For one thing, when any thread modifies a variable, the other threads are affected, as Listing 19.9 illustrates.

LISTING 19.9   A Comparison of Processes and Threads

```
01:   v = 100
02:   fork do
03:     puts "child process says v was #{v}"
04:     v += 1
05:     puts "child process has changed v to #{v}"
06:   end
07:
08:   Process.wait        # Let the child do its thing
09:   puts "parent process finds that v is #{v}"
10:   puts
11:
12:   v = 200
13:   child = Thread.new do
14:     puts "child thread says v was #{v}"
15:     v += 1
16:     puts "child thread has changed v to #{v}"
17:   end
18:
19:   child.join
20:   puts "parent thread finds that v is #{v}"
```

The output of Listing 19.9 looks like this.

```
child process says v was 100
child process has changed v to 101
parent process finds that v is 100

child thread says v was 200
child thread has changed v to 201
parent thread finds that v is 201
```

Variables defined locally in a thread block are an exception to the rule, because they belong to just one thread. That's good; threads have to be able to tell each other apart somehow. We're about to see an example of this.

A nice benefit of threading is the ease of housekeeping it implies. Since threads aren't processes, they don't turn into zombies. A threaded version of our simple Web server won't have to bother with catching SIGCHLD signals. Also, socket objects don't get duplicated, so they need to be closed only once, so to speak.

Listing 19.10 is a Web server that creates a separate thread to serve each new client.

LISTING 19.10   threaded-webserver.rb

```
01:   #!/usr/bin/env ruby
02:
03:   # threaded-webserver.rb:
```

continues

LISTING 19.10 Continued

```
04:    # Serves multiple clients simultaneously, with only one process.
05:
06:    require 'socket'
07:
08:    def main
09:      listener = TCPServer.new("localhost", (ARGV[0]||80).to_i)
10:
11:      loop do
12:        session = listener.accept
13:        Thread.new(session) do |s|
14:
15:          # Get a request from the client
16:          req = nil
17:          session.each do |line|
18:            if line =~ /^GET (.+) HTTP/
19:              req = $1
20:            end
21:            break if line.strip.empty?
22:          end
23:
24:          # Honor the request if possible
25:          if req
26:            session.puts http_file("." + req)
27:          else
28:            session.puts error_page("eh?", "I didn't understand that.")
29:          end
30:
31:          s.close
32:        end
33:      end
34:    end
35:    # Remainder of script is same as Listing 19.7, lines 33 onward.
```

The variable s introduced in line 13 refers to the new socket that was just created in the top-level thread. Since it is defined in the thread block (encompassing lines 13–32), each thread gets its own unique s. This is necessary because different threads will be talking with different clients, each through a unique socket, at the same time.

Passing Control Around

Threads are usually managed in such a way that the programmer doesn't have to put a lot of thought into it. One thread runs until Ruby's scheduler decides it is fair for another to have a turn. Occasionally a running thread will have to wait for something, perhaps a network event or a disk input/output event. In that case, control will generally be given to another thread right away to avoid wasting processor time. But tampering with this "natural order of things" is allowed, and the `Thread` class provides a number of class and instance methods that let you establish your own thread etiquette.

When one thread calls the `Thread.pass` method, it yields the rest of its turn to some other thread. The effect is temporary; another turn will come soon. In contrast, `Thread.stop` puts the currently running thread on indefinite hold. It will not proceed until some other thread invokes `Thread#run` or `Thread#wakeup` on it. The difference between the latter two methods is that `wakeup` merely makes the thread eligible to be scheduled (puts it back in line, so to speak), whereas `run` instructs the scheduler to start it running immediately.

`exit` may be called either as a class method or as an instance method. `Thread.exit` puts an end to the currently running thread (as opposed to just plain `exit`, that is, `Kernel.exit`, which applies to the entire program). `Thread#exit` is used by one thread when it wants to kill a *different* thread. `kill` is an alias for `exit`, allowing us to make a fairly natural-sounding distinction between the authoritarian `Thread#kill` and the polite, voluntary `Thread.exit`. These concepts are illustrated in Listing 19.11. It's a good idea to read this listing carefully, perhaps sketching out some predictions about its behavior, before you try to run it.

LISTING 19.11   An Example of Simple Thread Control

```
01:    thr = Thread.new do
02:      Thread.stop
03:      print "B1 "
04:      Thread.stop
05:      print "B2 "      # we never get here
06:    end
07:
08:    print "A1 "
09:    thr.run
10:    print "A2 "
11:    thr.kill
12:    print "A3\n"
    # Output: A1 B1 A2 A3
```

`Thread#alive?` returns *true* if a thread has not exited or been killed, and `Thread.list` returns an array of the threads that are alive. It's possible to iterate over that array and kill threads one by one, as Listing 19.12 shows.

LISTING 19.12   A Thread List Example

```
01:    # Start three threads.
02:
03:    ["Tom", "Dick", "Harry"].each  do |label|
04:      new_thread = Thread.new(label) do |me|
05:        counter = 1
```

continues

LISTING **19.12**   Continued

```
06:        loop do
07:          print "#{me}#{counter} "; STDOUT.flush
08:          counter += 1
09:          sleep .4
10:        end
11:      end
12:    end
13:
14:    # Let the other threads run for one second
15:    sleep 1
16:
17:    # ... then stop them.
18:    Thread.list.each do |t|
19:      t.kill
20:    end
21:
22:    print "\n AND I ONLY AM ESCAPED ALONE TO TELL THEE \n"

    # output:
      Tom1 Dick1 Harry1 Dick2 Tom2 Harry2 Dick3 Tom3 Harry3
```

The variable me is defined inside the thread block, so each thread has a separate copy of it; when the third thread assigns me to "Harry", the second thread's me still refers to "Dick". But did you notice what went wrong in the output? Contrary to appearances, there were not three threads in this example, but four; a top-level thread was responsible for creating the other three. When all the threads were killed, none were left to print the concluding message in line 22.

Thread.main tells us which is the top-level thread. To repair Listing 19.12, make line 19 conditional:

```
t.kill  unless t==Thread.main
```

Establishing a Pecking Order

When some threads require preferential scheduling, we give them a higher *priority*. Each thread starts with priority zero, but a different priority can be set with Thread#priority= and queried with Thread#priority. Higher values mean higher priority, which is backwards from the "niceness" convention in Unix. Priorities may be positive or negative; if maint is a thread designed to do some kind of low-urgency background maintenance work, then setting maint.priority=-10 (and leaving the rest at zero) will ensure that it will be allocated significant processor time only when the other threads have nothing in particular to do.

The Bathroom Pass

Remember what a grade school classroom is like? The classroom is full of desks and various educational accoutrements; students work together in a single body, in groups, or individually on different tasks; but there is only one bathroom down the hall, and only one student can use it at a time. Rather than letting fights develop around the bathroom door, the teacher keeps a hunk of wood hanging next to the chalkboard and maintains a simple rule: Nobody is allowed to leave for the bathroom unless in possession of that item.

A similar situation arises often in threaded scripts. There is some task that every thread may need to do now and then, but no two should be allowed to do that task at the same time. Perhaps a disk file exists that many threads use; it's fine if several threads read from the file at the same time, but problems arise when writes are attempted at the same time as reads or other writes. So writing to that file is a lot like occupying the bathroom, and what we need to preserve order is something analogous to the bathroom pass.

In threading jargon, the counterpart to the bathroom pass is called a *mutex* (short for *mutual exclusion*). When you create a Mutex object in Ruby, threads can attach blocks to it and be prevented from colliding with each other during the execution of those blocks. The method that accepts a block is Mutex#synchronize.

Listing 19.13 is a quick mutex example showing pairs of threads trying to do slow-motion screen output at the same time. Output is legible only when the mutex is used.

LISTING 19.13   An Example of Mutual Exclusion

```
01:    #!/usr/bin/env ruby
02:
03:    require 'thread'
04:
05:    def slow_output(msg)
06:      msg.each_byte do |b|
07:        print b.chr
08:        sleep .2
09:        STDOUT.flush
10:      end
11:    end
12:
13:    m = Mutex.new  # This is the bathroom pass!
14:
15:    print "\nWithout synchronization:\n"
16:    thr1 = Thread.new { slow_output "First " }
17:    thr2 = Thread.new { slow_output "Second " }
18:    thr1.join; thr2.join
19:
20:    print "\nWith synchronization:\n"
```

19

continues

LISTING 19.13 Continued

```
21:    thr3 = Thread.new { m.synchronize { slow_output "Third " } }
22:    thr4 = Thread.new { m.synchronize { slow_output "Fourth " } }
23:    thr3.join; thr4.join
24:
25:    print "\nAll done.\n"

       # output:
       Without synchronization:
       FSeicrosntd
       With synchronization:
       Third Fourth
       All done.
```

When to Thread and When to Fork

Are threads strictly necessary? Or, to shift the burden, if threading is so much easier and more efficient than process duplication, why bother learning to `fork`? There are two reasons: Process control is a more proven technology, and Ruby is still a young language.

There are essentially two ways for a language to implement threads. Ruby currently does it internally (employing *user-level* threads) so that the underlying operating system is not aware of anything fancy going on, but some systems allow for an intermediate threading model that works outside the interpreter (with *kernel-level* threads, or "lightweight processes," partially managed by the operating system). User-level threads are more portable across platforms, at least in theory, but they don't always switch among themselves quite as reliably, so they are occasionally susceptible to unnecessary delays. Ruby's threading implementation has been undergoing refinement, and it may also support the kernel-level model in the near future, but, even though threading works pretty well right now, some tasks still might be more effectively approached with old-fashioned process control.

Summary

Once you have mastered sockets and threads, you are in a position to be an original presence on the Internet. Yesterday you could act only as a user of others' services, but after today you are ready to invent and provide your own.

We aren't about to drop the topic of network services just yet. Tomorrow is devoted to the use of Ruby on the Web, but at a higher level; the emphasis will be not on the mechanics of the Web server itself (since we'll be using the free Apache server software rather than writing our own) but on the various ways that dynamic Web content can be provided to a server. That means learning what CGI and SHTML are and how to use them, along with some other less-known techniques.

Exercises

1. Write a `Datagram` class that would allow `get_via_UDP.rb` (Listing 19.4) to be written like this:

```
require 'socket'
require 'datagram'

sock = UDPSocket.new
sock.bind("localhost",inport)
dg = Datagram.new(sock.recvfrom(80))
print "contents: #{dg.contents}\n"
print "sender: #{dg.name} (#{dg.address}) on port #{dg.port}\n"

# Output:
  contents: Hello world
  sender: localhost (127.0.0.1) on port 1035
```

Hint: An `initialize` method and some attribute readers are enough to do the job.

2. Rewrite the `Spinner` class (Day 13, Listing 13.4), but using threads.

3. Sketch a strategy for a pair of chat scripts that would allow either participant to speak at any time.

Answers

1. As hinted, there isn't much required here.

```
class Datagram
  def initialize(info)
    @contents = info[0]
    @protocol, @port, @name, @address = info[1]
  end
  attr_reader :contents, :protocol, :port, :name, :address
end
```

More could be done, such as, perhaps, a nice `to_s` method and a `reply` method that accepts a string as a parameter and relays it to the sender of this datagram. But it's often a waste of time to write methods you don't need yet. They can be added as easily later.

2. One solution is given in Listing 19.14. Instance variables are automatically shared between the main thread and the spinner thread, making communication easy: setting `@running=false` tells the spinner to stop.

LISTING 19.14   A Threaded Spinner Class

```
01:    class Spinner
02:      Baton = '\|/-'
03:      def initialize
```

continues

LISTING **19.14**   Continued

```
04:        STDOUT.flush
05:        @running = true
06:        @spinthread = Thread.new do
07:          rotation = 0
08:          while @running
09:            STDERR.printf "%c\b", Baton[(rotation+=1) & 3]
10:            sleep .2
11:          end
12:          STDERR.printf " \b"  # erase the last baton character
13:        end
14:      end
15:
16:      def stop
17:        @running = false
18:        @spinthread.run     # prompt spinner to clean up
19:        @spinthread.join    # and wait for it to do so
20:      end
21:    end
```

Line 18 isn't strictly necessary, but it speeds things up a little; when quitting time comes, the spinner is likely to be taking a 0.2-second nap, so we wake it up to make it notice the change in @running right away.

But line 19 should not be neglected. Once the spinner thread wakes back up, there's no guarantee that it will finish its cleanup before the main program exits. Whenever that happens, all threads are forced to terminate whether they have finished their work or not.

3. The difficulty with letting either party talk at any time is that it's possible for one to interrupt the other while typing at the keyboard. Where should the incoming text be displayed? The cursor position is important to the typist. One solution is for each party to have a pair of windows, each running its own script: one for text entry and the other for displaying the entire conversation. This is easier than it sounds; the second script would listen on two sockets (or perhaps only one) and accept messages from both parties, and the first would blindly send messages.

A more sophisticated idea is to use two threads—one for text entry and the other for conversation display—and segregate the text output in some way. Our ANSI module from Day 12, with some enhancement, could maintain a text-entry area and a conversation-display area in the same window; Ruby's "curses" capability (which we have not discussed in this book) is easily powerful enough to do the job too. Even better, a window could be created using Ruby/Tk or another GUI library and divided into two areas. We'll come back to this idea on Day 21.

DAY 20

Working with the Web

For the Snark's a peculiar creature, that won't
Be caught in a commonplace way.
Do all that you know, and try all that you don't;
Not a chance must be wasted to-day!

—Lewis Carroll, *The Hunting of the Snark*

Today we take some introductory steps toward using Ruby to provide dynamic Web content. There are lots of ways to do it, and we'll experiment with several.

Since all of this depends on having access to a Web server, we'll also discuss relevant setup issues on Apache, the most popular Web server available free across most computer platforms.

We won't be going through the fundamentals of the Hypertext Markup Language (HTML) today. That is well covered in numerous books and in at least as many tutorials on the Web itself. We assume that you either already know something about HTML or are willing to pick up those fundamentals elsewhere.

Static Content Versus Dynamic Content

The World Wide Web (WWW) would function quite well as a large interconnected library, a collection of relatively static text pages embedded with links from one to another. In the early days of the Web, not much more than that was envisioned. Even graphics were considered inessential and dismissively filed under "bells and whistles." When information was to be added to the Web, it simply meant revising the text of an existing page, or adding a new one.

The idea of dynamic content came along a while later. When somebody accesses a Web page, why should the same thing happen every time? It is useful (or at least entertaining) to keep pages updated with current information and to provide various kinds of intelligent feedback to the browsing public.

Server-Side Versus Client-Side

A simple exercise in dynamic Web content is to make a page display the current time. But before tackling it, though, we must answer the question: Whose clock is authoritative? There is a *client* machine, from which somebody out there is surfing the Web, and a *server* machine, where the Web pages live. Each has its own clock, and the two are probably not in perfect agreement.

To display a Web page with the current time according to the client's clock, the usual procedure is to use JavaScript, the *de facto* native language of Web browsers. Here is complete HTML source code for such a page:

```
<html><body>
The time is: <b><script language="javascript">
  var the_time=new Date();
  document.write (the_time);
</script></b>
</body></html>
```

There are some pretty good reasons why this should be of little interest to us, though.

1. People surfing the Web probably already know what their own computers think the time is; if not, it's easy for them to find out. We don't provide much of a service by

giving the public what it already has. Any information that is interesting to a client is likely to exist at the server side, or someplace that the server can get to and the client can't. Otherwise, why does anyone visit our site in the first place?

2. Not all browsers support JavaScript, and among those that do, not all support it with the same functionality. Although there has been considerable work at standardization, there has unfortunately also been some work at intentional *non*standardization, depending on where you look and whom you ask.

3. Some surfers prefer to keep JavaScript locally disabled because of concerns about security ("Why should I let strangers run programs on my machine?"). If JavaScript is missing or turned off, our sample page will display "The time is:" and nothing else.

4. JavaScript is not Ruby!

So we'll stick with server-side dynamic content, mostly. It helps us to be more considerate to people out there who will browse our Web sites. We can make sure they get the right information no matter what browser they use or what settings they've chosen; in some cases it shouldn't even matter if they're using a text-only browser such as the venerable lynx.

Privileges at the Server

Oh yes—I neglected to mention the main attraction of JavaScript. It doesn't require special access to the Web server. JavaScript is just like any other text as far as the server is concerned; the browser does all the interpreting. If what you have is an account with an Internet service provider that allows you only to store pages, the client side is the only side you can use dynamically. But whenever somebody's Web browser neglects to provide the facilities and permission for your JavaScript code to run, you (or they, depending on your point of view) are just out of luck.

So it's necessary that we assume one more thing for the rest of today's lesson: You run your own Web server, or you have sufficient privilege on somebody else's to provide dynamic content. This means that either CGI or SHTML should be enabled, although the ability to create "cron jobs," which we'll briefly discuss later, can sometimes serve as a very limited substitute.

Since you were about to ask, CGI stands for "Common Gateway Interface" and is a way for entire Web pages to be generated on-the-fly. The abbreviation SHTML stands for "server-parsed HTML" and is a way to wedge chunks of dynamic content into otherwise static pages.

20

Configuring Apache: `httpd.conf`

As of this writing, the majority of active Web servers in the world are running Apache software. It's extensively documented, actively maintained, highly versatile, quite secure (depending on how it is configured, of course), and free. The actual program name of the server is `httpd`, for "HTTP daemon".

If you use Linux or any of the free BSD variants, it's almost certain that you already have a copy of Apache and don't need to download it from anywhere, although you may still want to go check out the current version if yours is very old. If you run Windows or practically anything else, there's an Apache for you, too; download it from `http://www.apache.org`. Discussion of Apache setup here is geared toward a Unix installation, but similar issues exist on other platforms.

Apache configuration settings are all specified in a single configuration file, `httpd.conf`. (In some earlier versions of Apache there were several files, but now they are combined.) It can usually be found in the `/usr/local/apache/conf` directory, although its location sometimes varies (invoke the command `locate httpd.conf` if you have trouble finding it). Log in as the privileged (root) user if necessary, load `httpd.conf` into a text editor, and read on. Don't worry; most of the file can be left alone. We'll change just a few things.

Choose a Root Directory for Web Documents

First, decide where you want Web documents to be kept. I like to maintain a special user account named `www` for this, with a `docs` subdirectory in its home directory. This makes it unnecessary to log in as the all-powerful and dangerous root user just to work on the Web site, and it keeps me from accidentally erasing Web files when I'm working as "myself."

Whichever directory you decide to use, Apache must be told the path to that directory. `DocumentRoot` is the entry for this purpose in `httpd.conf`. You may prefer to leave `DocumentRoot` at its default location or to put it in your own home directory.

To move `DocumentRoot`, search `httpd.conf` for text that looks like the following, and edit the `DocumentRoot` and `Directory` lines to reflect your choice.

```
#
# DocumentRoot: The directory out of which you will serve your
# documents. By default, all requests are taken from this directory, but
# symbolic links and aliases may be used to point to other locations.
#
DocumentRoot "/home/www/docs"
....


#
# This should be changed to whatever you set DocumentRoot to.
#
<Directory "/home/www/docs">
```

Enable SHTML

To make SHTML work, uncomment the appropriate `AddType` and `AddHandler` lines,

```
#
# To use server-parsed HTML files
#
AddType text/html .shtml
AddHandler server-parsed .shtml
```

and specify the `Includes` option for your main document directory:

```
# This should be changed to whatever you set DocumentRoot to.
#
<Directory "/home/www/docs">
...
    Options Indexes FollowSymLinks MultiViews Includes
```

The server also should be told to load `index.shtml` (if it's available) in preference to `index.html` when no filename is specified.

```
# DirectoryIndex: Name of the file or files to use as a pre-written HTML
# directory index.  Separate multiple entries with spaces.
#
<IfModule mod_dir.c>
    DirectoryIndex index.shtml index.html
</IfModule>
...
```

Enable CGI

To make CGI work, uncomment the CGI `AddHandler` line and add to it the standard file extensions for the languages you want to use (the important thing is that `.rb` should be there):

```
# To use CGI scripts:
#
AddHandler cgi-script .cgi .pl .rb
```

You need to keep CGI scripts in their own directory, which can be anywhere on the system. The Apache Web server does not allow CGI scripts to run if they are not in this directory. Modify the following lines after you've decided on a location; this example has it at `/home/www/cgi-bin`.

20

 **Caution**   Be careful with the trailing slash character. It should be in the `ScriptAlias` line but absent from the `Directory` line.

```
#
ScriptAlias /cgi-bin/ "/home/www/cgi-bin/"

# "/var/www/cgi-bin" should be changed to wherever your ScriptAliased
# CGI directory exists, if you have that configured.
#
<Directory "/home/www/cgi-bin">
    AllowOverride None
    Options None
    Order allow,deny
    Allow from all
</Directory>
```

Set a User ID

Give Apache access to the correct home directory by making it run as whatever user owns it.

```
# User/Group: The name (or #number) of the user/group to run httpd as.
# ...
User www
```

Activate the New Configuration

The Web server has to be started with the new configuration, or restarted if it's already running. Wait, don't reboot! First try Apache's supplied control script (again, as the root user):

```
# apachectl restart
```

This does exactly what we want: It starts the server if it isn't running, or restarts the server if it is. But sometimes a nonstandard Apache installation results in an `apachectl` script that doesn't work out of the box. In that case you can go find `apachectl` and tweak it, or (on Unix) you can perform the simplest trick that makes a running `httpd` consult its configuration file: send it a hangup signal.

```
# killall -1 httpd
```

All should be ready now. You can start populating `/home/www/docs` (or whatever your `DocumentRoot` directory is) with Web content.

Test Drives

Yesterday you saw what kind of output a Web server generates when it is delivering a page: a line identifying the HTTP protocol version, another line identifying the type of document to be delivered, a blank line, and finally the actual code to generate the page. (This is just a minimal description. Headers can contain extra information, such as a

`Content-length` line.) An HTML file normally doesn't include the header lines. For instance, this much HTML is sufficient to make a literal time appear in the browser window:

```
<html><body>
Current time: Sun Sep 16 12:46:46 CDT 2001
</body><html>
```

If you save these text lines in a file named `index.html` in your `DocumentRoot` directory and point a browser to `http://localhost`, the browser should display that same—and perpetually incorrect—time. (Actually, it's probably a good idea to do this now to make sure your basic server configuration is okay.)

Now let's try out three different ways of keeping the time dynamically updated.

Using Ruby to Generate an HTML File Directly

Static Web pages like the wrong-time page you just saw can be created with a text editor, but a Ruby script containing a series of `print` or `puts` statements, or a "here document" as described on Day 7, can do it a little better because the current time doesn't have to be hard-coded. Listing 20.1 shows how.

LISTING 20.1   approx-time.rb

```
01:    #!/usr/bin/env ruby
02:
03:    puts "<html><body>"
04:    puts "Time: <b>#{Time.now}</b><br>"
05:    puts "</body></html>"
```

Of course, this sends output to the screen and not to a file. We could modify it by creating a `File` object and printing there, or redirect its output when calling the script:

```
% ruby approx-time.rb > /home/www/docs/approx-time.html
```

It is conventional to redirect standard output when generating HTML instead of specifying a filename in the script. You'll see why shortly.

Under Unix, a "cron job" can be set up to run a program anytime you want, up to once every minute. We won't go into how the `crontab` command works (use `man crontab` to study the manual page if you're interested), but if you use it to tell cron to run `approx-time.rb` every few minutes, then every time a Web server loads `approx-time.html`, it will display a reasonably accurate time.

20

A `cron`-invoked Ruby script keeps track of the status of outgoing faxes where I work. Every five minutes it reads a log file, filters and formats its contents into HTML, and writes a locally available Web page so that senders can keep track of which faxes were sent successfully and which have been delayed because of busy phone lines and the like. This is the cheapest, most secure—and least interesting—way to put dynamic information on the Web. It requires no unusual setup of the Web server or the user's browser.

A First CGI Script

Using CGI is a little like what we did in the previous example, but with four important differences.

First, a CGI script is responsible for generating not only a Web page but also part of the associated HTTP header. The Web server will generate the first line on its own, but since it's legal for formats other than HTML to be produced by CGI scripts, the server relies on each CGI script to tell it what the `Content-type` line should say. Remember that there must be a blank line between the HTTP header and the rest of the output.

Second, a CGI script is not run at scheduled intervals but is invoked by the Web server whenever a client requests it.

Third, a CGI script *must* print to standard output, not to a file. The Web server captures that output before sending it back to the client, and if it's not at standard output, it gets lost.

Fourth, CGI gives scripts access to some session-specific information. But we'll talk about that in a few moments.

Listing 20.2 is a CGI version of the previous script (Listing 20.1).

LISTING 20.2   `cgi-bin/current-time.rb`

```
01:    #!/usr/local/bin/ruby
02:
03:    print "Content-type: text/html\r\n\r\n"
04:
05:    puts "<html><body>"
06:    puts "Current time: <b>#{Time.now}</b><br>"
07:    puts "</body></html>"
```

After saving this in your CGI directory, test it by pointing your browser to
`http://localhost/cgi-bin/current-time.rb`.

A First SHTML Script

Server-parsed HTML supports a mixture of static and dynamic content. As such, whenever we write SHTML, it is likely to end up in at least two pieces: a simple HTML file to hold the static parts, and one or more scripts to generate the dynamic parts. For our current task, only the time is dynamic, so we can make a single script that generates a time string (Listing 20.3), and do the rest in the static HTML file (Listing 20.4). As with CGI, the script must print to standard output.

LISTING 20.3   `print-time.rb`

```
01:    #!/usr/local/bin/ruby
02:    puts Time.now
```

The HTML file contains commands that indicate what scripts should be consulted and where their output should be inserted. These commands look a lot like HTML comments, ensuring that the client's browser won't display them if for some reason the server fails to do its parsing job. There are several directives that may be used in the commands, but we will concern ourselves only with `exec cmd`. Listing 20.4 is the static Web page that completes the example. It should be given an `.shtml` file extension.

Note

> The `.shtml` extension is necessary under the Web server setup shown in today's lesson. If the filename ends with `.html` instead, the page will be sent to the client verbatim, without processing. You can configure Apache to parse `.html` files too, but at a cost in performance (unless all pages on your server happen to require parsing).

20

LISTING 20.4   `current-time.shtml`

```
01:    <html><body>
02:    Date: <b><!--#exec cmd="./print-time.rb" --></b><br>
03:    <body></html>
```

Save this in the main document directory (not the CGI directory) and point your browser to `http://localhost/current-time.shtml` to verify that the current time is displayed as before.

Caution

It's possible for CGI and SHTML scripts to misbehave because the Web server is seeing a different system *PATH* than you expect. If you're having trouble making these examples work, try invoking the Ruby interpreter directly and specifying its exact location, for example:

```
<!--#exec cmd="/usr/local/bin/ruby print-time.rb" -->
```

It should be pointed out that when the Web server finds a command associated with `exec cmd`, it executes that command within a standard system shell. As a result, any command you could type in a terminal window can be carried out by the server in response to a command in your HTML page. Since there's already a Unix command to print the date (shockingly enough, it is called `date`), our trivial example could have got along without a separate Ruby script. This HTML code is enough to do the same job by itself:

```
<html><body>
Date: <b><!--#exec cmd="date" --></b><br>
<body></html>
```

Wait . . . did we say the Web server executes *any* command? If you're starting to worry about security, that concern is well placed. Apache is designed in such a way that pores in the security blanket are opened only to the minimal widths that you specify in its con-figuration file, and the Web server itself runs not as the root user but as somebody with very limited privileges (if you don't specify, that account is called *nobody*). Nonetheless, any opportunity for your anonymous clients to run code on the server carries a certain aura of risk with it. Understandably, many webmasters would never consider running a Web service on a computer that holds any sensitive information that shouldn't be avail-able on the Web.

Know Thy Client

It's a little-known fact that even when cookies are disabled, Web browsers quietly send some extra data with each page request. It's not really anything personal (your weight, sexual preference, and political opinions are not divulged), but innocuous stuff chosen to help content providers present their content well. Environment variables store the name of the browser, the Internet address the browser is operating from, the Web address (Uniform Resource Locator, or URL) of whatever page the browser had previously displayed, and a few other things. All CGI and SHTML scripts have access to this information.

If you're straining to think of a legitimate use for session information, imagine you work for a company that provides virus-scanning software for many computer platforms. When Joe User is having trouble installing the software and consults the company Web site's technical support page, he gets a popup menu: *Select your operating system*. But why ask a question when the answer is right in front of you? The `HTTP_USER_AGENT` environment variable can be consulted as follows:

```ruby
#!/usr/local/bin/ruby
print "Content-type: text/html\r\n\r\n"

case ENV['HTTP_USER_AGENT']
when /Win95/
  # generate one Web page...
when /Win98/
  # generate a different Web page...
  # (deal with other Windows variants...)
else
  # unsure, so generate the menu after all...
end
```

Environment variables can provide both security for your site and convenience for your clients. For example:

- The `HTTP_REFERER` environment variable tells you the URL of whatever page the client's browser had just visited. Consult it if you want to disallow access to a page that doesn't progress through an approved link, or if you want to give the user an intelligent "go back" link, or if you just want to keep statistics on how people are finding your site.

- `REMOTE_ADDR` makes it possible to provide different content to users in different networks (for instance, inside or outside a corporation), or even at individual locations.

- `HTTP_USER_AGENT` generally tells you not only what operating system the client has, but what kind of browser is being run on it. That can tip you off when certain HTML elements should be worked around because they are not supported. Might you not have an eccentric prospective client accessing your site from home, using that vintage 1995 browser he has never upgraded because his company's tech support staff doesn't make house calls? Do you want him to miss out on your sales pitch? One of those all-too-common "If you can't see this properly then upgrade your browser, luser!" messages is not likely to endear you to this person. Instead, consider silently providing the same content in a simpler form. If anybody is going to annoy and insult your customers, let it be your competitors.

20

Remember the Past

If your page contains form elements such as buttons, pop-up menus, and text entry areas, the environment contains records of whatever happened just a moment ago. In the simplest case, when the user clicks a "submit" button, the server generates the current page anew, with the environment variable QUERY_STRING reflecting the states of the form elements. When the page reloads, a Ruby script can grab that information. Listings 20.5 and 20.6 together provide an example.

LISTING 20.5   remember.shtml

```
01:    <html>
02:    <head><title>Short-term memory</title></head>
03:    <body>
04:
05:    <h1>Pick a number</h1>
06:    <center>
07:    <form>
08:      <select name="choice">
09:        <option value="one">one</value>
10:        <option value="two">two</value>
11:        <option value="three">three</value>
12:      </select>
13:      <input value="go" type="submit">
14:    </form>
15:    <hr>
16:    Your previous choice was:
17:    <!--#exec cmd="/usr/local/bin/ruby choice.rb"-->
18:    <center>
19:
20:    </body></html>
```

LISTING 20.6   choice.rb

```
01:    #!/usr/local/bin/ruby
02:
03:    # Use a regular expression to get the value of
04:    # the "choice" input into global var $1 ...
05:    ENV["QUERY_STRING"].split("&").grep(/^choice=(.+)$/)
06:
07:    # ... and print that value to stdout.
08:    # "to_s" is here because $1 might be nil.
09:    puts $1.to_s
```

Use DBM to Remember Old Session Information

As of version 1.7, Ruby supports a simple *persistent data* interface. Normally the contents of variables are lost after a program exits, but with persistent data, the program can store information, exit, and remember the information the next time it runs. Of course, you've been able to do this by writing files to disk and reading them later, but the DBM class provides a persistent object that acts like a hash, and doesn't require you to load or store anything explicitly. Here's some example DBM code you can run the old-fashioned way (no Web server necessary):

Note

It's outside the scope of this book, but Ruby also supports interaction with full-blown database systems such as Oracle, PostgreSQL, and MySQL.

```
fail "Sorry - need v1.7 of Ruby or later"   if RUBY_VERSION < "1.7"
require 'dbm'
database = DBM.new("ourdb")
puts "database['x'] == #{database['x']}"
database['x'] = "A Stored Value"
```

Output of first run:

```
database['x'] ==
```

Output of second run:

```
database['x'] == A Stored Value
```

You'll find that a file named ourdb.dbm in Unix, or ourdb.dir in Windows, has appeared in the current working directory after the first run.

The script in Listing 20.7 can be called to remind a client of the time of his or her last visit to your Web site. Separate times are stored for each client IP address.

LISTING 20.7   last-visit.rb

20

```
01:   #!/usr/local/bin/ruby
02:
03:   require 'dbm'
04:
05:   unless (remote = ENV["REMOTE_ADDR"]).nil?
06:     accesses = DBM.open("accesses")
07:
08:     last = accesses[remote]
```

continues

LISTING 20.7   Continued

```
09:
10:     if last.nil?
11:       puts "Apparently you have never visited this site!"
12:     else
13:       puts "You last visited this site at time #{last}."
14:     end
15:
16:     accesses[remote] = Time.now.to_s
17:   end
```

We need a little SHTML Web page (Listing 20.8) to call the script.

LISTING 20.8   test-dbm.shtml

```
01:   <html><body>
02:   <!--#exec cmd="last-visit.rb" -->
03:   <p>Actual content of the page would go here.</p>
04:   </body></html>
```

Now point your browser to http://localhost/test-dbm.shtml. Reload the page a few times and see how it changes.

Tip

If a CGI or SHTML script produces no output, it may contain an error in syntax or logic. But finding the problem can be tricky; a Web server normally won't display script error output. There may be a hint for you in the server's error log (a text file, typically found in /var/log/apache; see the Apache documentation for details), although it may turn out to be something unhelpful, such as "premature end of script headers". You might try to debug the script by running it directly from the command line, manually setting some shell environment variables if necessary. Both normal HTML output and error messages will appear at your console. Another idea is to redirect error output, as in the following command, so that it follows standard output, thus causing the browser to display exception messages along with the normal page content.

```
<!--#exec cmd="last-visit.rb 2>&1" -->
```

Object-Oriented CGI Support

HTML is not much fun to write by hand, and writing program code to produce it via `print` statements can be even less fun. Mistakes in the code might go unnoticed if you test on one browser and not others; malformed code might be interpreted charitably by one browser but cause another to crash.

The `CGI` class brings some order into the potential chaos of HTML generation by tying the page code into the structure of a Ruby program. One immediate benefit is that it enforces correct nesting of tags, so that mistakes like `<center><em>this</center></em>` can't happen. Here are two equivalent CGI scripts. The first, in Listing 20.9, is written the brute-force way:

LISTING 20.9   cgi-bin/cgi-test.rb

```
01:    #!/usr/local/bin/ruby
02:
03:    print "Content-type: text/HTML\r\n\r\n"
04:    puts " <html>"
05:    puts "    <head><title>A simple CGI page</title></head>"
06:    puts "    <body><h1>A large header</h1>"
07:    puts "       <p>Text of a paragraph</p>"
08:    puts "       <center>Centered and <em>emphasized</em></center>"
09:    puts "    </body>"
10:    puts " </html>"
```

The second, in Listing 20.10, takes advantage of a CGI object.

LISTING 20.10   cgi-bin/cgi-test-2.rb

```
01:    #!/usr/local/bin/ruby
02:
03:    require 'cgi'
04:    page = CGI.new "html3"
05:    page.out {
06:      page.html {
07:        page.head { page.title {"A simple CGI page"} } +
08:        page.body {
09:          page.h1 {"A large header"} +
10:          page.p {"Text of a paragraph"} +
11:          page.center{ "Centered and " + page.em{"emphasized"} }
12:        }
13:      }
14:    }
```

20

Both scripts produce a page like the one shown in Figure 20.1.

FIGURE 20.1

*Output of
Listings 20.9
and 20.10.*

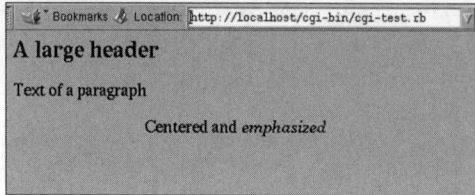

Tip

If you use your browser to look at the source of the Web page produced by Listing 20.10, what you see isn't very presentable. The entire HTML code unravels in one line. Wrapped to fit on our printed page, it looks like this:

```
<!DOCTYPE HTML PUBLIC "-//W3C//DTD HTML 3.2 Final//EN"><HTML><HEAD>
<TITLE>A simple CGI page</TITLE></HEAD><BODY><H1>A large header</H1><P>
Text of a paragraph</P><CENTER>Centered and <EM>emphasized</EM></CENTER>
</BODY></HTML>
```

The `CGI.pretty` class method takes a string of HTML text and reformats it with logical indentation. If we enclose lines 06–13 of Listing 20.10 in a `CGI.pretty()` call, the HTML that gets produced is more human-readable:

```
<!DOCTYPE HTML PUBLIC "-//W3C//DTD HTML 3.2 Final//EN">
<html>
  <head>
    <title>
      A simple CGI page
    </title>
  </head>
  <body>
    <h1>
      A large header
    </h1>
    <p>
      Text of a paragraph
    </p>
    <center>
      Centered and
      <em>
        emphasized
      </em>
    </center>
  </body>
</html>
```

Session Information Using the CGI Class

The "short-term memory" SHTML exercise (in the "Remember the Past" section earlier in today's lesson) is cleaner when written in the form of a single CGI script. There is no need to look through a QUERY_STRING to find out what button the user had previously pressed; the CGI object itself acts like a hash, allowing any piece of information to be looked up directly. Listing 20.11 by itself does the job of Listings 20.5 and 20.6 together. The resulting Web page is shown in Figure 20.2.

LISTING 20.11   cgi-bin/remember.rb

```
01:   #!/usr/local/bin/ruby
02:
03:   require 'cgi'
04:
05:   page = CGI.new("html3")
06:   page.out {
07:     page.html {
08:       page.head { page.title{"Short-term memory"} } +
09:         page.body {
10:         page.h1 {"Pick a number"} +
11:           page.center {
12:           page.form {
13:             page.popup_menu("choice","one","two","three" ) + " " +
14:             page.submit("go")
15:           } +
16:             page.hr +
17:             "Your previous choice was " + page["choice"].first.to_s
18:         } # end centering
19:       } # end body
20:     } # end html
21:   }
```

FIGURE 20.2

The Web page resulting from Listing 20.11.

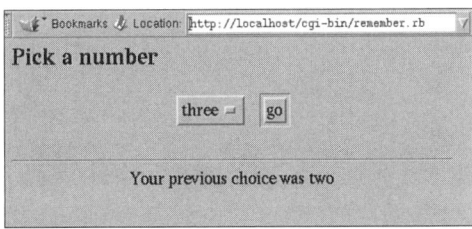

20

Notice the expression in line 17. page["choice"] returns *all* current values associated with the field name "choice" (which was defined in the popup menu on line 13), in array form. first is used to grab the first element of the array, because we know there is only one that we care about. Finally, to_s deals with the possibility of a nil by safely changing it to an empty string.

Persistent Session Information

As we've seen, HTML forms pass their information forward in time so that the next time a page is loaded, a CGI script can read it hash-style. But the information is transient. Consider this script in Listing 20.12:

LISTING 20.12 cgi-bin/transient.rb

```
01:   #!/usr/local/bin/ruby
02:
03:   require 'cgi'
04:
05:   page = CGI.new 'html3'
06:   username = page['ID_entry'].first
07:   if username.nil?
08:     page.out {
09:       page.html{
10:         page.p { "Please identify yourself:" } +
11:           page.form {
12:           page.text_field( "ID_entry" )
13:         }
14:       }
15:     }
16:   else
17:     page.out {
18:       page.html {
19:         "hello, #{username}."
20:       }
21:     }
22:   end
```

Users are prompted to enter identification into a text field when they first visit. Once that has been done, a greeting message appears. The problem is that if a user visits again tomorrow, or simply browses elsewhere and comes back in just a few seconds, the identification has to be re-entered. It was never stored anywhere.

One way to make session information persistent is with the CGI::Cookie class, as shown in Listing 20.13.

LISTING 20.13 cgi-bin/persistent.rb

```
01:   #!/usr/local/bin/ruby
02:
03:   require 'cgi'
04:
```

LISTING 20.13   Continued

```
05:    Cookie_name = 'macademia'
06:    Form_name   = 'userIDform'
07:    One_week    = 60*60*24*7     # a week, in seconds
08:
09:    page = CGI.new('html3')
10:
11:    # We'll accept two forms of identification.
12:    fresh_ID = page[Form_name].first
13:    cookie = page.cookies[Cookie_name].first
14:    old_ID = CGI::Cookie.parse(cookie)['userID'].first if cookie
15:
16:    # Use newly entered ID if available ...
17:    if fresh_ID
18:      cookie = CGI::Cookie.new( {'name'  => Cookie_name,
19:                                 'value' => ["userID=#{fresh_ID}"],
20:                                 'path'  => '/',
21:                                 'expires' => Time.now + One_week
22:                               })
23:      page.out('cookie' => [cookie]) {
24:        page.html {
25:          page.h2 {"Hello, new user #{fresh_ID}."}
26:        }
27:      }
28:
29:    # Failing that, try one taken from the cookie jar.
30:    elsif old_ID
31:      page.out {
32:        page.html {
33:          page.h2 {"Hello, established user #{old_ID}."}+
34:          page.p {"A little cookie told me who you were."}
35:        }
36:      }
37:
38:    # By now, we think this is the first visit, or cookies are disabled,
39:    # or we had a cookie on this user's machine but it expired.  So let's
40:    # ask who the user is.
41:    else
42:      page.out {
43:        page.html {
44:          page.p { "Kindly identify yourself." } +
45:          page.form { page.text_field( Form_name ) }
46:        }
47:      }
48:    end
```

20

The `page` and `page.cookies` objects are both hashlike, but they are of different types. The `page` object remembers nothing about the distant past, but it knows what happened a moment ago. In line 23, after the user has typed something into the identification box, it is stored as a cookie on the client's machine. So, even though `page[Form_name]` starts out empty when the user comes back to view this page tomorrow, the identification appears in `page.cookies[Cookie_name]`, and the user doesn't have to type it again.

Cookies are a little bit like DBM objects. Beyond a little bit of initial setup work, you don't have to think about the logic of how they store and retrieve information. There are a couple of differences to notice, however. One is that a cookie can be set to expire, whereas DBM information persists until erased. The other is more important: A cookie lives on the client's machine, whereas a DBM object is local to the Web server. In our example, this makes for a more reliable identification than if we tried to do it all by IP address at the server end, because different users of the same machine are likely to have their cookies stored in separate places. But it also implies a loss of control. Cookies, like JavaScript, can be disabled at the browser.

Embedded Ruby

Doesn't SHTML seem like a little too much work when you want to do something very simple? The logic of it is simple enough, yet every little piece of code has to be relegated to a separate script file.

But help has arrived. It's now possible to embed Ruby code in ordinary HTML pages, using Shugo Maeda's `eruby` package. It's freely available; check the Ruby Application Archive at `http://www.ruby-lang.org/en/raa.html` for a current download location, and follow the installation directions that come with it.

Once `eruby` is installed as a program, your Web server needs to know about it. For Apache, that means copying the `eruby` executable file into the `cgi-bin` directory (for security reasons, a mere symbolic link won't be good enough), adding the following lines to `httpd.conf`, and restarting `httpd` as discussed near the beginning of this chapter.

```
AddType application/x-httpd-eruby   .rhtml
Action  application/x-httpd-eruby  /cgi-bin/eruby
```

Now take any HTML file, give it an `.rhtml` filename extension, and infuse it with Ruby expressions. They will be newly processed every time a client loads the page.

See Listing 20.14 for an example `eruby` file. Enclosing a Ruby expression with `<%...%>` delimiters, as in lines 13–19, causes it simply to be evaluated. Enclosing it with <%=...%>, as in lines 10 and 11, causes that value to be converted to a string and inserted into the new HTML that eruby generates.

LISTING 20.14   test.rhtml

```
01:   <!-- point your browser at http://localhost/test.rhtml -->
02:
03:   <html>
04:     <head><title>An eruby test</title></head>
05:
06:   <body>
07:     <h1>Hello!</h1>
08:
09:     <%# Some tiny bits of embedded Ruby code: %>
10:     <p>This webserver uses Ruby version <%= RUBY_VERSION %>.</p>
11:     <p>The time is <%= Time.now %>.</p>
12:
13:     <%
14:        # Something a little sillier:
15:        words = %w{row row row your boat gently down the stream}
16:        words.size.downto(1) do |n|
17:          printf "%s<br>\n", words[0,n].join(" ")
18:        end
19:     %>
20:
21:   </body>
22:   </html>
```

Figure 20.3 shows the Web page generaged by Listing 20.14.

FIGURE 20.3

Web page produced by eruby *example in Listing 20.14.*

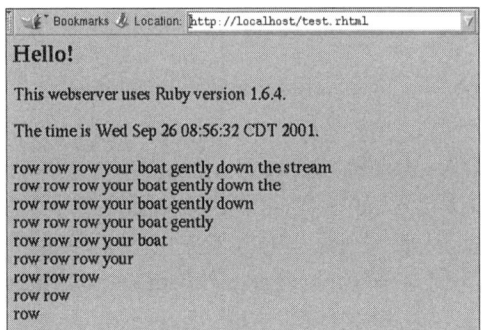

20

> **Where to Learn More**
>
> To read about a new and advanced way to use Ruby for dynamic Web content, check out the Interpreted Objects for Web Applications (IOWA) project at http://beta4.com/iowa/.
>
> The perfect source for learning all about the Web is the World Wide Web Consortium (W3C), whose Web site is at http://www.w3.org. There you'll find information about standardization, Web page structure, image formats, style sheets, XML, the history of the Web, and much more.

Summary

In this 20th day of learning Ruby, we learned about several ways of creating dynamic Web content. Stand-alone scripts (CGI) are the most popular and versatile way to do it, and Ruby provides a CGI class to make it even easier. SHTML or Embedded Ruby makes more sense when you want to insert a small amount of dynamic content (say, a custom access counter) into an otherwise conventional HTML page. In a pinch, you might be able to use Ruby to generate new static pages periodically and so keep them from going out of date.

We didn't do an exhaustive study of Ruby's CGI support or study HTML forms in great depth. We did walk through setting up an Apache Web server in a Unix environment, since so many of the world's Web sites run Apache on Linux.

Tomorrow will be our last Ruby lesson. As on Day 16, the emphasis will be on putting what we know to interesting use rather than learning new language concepts. First we'll get a little experience using Ruby for artificial intelligence, and then we'll build a two-party Internet chat program with a graphic interface.

Exercises

1. How can your CGI or SHTML script find out what the available environment variables are? *Hint:* Look at the Hash iterators.

2. Write an SHTML page and accompanying Ruby script (or a single eruby page, if you prefer) that produces messages like the following, based on the number of visits from the current IP address compared with the total number of visits.

   ```
   You seem to be responsible for 0.1% of the traffic on this page.
    Please visit more often.

   You seem to be responsible for 55.2% of the traffic on this page.
    Don't you have anything better to do?
   ```

   Hint: Use a single DBM object, with IP addresses for keys.

3. In our first "test drive," we discussed using a Unix cron job to make a script run at regular intervals. That might work when you have a Unix shell account on a Web server where you are not allowed to do CGI or SHTML scripting. But suppose you don't even have authority to run cron jobs? As a last resort in that case, you can trying using the `nohup` command to launch a script in such a way that it can keep running in the background after you log out. In this case it won't work to send the content to standard output, so a `File` object must be used.

Modify the `make_time_page.rb` script so that it can be used as indicated in the following code. It should run in an infinite loop, updating `index.html` at one-minute intervals, and not stopping until somebody kills it. (Be warned: That "somebody" might be a disapproving system administrator. Most sites require that you get permission to run long background jobs, even if they don't eat up lots of system resources.)

```
% nohup ruby make_time_page.rb &
[1] 25302                         (the process ID is returned)
% nohup: appending output to `nohup.out'
```

Log out, then log back in some other time. . .

```
% ps -u `whoami` | grep ruby (what Ruby processes am I running?)
25302 ?        00:00:00 ruby
% kill 25302
% ps -u `whoami` | grep ruby  (verify that it's gone)
%
```

Answers

1. `each_key` or `each_pair` can be used to iterate over the environment variables. Listing 20.15 shows another solution as a single `eruby` file; a two-piece SHTML solution would be similar.

LISTING 20.15   env.rhtml

```
01:   <html><head><title>eruby test</title></head>
02:   <body>
03:
04:     <h1>Environment variables</h1>
05:     <table>
06:     <%
07:       ENV.each_pair {|key,value|
08:         printf "<tr><td>%s</td><td>%s</td></tr>\n",
09:           key, value
10:       }
```

20

continues

LISTING 20.15   Continued

```
11:        %>
12:      </table>
13:
14:    </body>
15:  </html>
```

In the CGI solution in Listing 20.16, the ENV object is mapped directly to table rows.

LISTING 20.16   cgi-bin/env.rb

```
01:  #!/usr/local/bin/ruby
02:
03:  require 'cgi'
04:  page = CGI.new 'html3'
05:  page.out {
06:    page.html {
07:      page.head { page.title {"cgi test"} } +
08:      page.body {
09:        page.h1 {'Environment variables'} +
10:          page.table {
11:            ENV.map{ |k,v| page.tr{page.td{k}+page.td{v}} }.join
12:        }
13:      }
14:    }
15:  }
```

2. The solution is provided in two-piece SHTML form; see Listings 20.17 and 20.18. The same thing can be done in eruby by pasting the contents of count_relative.rb into the HTML file in place of the exec cmd line, and surrounding it with <%...%> delimiters. However, an advantage of keeping things like access counters in separate files is that they can be easily invoked from many different Web pages.

LISTING 20.17   count-relative.shtml

```
01:  <html><body>
02:
03:  <p>Please insert meaningful content here.</p>
04:
05:  <!--#exec cmd="./count-relative.rb"-->
06:  </body></html>
```

LISTING 20.18   count-relative.rb

```
01:  #!/usr/local/bin/ruby
02:  require 'dbm'
03:
04:  # Get the integer value associated with a key (default to 0)
05:  def ivalue(dbm,key)
06:    (dbm[key] || 0).to_i
07:  end
08:
09:  # Increment the integer value associated with a key.
10:  def increment(dbm,key)
11:    dbm[key] = ivalue(dbm, key)+1
12:  end
13:
14:  visits = DBM.new('visits')
15:  remote = ENV['REMOTE_ADDR'].to_s
16:  increment(visits, remote)
17:  increment(visits, 'total')
18:
19:  pct = (ivalue(visits,remote) * 100.0) / ivalue(visits,'total')
20:  printf "You seem to be responsible for %.1f%% ",  pct
21:  puts   "of the traffic on this page."
22:
23:  if pct < 10.0
24:    puts "Please visit more often."
25:  else
26:    puts "Don't you have anything better to do?"
27:  end
```

3. Although it takes a little Unix know-how to use the script in Listing 20.19, it's not all that hard to actually write it. Notice that we're not trapping any errors. If something went wrong with disk access, we would probably want our background jobs to stop running anyway while the system administrator got the problem cleared up.

LISTING 20.19   approx-time.rb

```
01:  #!/usr/local/bin/ruby
02:
03:  loop do
04:    out = File.new("/home/www/docs/index.html","w")
05:    out.puts "<html><body>"
06:    out.puts "Time: <b>#{Time.now}</b><br>"
07:    out.puts "</body></html>"
08:    out.close
09:    sleep 60
10:  end
```

20

DAY 21

Putting It Together (Part II)

A just machine to make big decisions

Programmed by fellows with compassion and vision. . .

—Donald Fagen, "IGY" (*The Nightfly,* 1982)

Today, just as on Day 16, there is no single organizing topic, and there are no exercises; rather, we practice our Ruby skills by walking together through two projects.

The first project is an exploration of rudimentary artificial intelligence. We write a script that takes advantage of past "experience," asks the user some questions about the current situation, and makes a decision—or more precisely, makes a prediction on which the user can base a decision.

The second project grows out of the discussion on Day 19 about online chat facilities. We had a pair of scripts that allowed for strictly alternating discussion (party A must send a message, then party B, then party A); today we'll come up with something that allows either party to speak at any time. It will also look nicer, because it will use the Tk windowing library.

Binary Decision Trees

Decision trees are an artificial intelligence (AI) technique used for making good decisions based on past experience. That experience need not be all from the life of one person; it can be gathered from anywhere, such as an informal survey, your personal observations, or statistics from any source you trust. To be useful for this technique, the information needs to be stored in the form of a list of discrete samples.

For example, suppose you're in the market for a car, new or used. You'd like to be able to benefit from the experiences of all your thousands of friends and acquaintances with the cars they've bought in the last few years. You ask them whether they've been happy with their cars and about the make, model, age, mileage, and the price they paid for the cars they bought. You also throw in a question about the color, although you suspect it is irrelevant.

Getting a few answers, you write them down in an organized way. Table 21.1 shows what the beginning of the list might look like.

TABLE 21.1 Survey Results About Acquaintances' Cars

Happy?	Make	Model	Age	Miles	Price	Color
Y	Mazda	Protégé	4	60000	7000	Tan
N	VW	Beetle	25	220000	2000	Blue
N	Ford	Contour	2	18000	11000	Red
Y	Dodge	Neon	0	0	14000	Black

Each line of the list is one sample. The answer to the happiness question *classifies* the sample; without it, the sample is useless. We refer to all the other pieces of a sample as *attributes*: a color attribute, a cost attribute, and so on.

Armed with the list, you visit some dealers and look at cars. Every time you see a car that looks interesting, you look through the list for something close. *Somebody was happy with one of these, but it was blue. Somebody else was unhappy with one, but it was a year older.* You find it difficult to make a good decision unless you find a sample that exactly matches the car you want to know about, though even in that lucky case you would feel obliged to keep looking for other samples that might contradict what the first one said. All the information in front of you ought to be useful somehow, but it's hard to and know what to do just by reading through the list.

What you need is a way to summarize the survey results into a few good generalizations. After all, there are probably some statistical trends in there. Maybe almost all the blue cars turned out to make their owners unhappy, or the Dodges tended to make their owners happy only if they were bought when less than three years old. Boiling down raw information into useful knowledge is a fundamental AI task.

A decision tree is a plan of which questions to ask and in which order. The sequence is not the same in every case; each question depends on the answer to the question before it. The example tree shown in Figure 21.1 is binary because its questions have yes/no answers.

FIGURE 21.1

Part of a decision tree: "Will I be happy buying this car?"

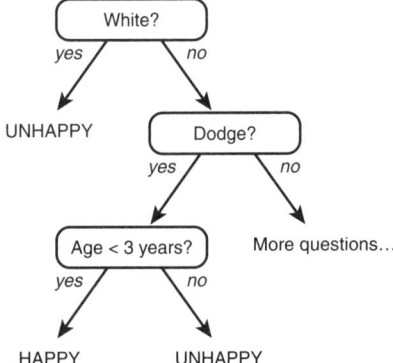

In general, decision trees may have multiple branches; that would allow us to ask just one question about the color of a vehicle instead of many. For our purposes, a binary tree is a little easier to think about. Normally we would need to assign values to attributes, but if they are binary, we consider only whether an attribute is present. Instead of an all-purpose color attribute, we talk about the blueness attribute, the whiteness attribute, the greenness attribute, and so on.

Final predictions of happiness and unhappiness, which we get to by answering questions and progressing to the outer edges of the tree, are by no means certain. We assume that the information we've gathered is valuable, but as we should be reminded by Bertrand Russell's famous illustration about the chicken,[1] we can never be sure the future will resemble the past. All intelligence, whether natural or artificial, aims to decide on courses of action based on the best guesses possible. You build a decision tree based on a group of preclassified samples (the survey results); those are called *training samples*. Later you'll want to use that tree to make a decision about a sample whose classification you don't have yet (a car you're considering buying). That sample is called a *test sample*.

21

---

[1] *"I've got it made. Every morning, the sun comes up, the farmer feeds me, my head does not get chopped off . . . "*

Script Overview

We'll create several new classes in this project.

First is the binary decision tree class, BDT. The job of a tree is to ask a series of questions and eventually return a classification. BDT will actually be a hollow shell of a class, with two subclasses: BDT_internal and BDT_leaf. The subclasses will offer the same methods but with different logic, as you'll see in a moment.

There also needs to be a class for the known samples. Each BDT_sample object will hold a few attributes ("blue", "dodge", "less than 3 years old", and so on) and a classification ("happy").

Finally, we'll make a class called BDT_set for grouping BDT_sample objects together. This might sound unnecessary, but it will be a convenient place to put most of the logic of tree building. For example, once we have collected a set of samples called the_samples, we'll want to be able to say the_tree=the_samples.make_tree and get a valid BDT object back.

Because all of these classes are designed to go together, we'll keep them in one file named bdt.rb.

The BDT Class and Its Relatives

The structure of a binary decision tree will be simpler than you might guess at first, because it will be recursive. This means we never have to think about how "deep" it is; a BDT object comprises one node and possibly references to its children. The children themselves, of course, are also BDT objects.

Thus, a tree with a hundred nodes is really a hundred BDT objects. But to use the tree, you consult only the BDT object associated with the top node. Unless it's an absurdly simple tree, it will start by asking you a question; based on your answer, it will prompt one of its children to ask you *its* question, and so on. Eventually a node that has no children of its own will be consulted, and that node will produce an answer instead of another question. Here's the BDT class:

```
class BDT
end
```

Don't be alarmed. Yes, that's right, there's nothing there; BDT exists only to clarify the relationship between two subclasses that we're about to create. Because those classes will share no common logic, there's really nothing to put inside the superclass.

A BDT_internal object corresponds to an internal node of the decision tree—that is, one with a pair of nodes below it. It has a question associated with it, plus references to those child nodes. When consulted for a classification, it first asks the user a question about one attribute, then consults one of its children based on what the user says.

Because this is a binary tree, we can get away with just two references to child nodes: @yes and @no. A general decision tree would instead need to employ some kind of container to keep track of an arbitrary number of children.

```
class BDT_internal < BDT
  def initialize(q,children)
    @question = q
    @yes, @no = children
  end

  def classify
    print @question,"? "
    if ($stdin.gets) =~ /^[yY]/
      @yes.classify
    else
      @no.classify
    end
  end
end
```

A `BDT_leaf` object is the last node visited when a test sample gets classified. There are no questions to ask, so the code can be very simple. Only one piece of data must be stored.

```
class BDT_leaf < BDT
  def initialize(c)  @classification=c  end
  def classify()     @classification    end
end
```

Had we decided on sticking with a single `BDT` class, we would have had to include some extra logic so that its objects could keep track of which kind they were. This isn't such a problem now, but if other methods are added later, things might get messier. The following class illustrates this alternative design idea.

```
# The road not taken:
# A less object-oriented approach
#      (to use this, you would need to make some
#         changes in the BDT_set class)
class BDT
  def initialize(label, children=nil)
    @label = label  # might be a question or a classification
    @yes,@no = children if children
  end
  def classify_interactively
    if @yes or @no  # See whether I'm an internal node
      print @label,"? "
      if ($stdin.gets) =~ /^[yY]/
        @yes.classify
      else
        @no.classify
```

21

```
          end
        else                    # It seems I'm a leaf node
          @label
        end
      end
    end
end
```

 Tip

> Establishing an inheritance relationship between the node classes is one
> way to help keep the code maintainable, because if we later find we have
> to add some methods that properly belong to both classes, that previously
> empty BDT class will be a ready-made place to put them. Also, the existence
> of the BDT class means we have a reliable way to test whether an object is a
> node of a binary decision tree:
>
> ```
> BDT_leaf.new('benign').is_a?(BDT)  #->  true
> ```
>
> But constructing scaffolding around code that doesn't yet exist, and may
> *never* exist, doesn't feel quite like the Ruby Way. If we choose not to define
> a BDT class, then the BDT_leaf and BDT_internal classes would be formally
> unrelated, but we could still informally test for an object's "type" based on
> which messages it responds to, like this:
>
> ```
> BDT_leaf.new('benign').respond_to?('classify')  #->  true
> ```
>
> Expressing logical relationships with an empty superclass is a technique that
> comes down from older OO languages like C++ and Java; Ruby supports but
> doesn't demand it. As always, you can do whatever helps you think most
> clearly.

The BDT_sample Class

We know that a training sample comprises a classification and some attributes. There
may be any number of attributes, but storing them in an array doesn't require knowing
how many there will be ahead of time. Writing the BDT_sample class is straightforward.
All we provide are an initialize method, to accept the necessary data, and a pair of
read-only accessors:

```
class BDT_sample
  def initialize(c, atr)  # single classification, array of attribs
    @classification = c
    @attributes = atr
  end
  attr_reader :classification, :attributes
end
```

A Mild Dose of Information Theory

Before implementing the `BDT_set` class, we will find it useful to teach the `Array` class a couple of special tricks.

```
class Array
  L2 = Math.log(2)  # a helpful constant

  def info_content
    total = self.sum
    return self.sum do |elt|
      if elt>0
        p = elt/total
        -p*(Math.log(p)/L2)
      else
        0
      end
    end
  end

  def sum  # The Ruby FAQ describes a more general way to do this.
    total = 0.0
    if block_given?
      self.each {|e| total += yield(e)}
    else
      self.each {|e| total += e}
    end
    total
  end

end
```

`Array#sum` is straightforward, but `Array#info_content` probably needs a little explaining.

Information content is at the heart of our tree-building strategy. Start with a set of test samples, and start breaking it up one attribute at a time. In our example, we might start by splitting the samples into Fords and non-Fords. The question, "Is the car a Ford?" becomes the top node of the tree, and we start building two new decision trees below it: a "yes" subtree based on the Fords and a "no" subtree based on the non-Fords.

It would take little effort to build a working decision tree if we didn't care about order in which the questions were to be asked. But the order is important, especially if there are many attributes to consider, and some of them are likely to be irrelevant. Suppose the fact that a car is painted blue really doesn't have anything to do with whether it makes its owner happy. Then splitting by blueness is likely to leave us with two sets of samples that have about the same happiness proportions as we started with, and we will have learned nothing. In fact, if the decision tree is built sensibly, it should never ask about the completely irrelevant attributes.

21

To make that a little more concrete, let's say we start with 1,000 samples. 100 have the blueness attribute, and 900 do not. 600 are classified as making their owners happy, and 400 are not. If the fact that a car is blue is completely unrelated to whether it makes the owner happy, then splitting up the samples according to blueness is likely to produce about a 60/40 (happy/unhappy) mix among the blues and a 540/360 mix among the non-blues. The ratios in the two sets will be the same and will match that of the unsplit set. Had we picked a more relevant attribute, we would have split the samples in a way that helped to segregate the classifications so that the proportion of happy buyers would be significantly higher in one set than in the other.

Information content is a way of quantifying this phenomenon. You can think of it as the amount of uncertainty involved when guessing the classification of a sample picked randomly out of a set. If almost all samples share the same classification, you have a good idea ahead of time what you're going to get, so there is not much mystery. But when there's a roughly even mix of classifications, the level of uncertainty is higher.

```
[999,1].info_content      #-> 0.01140775774
[485,515].info_content    #-> 0.9993506898
```

If we always limited our examples to two classifications, such as happy and unhappy, we probably could get by without quite as much fancy math as we're using. But `Array#info_content` as written is equipped to deal with multiple classifications:

```
[2,64,9].info_content     #-> 0.7017610237
```

When a set of samples is split by an attribute, each resulting subset has its own information content. The *expected* information content is just a weighted average of the information content values for the resulting subsets. This calculation is done in the `BDT_set#expected_info_content` method, which you can examine in Listing 21.1 later in this chapter. To decide which attribute to use, an expected information content is calculated for each possible split, and the split producing the smallest value (that is, the least apparent uncertainty) is deemed the best.

The `BDT_set` Class

Here's where the real AI happens. All the interesting logic of decision trees can be associated with sets of samples. We won't go exhaustively through its workings here, except to acknowledge that it is a modified version of the classic *DECISION-TREE-LEARNING* algorithm (Stuart Russell and Peter Norvig, *Artificial Intelligence,* Prentice Hall, 1995) and to highlight a few of the more interesting points.

> **Note**
>
> Those who are familiar with decision trees will notice two significant differ-
> ences between our algorithm and Russell and Norvig's original: Ours is only
> for trees with yes/no attributes, and it does not throw away attributes as it
> builds the tree. Instead, attribute selection is based purely on information
> gain, taking advantage of the fact that it is never profitable to split on the
> same attribute twice. We employ no test for being "out of attributes," nor
> do we explicitly test for the condition in which all samples in a set have the
> same classification; however, we stop recursing when no split remains that
> improves information content, and the effect is the same. The algorithm is
> simplified at the expense of efficiency, because unproductive splits will be
> repeatedly tried and rejected.

BDT_set#initialize accepts a filename when it is first called, because we will be feed-
ing it a file containing test samples. New BDT_sets will also be created later, however,
when the original gets split during the tree-building process, so BDT_set#initialize, as
follows, will also be ready to accept a BDT_sample array.

```
class BDT_set
  def initialize(source)
    if source.is_a?(String)  # treat as filename
      @samples = IO.readlines(source).map do |line|
        tokens = line.split(",").map{|t| t.strip}
        classification = tokens.delete_at(0)
        BDT_sample.new(classification, tokens)
      end
    else                      # treat as array of BDT_samples
      @samples = source
    end
  end
  attr_reader :samples
```

A file used to build a BDT_set has one sample per line. Each line is a comma-separated
list of a classification followed by any number of attributes. For example, to determine
what signs a baseball coach is sending to players, we might keep track of his antics for
part of a game, classifying by what happened on the next pitch:

```
steal, touch cap, brush across chest
no steal, touch elbow, touch cap, fold arms
hit and run, touch cap, brush across chest
steal, brush across chest, clap
...
```

21

`BDT_set#make_tree` is simpler than you might expect, but, as we've seen before, that is the nature of recursion.

```
class BDT_set
  ...
  def make_tree
    best = attributes.min do |a1,a2|
      expected_info_content(split(a1)) <=> expected_info_content(split(a2))
    end

    if expected_info_content(split(best)) < expected_info_content([self])
      BDT_internal.new(best,split(best).collect{|e| e.make_tree })
    else
      BDT_leaf.new((self.classification_totals.max{|x,y| x[1]<=>y[1]}).first)
    end
  end
end
```

The first part of `make_tree` is concerned with coming up with the best attribute to use when splitting the samples. It tests the expected information content of each possible split and chooses the attribute that results in a minimum value. `min` needs to be told what we mean by smallness, and we provide that information in an iterator block that works just like a sorting specification.

 Note

> Future versions of Ruby may allow a simpler form of the block given when finding a maximum or minimum, so that our code could read
> ```
> best = attributes.min_by {|a| expected_info_content(split(a))}
> ```

The second part of `make_tree` decides whether the best split seems profitable by comparing expected information content values from before and after. Based on that determination, it either makes an internal node using the chosen attribute and recursively builds two new decision trees from the split sample sets or ends the process by returning a leaf node with whatever classification predominates in the samples.

The classification line (`BDT_leaf.new...`) is rather dense. To understand it, you need to know that the `BDT_set#classification_totals` method returns a hash in which each classification is mapped to the number of samples with that classification.

```
{"manic"=>8, "happy"=>93, "unhappy"=>60}
```

The `max` method implicitly converts the hash to an array.

```
[["manic",8], ["happy",93], ["unhappy",60]]
```

Then it finds the biggest subarray, going by the second element of each.

```
["happy",93]
```

After extracting the `first` element of this array, we know that happiness is the predominant classification for this particular sample set.

The remaining details of the `BDT_set` class can be examined in Listing 21.1.

The Full Script

Here's a complete listing of `bdt.rb`, including the code we just discussed but with a couple of enhancements. The new `to_s` methods of `BDT_internal` and `BDT_leaf` make it possible to print a decision tree in a fairly intelligible indented format, and `BDT_set#initialize` can tolerate empty lines and comments in the training sample file.

LISTING 21.1   `bdt.rb`

```
001:   # bdt.rb
002:
003:   # Simplified binary decision trees.
004:   #
005:   # Classes
006:   #   BDT: A binary decision tree, which knows how to make
007:   #     a classification based on the user's answers to
008:   #     its questions
009:   #   BDT_leaf < BDT: leaf node
010:   #   BDT_internal < BDT: internal node
011:   #   BDT_sample: Single training sample comprising
012:   #     a classification and a set of attributes
013:   #   BDT_set: A set of samples, which knows how to
014:   #     build a decision tree out of itself
015:   #
016:   # Temporary enhancements to the Array class
017:   #   #sum
018:   #   #info_content
019:
020:
021:   # Methods to extend the Array class.
022:   class Array
023:     L2 = Math.log(2)  # a useful constant
024:
025:     # Use some magic math from information theory.
026:     def info_content
027:       total = self.sum
028:       return self.sum do |elt|
029:         if elt>0
030:           p = elt/total
031:           -p*(Math::log(p)/L2)
032:         else
033:           0.0
034:         end
035:       end
```

continues

LISTING 21.1 Continued

```
036:        end
037:
038:        def sum
039:          total = 0.0
040:          if block_given?
041:            self.each {|e| total += yield(e)}
042:          else
043:            self.each {|e| total += e}
044:          end
045:          return total
046:        end
047:      end
048:
049:      # Empty husk of a class to serve as a superclass for the
050:      # internal and leaf node types.  A decision tree is a
051:      # recursive structure, so to refer to a node is also
052:      # to refer to the entire tree below it.
053:
054:      class BDT
055:      end
056:
057:      # Internal decision tree node.
058:      class BDT_internal < BDT
059:        def initialize(question, children)
060:          @question = question
061:          @yes,@no = children
062:        end
063:
064:        # Interactively classify, based on user's responses.
065:        def classify
066:          print @question,"? "
067:          if ($stdin.gets) =~ /^[Yy]/
068:            return @yes.classify
069:          else
070:            return @no.classify
071:          end
072:        end
073:
074:        def to_s(logic="",indent="")
075:          indent + logic + "if " + @question + "\n" +
076:            @yes.to_s("then ", indent+"  ") +
077:            @no.to_s("else ", indent+"  ")
078:        end
079:        alias inspect to_s
080:      end
081:
082:      # Leaf decision tree node.
083:      class BDT_leaf < BDT
084:        def initialize(c)  @classification = c    end
```

LISTING 21.1   Continued

```
085:    def classify()      @classification       end
086:
087:    def to_s(logic="",indent="")
088:      indent + logic + @classification + "\n"
089:    end
090:    alias inspect to_s
091:  end
092:
093:  # A BDT_sample is a classification and an array of attributes.
094:  class BDT_sample
095:    def initialize(c, atr)
096:      @classification = c
097:      @attributes = atr
098:    end
099:    attr_reader :classification, :attributes
100:  end
101:
102:  # A BDT_set holds an array of samples. Since most of the
103:  # logic of decision trees pertains to sets of samples,
104:  # instance methods of this class do a lot of work.
105:  class BDT_set
106:    def initialize(source)
107:      if source.is_a?(String)  # treat argument as filename
108:        @samples = IO.readlines(source).map do |line|
109:          tokens = line.split(",").map{|t| t.strip}
110:          classification = tokens.delete_at(0)
111:          BDT_sample.new(classification, tokens)
112:        end
113:        # Get rid of lines that are empty or
114:        # contain comments (indicated by #).
115:        @samples.delete_if {|s| s.classification =~ /(^$)|(^#)/}
116:      else         # treat argument as array of BDT_samples
117:        @samples = source
118:      end
119:    end
120:    attr_reader :samples
121:
122:    def make_tree
123:      # Decide which attribute seems to give the best
124:      # possible split.
125:      best = attributes.min do |a1,a2|
126:        expected_info_content(split(a1)) <=>
127:          expected_info_content(split(a2))
128:      end
129:
130:      # Go deeper if the split seems profitable, else
131:      # return a leaf node with the predominant
132:      # classification for the set.
133:      if expected_info_content(split(best)) <
```

21

continues

LISTING 21.1   Continued

```
134:              expected_info_content([self])
135:          BDT_internal.new(best,split(best).
136:                  collect {|e| e.make_tree})
137:        else
138:          BDT_leaf.new((self.classification_totals.
139:              max {|x,y| x[1]<=>y[1]}).first)
140:        end
141:    end
142:
143:    # Return a list of all attributes that appear in the set.
144:    def attributes
145:      (@samples.map{|s| s.attributes}).flatten.uniq
146:    end
147:
148:    # Return a hash showing the number of samples for
149:    # each classification.
150:    def classification_totals
151:      h = Hash.new(0)
152:      @samples.each {|s| h[s.classification] += 1}
153:      h
154:    end
155:
156:    # Return expected information content of an array
157:    # of BDT_sets.
158:    def expected_info_content(sets)
159:      num_samples = sets.sum {|s| s.samples.size}
160:      sets.sum do |s|
161:        v = s.classification_totals.values
162:        v.info_content * v.sum / num_samples
163:      end
164:    end
165:
166:    # Return a pair of BDT_sets, reflecting a split of
167:    # self according to the given attribute.
168:    def split(atr)
169:      with = []; without = []
170:      @samples.each do |s|
171:        if s.attributes.include?(atr)
172:          with.push s
173:        else
174:          without.push s
175:        end
176:      end
177:      [BDT_set.new(with),BDT_set.new(without)]
178:    end
179:
180:    def inspect  # This was useful when debugging.
181:      @samples.map {|s| s.classification +
182:          ":  "+s.attributes.sort.join(",")}.
```

LISTING 21.1   Continued

```
183:            join("\n")
184:        end
185:
186:    end
```

A Test of Intelligence

Listing 21.2 shows a short script you can use to test `bdt.rb`.

LISTING 21.2   `bdt-test.rb`

```
01:    #!/usr/bin/env ruby
02:
03:    # A simple test of binary decision trees.
04:    # You must supply the name of a file containing training samples.
05:
06:    require 'bdt'
07:
08:    samples = BDT_set.new(ARGV[0])
09:    tree = samples.make_tree
10:    puts "Answer: #{tree.classify}"
```

Listing 21.3 is a file of test samples you can use to try it out. Suppose this is based on
past observations of various dogs; what you would like to predict is whether a dog that
looks threatening is actually going to bite you.

LISTING 21.3   `dog-bite.txt`

```
# Will this dog bite me?

No, dirty, showing teeth, hair raised, barking
Yes, growling, showing teeth, dirty, barking
No, collar, showing teeth, dirty, barking
No, barking, growling, clean, collar
Yes, growling, hair raised, barking
No, hair raised, collar, clean, barking
No, collar, clean, growling, barking
No, barking
Yes, showing teeth, dirty, barking, hair raised
No, dirty, collar, barking, showing teeth
Yes, barking, hair raised, dirty, showing teeth
```

If you feed this to `bdt-test.rb`, you'll find that the first question asked is always
whether the dog is wearing a collar. That's a reasonable question, because in the training

21

samples, the dogs with collars never bit anyone. You might also notice that regardless of your answers, you are never asked whether the dog is barking. If you examine the test samples yourself, it might take you a moment to see why asking that would be a waste of time; but our script figures that out all by itself. Instead of asking all possible questions and then trying to match the collected answers against the training samples, it saves you time by asking only the relevant questions, and in what seems to be an optimal order. That's artificial intelligence, wouldn't you say? But always keep in mind that the logic coming out can be no better than the information going in. We can only hope that our small set of observations is representative of how other dogs will act.

In the following example runs, you can see some of the generalizations that our script draws from these particular training samples. Dogs with collars are unlikely to bite; dogs without collars are likely to bite if they are growling or dirty.

```
C:\RUBY>ruby bdt-test.rb dog-bite.txt
collar? no
growling? yes
Answer: Yes

C:\RUBY>ruby bdt-test.rb dog-bite.txt
collar? yes
Answer: No

C:\RUBY>ruby bdt-test.rb dog-bite.txt
collar? no
growling? no
dirty? no
Answer: No
```

Ideas for Improvements and Enhancements

Where can we go from here? Our algorithm for building trees could be made more general. Instead of attributes that are simply either present or absent (blueness, whiteness), we could define attributes with multiple possible values (color=blue, color=white, and so on). Internal nodes could then have more than two children, making the trees "fatter but shorter." Fewer questions would have to be asked when classifying each new sample.

But there are practical limits to this. Some attributes, like the number of miles on a used car, have so many possible values that it's not useful to keep track of them all. If we split a set of samples by *exact* mileage, we would probably end up with no two samples in the same set. So in those cases, it makes sense to create some value ranges, more or less arbitrarily, and split samples into those ranges. This idea is illustrated in Figure 21.2.

FIGURE 21.2

Discretizing an attribute.

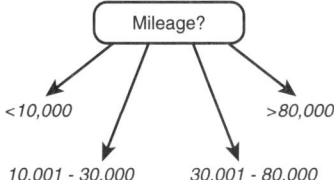

A simple algorithm for doing this *discretization* of an attribute might proceed by finding its minimum and maximum values according to the test samples, and setting a few partition points between them. It might be a good idea to adjust the partitions so that a roughly equal number of samples ends up in each range.

We might also reconsider our policy of asking the user questions when classifying a new sample. If we have a large set of test samples to classify, it is tedious to type in all those responses. Suppose we had two files, one containing preclassified training samples and another with unclassified test samples. What enhancements would be needed if we wanted to classify all the test samples without asking the user any questions?

Tk-Based Peer Chat

Back on Day 19 we toyed with the idea of chat scripts allowing people to type messages to each other over the Internet. Our implementation at the time was really barely functional; its main drawback was that any conversation had to be sequential, meaning that the parties—let's refer them to Alice and Bob—had to take turns speaking. Once Bob had sent a message, he was not allowed to send another one until Alice replied. Today we remedy that problem by resolving two little problems.

- When Alice is typing in a message, how can she receive a message from Bob? It would seem her script needs to be evaluating two separate gets expressions simultaneously, one of them referring to her keyboard and the other to a network socket.

- If a message from Bob comes while Alice is typing a message, where can Bob's message be displayed? Normally, a `puts` to standard output will drop text at the cursor point, but that's obviously going to cause havoc with Alice's typing. Incoming and outgoing messages will appear mixed together.

Both of these can be taken care of using techniques we've learned in this book. Getting simultaneous messages from two places just means doing two things at the same time, and we know that's easily accomplished by threading. Keeping incoming and outgoing messages apart is pretty simple if we use a graphical toolkit and maintain separate text widgets.

21

What Do We Mean by "Peer"?

Several popular chat services exist for general use. The best known is AOL Instant Messenger; another is Yahoo! Messenger. These use a central server, to which all conversing parties must connect, and through which all messages pass. The server keeps track of who is logged on, who is "visible" to whom, which users are holding private conversations, and so on.

A peer chat involves no such third central authority; connections between conversing parties are direct. In most ways, it's a simpler arrangement, but it implies a loss of symmetry. Instead of both parties filling a client (or, if you prefer, "caller") role by contacting the server, one party must call and the other must answer.

Note

> The distinciton between server and client is necessary only because we're using TCP. If we chose UDP instead, the very idea of connections would be irrelevant; the parties would just blindly send messages to each other, hoping that they would all arrive in sequence to make an intelligible conversation.

Imagine that it is Alice who calls Bob; then at the outset, Bob must play a server role. His script creates a TCPServer object that listens at a port. Alice starts by playing a client role; her script requests a connection to that port.

Fortunately, once a connection is made, each program has the same kind of TCPSocket object, and they can behave identically, as seen in Table 21.2.

TABLE 21.2   Client and Server Tasks in a Peer Chat Session

Server Tasks (Bob)	Client Tasks (Alice)
Create TCPServer for listening on a port.	
Accept a connection, to get a TCPSocket.	Connect to Bob's port, to get a TCPSocket.
Converse using the socket.	Converse using the socket.
Hang up when done talking.	Hang up when done talking.

The existence of a pair of sockets means there is no longer a need to remember who made the call and who answered it. The lack of symmetry between server and client scripts, then, is limited to the connection setup, and the first design decision will be how to exploit the overlap in the chatting logic.

Top-Level Scripts

The main scripts can be fairly simple if we factor out the entire conversation and concentrate on setting up the network connection. After all, that's the only thing that needs to be different between them. Listing 21.4 is the "answering" script, which corresponds to Bob in the foregoing discussion. Listing 21.5 is the "calling" script, which corresponds to Alice.

LISTING 21.4   `chat-answer.rb`

```
01:  #!/usr/bin/env ruby
02:  # command line arguments: [port [label]]
03:  require 'tk'
04:  require 'tkchat'
05:  require 'socket'
06:
07:  port, label = ARGV
08:  listener = TCPServer.new((port||10000).to_i)
09:  puts "Listening for incoming connection..."
10:  socket = listener.accept
11:  puts "Connection established."
12:  chat = TkChat.new(socket, label||'answered')
13:  END { chat.stop }
14:  Tk.mainloop
```

LISTING 21.5   `chat-call.rb`

```
01:  #!/usr/bin/env ruby
02:  # command line arguments: [address [port [label]]]
03:  require 'tk'
04:  require 'tkchat'
05:  require 'socket'
06:
07:  address, port, label = ARGV
08:  socket = TCPSocket.new(address||'localhost', (port||10000).to_i)
09:  chat = TkChat.new(socket, label||'called')
10:  END { chat.stop }
11:  Tk.mainloop
```

Two of the required files, `tk.rb` and `socket.rb`, are familiar—they are included free with Ruby—but `tkchat.rb` is something we will have to write.

In line 7 of both Listing 21.4 and Listing 21.5, we use multiple assignment to grab the command line arguments. The optional arguments will result in `nil` assignments to variables if they are omitted, but later they will be given default values if necessary (see lines 8 and 12 of Listing 21.4 and lines 8–9 of Listing 21.5).

21

By the time `chat-answer.rb` gets to line 12 and `chat-call.rb` gets to line 9, a socket exists for each. Conversation as equals is ready to begin, so the rest of the code can be identical. An object of the `TkChat` class is created for each party. The `TkChat` interface is simple; a "chat object" is created from a socket. We also provide the label that will appear at the top of the chat window. After the conversation ends, `TkChat#stop` is called to do any necessary cleanup. But there is no `TkChat#start` method; once the chat object exists, it is `Tk.mainloop` that gets event handling underway.

Remember that `Tk.mainloop` never exits, so it is not helpful to simply drop a `chat.stop` line in at the end. Instead, we use an `END` block to make sure `chat.stop` will get special treatment at program exit time, and we also place it *above* the `Tk.mainloop` call (otherwise, the interpreter would ignore it).

Now, about handling the conversation. . .

The `TkChat` Class

`TkChat` needs just two instance methods to satisfy the interface we've designed for it: `initialize` and `stop`. The general layout can be something similar to the following.

```
class TkChat
  def initialize(socket, label)
    create and display the necessary Tk frames and widgets
    define event bindings so messages go where they should
    start a thread for listening on the socket
  end

  def stop
    stop the listener thread
    close the socket
  end
end
```

It's apparent that we will need at least two instance variables so that the `stop` method can do its job when the time comes: One variable will refer to the socket, another to the listener thread.

Most of the work of building a `Tk` application is in designing the widgets and their layout. In this class we'll keep it fairly simple. In the root window, there will be an input area (a text entry field, plus "send" and "quit" buttons) and an output area (where messages from both parties will be displayed). These areas can be organized as frames and named `inframe` and `outframe` respectively. Listing 21.6 shows a working `TkChat` class.

LISTING 21.6   tkchat.rb

```
01:   # TkChat class for implementing Tk-based peer chat scripts.
02:
03:   require 'tk'
04:   require 'socket'
05:   require 'thread'     # because we'll need a mutex
06:
07:   class TkChat
08:
09:     def initialize(socket, window_title)
10:       @socket = socket
11:       @append_mutex = Mutex.new
12:
13:       # Create the input and output area frames.
14:       root = TkRoot.new {title window_title}
15:       outframe = TkFrame.new(root).
16:         pack('side'=>'top','fill'=>'both', 'expand'=>true)
17:       inframe = TkFrame.new(root).
18:         pack('side'=>'bottom','fill'=>'both')
19:
20:       # Create the various widgets.
21:       inbox = TkEntry.new(inframe)
22:       input_text = TkVariable.new
23:       inbox.textvariable input_text
24:       @outbox = TkText.new(outframe) {fg 'white'; bg 'black';
25:         font '-*-times-r-*-*—*-180-*-*-*-*-*-*';
26:         width 30; height 10; state 'disable'; wrap 'word'}
27:       @bar = TkScrollbar.new(outframe)
28:       send_btn = TkButton.new(inframe) {text 'Send'}
29:       quit_btn = TkButton.new(inframe) {text 'Quit'}
30:
31:       # Define actions for buttons, and bind Return key with sending.
32:       send_msg = proc do
33:         message = window_title + ': ' + input_text.value + "\n"
34:         inbox.delete(0, 'end')
35:         append(message, 'white')
36:         socket.puts message
37:       end
38:       send_btn.command send_msg
39:       quit_btn.command 'exit'
40:       root.bind('Return') {send_msg.call}
41:
42:       # Associate the actions of the listbox and slider bar.
43:       @bar.command(proc {|args| @outbox.yview *args})
44:       @outbox.yscrollcommand(proc {|first, last| @bar.set(first, last)})
45:
46:       # Pack the widgets.
47:       inbox.pack('side'=>'top', 'fill'=>'both', 'expand'=>true).focus
```

continues

21

LISTING 21.6 Continued

```
48:        send_btn.pack('side'=>'left')
49:        quit_btn.pack('side'=>'right')
50:        @outbox.pack('side'=>'left', 'fill'=>'both', 'expand'=>true)
51:        @bar.pack('side'=>'right', 'fill'=>'both')
52:
53:        # Start the thread that will receive messages from the peer.
54:        @msg_acceptor = Thread.new do
55:          loop do
56:            message = @socket.gets
57:            append(message,'yellow')
58:          end
59:        end
60:      end
61:
62:      def stop
63:        @msg_acceptor.kill   # Stop the listening thread.
64:        @socket.close
65:      end
66:
67:      private
68:      def append(msg,color)
69:        # The mutex ensures that only one thread at a time
70:        # can insert text.
71:        @append_mutex.synchronize do
72:          tag = TkTextTag.new(@outbox, {'foreground'=>color})
73:          @outbox.configure('state', 'normal')
74:          @outbox.insert('end', msg, tag)
75:          @outbox.configure('state', 'disable')
76:        end
77:        # If conversation has strayed off the bottom of the window,
78:        # automatically scroll downward.
79:        @outbox.yview('moveto', 1)
80:        first,last = @bar.get
81:        if (offset = 1.0 - last) > 0
82:          @bar.set(first+offset, 1.0)
83:        end
84:      end
85:
86:    end
```

Testing the Scripts

To chat with yourself on one machine, start `chat-listen.rb` and then `chat-call.rb`. The order is important (review Day 19 if you don't understand why). Figure 21.3 shows a test conversation.

FIGURE 21.3

Test conversation on one machine.

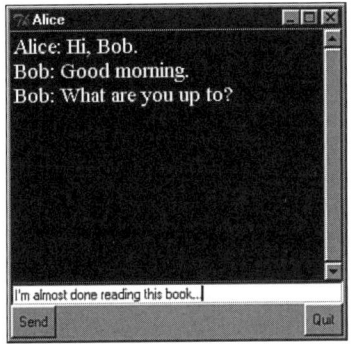
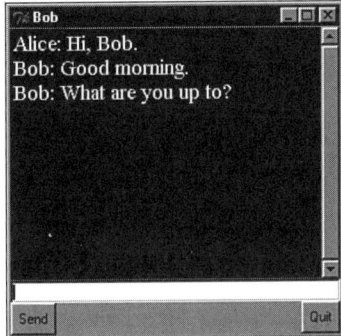

The commands used to start the conversation were

```
% ruby chat1.rb 10000 Alice &
% ruby chat2.rb localhost 10000 Bob
```

It's possible to start both scripts from the same command window. In Unix, place an ampersand (&) at the end of the first command so that the command shell doesn't wait for it to finish before letting you start the second. In Windows, the ampersand is not supported; you can use the rubyw interpreter instead of ruby, but only after disabling the puts lines in chat-answer.rb, because there is no standard output for rubyw. We'll discuss this more in just a moment.

To conduct a conversation across a network, just change the localhost reference in chat-call.rb to the IP address or hostname of whatever computer is running chat-answer.rb. If port 10000 doesn't work, you can change that too, but make it the same for both scripts. The Alice and Bob arguments are optional; they determine what text appears in the title bars of the chat windows.

Ideas for Improvements and Enhancements

In chat-answer.rb, the "Listening. . . established" messages appear at standard output. But if you're using rubyw on a Windows machine, that output cannot be used. A better use of Tk would be to display that message in a window that contains a Cancel button so the user has a way to stop the program before a connection is made. What changes would be needed to support this? Notice that the creation of a TkChat object forces the creation of a TkRoot object. Would our design would be more flexible if TkChat#initialize expected to be given an existing Tk window and did not create its own?

21

Privacy could be improved. We're sending our strings in plain text. Anybody sniffing network traffic, perhaps using a tool like tcpdump, will be able to eavesdrop. We have the opportunity for greater privacy than if we were using somebody else's server to mediate our conversations, but we aren't yet taking advantage of it. Can you think of a way to add simple encryption?

Finally, when one party clicks the Quit button, the other doesn't know about it until he or she tries to send a message. At that time, a Tk error box pops up complaining about a "broken pipe." With some effort it should be possible to establish a protocol notifying one party when the other is unavailable. (Perhaps the Quit binding could include an instruction to send a special message.)

Summary

How's your bag of tricks? By now you've seen enough Ruby code and concepts to give you the confidence to dive into new problems. Programming tasks can be difficult, but many of them are difficult in ways that other programmers have seen before, and Ruby is designed to help you minimize the distress, organize your thinking, and come up with the simplest solutions that actually work.

Ruby was almost unknown to the general public—outside of Japan, that is—as recently as a year ago, but more Web resources are gradually appearing, and several books on Ruby now exist or will soon be on the bookstore shelves, including

- *The Ruby Way*, Hal Fulton (Sams, 2001), ISBN 0672320835.
- *Programming Ruby*, Dave Thomas and Andy Hunt (Addison-Wesley, 2000), ISBN 0201710897.
- *Ruby in a Nutshell*, Matsumoto Yukihiro (O'Reilly and Associates, 2001), ISBN 0596002149.
- *Ruby Developer's Guide*, Michael Neumann, Robert Feldt and Lyle Johnson (Syngress, 2002), ISBN 1928994644.

Here are some Web resources you can consult:

- http://www.ruby-lang.org, the Mother of All Ruby Web Sites.
- http://www.rubygarden.org, news portal and home of the *Wiki*.
- http://www.rubycookbook.org, a place for sharing code examples.
- http://www.rubycentral.com, a site run by Dave Thomas and Andy Hunt. The Ruby FAQ is here.
- http://www.hypermetrics.com/ruby.html, Hal Fulton's site.

Go to it! May as much of your work as possible, from this day forward, feel like play.

Appendices

A   `irb` Results

B   Installation Help

C   Debugging, With and Without a Debugger

D   Essential Vocabulary

APPENDIX A

irb Results

Here's a transcript of the irb session described near the end of Day 1.

```
irb(main):001:0> 99 < 100
true
irb(main):002:0> 99 <= 100
true
irb(main):003:0> 100 <= 100
true
irb(main):004:0> 100 == 100
true
irb(main):005:0> 100 = 100
SyntaxError: compile error
(irb):5: parse error
100 = 100
    ^
        from (irb):5
irb(main):006:0> perfect_score = 100
100
irb(main):007:0> "99" < 100
TypeError: failed to convert Fixnum into String
        from (irb):7:in `<=>'
        from (irb):7:in `<'
        from (irb):7
```

```
irb(main):008:0> "99".type
String
irb(main):009:0> 100.type
Fixnum
irb(main):010:0> "99".length
2
irb(main):011:0> 100.length
NameError: undefined method `length' for 100:Fixnum
        from (irb):11
irb(main):012:0> "99" < "100"
false
irb(main):013:0> "99" > "100"
true
irb(main):014:0> 99 + 100
199
irb(main):015:0> "99" + "100"
"99100"
irb(main):016:0> "99".to_i + "100".to_i
199
irb(main):017:0> 99.to_s + 100.to_s
"99100"
irb(main):018:0> 99 <=> 100
-1
irb(main):019:0> 100 <=> 100
0
irb(main):020:0> 100 <=> 99
1
irb(main):021:0> 99.nonzero?
99
irb(main):022:0> "99".nonzero?
NameError: undefined method `nonzero?' for "99":String
        from (irb):22
irb(main):023:0> "99".methods
["[]=", "tosjis", "tojis", "kconv", "unpack", "slice!", "sum", "each_line",
"delete!", "tr!", "squeeze", "tr_s", "chomp!", "strip!", "sub!", "chomp",
"gsub", "center", "ljust", "intern", "clone", "eql?", "size", "succ", "next",
"upto", "rindex", "to_i", "to_f", "to_s", "dump", "downcase", "swapcase",
"downcase!", "swapcase!", "oct", "reverse", "concat", "<<", "<=>", "==", "===",
"%", "toeuc", "slice", "each_byte", "each", "squeeze!", "tr_s!", "count",
"delete", "tr", "chop!", "gsub!", "strip", "chop", "sub", "rjust", "scan",
"include?", "dup", "hash", "length", "empty?", "succ!", "next!", "index",
"replace", "to_str", "inspect", "upcase", "capitalize", "upcase!",
"capitalize!", "hex", "split", "reverse!", "crypt", "*", "+", "=~", "~", "[]",
"each_with_index", "member?", "max", "min", "map", "collect", "reject",
"select", "find_all", "detect", "find", "grep", "sort", "entries", "to_a",
"<=", "between?", "<", ">", ">=", "respond_to?", "kind_of?", "private_methods",
"methods", "frozen?", "taint", "type", "instance_eval", "extend", "method",
"is_a?", "instance_variables", "public_methods", "tainted?", "class",
"__send__", "singleton_methods", "untaint", "id", "nil?", "display",
"instance_of?", "protected_methods", "freeze", "__id__", "equal?", "send"]
irb(main):024:0> "99".methods.include? "nonzero?"
false
```

APPENDIX B

Installation Help

We'll divide these instructions between Unix and Windows, the operating systems in which Ruby is most used. Current and future releases for other platforms should come with their own specialized documentation.

Unix

These instructions apply to most Unix derivatives, including the commonly encountered Linux and FreeBSD. Before going any further, you must decide whether you want to install a precompiled package or to compile from source code. If you go with a precompiled package (a Red Hat RPM file, for instance), you probably don't need any help from here, so the instructions that follow assume you will be compiling from source. Don't be afraid; it's not very hard — just, well, sort of interesting. Your operating system almost certainly came with the right tools, so you can do it all as described in the following steps. You tend to get a better installation this way insofar as it is tailored to your system.

The shell prompts shown in the following steps indicate who the user is logged in as. This may or may not be how your shell prompt is set up, but we'll want to illustrate the distinction between user accounts when we get to Step 6.

Step 1. Download the Source Code

Point a Web browser to http://www.ruby-lang.org to get the source code. Source file archives are named with this convention:

```
ruby-version.tar.gz
```

As of the time of this writing, the "stable" version is 1.6.6, so we'll refer from here on out to ruby-1.6.6.tar.gz. Download this file or whatever is current, and put it in the disk location of your choice.

Note

There are also usually one or more "bleeding edge" versions of the interpreter source available. The minor version number is even for stable release versions and odd for development versions, so 1.7. x versions are available now, and the next stable version considered suitable for public consumption should be 1.8.0.

Step 2. Unpack the Archive

Modern incarnations of GNU tar are able to both decompress an archive and break it apart in response to a single command:

```
[you@yourhost]$ tar xzf ruby-1.6.6.tar.gz
```

If your system is using an older version of tar that balks at the z option, you'll have to unzip and untar separately:

```
[you@yourhost]$ gunzip ruby-1.6.6.tar.gz
[you@yourhost]$ tar xf ruby-1.6.6.tar
```

Or you can say gzcat ruby-1.6.6.tar.gz | tar xf - instead, which effectively performs the preceding steps in sequence, but uses less disk space because it leaves the original file compressed when you're done.

A new subdirectory ruby-1.6.6 will have appeared in your current directory. Move there before going on to the next step:

```
[you@yourhost]$ cd ruby-1.6.6
```

Step 3. Prepare for Compiling

Here's the part that is most valuable about compiling from source instead of just slapping a prefab interpreter into place. The configure script does some detailed reconnaissance and prepares a makefile suited to your compiler and hardware.

```
[you@yourhost]$ ./configure
creating cache ./config.cache
checking host system type... i686-pc-linux
checking target system type... i686-pc-linux
  ...
```

It will take a little while for `configure` to perform all its tests. If it reports errors, you may need to check your compiler installation. Otherwise, you can press on. (There are some very careful people who would insist on examining and tweaking the makefile at this point, but do you really have the patience? Neither do I.)

Step 4. make the Interpreter

Pull that big cast iron lever and watch the gears start to turn:

```
[you@yourhost]$ make
gcc -g -O2 -I. -I. -I/usr/local/include -c array.c
gcc -g -O2 -I. -I. -I/usr/local/include -c bignum.c
gcc -g -O2 -I. -I. -I/usr/local/include -c class.c
  ...
```

You can generally ignore any warnings if you see them scroll by. The `make` utility won't stop unless it encounters an actual "error," which is more serious than a warning.

Step 5. Test Before Installing

It's a good idea to run a battery of tests on the new interpreter before you install it. All you need to do for this is ask for another `make`, with an added argument:

```
[you@yourhost]$ make test
```

After a short while, you should see the message `test succeeded`.

Step 6a. Install (If You're the Administrator)

You might be the administrator of this Unix machine. Of course, if you own it, you probably also administrate it. That's just a question of putting on your administrator hat, which you do by issuing the `su` (substitute user, or super user) command. This is sometimes called "becoming root." Once the administrator's hat is on, you install Ruby by entering the command `make install`. Afterward, be sure to `exit` so as to take the administrator hat back off.

```
[you@yourhost]$ su
Password: youradminpassword
[root@yourhost]$ make install
./miniruby ./instruby.rb
ruby -> /usr/local/bin/ruby
chmod 0755 /usr/local/bin/ruby
  ...
[root@yourhost]$ exit
[you@yourhost]$
```

Once this is done, anyone with an account on this computer should be able to use Ruby.

Step 6b. Update PATH (If You're *Not* the Administrator)

Maybe you are not the administrator of this machine, or maybe you're just experimenting with Ruby and don't want to finish the installation just yet. In either of these cases, you can use Ruby right where it is. You just have to make sure the interpreter is in your executable path.

If you were in the directory /home/you/ruby-1.6.6 when compiling the interpreter, and you're using some variant on the sh shell (this includes bash, the most common for Linux), then you can add a line like the following to your personal configuration file, which is typically ~/.profile or ~./bashrc.

```
export PATH=${PATH}:/home/you/ruby-1.6.6
```

csh-derived shells (including tcsh) use a different syntax as shown here:

```
setenv PATH "$PATH":/home/you/ruby-1.6.6
```

They will generally look for path info in ~/.cshrc or ~/.tcshrc.

Exit the current shell, log in again, and your PATH should be correct.

Step 7. Test Accessibility

Verify that Ruby is where you can get at it.

```
[you@yourhost]$ ruby -v
ruby 1.6.6 (2001-12-26) [i686-linux]
```

If you see version information similar to the above, congratulations; you have a working Ruby interpreter. If instead you see an error message like bash: ruby: command not found, you should have another look at how you set up your PATH. You can also examine its contents directly via echo $PATH in most shells.

Step 8. Set Up the emacs Ruby Mode (Optional)

If you're an emacs user, you'll want smart indenting and syntax highlighting in place when you edit scripts. The logic for this is found in one of the files you unpacked earlier. Look for misc/ruby-mode.el.

If you have done a shared Ruby installation (as in Step 6a), make yourself root again—just long enough to copy ruby-mode.el to the /usr/share/emacs/site-list/ directory. Otherwise you can copy it to some other directory that belongs to you, or you can leave it where it is.

Then you need to tell emacs how to recognize a Ruby file when it sees one. Either create a new ~/.emacs file or edit the existing one, placing these lines at the top (and adding path information to the first line if needed):

```
(autoload 'ruby-mode "ruby-mode.el" "Ruby editing mode." t)
(setq auto-mode-alist
      (cons '("\\.rb$" . ruby-mode) auto-mode-alist))
(setq interpreter-mode-alist
      (cons '("ruby" . ruby-mode) interpreter-mode-alist))
```

Now, whenever emacs loads a Ruby file, it should automatically switch into Ruby mode. To switch modes manually, press Esc, press X, type **ruby-mode**, and press Enter.

Microsoft Windows

It's possible to compile a Ruby interpreter in Windows just as in Unix, but it is much less commonly done, because an out-of-the-box Windows machine does not provide any kind of compiler. In most cases, Windows users prefer to install a canned interpreter package, often based on the Cygwin compatibility library.

The "One-Click" Installer

A convenient precompiled package has been prepared by David Thomas and Andrew Hunt (also known as "the Pragmatic Programmers"). At the time of this writing the package can be found at http://www.rubycentral.com, under the One-Click Windows Installer link. Use your Web browser to download the installer executable (currently ruby165-2.exe) to your desktop, then double-click it and follow the simple instructions. This is a slick automatic installer that sets up a full Ruby environment, including Tk libraries and automatic file associations for text and graphic scripts using the .rb and .rbw file extensions, respectively. It also allows for a clean deinstallation later if you need it, by clicking Start, Settings, Control Panel, Add/Remove Programs, and then selecting Ruby from the list.

Unix Wannabe Installation for Windows

An alternative way to install Ruby on Windows is to start with the compatibility layer. If you want to try this slightly crazy but very cool thing, go to http://www.cygwin.com. Click any one of the many Install Cygwin Now! buttons on the Web page to download a setup.exe program of about 200KB. Running that setup.exe downloads and installs the Cygwin files themselves. There's a lot to download (hopefully you'll be able to do it over something faster than an analog modem), but it gives you a window you can open into a startlingly Unix-like environment, complete with a bash shell, real GNU compiler, and most of the familiar tools.

Now you can pretend you have a Unix machine and download and compile the interpreter source as described at the beginning of this appendix.

APPENDIX C

Debugging, With and Without a Debugger

Things can go wrong when you're programming in any language. Good programming practices minimize the risk of bugs, but do not eradicate them entirely. Where do you turn if you've written a script and it doesn't behave as you expected? Lots of beginners (and occasionally, more experienced folks) jump in and make random changes hoping that one will make the difference, but there's no need to act in such desperation. Ruby can help you out in a couple of nice ways.

Stack Traces

When a script fails with an exception message, that message provides a description of the problem, in terms that may or may not make immediate sense to you. An exception message appears along with something called a *stack trace*, which is a kind of history of method calls going back to the top-level script.

The script in Listing C.1 has a problem (besides being obfuscated, contrived, and otherwise useless, that is) that prevents it from running to completion.

LISTING C.1   div0.rb

```
#!/usr/bin/env ruby

def foo
  return 4.0/baz(20)
end

def baz(n)
  sum = 0
  n.times do |i|
    sum += quux(i)
  end
  return n + sum
end

def quux(v)
  return 9/(5-v)
end

puts foo
```

The Ruby interpreter produces the following information when trying to run the script:

```
~/testcode:>ruby div0.rb
div0.rb:16:in `/': divided by 0 (ZeroDivisionError)
        from div0.rb:16:in `quux'
        from div0.rb:10:in `baz'
        from div0.rb:9:in `times'
        from div0.rb:9:in `baz'
        from div0.rb:4:in `foo'
        from div0.rb:19
```

What does it all mean? Reading from top to bottom, we first see the exception message: that in method quux, line 16, there was a division-by-zero error. The subsequent lines make up the stack trace. From the first line of the stack trace we see that the error happened in method quux, line 16. quux had been invoked in method baz, line 10, which had in turn been invoked in a times iterator that started on line 9, and so on until we reach the top-level logic of the script.

That's pretty informative, although it isn't quite a complete history. How many times had the iterator block been executed before failure? What were the values of the variables n and i? What values had quux been returning in previous trips through the iterator block, if any? Ruby has a built-in debugger feature that can answer all those questions, and we'll talk about it shortly. But to suggest that you need to use a debugger every time you run into trouble is probably a disservice to you. A little thought and some well-placed extra lines of code might help you find bugs faster.

Inline Diagnostics

Although some consider it a haphazard and undisciplined practice, inserting a few STDERR.print statements at strategic places is often enough to clue you in to what is going wrong with an errant script. When method bodies are relatively small (as they generally should be), a stack trace can help you see where those strategic places are.

Upon examination of the stack trace in the previous section, it seems likely that a diagnostic message in the times iterator block, such as the following, would be helpful:

```
n.times do |i|
  STDERR.puts "i == #{i}"
  sum += quux(i)
end
```

Now, when you run the script, the following extra output discloses the value of i being fed to quux:

```
~/testcode:>ruby div0.rb
i == 0
i == 1
i == 2
i == 3
i == 4
i == 5
div0.rb:17:in `/': divided by 0 (ZeroDivisionError) ...
```

The problem occurs when i refers to 5. Assuming you're reasonably alert, it is now plain to you that quux was trying to do integer division by 5-5.

It would probably have been equally effective to put a diagnostic message in quux itself:

```
def quux(v)
  STDERR.puts "v == #{v}"
  return 9/(5-v)
end
```

Diagnostic lines can be removed from a script once a problem has been corrected, but it's possible you will need them again later. It's kind of painful to type them in once they've been erased, so some programmers *comment them out* so that they can be *uncommented* again later if necessary. A more foresighted approach is to make them conditional on the global $DEBUG variable:

```
STDERR.puts "made it to line #{__LINE__} of file #{__FILE__}" if $DEBUG
```

This way you can activate all debugging output at once with the -d command line switch. Be sure that the switch goes to the ruby interpreter and not to your script:

```
% ruby -d yourscript arg1 arg2     #This is right.

% ruby yourscript -d arg1 arg2     #This is wrong.
```

If your scripts are executable, so you're not explicitly invoking the interpreter from the command line, you can activate the debugging flag on the "shebang" line instead.

```
#!/usr/bin/env ruby -d
```

But if you want to leave debugging lines in your scripts, keep in mind that performance can suffer because $DEBUG keeps being reevaluated.

The Built-In Debugger

Put -r debug (the space is optional; -rdebug works too) on the Ruby command line with a script name, and you get access to lots of diagnostic tools, making it unnecessary to sprinkle your code with diagnostic messages.

The debugger gives you what amounts to an intelligent pause control, letting you freeze a script's execution and examine the contents of variables at any time. How that pause control is invoked can vary depending on your needs.

Any time you're in the debugger, you can enter an h (for *help*) command to get a list, like the following, of all the things you can do there.

```
~/testcode:>ruby -r debug div0.rb
Debug.rb
Emacs support available.

div0.rb:3:def foo
(rdb:1) h
Debugger help v.-0.002b
Commands
  b[reak] [file|method:]<line|method>
                          set breakpoint to some position
  wat[ch] <expression>    set watchpoint to some expression
  cat[ch] <an Exception>  set catchpoint to an exception
  b[reak]                 list breakpoints
  cat[ch]                 show catchpoint
  del[ete][ nnn]          delete some or all breakpoints
  disp[lay] <expression>  add expression into display expression list
  undisp[lay][ nnn]       delete one particular or all display expressions
  c[ont]                  run until program ends or hit breakpoint
  s[tep][ nnn]            step (into methods) one line or till line nnn
  n[ext][ nnn]            go over one line or till line nnn
  w[here]                 display frames
  f[rame]                 alias for where
  l[ist][ (-|nn-mm)]      list program, - lists backwards
                          nn-mm lists given lines
  up[ nn]                 move to higher frame
  down[ nn]               move to lower frame
  fin[ish]                return to outer frame
```

```
tr[ace] (on|off)           set trace mode of current thread
tr[ace] (on|off) all       set trace mode of all threads
q[uit]                     exit from debugger
v[ar] g[lobal]             show global variables
v[ar] l[ocal]              show local variables
v[ar] i[nstance] <object>  show instance variables of object
v[ar] c[onst] <object>     show constants of object
m[ethod] i[nstance] <obj>  show methods of object
m[ethod] <class|module>    show instance methods of class or module
th[read] l[ist]            list all threads
th[read] c[ur[rent]]       show current thread
th[read] [sw[itch]] <nnn>  switch thread context to nnn
th[read] stop <nnn>        stop thread nnn
th[read] resume <nnn>      resume thread nnn
p expression               evaluate expression and print its value
h[elp]                     print this help
<everything else>          evaluate
(rdb:1)
```

Some of the commands used most often with debuggers include the following:

Command	Meaning
l	List
n	Next
s	Step
b	Breakpoint
wat	Watchpoint
c	Continue
disp	Display

Let's see how these can help us analyze our faulty script.

The debugger maintains a "program counter," which keeps track of whatever line is going to be looked at next. The *list* command uses this to show you where you are, along with a little bit of context (that is, a few lines of the script taken from before and after the program counter):

```
(rdb:1) l
[-2, 7] in div0.rb
   1
   2
=> 3  def foo
   4    return 4.0/baz(20)
   5  end
   6
   7  def baz(n)
```

A *breakpoint* is a little stop sign in your code. The continue command tells the debugger to execute your script till it gets to a breakpoint, then stop and wait for further instructions. You can specify a line number or a method name as a breakpoint, as the following code shows.

```
(rdb:1) b 19
Set breakpoint 2 at div0.rb:19
(rdb:1) b
Breakpoints:
  2 div0.rb:19
(rdb:1) c
Breakpoint 2, toplevel at div0.rb:19
div0.rb:19:puts foo
(rdb:1) l
[14, 23] in div0.rb
   14
   15  def quux(v)
   16    return 9/(5-v)
   17  end
   18
=> 19  puts foo
```

The *step* and *next* commands move forward in your script and then stop. The difference between them is that *next* will execute the next line, no matter what it is, and not stop until the line is completely executed, including all method calls. The *step* command, on the other hand, executes the entire next line only if it does not involve calling a method. If the next line contains a method call, the *step* command "steps into" that method, stopping at the method's first line so that you can see what happens in it.

In the preceding example, it would not have been helpful to issue a *next* command with the program counter on line 19 as shown because that would have required the foo method to be executed in its entirety; the script would have halted with the division-by-zero message, but we still wouldn't know why it happened. We'd probably use the q command to quit the debugger, and start over. Instead we should take some *step*s into foo:

```
(rdb:1) s
div0.rb:4:  return 4.0/baz(20)
(rdb:1) s
div0.rb:8:  sum = 0
(rdb:1) s
div0.rb:9:  n.times do |i|
(rdb:1) s
div0.rb:10:    sum += quux(i)
(rdb:1) s
div0.rb:16:  return 9/(5-v)
(rdb:1) s
div0.rb:10:    sum += quux(i)
(rdb:1) s
div0.rb:16:  return 9/(5-v)
(rdb:1) s
div0.rb:10:    sum += quux(i)
```

Since foo invokes baz and baz invokes quux, we are actually stepping through all these methods. Obviously the last few steps have taken us into in a repetitive area of the script,—that is, the iterator loop—but the debugger isn't telling us which iteration is which. So now we'd like to know the value of the local variable i. It's in scope for line 10 of the script, and that is where the program counter is; so we can evaluate i just by entering the name, as follows:

```
(rdb:1) i
2
```

Note

> Ambiguity is a problem when you have a variable name that looks like a debugger command. In that case, you can issue the p command on the variable. For example, to see the value of a variable named disp, say **p disp**.

C

The variable v is in scope only for the quux method. Asking for its value with the program counter on line 10 will make the debugger complain:

```
(rdb:1) v
(eval):1:in `baz': undefined local variable or method `v' for
➡#<Object:0x401b5b28>
        from div0.rb:10:in `baz'
        from div0.rb:9:in `times'
        from div0.rb:9:in `baz'
        from div0.rb:4:in `foo'
        from div0.rb:19
```

A more sensible way to keep an eye on variables is to add them to a display list. Every time the debugger stops for a command, it finds values for everything in the display list, quietly omitting whatever is out of scope. Watch what happens when we put v and i in the list, and then start stepping through the script some more:

```
(rdb:1) disp i
1: i = 2
(rdb:1) disp v
2: v =
(rdb:1) s
div0.rb:16:   return 9/(5-v)
1: i =
2: v = 2
(rdb:1) s
div0.rb:10:     sum += quux(i)
1: i = 3
2: v =
```

The display list need not be confined to simple variable names. You're allowed to enter more complex expressions, and the debugger evaluates them whenever possible. So disp_5-v is a sensible thing to ask for, since that shows you what is being divided by every time you reach line 16. But disp i+v can never turn up anything useful, since those variables are never in scope at the same time.

You can speed up the stepping process by providing an argument. s s 10 makes the debugger take 10 steps, then process its display list. (You can also provide such an argument to n, the *next* command).

Watchpoints logically combine the breakpoint and display list ideas. Suppose we already suspect that problems occur when v is 5 in the quux method. Defining the watchpoint v==5 and issuing a continue instruction will take us directly to the problem area without bothering with all the steps between.

```
~/testcode:>ruby -rdebug div0.rb
Debug.rb
Emacs support available.

div0.rb:3:def foo
(rdb:1) wat v==5
Set watchpoint 1
(rdb:1) c
Watchpoint 1, quux at div0.rb:quux
div0.rb:15:def quux(v)
(rdb:1) l
[10, 19] in div0.rb
   10      sum += quux(i)
   11    end
   12    return n + sum
   13  end
   14
=> 15  def quux(v)
   16    return 9/(5-v)
   17  end
   18
   19  puts foo
(rdb:1) v
5
```

The debugger can do much more than you've seen here, but this should be enough to get you started if you are interested. Many programmers never use a debugger, but depending on your turn of mind and your background, it may be just the thing for you.

APPENDIX **D**

Essential Vocabulary

This appendix lists much of Ruby's essential vocabulary: reserved words, standard method names, and class and module names that are built into Ruby or accessible from standard libraries. The meanings of the names are not documented here, although many are discussed elsewhere in this book; consult Ruby reference materials online at `http://www.ruby-lang.org` for further information.

Some words have intrinsic meaning to Ruby and should not be used to mean something else. There is no strict enforcement of this guideline; if the interpreter doesn't see an ambiguity right away, you can try to use a reserved word to name anything you want, but the results will probably be unsatisfactory. For instance, you're allowed to name a method `def`, as shown here, but you might have a hard time calling it later.

```
# a legal but useless method definition
def def(def)
  "def"
end
```

Ruby has fewer reserved words than you find in some languages. Table D.1 is a complete list.

TABLE D.1 Reserved Words in Ruby

alias	and	begin	BEGIN	break	case	class
def	defined?	do	else	elsif	end	END
ensure	false	__FILE__	for	if	in	__LINE__
module	next	nil	not	or	redo	rescue
retry	return	self	super	then	true	undef
unless	until	when	while	yield		

Standard Method Names

The names in Table D.2 are not reserved words. They are, however, names of standard methods provided by the Kernel module and the Class and Object classes, and nearly every possible Ruby script depends on one or more of them. Using them in a way inconsistent with their conventional meanings can be dangerous.

TABLE D.2 Standard Method Names

autoload	at_exit	ancestors
abort	block_given?	binding
chomp!	class_eval	const_get
const_set	catch	caller
chomp	chop	class_variables
const_defined?	constants	callcc
clone	chop!	class
dup	display	equal?
eval	exit!	eql?
exec	extend	exit
freeze	format	frozen?
fail	fork	gsub!
getc	gets	global_variables
gsub	hash	included_modules
id	include?	__id__
is_a?	instance_variables	instance_of?
instance_methods	instance_method	instance_eval
iterator?	inspect	kind_of?
local_variables	load	lambda
loop	method	methods
method_defined?	module_eval	method_missing
nesting	nil?	new
name	open	protected_instance_methods
print	proc	public_class_method
private_instance_methods	protected_methods	public_methods
putc	public_instance_methods	private_class_method
puts	printf	private_methods
p	readline	rand
require	respond_to?	raise
readlines	superclass	split

TABLE D.2   Continued

scan	select	singleton_methods
singleton_method_added	singleton_method_removed	srand
sub!	singleton_method_undefined	set_trace_func
syscall	sub	__send__
system	sleep	send
sprintf	taint	type
throw	to_a	tainted?
trace_var	to_s	test
trap	untrace_var	untaint

Standard Class and Module Names

The names in Table D.3 belong to supplied classes and modules. Those accompanied by a parenthesized library name are not built into Ruby and must be accessed from a standard library. For example, the `Mutex` class exists only for scripts that explicitly require `'thread'`.

TABLE D.3   Standard Class and Module Names

Class or Module	Library	Class or Module	Library
Array		Bignum	
Binding		BasicSocket	(socket)
Class		CGI	(cgi)
CGI::Session	(cgi)	Complex	(complex)
ConditionVariable	(thread)	Comparable	
Dir		Date	(date)
Enumerable		Errno	
English	(English)	Exeption	
File		FileTest	
File::Stat		Fixnum	
Float		Find	(find)
GetoptLong	(getoptlong)	GC	
Hash		IO	
IPSocket	(socket)	Integer	
Kernel		Mutex	(thread)
mkmf	(mkmf)	Method	
MatchData		Module	
Math		Marshal	
Net::SMTP	(net/smtp)	NilClass	
Net::APOP	(net/pop)	Net::Telnet	(net/telnet)
Net::FTP	(net/ftp)	Net::HTTP	(net/http)
Net::HTTPResponse	(net/http)	Net::POP	(net/pop)
Net::POPMail	(net/pop)	Numeric	
Object		ObjectSpace	

continues

TABLE D.3   Continued

Class or Module	Library	Class or Module	Library
Proc		PStore	(*pstore*)
ParseDate	(*parsedate*)	Process	
profile	(*profile*)	Regexp	
Range		String	
Struct		Socket	(*socket*)
SOCKSSocket	(*socket*)	Time	
ThreadGroup		Thread	
TCPServer	(*socket*)	TCPSocket	(*socket*)
timeout	(*timeout*)	Tempfile	(*tempfile*)
UNIXServer	(*socket*)	UNIXSocket	(*socket*)
UDPSocket	(*socket*)	WeakRef	(*weakref*)

INDEX

SYMBOLS

! (not operator), 77, 146

#! (shebang line), 20–21

#? (regular antigreedy match variable), 172

#{...} (variable reference indicator), 18

$

    global variable indicator, 107

    regular expression line end, 168

$! (load path global variable), 213

$& (regular expression most recent match variable), 171

$' (regular expression after match variable), 171

$:

    extension directory list variable, 209

    directory path (global variable) indicator, 212

$` (regular expression before match variable), 171

$1, $2, etc. (regular expression backreferencing), 176–177

$DEBUG (global variable), 108

$defout variable, 115

$stderr variable, 115

$stdin variable, 115

$stdout variable, 115

% (modulus operator), 76

%c (printf character parameter), 121

%d (printf decimal parameter), 121

%f (printf floating-point parameter), 121

%s (printf string parameter), 121

& (array instance method), 63

& proc object indicator, 299

&& (and operator), 146

*

    multiplied_by, 323

    regular expression repetition test, 170

+

    plus, 323

    regular expression repetition test, 170

-

    minus, 323, 324

    character range, 166

-@ (unary minus operator), 324

-d (command line debugging switch), 108, 116

-e (evaluate switch), 15

-v (version switch), 14

.

    current directory indicator, 209, 434

    regular expression wildcard character, 165

.rb file extension, 205

/
  divided by, 323
  regular expression delim-
    iters, 164
  Unix directory separator, 267
**/i (regular expression case
insensitivity), 178**
**/x (regular expression
extended legibility), 178**
**/m (regular multiline match-
ing), 178**
**< (class inheritance indica-
tor), 187**
**=~, regular expression
matching operator, 164**
[], character class, 166
^

  negate character, 166
  regular expression line
    start, 168
?

  character literal, 56
  regular expression repeti-
    tion test, 170
**@ instance variable indica-
tor, 94**
****

  DOS directory separator),
    267
  escaping forward and
    backward slashes, 165
\a (alarm bell character), 18
**\A (regular expression line
end), 168**
**\b (regular expression word
boundary), 169**
**\B (regular expression word
nonboundary), 169**
**\n (linefeed character), 73,
18**
\t (tab stop character), 18
**\z (regular expression line
start), 168**

**{ ... } code block delim-
iters, 296**
<< operator, 120
::

  scope operator, 104
  outer Inner class connec-
    tor, 230
**` (backtick shell script com-
mand indicator), 271**
|

  pipe, 271, 272–275
  regular expression alterna-
    tive indicator, 176
|| (or operator), 146

A

abstraction
  choosing level of,
    215–217
  defined, 214
  in Ruby versus C, 2–5
  under- and overabstrac-
    tion, 214–215
accelerator group
  in Gtk, 409
accelerators
  defined, 409
access control
  methods, 105
aliases, 73
aliasing
  of methods, 318
  and overriding, 236
ambiguity
  resolving, 52–53
    domain knowledge, 53
    parentheses, 53
    precedence rules, 53
ampersand operator (&), 144

and operator, 146
ANSI terminal
  configuring, 255
Apache, 449, 457, 468
  activating, 454
  configuring, 452–454
    enabling CGI, 453
    enabling SHTML, 453
    setting user ID, 454
  design of, 458
  HTTP daemon, 452
ARGF, 173
arguments
  in overridden methods,
    239
Array class
  enhancements for binary
    decision trees, 481
arrays
  built-in methods
    flatten, 62
  containing other arrays,
    61–62
    as matrices, 61
    flattening, 62
    matrix class, 62
    parentheses, 61
    syntax, 61
  defined, 59
  growing, 60
  instance methods
    &, 63
    <<, 61
    +, 61
    compact, 63
    grep, 64
    max, 63
    min, 63
    sort, 63
    uniq, 63
  iteration of, 323
  in matrices, 315–316

square bracket notation, 60
subarray indices, 60
subarray replacement, 60
syntax, 60
w syntax, 60
artificial intelligence (AI)
decision tree, 476
assignment
chained, 152
multiple, 153–154
irb, 153
swapping values, 153
associative array. *See* **hashes**
attributes
in binary decision trees, 476
readers, 319

B

basename method, 126
BDT_sample class, 480
Berners-Lee, Tim, 450
Bignum, 141
binary arithmetic, 143–146
bdt.rb, 485–489
efficient storage, 145
Fixnum, 145
operations, 143–144
bitwise and, 144
bitwise or, 143
exclusive or, 144
negations, 144
shifts, 144
operators
<< and >>, 144
ampersand (&), 144
hat (^), 144
tilde (~), 144
testing, 487–490

binary decision tree
attributes, 477
defined, 475
implementing AI logic, 482–485
improvements and enhancements, 490–491
information content, 481
expected, 482
order, 481–482
relationship between node classes, 480
sample
as attributes, 476
classifying, 476
sample sets, 482–485
structure
BDT objects, 478
internal nodes, 478
leaf nodes, 479
bin containers
in Gtk, 394
blocks. *See* **code blocks**
boolean expressions, 76–77
of regular expressions, 165
Boolean logic, 146–148
short-circuit evaluation, 147–148
testing conditions, 146–147
Box containers
border_width, 397
in Gtk, 395–399
set_homogeneous, 397
set_spacing, 397
breakpoint, 514
browsers, 450, 451, 459, 466
BSD, Apache for, 452
bugs, and Ruby, 509–516

C

capitalize method, 58
case statement
getting a value from, 84
center method, 58
CGI (Common Gateway Interface), 451, 457, 470
enabling, 453–454
errors, 462
object-oriented support, 463–468
PATH problems, 458
script, 456–457
session information, 458–459
CGI class, 463
CGI::Cookie class, 466
characters
as ASCII numbers, 56
as tiny strings, 56
character literal, 56–57
chr method, 56
omitting length parameters, 56
syntax, 56
versus substrings, 56
character classes, 165–166
character ranges, 166
character repetition, 169–172
chat
central server, 492
chat-answer.rb, 493
chat-call.rb, 493
improvements and enhancements, 497–498
peer, 491, 492
problems, 491
testing
across a network, 497
on one machine, 496–497
TKChat class, 494–496

check button. *See* **check box**
check box
   in Tk, 366
   in Gtk, 403–405
child process
   controlling, 283
   created using `fork`,
      278–281
   created using `popen`, 276,
      281–283
   defined, 272
   process waiting, 438–440
   `SIGCHILD` signals, 438
   waiting for, 277
   zombie processes, 438
`chomp` methods, 79
class constants, 103
   local scope, 104
   scope operator, 104
classification
   in binary decision tress,
      476
class methods, 123–127, 301
   `file.exists?`, 269
   `file.directory?`, 269
   `file.executable?`, 269
   `file.writable?`, 269
   `Find.find`, 268
class/module distinctions,
   224–225
   abstraction process, 225
   choice guidelines, 224
   object-oriented program-
      ming convention, 234
   one file per class, 234–235
   one-use modules, 235
class variables, 128–129
classes
   as modules. *See* modules,
      classes as
   CGI, 463

`CGI::Cookie`, 466
defining, 186–187
   inside classes, 232–234
   inside modules,
      233–234
designing for clarity and
   reuse, 223–229
distribution across pro-
   gram files, 234
dynamic modification,
   291–292
   dangers of, 292
embedding. *See* embedded
   classes and modules
inheritance. *See* inheritance
inner, 230
interface, 313–314
IO
   control methods, 114
   iterated communication
      methods, 114
   one-shot communica-
      tion methods, 114
matrix, 62, 315
`mutex`, 446
methods for. *See* class
   methods
named with noun, 224
outer, 230
procedure objects,
   293–295
   methods, 294–295
   syntax, 293–294
stress methods in, 314
"stub," 206
`TCPServer`, 428
`TCPSocket`, 428
`Thread`, 442–444
`UDPSocket`, 431
versus modules, 196, 224

client, 450
`closed?` method, 120
closure
   defined, 365
code blocks, 296–297
   `BEGIN` keyword, 303
   { ... } as delimiters, 296
   do ... end delimiters, 296
   `END` keyword, 303
   evaluation of, 296–297
   signal trapping, 303
code reusability, 229
command line, 15
   `-d` flag, 116
command line arguments,
   127–128
   `ARGV` array, 128
   `-d` flag, 128
   `showargs` script, 128
compact method, 63
comparisons
   between integers and
      strings, 57
complex coding, 375
constants
   capitalization, 103
   class. *See* class constants
   classless, 104
   naming conventions, 103
containers, 51
   arrays, 59–64
   FIFOs, 62
   hashes, 64–66
   methods that use regexes,
      178
   ranges, 54, 66
   stacks, 63
   strings, 54
content
   Web pages
      dynamic. *See* dynamic
         content
      static, 450

count method, 58
cron jobs, 451, 455
Ctrl+D, EOF character (Unix), 21
Ctrl+Z, EOF character (Windows), 21
cyclone. *See* @, instance variable indicator

D

datagrams. *See* sockets, UDP
DBM, 461–462
decision tree
  binary (*see* binary decision tree)
  defined, 477
  test sample, 477
  training sample, 477
delete method, 58
design, from the top down, 350
destructive methods, 155–157
dialogs
  in Gtk, 403
  modal, 403
dictionary. *See* hashes
Dir class, 126–127
directory? Method, 126
dirname method, 126
discretization, of an attribute, 491
do ... end blocks, 71–72
$defout variable, 115
$stderr variable, 115
$stdin variable, 115, 116
$stdout variable, 115

domain knowledge
  for resolving ambiguity, 53
downcase method, 58
downto statement, 72
dynamic content, 470
  CGI script, 456–457
  client-side, 450
  Java Script, 450
  server-side, 450
  SHTML, 457
  versus static content, 450
  using Ruby to generate an HTML file directly, 455–456

E

each statement, 70, 71
each_byte method, 73
each_index statement, 74
each_key method, 74–75
each_line statements, 73–74
each_pair method, 74
each_value method, 75
each_with_index statement, 74
EDIT text editor, 15
else statements, 78
elseif statements, 83
emacs text editor, 16
embedded classes and modules
  classes within classes, 230–231
    creating instances of, 230
    Outer::Inner notation, 230
  embedded, 229

include statements, 229
  modules mixing in modules, 231
embedding classes and modules
  classes defined inside classes, 233–234
  inner classes versus inheritance, 233–234
  classes defined inside modules, 232–233
  namespaces, 231
environment variables
  for Web session information, 458–459
entry widgets and buttons, 362
EOF (end-of-file) character, 21–22
eof? method, 120
errors, 130–132
  rescue method, 130–131
  division-by-zero, 510
event loop, 356
examples
  anagram tester, 362–366
    in Gtk, 395–398
  binary decision tree, 476–491
  burger stand, 403–405
  Dish class, 206–208
  IntegerMatrix class, 315–331
    accessing dimensions, 318–319
    constructors, 326–331
    initialization, 315–316
    math operations, 322
    multipurpose class, 324–326
    providing iterators, 321–322

storing and retrieving
elements, 316–318
viewing a matrix as a
whole, 319–321
interactive process killer,
348
in action, 354
design, 350–352
script, 352–353
keyboard accelerator,
408–409
message box, 403
odd-position elements, 81
Philosopher class,
123–125, 128–129
recording media module,
226
scrollable window, 411
temperature class, 96–97,
99–100, 100–106
text editor
simple, 409–411
enhanced, 411–419
text filter, 78–80
Tk-based peer chat,
491–498
unjumbler, 337
getting permutations,
338–341
improving perfor-
mance, 346–347
single-match version,
345–346
script, 343–344
word recognition,
341–343, 344–345
user survey, 367–374
Violin class, 190–194
exceptions, 130–132
Load error, 17
rescue method, 130–131
exists? method, 126

expressions
grouping, 86
refactoring code, 84–86
parentheses, 85
shorthand syntax, 85
extensions, 204
compiled
C (language), 209
shared object files, 209
core library, 212
cgi.rb file, 212
irb.rb file, 212
English.rb file, 212–213
load method, 210

F

**F6, EOF character
(Windows), 21**
factorials, 247–250
defined, 248
Fibonacci sequence
iterative solution, 252
misapplication of recur-
sion, 252
FIFOs
pop, 62
push, 62
shift, 62
unshift, 62
first in, first out. *See* **FIFOs**
cgi.rb file, 212
and require, 212
extension loading, 212
English.rb class, 212–213
aliases for global vari-
ables, 213
File class
basename method, 126
directory?, 126
dirname, 126

exists?, 126
mtime, 126
new
filename argument, 117
mode arguments, 117
open method, 117, 126,
298
read, 125
readlines, 125–126
rename, 125
size, 126
split, 126
writable?, 126
zero?, 126
filename extensions
.dll, 209
.so, 209
files
append (a) mode, 117
closing, 117
default mode, 117
device files, 117
File object, 117
new method, 117
open method, 117
opening, 117
read-only (r) mode, 117
read/write (rt) mode, 117
writing (w) mode, 117
fill method, 316
first in, first out. *See* **FIFOs**
Fixnum, 145
floating-point literals
notation, 139–140
precision, 140
floats, 139
converging integers to,
to_f method, 98
division of, 98
flow control, 76–88
conditionals, 76–78
Boolean expressions,
76–77

case statements, 84
else statements, 78
if ... end blocks, 77–78
if modifier, 77–78
multiple, 83–84
negating expressions, 77
nil values, 77
non-Boolean expressions, 77
shorthand syntax, 85
true/false evaluations, 76–77
unless modifier, 77
interruption, 80–81
looping versus iteration, 86
loops
break statement, 81
infinite loops, 80
next statement, 81
redo statement, 81
while statement, 78
select iterator, 76
for statements, 71
forks
disadvantages of, 440
spinner example, 279–281
versus threads, 440, 446
formatted output, 121–123
functional methods, 155–157
chaining nondestructive methods, 155
garbage collection, 155
functional programming style, 155–156
functions, 100

G

garbage collection
chaining nondestructive methods, 155
general case
designing for, 213–217
geometry managers, 360–362
defined, 360
grid method, 361
nested containers, 362
pack method
allocation rectangle, 361
place method, 361
get method, 317, 318
global variable, 107–108
$ indicator, 107
$DEBUG, 108, 116
$defout, 115
$: extension directory list, 209
$: path list, 212
$stderr, 115
$stdin, 115
$stdout, 115
syntax, 107
universal scope, 107
versus top-level constants, 108
versus top-level instance variables, 107–108
glue languages, 266
graphics tool kits. *See* **Tk, Gtk**
greedy matches. *See* **regular expressions, greed**
grep method, 64
grid method, 361

Gtk, 114
defined, 389
designing multiple windows, 400–403
exit method, 393
file selector, 416–419
HSeparator, 408
installation
under Unix, 390–391
under Windows, 391–392
main_quit method, 393
message boxes in, 403–403
scripts, 392–394
signal connect method, 393
toggle button, 408–409
widgets
accelerator group, 409
Bin containers, 394
Box containers, 395–399
check_button, 403
pack_end, 398
pack_start, 398
radio button, 403
scrollable window, 411
table containers, 399
text, 409–411
windows
modal dialogs, 403
subclasses, 400
table layout, 400–402
GUI (Graphical User Interface)
event loop, 356
multiple-document interface (MDI), 356
single-document interface (SDI), 356
widgets, 356
windows, 356

H

hashes
default values, 64
instance methods
key?, 65
keys, 65
to_a, 66
value?, 65
values, 65
iterators for, 74, 75
keys, 64
syntax, 64
values, 64
hat operator (^), 144
HBox
in Gtk, 395
high-level languages
compared to VHLLs, 3
HSeparator
in Gtk, 408
HTML, 455, 456, 459, 466, 468
embedded Ruby, 468
generated by Ruby, 455
server-parsed. *See*
SHTML
HTTP
current working directory
stipulation, 434
default port 80, 434
GET command, 434, 435
headers in, 436
loops and, 435
return values from, 436
security precautions, 434
httpd. *See* **Apache**
**HTTP_REFERER environment
variable, 459**
**HTTP_USER_AGENT environ-
ment variable, 459**
hypertext, 450

I

if ... end blocks, 77–78
if statements, 77–78, 84
imperative style, 155–157
changers of, 156–157
include keyword, 195
versus require, 211
include? method, 59
index method, 59
inequality test, 80
infinite loops, 80
infinity, 84
information content, 481
inheritance
advantages of, 187
< class inheritance indica-
tor, 187
class constants, 189
container class iteration,
297–298
creating, 187
in object-oriented pro-
gramming, 187
"is a" relationships, 194
mixing modules, 197
multiple, 196
overriding methods, 193
resolving method calls,
193–194, 197–198
shared class constants, 188
shared class variables,
188, 189
shared methods, 188–189
subclasses, 188, 189
superclasses, 187, 189
syntax, 187
tune method example,
193–194
Violin class example,
189–193

**initialize method,
105–106, 318, 327**
number of arguments for,
106
input/output methods. *See*
methods, input/output
**inspect method, 320–321,
326**
instance variables, 94–95
@ indicator, 94
object scope, 94
syntax, 94
top level visibility,
107–108
integer class methods
downto, 72
times, 72
upto, 72
integer literals, 138–139
bases, 139
**IntegerMatrix#initialize
method, 327**
**IntegerMatrix#plus method,
324**
integers
converting floats to integers
ceil, 98
floor, 98
round, 98
rounding, 98
to_I, 98
division of, 98
interfaces, 331
of a class, 313–314
design, 313–327
Internet
chat services
AOL Instant
Messenger, 492
Yahoo! Messenger, 492
TCP, 492
UDP, 492

Internet Service Provider (ISP), 451

IO class

  choose method, 300

  readlines method, 300–301

  select method, 300, 301

IO class methods

  <<, 119

  closed?, 120

  eof?, 120

  getc, 118

  gets, 118

  lineno, 118

  pos, 118

  pos=, 119

  print, 119

  read, 119

  readlines, 119

  rewind, 119

  ungetc, 118

  write, 119

IO.pipe method, 277–278

IO.popen method

  new process in same script, 275

  process in different script, 272

  spinner example, 281–283

IP address, 461

irb (interactive ruby interpreter), 22–23, 212

  example session, 501–502

"is-a" relation, 238

iteration, 69–76. *See also* **iterators**

  of arrays, 323

  for hashes, 74–76

  of matrices, 321–322

  for numbers, 72–73

  for statements, 71

  for strings, 73–74

  syntax of, 70

  versus looping, 86

  versus recursion, 248

iterators, 289–302, 321

  adding to standard classes, 299–301

  concept of, 295–297

  converting between proc objects and blocks, 299

  defined, 70

  downto, 72

  each, 70–72

    alternate form of, 71

    do ... end blocks, 71–72

  each_byte, 73

    alias for, 73

    \n line feed characters, 73

    long string, 73

  each_index, 74

  each_key, 74–75

  each_pair, 74–76

  each_value, 74–75

  each_with_index, 74

  for inherited classes, 297–298

  hybrid, 299

    yield keyword, 299

  life without, 290–295

  map, 75–76

  select, 75

  step, 72, 73

  times, 72

  upto, 72, 73

  usefulness of, 301

  variation on calls, 71

J

JavaScript, 450, 451

jed text editor, 16

joe text editor, 16

K

Kernel class

  block_given? method, 298

  eval method, 292

  fork method, 276, 298

  open method, 283

  raise method, 317

Kernel module, 205

key? method, 65

keys method, 65

keywords

  BEGIN, 303

  include, 195, 207

  END, 303

  private, 105

  super, 238

  yield, 299

kind_of? method, 325

L

last in, first out. *See* **stacks**

layout manager. *See* **geometry managers**

lazy evaluation. *See* **short-circuit evaluation**

lineno, 118

Linux, Apache for, 452

list box

  in Tk, 366, 373–374

ljust method, 58

local variables

  block scope for, 151

Load Error exception, 209

load method

  versus require, 210

looping

  versus iteration, 86

loops, 78

Lynx, 451

M

Maeda, Shugo, 468
`map` **method, 316, 323**
`map` **statements, 75–76**
matrices
  addition, 324
  math operations, 322–328
  multiplication by scalar,
    322–326
Matsumoto, Yukihiro
  (Matz), 313
max method, 63
memoization, 252–254
memory space, 120–121
  `ARGF` object, 120
  large files, 120
  read methods and, 120
menus
  in Tk, 375
metasyntactic variables, 109
method overloading, 315
methods, 100, 235–236
  accessors, 99–100, 319
    `attr_accessor`, 99
    `attr_reader`, 99
    `attr_writer`, 99
  aliasing of, 318
  argument passing, 192
  built-in
    &, 63
    <<, 61
    +, 61
    array, 61, 63–64
    `capitalize`, 58
    `ceil`, 98
    `center`, 58
    `chr`, 56
    `compact`, 63
    `count`, 58
    `delete`, 58
    `downcase`, 58
    file methods, 125–126

`flatten`, 62
`floor`, 98
`format`. *See* `sprintf`
`grep`, 64
hash methods, 65–66
`initialize`, 105–106
`key?`, 65
`keys`, 65
`ljust`, 58
`max`, 63
`min`, 63
number methods, 98
`printf`, 121–123
`rjust`, 58
`round`, 98
`slice`, 55
`sort`, 63
`sprintf`, 121, 122–123
string methods, 58–59,
  163
`swapcase`, 58
`to_a`, 66
`to_f`, 98
`to_i`, 98
`uniq`, 63
`upcase`, 58
`value?`, 65
`values`, 65
class methods. *See* class
  methods
constructor, 326–331
  `new`, 326, 327
dot notation, 55
excess number of, 314
file
  `closed?`, 120
  `eof`, 120
  `getc`, 118
  `gets`, 118
  `lineno`, 118
  `pos`, 118
  `ungetc`, 118

`fill`, 316
`get`, 317, 318
hiding
  `private` keyword, 105
  syntax, 105
`initialize`, 318
input/output, 117–120
  <<, 119
  `closed?`, 120
  `eof?`, 118
  `getc`, 118
  `gets`, 118
  `lineno`, 118
  `pos`, 118
  `pos=`, 119
  `print`, 119
  `read`, 119
  `readlines`, 119
  `rewind`, 119
  `ungetc`, 118
  `write`, 119
`inspect`, 320–321, 331
instance. *See also* instance
  methods
  `initialize`, 326, 327
`is_a?`, 325
`kernel.raise`, 317
`kind_of?`, 325
`map`, 316, 323
naming conventions
  equal signs in, 98–99
`object#type`, 324
organization of, 314–315
output formatting, 121
overloading, 315
overriding, 193, 235, 236,
  237–238
`put`, 317, 318
reader, 319
`reverse`, 18
shared. *See* inheritance,
  shared methods

sugaring syntax, 55
to_i, 318
to_s, 320–321, 331
Microsoft Windows
Ruby installation under, 507
min method, 63
minus, 326
minus_matrix method, 325
mixing in modules, 231–232
modal window, defined, 356
modules, 195–196, 229–234
accessing methods in, 195
classes as, 195
code reusability, 229
defined inside, 232–233
design example, 226
designing for clarity and reuse, 223–229
distinguishing from classes, 196
distribution across program file, 234
embedding. *See* embedded classes and modules
include derective, 195, 207, 208
Kernel, 205
level of abstraction, 225
mixins, 207
named with adjectives, 224
no instances of, 195
versus classes, 224–225
modules mixing in modules, 231
mtime method, 126
multiple inheritance. *See* **inheritance, multiple**
Mutex class, 446
MySQL, 461

N

naming conventions
constants, 103
methods, 98
variables
descriptive names, 109
meaningful names, 108
small names, 109
nedit text editor, 16
(^) negation in a character class, 166
new method, 326, 327
for opening a file, 117
nil values, 77
nongreedy. *See* **regular expressions, greed**
nonmodal window
defined, 356
not operator, 146
Notepad text editor, 15
numbers, 138–148
binary arithmetic. *See* binary arithmetic
Boolean logic. *See* Boolean logic
Float class, 142
floating-point literals, 139–140
integer literals, 138–139
overflows, 142
presentation, 142–143
printf, 142
sprintf, 142
storage, 140–142
Bignum, 141
in C, 140

O

Object#is_a?, 325
Object Linking and Embedding (OLE), 267
object-oriented (OO) programming, 194, 195, 196
and inheritance, 187
and reusability, 229
object variable. *See* **instance variable**
objects
adding methods to, 289–297
characteristics of, 93
containers for, 51
arrays, 59–64
FIFOs, 62
hashes, 64–66
ranges, 66
stacks, 63
ranges, 54
regexes and matches as, 180–181
strings, 54–55
one-way pipes. *See* **FIFOs**
open method, 117, 126
operating systems, 459
calling external programs from scripts, 269–271
communication between processes
fork, 278
controlling child processes, 283
conversations between processes, 272–275
popen, 272, 275–276
gathering information, 267–269
interaction with, 265–283
pipes, 271
portability of Ruby, 266–267

operators
  as method calls, 100
  different meanings of, 100
  user defined methods for,
    100–103
    Boolean expressions,
      101
    comparisons, 101, 102
    disadvantages, 102
overriding
  and aliasing, 236
overriding methods. *See*
methods, overriding
  -w flag, 236
  aliases, 236
  argument handling, 239
  inherited methods, 237
    "is" relationships, 238
    super keyword, 238
Oracle, 461
or operator, 146

P

pack_end, 398
pack method, 361
pack_start, 398
parent process
  defined, 272
parentheses
  to remove ambiguity, 53
PATH variable, 267
  Unix naming conventions,
    267
pattern, 163
pattern matching. *See* **regu-**
  lar expressions
Perl, 55
permutations, 338–341

**PFE (Programmer's File
  Editor), 15**
pico text editor, 16
pipes
  IO.popen method,
    281–283
  STDOUT buffering, 273
  with fork, 277–278
place method, 361
plus, 326
plus_matrix, 324
pop, 62
ports
  numbers for, 430
  on Unix, 428
  on Windows, 428
pos, 118
pos=, 119
position anchors, 168–169
PostgreSQL, 461
precedence rules
  for resolving ambiguity,
    53
**principle of least surprise
  (POLS), 12**
print method, 119
  length, 122
printf method
  C language origins, 121
  decimals, 121
  %c, 121
  %d, 121
  %f, 121
  %s, 121
Proc class, 293–295
  passing to iterators, 299
  Proc#arity method, 295
  Proc#call method, 294
    parameters, 294
    syntax, 293–294
procedure objects. *See* **Proc
  class**

Process class
  kill method, 279, 303
  wait method, 277
  waitpid method, 277
process duplication, 440
processes
  child, 272, 275–276
  communication between,
    272
    fork method, 278
  controlling child process-
    es, 283
  parent, 272
  popen method, 272–275,
    275–276
  runaway, 281
program organization
  defined, 185
program versus script, 14
programming
  resolving ambiguity,
    52–53
programming style, 155–157
  destructive methods,
    155–157
  functional methods,
    155–157
  functional style, 155–156
  garbage collection, 155
  imperative style, 155–157
    changers of, 156–157
push, 62
put method, 317, 318

R

radio button
  in Tk, 366
  in Gtk, 403–405

ranges
exclude endpoint, 66
`start ... end` point, 66
strings in, 66
syntax, 66
`read` method, 119, 125
and memory space, 120
for large files, 120
loops, 120
`num-byte` parameter, 120
reader method, 319
**`readlines` method, 119,
125–126**
and memory space, 120
for large files, 120
loops, 120
`num-byte` parameter, 120
recursion
base case, 249
disadvantages of, 249–250
efficiency concerns,
250–252
explained, 249
factorial example, 249
Fibonacci sequence exam-
ple, 250–252
memoization, 252–254
performance checking,
252
Towers of Hanoi puzzle,
254–260
versus iteration, 248
recursive functions, 250
permutation sets as, 338
`Regex` class, 164
`gsub` method, 179–180
`sub` method, 179–180
regular expression, 163–164.
See also **`Regex` class**
and `ARGF`, 173
backreferencing, 177,
179–180
. dot character, 165

character classes,
165–166, 167
abbreviations, 167
character recognition,
166
ranges, 166
character repetition,
169–172
for date fields, 170
repetition tests, 170
container methods, 178
escaping special charac-
ters, 165, 166
greed, 171–172
grouping, 172–177
and memory, 176–177
with alteration, 176
with repetition,
172–175
`gsub` method, 179
match objects, 180
outside of, 168
position anchors, 168–169
$ regular expression
line end, 168
\Z regular expression
line end, 168
^ regular expression
line start, 168
\A regular expression
line start, 168
\b word boundary, 169
\B word nonboundary,
169
regex objects, 180
special characters, 166
sub method, 179
switches, 177
case insensitive, 178
extended legibility, 178
multilane matching,
178
wildcards, 165

**`REMOTE_ADDR` environment
variable, 459**
rename method, 125
repetition, 172
greedy matches, 172
repetition method
arguments for, 208–209
default directory, 209
directory search order,
209
extension directory,
209
file names, 208
`.rb` file name exten-
sions, 208
extensions, 208
`$:` global variable, 209
path information,
208–209
before including module,
208
binary files, 209
C extensions, 209
`Kernel` module, 205
local variable access, 210
versus `include`, 211
versus `load`, 210
reserved words, 518
`reverse` method, 18
`rewind` method, 119
`rindex` method, 59
`rjust` method, 58
root user, 452
Ruby, 449, 451, 455–456
advantages of, 11–14
free, 12
gives immediate feed-
back, 12
GTK support, 13
intuitive syntax, 12
object-oriented, 13
portable, 12–13

regular expressions, 14
scripting language,
    13–14
small size, 12
TK support, 13
application archive,
    468–470
and CGI support, 470
and dynamic content, 470
embedded (eruby), 468
as a "glue language," 266
debugger feature, 510,
    512–516
debugging, 509–516
    built-in debugger,
        512–516
    diagnostics, 511–512
    stack traces, 509–510
enhancement possibilities,
    347–348
essential vocabulary,
    517–520
installation
    archive unpacking, 504
    compiler preparing,
        504–505
    downloading source
        code, 504
    emacs Ruby mode,
        506–507
    for Microsoft
        Windows, 507
    making the interpreter,
        505
    one-click installation,
        507
    path update, 506
    testing accessibility,
        506
    testing the interpreter,
        505
    under Unix, 503–507
    Unix simulation, 507

interpreter, 511
multiple inheritance, 228
numbers. *See* numbers
Object Linking and
    Embedding (OLE) sup-
    port, 267
portability issues,
    266–267, 270
proposed extensions to,
    301
run from command line.
    See command line
run interactively, 21–24
standard class and module
    names, 519–520
standard method names,
    518–519
and static content, 470
systems programming
    %x command, 271
    backticks, 271
    calling programs from
        scripts, 269–272
    class methods,
        267–269
    controlling child
        processes, 283
    Dir.entries, 267–268
    ENV objects
    FileTest module meth-
        ods, 269
    "glue languages," 266
    IO.pipe method,
        277–278
    IO.popen method, 272,
        275–276, 281–283
    Kernel.fork method,
        276
    Kernel.open method,
        283
    parallelized scripts,
        266

PATH variable, 267
    pipes, 271, 281–283
    processes, 275–277
    security issues, 271
    system method,
        269–271
    Unix versus Windows,
        266
    Unix origins of, 266–267
**Ruby Application Archive
    (RAA), 12, 13**
Ruby installation
    irb application, 212
    cgi.rb, 212
    core library, 212
    English.rb file, 212–213
    installation directory, 212
    irb.rb, 212
    irb subdirectory, 212
Ruby language
    examining the installation,
        211
    runtime extension of,
        205–209
Ruby Way, defined, 5
runtime extensions
    require method. *See*
        require method

S

scientific notation, 139–140
scripts
    comments, 52
    eval.rb, 23
    first.rb, 16
    parallelized, 266
    versus irb sessions, 52
scrollbar
    widget in Tk, 367, 374
select statements, 75

session
    defined, 351
    Unix logon, 350
session information, 458
    environment variables, 459
    form element status, 460
    object-oriented CGI support, 463–468
    persistent, 466–468
    using DBM, 461–462
    using the CGI class, 465
server, 450
shebang line, 20–21
shift, 62
shift operator (<<, >>), 144–145
short-circuit evaluation, 147
shortcuts, 151–154
    chained assignments, 152
    multiple assignments, 153–154
        `irb`, 153
        swapping values, 153
    variable modification, 151–152
SHTML (server-parsed HTML), 451, 465
    enabling, 453
    errors, 462
    `PATH` problems, 458
    script, 457–458
    session information, 458–459
simple, 164–168
    alternate delimiters, 164
    / delimiter, 164
    regex literals, 164
`size` method, 126
`sort` method, 63
sockets
    concurrent sessions, 438–439
        forking new processes, 438

    process control, 438–439
    phone company principle of, 428
    ports
        on Unix, 428
        on Windows, 428
    post office principle of, 428
    TCP (Transmission Control Protocol), 428–430
        Quitting, 433
        Web servers and. *See* Web servers
    threads. *See* threads
    two-way communications, 432–433
    UDP (User Datagram Protocol), 428, 430–432
        connectionless state, 431
        infrequency of use, 431
        return values from, 431
        unreliability of, 432
`split` method, 63
`sprintf`, 121–123
stacks, 63
stack traces, 509–511
static content, 470
    versus dynamic content, 450
`STDERR`, 114
    to facilitate debugging, 274–275
    `STDERR.print` statements, 511
`STDIN`, 114
`STDOUT`, 114
    nonbuffered, 273
streams, 113–116
    different receivers, 115
    `$DEBUG` variable, 116

    global `$defout` variable, 115–116
    global `$stdin`, `$stdout`, and `$stderr` variables, 115
    GUI application, 114
    IO class
        control methods, 114
        iterated communication methods, 114
        on-shot communication methods, 114
        omitting receivers, 114–115
        redirection, 115–116
        standard streams, 114–116
        `STDERR`, 114
        `STDIN`, 114
        `STDOUT`, 114
`String#include?` method, 163
string literals
    delimiting, 149
    here documents, 149–150
    special characters, 148–149
        `#{...}`, 149
        `%`, 149
        `|`, 149
        `\a`, 149
        `\n`, 148
        operator <<, 149
        `Q`, 149
    specifying a string, 148
strings, 54–55, 148–150
    counting from, 54
    defined, 54
    equality of, 54
    instance methods, 58
    literals, 148
    pattern matching. *See* regular expressions

square bracket notation, 54
substrings, 54–55, 57
syntax, 54
strip method, 59
strudel. *See* @, **instance variable indicator**
subclasses. *See* **inheritance, subclasses**
substrings
specifying by matching, 57
specifying by position, 54–55
counting from, 54
indices, 54
modification, 54
square bracket notation, 54
versus characters, 56–57
sugaring
syntax, 55
superclasses. *See* **inheritance, subclasses**
swapcase method, 58
switches, 177–178
syntax sugar
defined, 55
syntax sugaring, 71

T

table containers
in Gtk, 399
Task Scheduler, 456
Tcl (Tool Command Language). *See* **Tk, history**
TCP (Transmission Control Protocol), 428–430
in chat, 492
simple Web server, 433–438
sockets, 428

"Hello, World" using, 429
chat session, 432–433
TCPServer class, 429
object, 492
TCPSocket class, 429
object, 492
text
widgets in Tk for, 375
text editors
BBEdit, 16
DOS, 15
EDIT, 15
emacs, 16
joe, 16
Mac OS X, 16
Notepad, 15
pico, 16
PFE (Programmer's File Editor), 15
Unix, 15
vi, 15–16
vim, 16
Windows, 15
threads, 440–446
control methods, 442–444
versus forks, 440–441, 446
mutex (mutual exclusion), 446
priority, 444
process control, 441
variables within, 441
Thread class
alive? method, 443
exit method, 443
kill method, 443
main method, 444
Mutex class and, 446
pass method, 443
priority method, 444
stop method, 443
tilde operator (~), 144
times statements, 72

Tk, 114
advantages of, 357
binding code, 357
chat application, 491–498
defined, 357
disadvantages of, 357
history, 357
widgets, 356
allocation rectangle, 361
anchor point, 361
check button (check box), 366
class names, 358
drawing, 375
expand option, 361
fill option, 361
list box, 366, 373–374
mainloop method, 359
menus, 375
multiline text, 375
pack method, 359, 360
padx option, 361
pady option, 361
photo image, 375
radio button, 366
root object, 358–360
scrollbar, 367, 374
text widgets, 375
top-level windows, 358
to_a method, 66
toggle button
in Gtk, 408–409
to_i method, 317
to_s method, 320–321
Towers of Hanoi, 254–260
tr method, 59

U

UDP (User Datagram
  Protocol)
  "Hello, World" using,
    430–432
  sockets, 428
UDPSocket class, 431
ungetc, 118
uniq method, 63
Unix, 458, 461
  Apache for, 452
  ports, 428
  Ruby installation under,
    503–507
  sockets, 428
  tools, 348–349
  word recognition, 341–343
unless statement, 77
unshift, 62
upcase method, 58
upto method, 72
URL, 459
user ID, 454

V

value? method, 65
values method, 65
variable assignment
  inside a block, 151
variables
  assignment, 17–18
  class. See global variables
  global. See global vari-
    ables

  in debuggers, 515–516
  instance, 94
  local scope, 94
  metasyntactic, 109
  name assignment, 155
  naming conventions,
    meaningful names, 108
  out of scope, 94
  reference, 17–18
  require and, 210
VBox
  in Gtk, 395
very high-level Languages
  (VHLLs)
  characteristics of, 2
  compared to high-level
    languages, 2–5
  need for, 2
vi text editor, 15–16
vim text editor, 16

W

watchpoints, 516
Web documents
  root directory, 452
Web servers, 433–438, 449,
  454, 456, 458, 468
  concurrent sessions
    using forks, 438–440
    using threads, 441–442
  cookies, 466
  HTTP implementation for,
    434
  session information. See
    session information
website, 517

whirl. See @ instance variable indicator
widgets. See TK, widgets;
  Gtk, widgets
wildcards, for regular
  expressions, 165
Win_cron, 456
Windows, 456, 461
  Apache for, 452
  in Gtk, 400–403
  ports, 428
  sockets, 428
window class
  subclasses
    dialog, 403
word recognition
  with dictionary file,
    346–347
  portable function for,
    343–344
  under Unix, 341–343
World Wide Web (WWW),
  time displayer, 450–451
World Wide Web
  Consortium (W3C), 470
writable? method, 116
write method, 119
xcoral text editor, 16
zero? method, 126